BROOKLYN
DETAILED SKETCH OF THE NORTH SIDE OF THE STREET.
VIEW FROM TRINITY CHURCH, LOOKING DOWN WALL
BRO

R D Calkins
Dean's Office
DETAILED SKETCH OF THE SOUTH SIDE OF THE STREET
STREET WITH SKETCHES OF THE BUILDINGS ON EACH SIDE.

THE NEW YORK MONEY MARKET

PREPARED UNDER THE AUSPICES OF THE

COLUMBIA UNIVERSITY COUNCIL FOR RESEARCH IN THE SOCIAL SCIENCES

EDITED BY

BENJAMIN HAGGOTT BECKHART

ASSOCIATE PROFESSOR OF BANKING IN COLUMBIA UNIVERSITY

VOLUME I

BY

MARGARET G. MYERS

Courtesy New York Historical Society

WALL STREET ABOUT 1845

The New York Money Market

VOLUME I

ORIGINS AND DEVELOPMENT

BY

MARGARET G. MYERS

NEW YORK

COLUMBIA UNIVERSITY PRESS

1931

PUBLISHED OCTOBER, 1931

PRINTED IN THE UNITED STATES OF AMERICA
GEORGE GRADY PRESS NEW YORK

PREFACE

The history of the New York Money Market before 1913 falls naturally into two parts, with the dividing line at 1863. That year marked the passage of the National Bank Act, a law which materially changed the structure of the financial organization of the United States. The effects of that measure were felt in every phase of money market activity, creating many new problems, and giving a different guise to old ones. Besides this fundamental change in the banking system, the Civil War gave rise to important alterations in the economic life of the nation and left a heritage of monetary problems in connection with the public debt, the issue and redemption of greenbacks, and the resumption of specie payments, which differed in degree, if not in kind, from the problems which had engaged the financial community before the War. The period from 1863 to 1913 was dominated by the existence of the national banking system and was brought to a conclusion by the passage of the Federal Reserve Act. This new legislation, which closely coincided with the outbreak of the World War, produced another radical break in the continuity of the money market's history.

A topical arrangement has been used within each of the two periods covered by this volume. This has the advantage of permitting a complete discussion of each phase of the money market's activity—the call loan market, the commercial-paper market, the investment market, and the relation of the banks and the treasury to the money market. A chronological arrangement would have obscured the development of each part by placing the subjects in a purely fortuitous time sequence. The topical arrangement has, on the other hand, a very real disadvantage in picturing the evolution of the money market as a number of parallel streams of events, rather than as one broad stream in which many currents mingle. In order to overcome this drawback, numerous cross references have been used in each chapter, linking contemporaneous developments.

It is difficult to find a satisfactory definition for the term money market. Colloquial usage frequently narrows its meaning to the call money market alone, thus referring to the salient feature of the New York money market, rather than to the market as a whole. This definition is too narrow. Defining the money market as the market for surplus funds is, on the other hand, somewhat too broad and too vague to be satisfactory, for everything hinges upon the meaning given to the adjective "surplus." Bagehot's phrase "borrowed funds" seems preferable, for it involves the essential idea of the transfer of funds from the person who lends to the person who borrows, whether the period for which the transfer is made be long, as in the case of investment funds, or short, as in the commercial-paper and call loan markets. It includes all the funds available for productive, commercial or speculative purposes, as well as the mechanism by which these funds are gathered together from holders not immediately requiring their use, and redistributed in answer to the needs of various classes of borrowers. With this broad definition of the money market to serve as a working base, it will be possible to set forth on the study and to select the features of its history which are of most significance.

The author is indebted to many persons for assistance in various stages of the work. Dr. B. M. Anderson, Jr., Professor William Adams Brown, Jr., Mr. J. Edward Meeker, the Honorable Edmund Platt, Mrs. Helen Slade, Professor James G. Smith, Professor T. W. Van Metre, and Miss Caroline Whitney, contributed valuable criticisms of the manuscript. Mr. Gilbert Sussman aided in gathering the material. The staff of the Economics Division of the New York Public Library gave constant and expert assistance. Professor E. R. A. Seligman kindly permitted the author to use his collection of economic and financial monographs. Special acknowledgment is due Professor H. Parker Willis in whose seminar the work was carried forward.

This volume is the first in a series of two studies of the New York money market conducted under the auspices of the Council for Research in the Social Sciences of Columbia University and under the immediate supervision of a subcommittee on economics composed of Professors R. C. McCrea, W. C. Mitchell, and E. R. A. Seligman. The generous support of the Council and the coöperative attitude of the members of the subcommittee on economics have greatly facilitated the work.

MARGARET G. MYERS

New York City
June, 1931

CONTENTS

Part I. The Development of the New York Money Market to 1863

ILLUSTRATIONS

CHARTS

PART I

THE DEVELOPMENT OF THE NEW YORK MONEY MARKET TO 1863

CHAPTER I

NEW YORK BECOMES THE NATION'S MONEY MARKET

Philadelphia the first financial center of the country

There was no money market on this side of the Atlantic until after the Revolution. When the American colonies repudiated their allegiance to the British crown, the act had implications which extended far beyond the realm of politics. It cut them off at once from the financial resources of the mother country and forced them to develop monetary and credit institutions of their own. Banks and stock exchanges had been unknown in the colonies, and the process of creating them was contemporaneous with the creation of the new Federal government. It was for this reason that the first money market in America developed in Philadelphia rather than in New York. The failure of the American army to force the British out of New York had necessitated the temporary location of the government in Philadelphia. There the Bank of Pennsylvania, the first commercial banking institution in the country, was established in 1781 by Robert Morris and a group of associates, to afford credit facilities for the embarrassed Continental Congress. The Bank was of such material assistance in the purchase of supplies and the paying of the army that Congress was persuaded to grant a national charter to the Bank of North America in 1784. In return for this valuable privilege, the new bank was required to make loans to the government and to discount its paper.

Still another advantage was added to that which Philadelphia possessed in having the only nationally-chartered bank in the country. The capital of the Federal government had been established originally in New York in 1787, and there the first President had been inaugurated and the first Congress assembled. In 1790, as the result of a bargain over the funding of the public debt, the capital was removed to Philadelphia for a period of ten years. It was in the latter city, therefore, that the head office of the Bank of the United States was established in 1791, an event which enormously increased Philadelphia's prestige in the field of finance. Philadelphia was now the undisputed banking center of the country. A Stock Exchange was organized, and Philadelphia quotations were published throughout the country; sterling exchange rates originated in Philadelphia, and domestic exchange rates were ordinarily given in terms of Philadelphia values. When New York wished to organize a bank and a Stock Exchange of her own, she was obliged to model them after the Philadelphia institutions.

While accidents of war and politics had been responsible for the first impetus towards the establishment of Philadelphia as the financial center of the country, her financial primacy in this early period rested upon a more secure foundation of commercial supremacy. A greater volume of exports was shipped from her port than from any other city in the country, and to it came a greater volume of foreign imports. In domestic, as well as in foreign trade, the position of Philadelphia was unchallenged. If this leadership in trade could have been maintained, Philadelphia would never have been compelled to relinquish her financial leadership, for as Walter Bagehot said, in explaining the position of London: "When a trade has settled in any one spot, it is very difficult for another to oust it—impossible unless the second place possesses some very great intrinsic advantages."

New York did possess very great intrinsic advantages; the excellence of her harbor facilities, and her strategic location at the mouth of the Hudson, convenient both to New England and to the new West, were factors with which Philadelphia could not compete. These superior attractions first made themselves felt in the sphere of foreign trade. As early as 1796, imports into Philadelphia had been exceeded by those into New York, and in the next year Philadelphia lost first place in exports. It was more difficult for New York to win the domestic trade. As long as the South, which traded largely with Philadelphia, was more important than the West, the position of Philadelphia was secure and it was not until the first quarter of the nineteenth century that the West outstripped the South and threw the balance in favor of New York.

Influence of Bank of the United States

In the growing rivalry between the two cities, relations between the Bank of the United States controlled in Philadelphia, and the state-chartered banks which had been established in New York, were not always of the friendliest. The share of the 10 millions of capital which had been allotted to the New York branch of the Bank of the United States was only 1.8 millions, while to the main office at Philadelphia, 4.7 millions had been apportioned. As the volume of business in New York grew, the resentment over this apparent injustice increased, and whenever the New York branch was unable to meet the wishes of a prospective borrower, the limitation of working capital was blamed. The branch in New York also brought upon itself the bitter opposition of the state banks by its "unreasonable" practice of sending home their notes for redemption, instead of paying them out over its counter and helping them to remain in circulation. John Jacob Astor was another of the bitter enemies of the branch, even offering to lend to the government himself, as an inducement to refuse to recharter the Bank. New York did not rally to the Bank's defense when the charter expired.

When the course of events during the War of 1812 convinced even those who had opposed the first Bank of the United States that a similar institution was necessary, the prestige of Philadelphia was still sufficient to procure the head office. During the debate on the new bank charter in the House of Representatives, Mr. Wright of Maryland moved that the Bank be located in Washington since "the motive for fixing the old Bank of the United States at Philadelphia was the same that ought now to place the present bank here, to wit, that it is the seat of government." Mr. Robertson of Louisiana agreed; he could see no strong reason for preferring Philadelphia, because "if the object was to select a city on account of its commerce, Philadelphia was not the most commercial city, and if that reason carried the bank from the seat of Government, the same reason would prevent its being located at Philadelphia. . . . However, . . . as a place of greater commerce, he preferred Philadelphia to Washington." Even Mr. Fisk of New York agreed to the location of the Bank in Philadelphia "in preference to New York and other places" because it was "a place of greater security and greater wealth" and was "more central to the commercial transactions and wealth of the country."[1] Nor was there any effort on the part of private citizens of New York City to obtain the Bank. John Jacob Astor, who had bitterly opposed the first Bank, wrote blandly to Mr. Girard to inquire if the latter would be interested in petitioning with him for a charter for the second Bank, and received the characteristic reply that "it is not probable that I will become one of the applicants for a charter unless the mother Bank is established in Philadelphia." It is to be noted that Girard was as good as his word, and with Parish and Astor came to the rescue of the new institution by taking the last three millions of its stock when the public could not be induced to subscribe.[2]

Upon the establishment of the head office of the second Bank of the United States in Philadelphia, there occurred a separation between the political and financial capitals of the country which is peculiar to America. In Europe the two are usually the same; London, Paris, Berlin, are the seats both of the government and of the money market. The division of these functions between two cities in the United States was due to the fact that Washington, the political capital, was a creation for a special purpose, and had its origin after the financial life of the country had become concentrated in Philadelphia.

New York outstrips Philadelphia

The location of the second Bank of the United States in Philadelphia was of great advantage, but by itself it was not enough to retain for Philadelphia its ancient prestige. New York, which had already taken precedence over her rival in both

[1] Annals of Congress, 13 Congress, Vol. III, pp. 563, 1043; 14 Congress, 1 Session, p. 1120.

[2] McMaster, *Life and Times of Stephen Girard*, pp. 286-88. Astor became one of the government-appointed directors of the Bank.

the import and export branches of the foreign trade, was now taking first place in domestic trade as well. The "intrinsic advantages" of her location became more and more apparent as the frontier was pushed westward. The building of the Erie Canal opened the port of New York to the important area being developed in the Ohio territory, and brought to her harbor the grain and other farm products which formed so large a part of the total export trade. Pennsylvania's canal system was not only later in being built, but when completed was both longer and more expensive than that of New York.[3] In spite of the strenuous efforts of Pennsylvania, it was impossible for her to turn the course of trade away from New York and back to Philadelphia, and the latter city saw her rival forging rapidly ahead in trade with the interior of the country as she had already done in the trade with other countries.[4]

The advantages which made New York the center for the distribution of foreign goods made it also a desirable distributing center for the shipment of domestic manufactured goods. In this field New York soon outstripped Massachusetts and Pennsylvania, the two states in which manufactures had obtained a start. In 1824 the Secretary of State of the United States estimated that in New York the total investment of capital in manufacturing enterprises was about 7.8 millions of dollars compared with 6.3 millions in Pennsylvania, 5.7 millions in Maryland, and 4.5 millions in Massachusetts. By 1840 the manufacturing capital of New York had grown to 55 millions, nearly one-fifth of the total for the country, while Massachusetts, the nearest rival, had 42 millions, and Pennsylvania only 31 millions.[5]

[3] See p. 20 below, for discussion of the financing of these improvements.

[4] From the *Pittsburgh Gazette* of December 30, 1831, quoted in the *American Railroad Journal,* Vol. I, No. 2, p. 21. "Before the Ohio canal was made, and when produce from that part of Ohio was sent to market by *common roads,* Pittsburgh, Philadelphia and Baltimore were the usual destinations of all the surplus productions of this section of the country. There being no other mode of conveyance than these ordinary roads, produce naturally sought the *nearest* market. The completion of the Ohio canal has produced an entire change in this respect. Owners of produce now find it cheaper to send their property seven or eight hundred miles to New York, by canal and lake navigation, than five hundred miles to Philadelphia, part of the distance by common roads. If a Railroad or Canal is once completed hence to the Ohio canal, the inequality which now exists will be corrected, and produce will *again* seek the *nearest* market."

[5] *United States Census,* 1840.

The growth in trade was reflected in the growth of the population of these three largest cities. The city of Philadelphia was largest until the decade between 1810 and 1820. Boston was left far behind by both, and after 1800, the third position in point of size was held by Baltimore.[6]

POPULATION OF CITIES AT EACH CENSUS, 1791 TO 1850

Cities	*1791*	*1800*	*1810*	*1820*	*1830*	*1840*	*1850*
Baltimore . . .	13,503	26,114	35,583	62,738	80,625	102,313	169,054
Boston	18,038	24,937	34,381	43,298	61,392	93,383	136,881
New York . . .	33,131	60,489	96,373	123,706	202,589	312,710	515,547
Philadelphia . .	42,520	69,403	91,874	112,772	161,410	220,423	340,045

With the course of trade flowing inexorably through New York, it was only a question of time until New York should be able to wrest from Philadelphia the first rank in finance. The first section of the money market to transfer the major part of its activities to New York from Philadelphia was the Stock Exchange. The first in America had been organized there and it had long been the primary market for securities. During the period of heavy borrowing by the state governments, beginning with the successful flotation of the Erie Canal bonds in New York state, the Stock Exchange in New York rapidly passed that of Philadelphia in volume of trading and New York quotations thereupon became the standard for the country.[7]

In the commercial credit field, owing to the influence of the second Bank of the United States, Philadelphia retained its prestige longer than in any other. While New York had a market for such paper in its banks, the bankers who comprised the market were a group of scattered individuals without organization, and they could not exert the same influence as the

[6] United States Census, 1850.

[7] Not long after the transfer to New York of the greater part of stock dealings, came the development of the call loan market from the funds which were finding their way to the city in increasing volume. It is not correct to say that the call loan market was moved from Philadelphia, for it apparently never had had an existence there, but its development was a significant factor in giving New York the financial leadership which had belonged to Philadelphia.

Bank of the United States, which was not only wealthy and powerful, but had the further advantage of branches set in strategic positions throughout the country. It was not until 1836, when the national charter of the Bank lapsed, that New York City finally achieved supremacy in this phase of money-market activity. Philadelphia had lost her last claim to that position, and henceforth New York had no effective rival.[8]

[8] The shift from Philadelphia to New York of the principal money market of the country, is illustrated by a report made to the Senate by the Secretary of the Treasury in 1838, on the rates of exchange and the prices of bank notes. The earliest year covered by the tables is 1814, and from that year to 1824 the quotations represent Philadelphia prices only. But by 1825 the prices at New York had evidently attained an importance equal to those in Philadelphia, and for every year thereafter down to 1838, when the report was published, quotations of both foreign and domestic exchange are given for New York also. (25 Congress, 2 Session, Senate Document 457.)

CHAPTER II

THE ORIGIN OF THE INVESTMENT MARKET

The early money market of New York was an amorphous structure, out of which slowly crystallized the various institutions existing at the present time. Each arose in answer to the demand for a particular type of fund. To meet the long-term requirements of industry, production and government, the investment market was developed; to meet the needs of trade and commerce, the commercial paper market and the foreign exchange market grew up, and to meet the demand for speculative borrowing, the call loan market came into existence. But in the early stages of their growth these markets overlapped and were hardly distinguishable from one another. The first stockbrokers were merchants who found it profitable, because of the increasing trade in securities, to drop other interests and devote themselves to stockjobbing; the first foreign exchange dealers were importers whose foreign banking connections grew out of their overseas trade; the first note brokers were private bankers who ultimately concentrated their energies on that particular form of lending.[1] The evolution of the money market, in other words, has followed the law of evolution in general, and has been marked by continuous differentiation of function.

The first of the specialized markets to develop from the unorganized borrowing and lending of funds in New York City, was the market for securities. There had been nothing to deserve the name of investment market in the United States, either in Philadelphia or in New York, until the funding of the miscellaneous state debts into obligations of the Federal government created an easily transferred medium for the investment of funds,

[1] About 1820, one of the partners in the linen firm which eventually became the banking house of Brown Brothers, wrote: "As respects stocks, I have made up my mind to keep clear of them. . . . Stockjobbing is a trade of itself and only suits them that make a trade of it." Brown, *One Hundred Years of Merchant Banking*, p. 69.

about which a market could be organized. Before that time there had been neither government bonds nor shares in business enterprises. The Colonies had resorted largely to irredeemable paper currency as a method of public financing, since their credit was not good enough to permit the issue of bonds.[2] Industry was carried on largely by means of partnership, with the partners supplying the needed capital. The corporate form of organization made slow progress; none of the Colonies had a general incorporation law, and few of them had issued special charters for business corporations. Nor is it probable that they would have respected each others' charters if any had been granted. In the whole Colonial period only six American charters had been issued for business purposes and most companies so incorporated had ceased to exist by 1776. To the small investor, loans on local real estate or a share in a ship offered the most profitable opening. In New England, savings could be placed with a shipowner like Elias Haskett Derby of Salem; in the South, in such enterprises as the partnership formed for making the Yazoo land purchase, into which only one man put more than £2,000, and two put in less than £200. Men of large wealth had little alternative but to go into trade for themselves, in order to make profitable use of their funds.[3] Although the Continental Congress had been forced to borrow frequently during, and immediately after, the Revolution, these credits had been extended either by foreigners in such a way that none of the securities came upon the market at home, or by banks in the form of short-term credits.[4]

First American securities provided by funding of government debt

With the establishment of the Federal government and the success of Hamilton's funding plan for the domestic debt, there were created the first securities available for investors. The

[2] Pitkin, *Statistical View of the Commerce of the United States of America*, pp. 413-15 (1835).

[3] Baldwin, *American Business Corporations before 1789. One Hundred Years of American Commerce*, Vol. I, p. 68.

[4] American State Papers on Finance, Vol. I, pp. 26, 181.

total amount of debt funded into the new Federal securities during 1790 was 31.8 million dollars.[5] Public interest in the new issues was intense, and during the next few years, the vicissitudes of "the Stock"[6] kept the public in a furor of excitement. The course of price quotations indicates the wide range which they covered.

PRICE OF UNITED STATES GOVERNMENT 6'S[7]

Months	1791		1792	
	Low	*High*	*Low*	*High*
January	84	87	117	129
February	86	88	120	127
March	85	86	105	125
April	85	86	100	105
May	86	86	105	112
June	86	90	105	112
July	89	100	105	107
August	100	113	107	110
September	103	106	110	111
October	103	110	107	110
November	107	111	106	107
December	111	115	100	106

The feverish interest in United States securities had scarcely died down when a new type of stock was put upon the market. Two new bank stocks became available in 1791, that of the Bank of the United States, capitalized at ten millions, and the half million increase in stock of the Bank of New York. Subscription books for the former were opened in Philadelphia in July, and closed in an hour with an oversubscription of 20 per cent, while in August the new stock of the Bank of New York was taken in five minutes. Within a week quotations for the latter had risen from 100 to 280, and by the middle of August had fallen back to par again.[8] During the first three months of

[5] 28 Congress, 1 Session, Executive Document 15, p. 120.

[6] The terms "stocks," "bonds" and "shares" were used indiscriminately at this time.

[7] 28 Congress, 1 Session, Executive Document 15, pp. 231-32. The quotations as given by the *Gazette of the United States* were in shillings and have been converted into percentage of par; 20 shillings being equivalent to 100 per cent.

[8] Davis, *Eighteenth Century Business Corporations in the United States*, pp. 46-60.

1792 there was a temporary cessation of the speculative excitement, and in April Hamilton seized the opportunity to redeem government stock at the more moderate prices then prevailing. In May there was a renewed rise in prices, and considerable disorder in the markets of both New York and Philadelphia.[9]

The eagerness with which the public seized upon this opportunity to purchase stocks should not be ascribed to a purely speculative enthusiasm. It gives evidence that there was in the country a considerable volume of savings awaiting opportunity for profitable investment on the part of small capitalists—not enough to supply all the new capital needed by the country, of course, but more than enough to supply the small part of that need which took the attractive guise of negotiable securities. The obligations of the government, as well as bank and insurance stocks, were eagerly absorbed by genuine investors, and the domestic demand for loan issues of the Treasury continued to be greater than the supply. No new foreign loans had to be floated by the government after the finances were once set in order. Short credits were furnished to the Treasury by the banks during the decade of the nineties, and in 1798, when a longer loan became necessary, Secretary Wolcott was able to secure more than six millions of dollars directly from individuals, without utilizing the banks even as agents for its distribution.[10]

Slow increase of corporate securities

The volume of corporation securities on the market was still very small. An increasing number of business enterprises was being organized under charters of incorporation, but few of the securities issued found their way to a central market. The total number of charters for business corporations in each five-year period before 1800 was as follows:[11]

[9] 28 Congress, 1 Session, Executive Document 15, p. 120. McMaster, *History of the People of the United States*, Vol. I, p. 38.

[10] 28 Congress, 1 Session, Executive Document 15, p. 448.

[11] Davis, *Eighteenth Century Business Corporations in the United States*, p. 24. The figures after 1800 are not available.

From 1781 to 1785 inclusive	....	11
From 1786 to 1790 "	....	22
From 1791 to 1795 "	....	114
From 1796 to 1800 "	....	181

Nearly every one of these companies had secured its charter by special act of a state legislature. The necessity for such action tended to discourage incorporation by making it a lengthy and expensive process. Moreover the issuance of a charter had long been looked upon as a royal prerogative, carrying with it monopoly privileges, which were frowned upon in a society setting out to be democratic. As late as 1827, a pamphlet on the "Use and Abuse of Incorporation" could argue that "every act of incorporation for the purpose of pecuniary profit, carries with it such [*i. e.* monopolistic] privileges,"[12] and in 1850 Nathan Appleton still felt obliged to write a defense of incorporation as a method of carrying on manufacturing. This popular hostility to corporations explains in part the slow increase of such securities. No general incorporation law for business activities existed in any state until the Act of 1795 in North Carolina, applying only to canal companies, set a precedent which was grudgingly followed by other states. New York enacted a general law for the incorporation of manufacturing concerns in 1811, and in 1838 a free incorporation law for banks.[13]

Of the business corporations which were formed in the years before 1800 the majority were organized for purposes of local improvement. Two-thirds of all the charters granted were for the construction of local highways—roads, canals, and bridges; while another tenth were for local public service enterprises—water supply and docks. The par value of many of the shares was small, from twenty to fifty dollars, which brought them within the reach of the local investor most apt to be interested in the object of their issue. There was the less need for resort to a large central market for funds since the total capitalization of many of these corporations was small. A few banks had nominal

[12] *Letter on the Use and Abuse of Incorporation*, New York (1827).
[13] Callendar, *State Enterprise and Corporations*, pp. 147-50.

capitals of as much as $1,000,000, and a few other banks and insurance companies were capitalized at $500,000; but the great majority of the corporations were capitalized at sums which fell between $100,000 and $500,000.[14]

Even the growth of manufacturing did not bring any proportionate increase in the offering of industrial securities. The commercial isolation of the country during the War of 1812 brought about so pressing a need for manufactured goods that the Secretary of the Treasury proposed a revolving fund supplied by the government, to be loaned without interest to manufacturers. About the same time discouraged New England sea captains and shipowners turned to manufacturing as an outlet for their energies and funds, and in Massachusetts, by 1815, the number of manufacturing companies was actually greater than the number of transportation companies. As the East India trade waned, Providence and Salem also turned to manufacturing. By 1820 the manufacturing capital of the country was estimated at 50 millions, and it more than doubled during each decade thereafter, amounting to one billion dollars in 1860.[15] However, the manufacturing companies seldom found it necessary to turn to the investment market for funds. Many had been organized originally as small concerns, and had grown by a process of accretion. Owners plowed their profits back into the business, and employees invested their small savings in the factories with whose management they were well acquainted. Few business enterprises were organized originally as corporations with any large amount of capital; those which sought to float stock in New York were more than apt to be speculative ventures which could not secure capital at home. Even in Boston, which was then nearer to the manufacturing center of the country than New York, no shares of industrial corporations appeared on the Exchange until 1827, and in 1830 there were only six industrials listed. The first industrial shares did not appear on the New

[14] Davis, *Eighteenth Century Business Corporations in the United States*, pp. 290-297.

[15] About one and one-half billion dollars had been invested in railroads by 1860.

York Stock Exchange until 1831 when the New York Gas Light Company stocks were sold; Schuylkill Coal appeared in 1832.[16] By 1855 the list included eight coal and mining companies, three gas lighting companies, and four others, but its length was insignificant as compared with that of the rails. Industrial shares played a very small part, therefore, in the history of the investment market before 1863.[17]

First organization of brokers

The first trading in securities was carried on by merchants and by auctioneers as a part of their regular business in other commodities. By 1792 the activity in Wall Street was sufficient to produce a group of specialists in stock trading. When five of the auctioneers, seeing a part of their business about to be taken from their hands, proposed to establish a daily regular auction of stocks, the brokers were forced into a compact for self-defense, and drew up the first informal agreement for a Stock Exchange. They mutually promised not to patronize the auctioneers, not to charge a commission of less than one-fourth of one per cent,[18] and to give each other preference in sales. This effectually nipped the scheme of the auctioneers, and since the one-way type of market which they were able to offer to investors was less satisfactory than the two-way market provided by brokers, the market was practically left to the brokers.[19]

After the first few exciting years which followed Hamilton's funding operations, there was a decided slump in stock trading. Persons fortunate enough to hold shares of the public debt were not inclined to sell them, and the price remained well above the point at which the Sinking Fund Commissioners hoped to redeem the debt. With so little trading in the market, many of the

[16] *New York Evening Post,* Oct. 14, 1831, and Nov. 21, 1832. See pp. 431-32 below for list of securities traded in New York during 1835. There was no formal listing of securities at this early date; at the request of two or three members any stock might be opened to trading.

[17] Callendar, op. cit. p. 150. *New York Times,* March 9, 1857, p. 4.

[18] The commission was based upon the selling value of the stock until Nov. 7, 1840, when it was changed to ¼ of 1 per cent of the par value. *New York Evening Post* that date.

[19] Lamb, *Wall Street in History,* p. 72. Hemming, *History of the New York Stock Exchange,* p. 11. Meeker, *The Work of the Stock Exchange,* pp. 45, 108.

brokers were glad to resume their former occupations as merchants, or to accept bets on political controversies, foreign and domestic, in order to eke out their scanty commissions.[20]

The entrance of the government into the money market as a heavy borrower had been the basis for the establishment of the framework of an investment market in 1792, but it did not provide enough material to fill in that framework and make a permanent structure. The government was paying off its former foreign loans, or refunding them into domestic loans, rather than issuing new securities.[21] It was not until the renewed borrowing by the Treasury during the War of 1812 that the market revived. A period of activity in the flotation of Treasury issues was inaugurated which increased the public debt from 56 millions of dollars in 1813, to 123 millions in 1817, doubling the volume of government securities outstanding. European capital markets were unable or unwilling to render assistance and the securities were offered to the American public by the method of inviting bids.[22] Moreover the close of the war brought an end to the business depression, and the suspension of specie payments removed any check to speculation which the limitations on bank credit might have exercised with the result that there was another boom in the stock market. Increased business warranted a more formal organization of the brokers, and in 1817 William Lamb was sent to Philadelphia to inquire how the Exchange, organized in that city about 1800, did its work. A constitution was drawn up for New York similar to that of Philadelphia, and 7 firms and 13 individuals became members of the new Board of Brokers, paying an initiation fee of $25. By 1820 the membership had increased to 39 individuals, and the fee to $100.[23]

The trading list at that time was long in comparison with the list of 1792, but contained only the stocks of Federal and state governments, banks and insurance companies. No industrial or

[20] Stedman, *History of the New York Stock Exchange*, p. 35. Seybert, *Statistical Annals*, p. 737 (1818).

[21] 28 Congress, 1 Session, Executive Document 15, pp. 418, 427, 483.

[22] 28 Congress, 1 Session, Executive Document 15, p. 548, 570. *American State Papers on Finance*, Vol. III, pp. 121, ,129. For further details, see p. 150 below.

[23] Hemming, op. cit. p. 11. Lamb, op. cit. p. 72.

railroad shares were included. Those which today would probably fall into the public utility class, such as water companies, were frequently issued by the state governments and listed therefore as state stocks. At first most of the actual trading was done at the daily roll call of listed stocks, during which the brokers stood respectfully, with high hats removed. A fine of six cents was exacted from a member who did not attend the session.[24] On some days during the year 1827 the total sales on the Board were as low as 14 shares; 100 shares appears to have been a fair day's trading. During a flurry of selling in 1828 the daily turnover of stocks reached 600 and 700 shares, but it soon sank to the former low levels. During 1830 and 1831 a higher general level was maintained, and "thousand-share days" were not uncommon.[25]

Besides the decorous buying and selling which was carried on within the Exchange, there was always a certain amount of street selling which could not be brought under its control, and which was at times reported to be as large as that at the Board. The prices, in any case, were those set by the Board at its morning call. The relation between the sales in and out of the Exchange was thus described in 1836: "One great object of meeting together in the morning as a board, is to ascertain who desires to buy and sell a particular stock, which buying and selling, to a great extent, is done publicly in the street, or at the exchange, after the board adjourns, and after the prices of the morning are made known to those, out of the board, who may desire to buy or sell."[26]

Renewal of capital importation after 1815

Although its growth was rapid after 1815, the Stock Exchange reflected only one aspect of the increasing activity of the investment market. Even more important than security trading at home was the renewed importation of capital from abroad. In any rapidly developing country there is an intense demand for

[24] Stedman, op. cit. p. 65.
[25] *Journal of Commerce*, passim.
[26] New York State Assembly Document 291, March 23, 1836.

funds with which to establish industry and transportation, a demand which is inevitably greater than the ability of domestic saving to supply. The high rate of interest which is the effect of this wide margin between the demand and supply attracts investors from other countries, and the history of the investment market in the importing nation must concern itself largely with the manner in which this importation of capital takes place, as well as with the use to which the imported funds are put.

After the Revolution until about 1815, the European investor was little interested in American loans. He was too much occupied with the wars being waged by his various governments to take an interest in financial possibilities of doubtful credit thousands of miles away. There was probably less investment by foreigners in American securities during these years than in any other period of our history. Some of the government bonds purchased prior to 1800 continued to be held abroad, but the total amount declined from 32 millions of dollars' worth in 1803, to 25 millions in 1818. A few shares of the stock of the Bank of North America were held abroad, and by 1811, 7 of the 10 millions of dollars of the capital stock of the Bank of the United States had passed across the ocean, Sir Francis Baring alone having taken 2,220 shares of the latter in 1802. Dutch investors also held some Connecticut canal stock and stock in the New Jersey Manufacturing Company.[27]

The end of the Napoleonic wars brought about a cessation of borrowing by the British government, which made possible the diversion of savings to other uses. The investment needs of the United States, following a long depression and its own costly war, were many, and beyond the scope of the domestic funds available. It was inevitable therefore that the entrepreneurs of the United States and the investors of England should find cooperation profitable. One of the first direct investments of British funds after the war was that in the stock of the second Bank of the United States. The subscription books had been opened in July,

[27] Davis, *Eighteenth Century Business Corporations in the United States*, p. 297. Seybert, *Statistical Annals*, pp. 736, 757 (1818). *American State Papers on Finance*, Vol. II, p. 453.

1816, and, with the help of several leading American capitalists, the stock had been subscribed in full at home.[28] Foreign capitalists soon discovered it and by 1820 English investment in the Bank had reached the sum of 3 million dollars. By 1831, 8 millions of the total 35 millions of capital were held in England.[29] In 1839, on the eve of its final liquidation, one-half of its capital stock was held abroad and one-fourth of all the stockholders were resident in the British Isles; forty-two of them, to the horror of the Congress which was investigating the subject, bore titles of nobility.[30]

The bonds of the Federal government were also being exported to England more rapidly than before. Although the loans were floated in this country and the initial sale was to American investors, many of the bonds were soon resold to foreigners. Of all the debt falling due between 1825 and 1827, one-third was payable abroad, and in 1828, fourteen million dollars' worth of government securities, nearly one-fourth of a total public debt of about sixty millions, was held in England alone.[31]

Issue of state stocks: their export

When in the years between 1830 and 1840 state stocks began to be issued in great volume, the European investor became a prominent factor in this field also. The excellent returns accruing to foreigners from stock of the First and Second Banks of the United States, and the increasing credit of the central government arising from a rapid retirement of the public debt after 1817, combined with the obvious prosperity and enterprise of the country, made European investors somewhat indiscriminate in their eagerness for other forms of American securities. As the states began to issue bonds to finance all sorts of improvements, the foreign investor was little inclined to view them with a

[28] See p. 6 above.

[29] *Niles' Register*, Vol. XI, p. 16; Vol. XII, pp. 60, 159, 208; Vol. XLI, p. 112.

[30] "To wit: 2 earls, 2 marquises, 8 counts and countesses, 2 lords, and 28 knights, barons and baronets". Secretary of the Treasury, *Report on State Banks*, 1839, p. 347.

[31] Secretary of the Treasury, *Report*, Oct. 15, 1828. Seybert, *Statistical Annals*, (1818).

critical eye, or to remember, as unkind circumstances later forced him to do, that "there was a long distance between Massachusetts and Mississippi financially as well as geographically.[32]

In order to understand this flood of state securities which began about 1825 and continued with increasing turbulence until the debâcle of 1840, it is necessary to recall the economic and political changes going on within the country. Foremost of these was the redistribution of population, with the center shifting steadily westward. Ohio had been admitted to the Union in 1803, Indiana in 1816 and Illinois in 1818. The number of acres under cultivation increased proportionately, and a steadily increasing stream of agricultural products went from them back towards the seaboard, for consumption there or shipment to Europe. The extension of the frontier instituted a bitter rivalry among the Atlantic states for their share in the lucrative trade with the West, a competition which resolved itself into the question of which could offer the cheapest transportation facilities to the western farmers in the marketing of their crops. New York, Pennsylvania and Maryland were the foremost in this contest, and involved themselves in the expenditure of millions of dollars for roads, canals, and eventually railroads, in their efforts to increase their own trade and diminish that of their rivals.

The undertaking of internal improvements by the states rather than by the central government, which had important consequences for the security holders, had been induced by a number of factors. Jacksonian democracy and a great tenderness for states' rights had taken the place of the federalist principle of strong centralization.[33] The states became the centers of administrative activity, and since the day of the great public utility corporation had not yet arrived, they found themselves forced to undertake the burden of providing public utilities, with only occasional aid from the Federal treasury. In its zeal to outdo a rival, a state frequently engaged in projects which would hardly

[32] Porter, *State Debts and Repudiation*, p. 590.

[33] Secretary of the Treasury, *Report on Finances*, 1826, pp. 37-39; 1828, p. 10; 1829, p. 3; 1831, p. 7, gives details of Federal aid to internal improvements in these years.

have appealed to the more sober view of a central government unconcerned with state rivalries, or to the managers of a corporation bound to earn dividends.

The first of the large internal improvements of this period, and in many ways the most successful, was the building of the Erie Canal in New York. Begun in 1817, it was carried on in the face of tremendous political opposition, and at a terrifying cost, to its completion in 1825. It was an immediate success, not only in its purpose of attracting the trade of the middle West, but equally so from a financial standpoint. During the first year of operation it was self-supporting, and within ten years it had redeemed at a premium the state bonds issued for its construction. Shipping costs were reduced at the same time that the price of wheat was being increased by the wider market, so that the value of the western lands was enormously enhanced, and a constantly increasing acreage sent its produce eastward.

Philadelphia and Baltimore watched with anxiety and envy the building of this waterway to the port of New York. In 1824 a Society for the Promotion of Internal Improvements had been formed in Philadelphia, and it was largely due to its efforts that Pennslyvania was persuaded to begin an elaborate course of canal and horse-power railway, to connect the Ohio river valley with the coast by way of Pittsburgh and Johnstown to Philadelphia. "At length the noble example set by the State of New York, in the Erie and Hudson Canal, aroused the energies of our citizens," as Mathew Carey diplomatically phrased it, and by 1829 Pennsylvania could point to its Chesapeake and Delaware Canal as a worthy rival to the Erie.[34]

Maryland refused to be outdone in the matter of canals, and started, on July 4, 1828, with music and a parade to dig the Chesapeake and Ohio Canal, in order to get her share of the Western trade. On the same day, with more music and parade, a railroad was started by a group which was convinced that the canal was already outmoded as a means of transportation. This

[34] Callendar, *State Enterprise and Corporations*, p. 143. Carey, *Brief View of the System of Internal Improvements of the State of Pennsylvania* (1831).

was the Baltimore and Ohio Railroad, and it became so popular that the canal was never finished.[35]

The states of the Middle West were quick to see the advantages to be gained from full use of the canals being built to the coast, and they proceeded to build connecting waterways which would make the water route available to shippers in all parts of their territory. Although their coastwise shipping made less necessary the construction of canals, the Southern states were stimulated by the ease with which securities could be floated in New York and London to issue them for large state banks, as well as for public improvements. Only the New England states escaped the craze for borrowing which seemed to have descended upon the country.

There was at this time in New York City no group of bankers which corresponded to what we know today as investment bankers. The investment function was exercised by commercial bankers, who combined the investment business with their commercial banking business, and by brokerage houses. It had long been customary for these commercial banks, both those which were incorporated and those which operated as private banks, to purchase large blocks of securities and resell them in smaller lots, or to take the securities as agent for the issuing corporation, and sell them on commission. Stephen Girard in Philadelphia and John Jacob Astor in New York had frequently handled government bonds on such terms, and during the rapid flotations of securities which marked the decade of the 1830's many other banking houses joined in this lucrative business. Astor and Sons; Brown Brothers and Company; Prime, Ward and King; Nevins, Townsend and Company; Morris Canal and Banking Company, were among the private banks and brokerage houses whose names are frequently met in the history of security issues by the states while, among the incorporated banks, the Bank of the Manhattan Company and the Phenix Bank were prominent.

Some of the securities were sold through the Bank of the

[35] Jenks, *Migration of British Capital*, p. 74. 27 Congress, 3 Session, House Report 296, p. 57.

United States and through the private firm of Thomas Biddle and Company in Philadelphia, which was owned by the brother of Nicholas Biddle, President of the Bank of the United States. The connection, personal and banking, between the Biddles and the Barings of London was also of especial advantage at this time, since it enabled securities destined to be sold in London to be handled in expeditious fashion. Even more direct was the sale of state issues to branches of foreign houses, or to their representatives in New York. In 1837 S. V. S. Wilder was the New York agent of the French house of Hottinguer, and Auguste Belmont of Rothschild's.[36] All foreign connections, in this period when one of the chief functions of the investment banker was to arrange for the sale of the securities abroad, were valuable.

The first important issue of state securities was the New York 6's, which appeared in 1817. In the next eight years $7,000,000 of New York canal stocks appeared on the market, with so high a credit rating that in 1822 Messrs. Astor and Son took $250,000 worth at 7 per cent premium, and in 1823, two large Albany banks took $300,000 at 5 per cent advance.[37] But after 1825 the plan of creating with each new debt, provision for its payment, was abandoned, and New York must be added to the list of recklessly borrowing states. By 1840 its outstanding debt was nearly 17 millions, at the very time that the revenues from canal tolls were declining.

Like New York, Pennsylvania issued its own stock to finance the construction of canals and railways. Thirty-four millions of the total state debt of $36,000,000, had been issued for this transportation system alone and it was probably true, as Carey boasted, that "No nation has ever expended so much money on such vast useful improvements in the same space of time."[38] His boastfulness was somewhat premature, for when the second

[36] Jenks, *Migration of British Capital*, p. 359, note 12. *Niles' Register*, Vol. XLVIII, p. 250. 27 Congress, 3 Session, House Report 296, p. 94. New York State Comptroller, *Report*, 1843. *Financial Register*, Vol. I, p. 301.

[37] *Niles' Register*, Vol. XXIII, pp. 96, 290. Pitkin, *Statistical View*, pp. 546-549 (1835).

[38] Carey, *Brief View of the System of Internal Improvement of the State of Pennsylvania* (1831), 27 Congress, 3 Session, House Report 296, p. 54.

series of bankruptcies began, in 1839-1840, the state was so impoverished that it was obliged to stop the payment of interest, and for a time there was doubt as to the ultimate redemption of the securities. Eventually all of its obligations were made good.

The construction of the Chesapeake and Ohio Canal was undertaken by a private company, but was heavily subsidized by municipal, state and national governments. Of its original capital of $3,600,000, $1,000,000 each had been subscribed by the national government and the city of Washington, $500,000 by the state of Maryland, $250,000 each by the cities of Georgetown and Alexandria, and only $600,000, or one-sixth of the total, by individuals. The three cities sent a representative to New York early in 1830 to borrow money with which to pay their subscriptions, and obtained it easily at less than 6 per cent, from Dutch agents. The state of Maryland subscribed $2,000,000 more in mortgages in 1833, and between 1836 and 1839 issued $4,375,000 of "preferred stock" for a further subscription, making a total state indebtedness of nearly $7,000,000 incurred for this one canal which was never entirely completed.[39]

A frequent procedure among western states which wished to float bonds was for the state legislature to vote authorization and then to enter into a contract with an eastern banker, either for the sale of the bonds outright to him at a profitable discount, or for the sale of the bonds to other investors by the banker as agent —at, of course, a lucrative commission. In 1825, when Ohio was contemplating internal improvements on a large scale, she sent commissioners to New York to get the lay of the financial land. The four great powers of Wall Street, Nathaniel Prime, J. J. Astor, John Robins, and John Hone, after a conference which is alleged to have lasted for two days and a night, came forth with an ultimatum regarding the concessions to be enacted into the statute, and were able to enforce their terms before the requested loan of $400,000 was forthcoming.[40] After that first

[39] Letter from J. J. Speed, Esq., of Baltimore, to the representatives of Maryland in the Congress of the United States on the subject of the Canal; 27 Congress, 3 Session, House Report 296, pp. 55, 56.

[40] Barrett, *The Old Merchants of New York City*, I, p. 391.

loan, the Ohio canal commissioners generally advertised for sealed bids on each offering, placing notices in the newspapers of New York in ample time for the news to reach Europe. The Bank of the Manhattan Company acted as New York agents for the commissioners, paying interest, making transfers, and placing the proceeds of the sales to the credit of the state. When in 1831, Ohio entered upon a rather reckless policy of subsidizing private companies engaged in the construction of public works, brokers were employed instead of the Bank, and in 1842, when the state's credit was very low, Baring Brothers bought small lots of the bonds direct, at a heavy discount.[41]

In its turn, Indiana undertook the building of the Wabash and Erie Canal, and issued nearly ten millions' worth of bonds between 1832 and 1836 for that purpose. Illinois started boldly on another ten-million-dollar program for internal improvements including the Illinois and Michigan Canal, with connecting railroads. Both states became involved in financial difficulties by thus allowing themselves to be "allured from the path of wisdom and economy by the seductive spirit of speculation and the wild fury of popular delusion."[42] They were unable to carry out the elaborate plans which they had made for opening a channel to the Erie Canal and the East, and by 1841 the two states were reduced to issuing new bonds in order to pay interest on the old.[43]

Michigan had a most unfortunate experience in her efforts to provide internal improvements. Her first legislature, meeting in 1837, was anxious to show that the new state was in full accord with the spirit of the times, and authorized a bond issue of 5 millions to be expended upon public works. The banks of the country had just suspended specie payments, and no one in New York was willing to buy the bonds outright at par. However, the Morris Canal and Banking Company of New York

[41] Bogart, *Internal Improvements and State Debt in Ohio*, p. 162.

[42] Governor Carlin, of Illinois, quoted in "Debts of the States", *North American Review*, 1844. Stocks of the State Bank of Indiana, sold in London after 1834, maintained their credit throughout. McCulloch, *Men and Measures of Half a Century*, p. 115.

[43] 27 Congress, 3 Session, House Report 296, pp. 86-89.

offered to act as agent in their sale, at a commission of 2.5 per cent. By November, 1838, the Company had disposed of more than a million dollars' worth of the bonds, and deposited the proceeds to the credit of the state. But the

STATE DEBTS, JANUARY, 1843*

State	(In millions of dollars)			Population (In thousands)
	Direct debt	Floating debt and loans of credit	Total liabilities	
Maine	1.7	0.1	1.8	502
New Hampshire				285
Vermont				292
Massachusetts	1.4	5.4	6.7	738
Connecticut				310
Rhode Island				109
New York	19.5	5.2	24.7	2,429
New Jersey				373
Pennsylvania	37.9	2.0	39.9	1,724
Delaware				78
Maryland	10.0	10.0	20.0	470
Virginia	7.4	2.9	10.3	1,240
North Carolina		1.1	1.1	753
South Carolina	0.8	4.8	5.6	594
Georgia	1.6	1.7	3.2	691
Kentucky	3.8	0.04	3.8	780
Tennessee	1.5	1.5	3.0	829
Ohio	16.2	3.0	19.2	1,519
Louisiana	1.2	19.2	20.4	352
Indiana	12.7	2.4	15.1	686
Mississippi		7.0	7.0	376
Illinois	13.8	5.0	18.8	476
Alabama		15.7	15.7	591
Missouri	0.9		0.9	384
Arkansas		3.5	3.5	98
Michigan	5.4	0.2	5.6	212
Florida		3.9	3.9	54
Wisconsin	0.1		0.1	31
Iowa				43
District of Columbia	1.4		1.4	44
TOTAL	137.1	94.5	231.6	17,063

* 27 Congress, 3 Session, House Report 296, p. 117 [from the *Democratic Review*].

Company then found itself in difficulties, and suggested to the Governor that he turn over the rest of the bonds to the Bank of the United States of Pennsylvania, receiving in exchange its guarantee for three-fourths of their par value to be paid over a period of years. The Morris Canal Company guaranteed the other fourth, minus its commission. The bonds were pledged by the Bank of the United States of Pennsylvania to various banking houses in Europe to secure the short-term credits which the Bank was then acquiring. A few months later the Bank failed, leaving European investors in the uncomfortable position of holding bonds for which the state had received about one-third of the face value, and which it refused to redeem except on that basis.[44]

The southern states had fully as many difficulties with the final disposition of their bonds as did Michigan. Louisiana was the first to enter the London market for funds, with state bonds issued for the purpose of establishing banks. The banks were well managed and the bonds, which were made payable in England, retained their high credit until the banks became involved in the cotton speculation of 1837-1839, when they found their capital impaired.[45] Mississippi, Tennessee, and Kentucky came into the market rather late, when the first enthusiasm of the foreign investors had passed, but they were still able to dispose of their bonds at par. Mississippi and Kentucky contracted with the United States Bank for the sale of their bonds, Tennessee with a New York banker. Many of the southern bonds went to Europe and England, where they were converted into sterling bonds with the interest and principal payable in London. Hope and Company of Amsterdam held a large number of the Mississippi bonds at the time of their repudiation in 1841.[46]

The total amount of state issues from 1820-1838 is given in the following table:

[44] Curtis, *Debts of the States*, pp. 134-36. Scott, *Repudiation of State Debts*, p. 161.

[45] Curtis, op. cit., p. 137. *Niles' Register*, Vol. XXVII, p. 154.

[46] Curtis, op. cit., p. 40. *Financial Register*, Vol. II, pp. 28-30. Scott, op. cit., p. 37.

STATE BOND ISSUES

Years	*Amount*
1820–1825	$12,791,000
1825–1830	13,680,000
1830–1835	40,013,000
1835–1838	107,824,000
TOTAL	$174,308,000

The purposes for which the stock still outstanding in 1838 had been issued, were:[47]

Purpose	*Amount*	*Per cent of total*
Banking	$52,640,000	35
Canals	60,202,000	31
Railroads	42,871,000	25
Turnpikes	6,619,000	4
Miscellaneous	8,475,000	5
TOTAL	$170,808,000	100

While the total amount of these securities marketed in England cannot be precisely determined, several estimates are available. Representative Garland, speaking in Congress in 1838, stated that of all the state securities then outstanding, 86 millions, or almost exactly half, were held in England. In addition to these he listed 24 millions of bank, life insurance, railroad, and other securities issued by private companies which were held in that country, making a total of 110 millions. A second estimate from Elliott's *Funding System* gives 30 million pounds, approximately 145 million dollars, as the total of American loans contracted in England between 1818 and 1838. This is a somewhat more generous figure than that of Representative Garland, but if the stocks which were redeemed or sent back during those years were

[47] Tenth Census, 1880, Vol. VII, p. 523. This total is the amount of debt outstanding in 1838, and does not therefore equal the total of stock issued.

subtracted from this figure, the remaining total would probably not be different from Mr. Garland's.[48] A third and still larger figure for the total was given in 1842. Representative Johnson, in an official report to the Treasury, set the total foreign holdings of state and municipal securities at 150 millions.[49]

We have seen something of the way in which the transfer of securities was effected; it remains to look at the other side of the picture and to see how they were paid for. The close connection which exists between the different branches of the money market is nicely illuminated by such an inquiry, for a large part of the securities which were exported from the United States to Great Britain were paid for in short-term credits used to finance the shipment of goods from Great Britain to the United States.[50] The immediate method of payment was by permitting the American importer to purchase merchandise against letters of credit, a process which kept the exchanges in favor of the United States.

When the top-heavy credit structure finally began to totter in 1837, it was in the commercial-paper market that the first difficulties arose; cotton houses in New Orleans, and their correspondents in New York to which a disproportionate amount of credit had been extended, began to fail; specie began to flow towards England in alarming volume. The banks of New York were forced to suspend specie payments and those in the rest of the country soon followed. But the export of securities, which was really the foundation for the extension of all these other credits, was not at once interrupted.[51] During 1838 and the early part of 1839 the credit of the states was still good in the London market, and a number of issues were floated there. By August of the latter year, the situation had changed. Illinois was able to dispose of only a part of her 8 per cent bonds and then only

[48] Jenks, op. cit., p. 64. 28 Congress, 1 Session, Executive Document 15, p. 1170. *Financial Register,* Vol. II, p. 141.

[49] 27 Congress, 3 Session, House Report 296, p. 7.

[50] See p. 64 below.

[51] *The New York Evening Post,* in commenting on the continued flow of English funds into American stocks, suggested that it was caused by a want of confidence in the future stability of English securities, and added that there was no doubt that "American stock is the best security in the world." (March 28, 1837.)

at a discount of 17 and 18 per cent.[52] During the same summer, Indiana 5's were sold in New York at 50, and Illinois 6's at 60, and only a small amount could be sold at that price. By February of 1840 Mr. Jaudon of the United States Bank of Pennsylvania was unable to sell a million of the Maryland canal bonds in London at any price. Since they could no longer borrow to pay the accumulating interest charges, nine states stopped payment of interest during 1841 and 1842. Three of them also declined to repay the principal in whole or in part, Mississippi openly repudiating the whole of her 5-million-dollar bond issue of 1838, on the high moral ground that she would not make serfs of her children. Michigan refused to pay that part of her debt which represented funds out of which she had undoubtedly been swindled by her agents. Florida claimed that she had not had legal power to contract the debt. Six other states simply said that they had no money with which to pay dividends, although they had honorable intentions of resuming payment as soon as possible.[53] There was considerable truth in the gloomy summary of events given by Senator Benton in 1840.[54]

> The goods are worn out; the paper money has returned to the place from whence it came; the operation is over, and nothing remains to the transactions but the 170 millions of debt, its devouring interest, and the banks, canals, and roads which represent it. The whole of these banks have failed once, and most of them twice, in two years; the greater part of the roads and canals are unfinished, and of those finished, several are unproductive.

It was obvious that no more state bonds could be floated at home or abroad. The credit of the states might have been restored through the assumption of their debts by the Federal government, as had been done, under very different circumstances, in 1792. Congress spent many hours in bitter debate over the plan and English holders of American securities wrote letters and pamphlets in its favor, but the proposition was never able to gain enough votes for enactment. The only relief offered by the

[52] *Niles' Register*, Vol. LVIII, p. 384.
[53] Jenks, op. cit., p. 103.
[54] Quoted in Tenth Census, 1880, Vol. VII, p. 527.

government was a national bankruptcy act which eased the position of the American debtor, but was small comfort to his English creditor.[55]

Although a large amount of these stocks was held in the United States, they played a disproportionately small rôle in the market. Very little business on the New York exchange was carried on in state stocks, and the volume of trading gives no clue to the amount of capital funds being absorbed by the states. A great many of the stocks were held for years in the vaults of banks in New York and other states as security for their note circulation.[56] With the foreign market closed, therefore, the era of internal improvements by the states was brought abruptly to an end. While they were struggling to pay debts already accumulated, large private corporations arose to take over the functions formerly exercised by the states, and the building of the railroads, which proceeded rapidly after 1840, was almost entirely in private hands.[57]

The railroad era

The business in railroad securities was chiefly responsible for the activity on the Stock Exchange in the expansion of 1834-1837. On November 5, 1834, the turnover of shares reached a total of 8,700; throughout the autumn it was often 5,000 shares daily. After the panic of 1837, and during the early 1840's, the totals sank back to 2,000 and 3,000 shares.[58] Indeed the activity of trading in the rails provided business enough for a rival organization, the New Board of Brokers, which offered effective competition to the Old Board.

The addition of railroad stocks to the usual list had begun with the Mohawk and Hudson, in August, 1830. Two other lines were

[55] The law permitted bankrupts after assigning all their property to their creditors pro rata to be declared debt free. The Act was repealed in 1843. United States Statutes at Large, 27 Congress, 1 Session, Chapter IX.

[56] Message of Governor Horatio Seymour of New York, June 1, 1853. 10 millions of the total 23 millions of New York state stocks were held by banks against note circulation.

[57] Porter, op. cit., p. 590. Adams, *Public Debts*, p. 339.

[58] *Journal of Commerce*, passim.

in existence at that time, the Baltimore and Ohio, and a road between Charleston and Hamburgh in South Carolina.

SHARES TRADED ON NEW YORK STOCK EXCHANGE, MAY 31, 1831

Name of share	*Amount*
United States 4's	1,880
United States Bank	70
Manhattan Bank	30
Union Bank	17
Delaware and Hudson Canal	264
Butchers and Drovers Bank	325
Morris Canal	75
Farmers Loan Co.	100
Aetna Insurance	25
Brooklyn Insurance Co.	43
Catskill Railroad	50
Ithaca and Oswego Railroad	40
TOTAL	2,919

Horse power was used on these early roads, and passengers were permitted to use their own carriages on the rails. But during 1830 and 1831, when it became evident that steam locomotives would soon take the place of horses, the public imagination was touched and its speculative propensities fired. In 1831 the *Journal of Commerce* remarked sourly that "railroads are all the go now, and more charters, involving some millions of expenditures, are wanted, not only for the general benefit, but to give scope to speculation, which is quite too much pent up within the limits of the present small companies." The wanted capital was soon forthcoming in spite of journalistic disapproval. Part of it came from the state legislatures before 1838, but most of it from individuals. By 1840 there were 2,800 miles of road in operation; by 1850 the length had more than trebled, and by 1860 it had trebled again, reaching the total length of 30,600 miles before the Civil War interfered with its rapid growth. It had cost about one and one-half billion dollars to lay the tracks.[59]

[59] *Journal of Commerce*, March 9, 1831. Stedman, op. cit. p. 87. Henry Poor, *Influence of the Railroads*, p. 10.

With the entrance of railroad securities into the market, there began also a long series of spectacular exploits on the part of railroad stock manipulators. Jacob Little opened with a corner in Morris Canal in 1835; Jacob Barker, Daniel Drew, Jim Fisk, Astor, and Vanderbilt were worthy successors. These men undoubtedly possessed a type of intelligence, and an acquisitive instinct superior to that of many of their fellows. To the investment market of New York, however, they contributed nothing, and may even be considered to have damaged its power and its prestige. The details of their maneuvers have many times been recounted and are dramatic and intriguing. In a study of the money market they have no place, for although the conscientious reader could undoubtedly discover a moral to adorn every such tale, the moral is applicable not so much to the organization of the money market as to the general code of business ethics which permitted such abuses.[60]

When the period of rapid railroad expansion began, domestic investors were unable to supply the amount of funds required, and the railroad companies followed the example of the states and turned to London.[61] Even before the English investor had ceased to absorb the bonds of the American states, he had begun to experiment with American railway securities, although at first there was considerable suspicion of them. The London *Times* warned its readers in 1838 against "American private enterprises such as coal-mining, railroad and canal companies. . . . We have never thought highly of any of the American securities, but against such as these especially the public ought to be upon their guard." Within a few years, however, the state stock had lost even such shreds of reputation as the *Times* had been willing to allow it, while the railroads and other corporate securities had grown in favor.[62] The first rail stock to appear on the London

[60] Hemming, *History of the New York Stock Exchange*, p. 16. *Stocks and Stock-Jobbing in Wall Street* (1848). Stedman, op. cit. p. 102. Clews, *Fifty Years in Wall Street*, pp. 105, 110, 505. Clew's book is an excellent example of the matter-of-fact way in which these exploits were regarded by their contemporaries.

[61] Hemming, op. cit., p. 16. Jenks, op. cit., p. 368, Note 11.

[62] Quoted by the *Financial Register*, Vol. II, p. 188 from London *Times* of July 23, 1838.

market was the Camden and Amboy in 1838, which was soon followed by the Lehigh, the Harrisburg and Lancaster, the Reading, and others. Although there was a recognized market for American rails in London by 1840, it was some time before the foreign demand for rails acquired momentum. Between 1838 and 1849, the amount of new foreign capital invested in American enterprises was probably less than 40 millions of dollars.[63] After 1850 many of the issues of railroad securities were floated in London originally in order to take advantage of the lower rate of interest. During June, 1852, for example, arrangements with London bankers were made by the Illinois Railroad for a loan of 5 millions, by the Erie for 2 or 3 millions, and by the Pennsylvania for 3 millions. The last one in particular occasioned resentment among New York houses which found themselves outbid by their English competitors.[64]

The total amount of American securities held in England increased more rapidly between 1850 and 1860 than in any other decade before the Civil War.[65] In 1853 there appeared an estimate by the Secretary of the Treasury, based upon returns from a large number of officials and corporations. State securities held first place in volume, but they consisted largely of the repudiated issues before 1840, which were still in the unwilling hands of their purchasers; the railroad securities which ranked second in amount had all been purchased after 1838, and most of them after 1840.

The miscellaneous item is probably too small, since it included reports from only fifteen corporations. The figure for canal and navigation companies also seems small until one recalls that most of the indebtedness incurred for canal building was included under the head of state bonds. It was to be expected that the largest foreign holdings of bank stocks would be found in the

[63] Bullock, Williams and Tucker, "The Balance of Trade in the United States," *Review of Economic Statistics*, 1919.

[64] *New York Times*, June 28, July 1, 1852. Stedman, op. cit., p. 102.

[65] In 1851 it was estimated by a writer in New York at $225,000,000. This figure included state, federal, county and city debts, as well as 20 millions of the outstanding 40 millions of railroad securities. No attempt was made to supplement this with an estimate of the amount of short-term credits due to English bankers. *New York Times*, Nov. 25, 1851.

case of banks in the larger cities. In New Orleans, for example, 28 per cent of the total bank capital was foreign-owned.

The separate items of this estimate were as follows:[66]

AMERICAN SECURITIES OWNED ABROAD IN 1853

Issued by	*Total outstanding*	*Foreign-owned*	*Per cent foreign-owned*
United States	$58,205,000	$27,000,000	46
States	190,718,000	110,972,000	58
Counties and cities	93,280,000	21,462,000	23
Railroad bonds	170,112,000	43,889,000	26
Railroad stocks	309,894,000	8,026,000	3
Banks and insurance	279,555,000	7,067,000	3
Canal and navigation	58,019,000	2,522,000	4
Miscellaneous	18,784,000	1,068,000	6
TOTAL	$1,178,567,000	$222,006,000	18

During 1854 and 1855, when the Crimean War was being waged by England, France, and Russia, many American securities were returned to this country.[67] In spite of this the official estimate of American securities held abroad in 1856 was higher than for 1853. The chief reduction had been in Federal bonds, many of which had been voluntarily redeemed by the government at a high premium. The greatest increase was in railroad bonds. The total funded indebtedness of the country, including only the industrial companies of the first report, was estimated at 1,408 millions of dollars, and the total amount owned by foreigners (accepting the previous estimate of 111 millions of dollars as the amount of state stock held abroad) was set at 240 millions of dollars.[68]

A new official estimate by the Secretary of the Treasury for 1860 set the total foreign investment in this country at 400 millions of dollars in that year. The railroad securities headed

[66] 33 Congress, 2 Session, Executive Document 42.

[67] Hunt's *Merchants' Magazine*, Vol. 28, p. 74; Vol. 23, p. 529. *Bankers' Magazine*, Vol. 9, p. 79.

the list, as many of the state bonds had been by this time returned and exchanged for the more popular rails, and only a few small state issues were floated abroad during the 1850's.

By 1860 the English investor was too much concerned over the possibility of Civil War in the United States to be willing to risk his capital in further investment here, either in government or railroad securities. The proceeds of sales of English goods, which would ordinarily have been invested in American securities in large amounts, were permitted to pile up as bank balances, and were finally withdrawn entirely.[69] Moreover, many securities already held in England were returned, and between 1860 and 1863 the result of a decade of capital importation was undone, and the volume of American securities held abroad dropped to about 200 millions of dollars, where it had stood at the beginning of the decade.[70] A comparatively small amount of Confederate securities was taken by English investors, and on the whole the War of 1861, like the War of 1812, had to be financed without help from abroad.

Technique of trading on the early Stock Exchange

The technique of investing funds at the New York Stock Exchange had undergone changes in many details since the first informal selling under the buttonwood tree in Wall Street, and the process of trading in stocks and bonds is as different as the types of securities traded. One of the points which has been changed by both law and custom is the period of time within which sales are completed. By-laws adopted in 1817 by the

[68] The *New York Herald* considered these figures far too small; its estimate of the total funded indebtedness of the country was 2,500 millions, and the amount held abroad was set at 500 millions, more than twice the official figure. The interest on so large a foreign debt would absorb 35 millions annually, nearly one-third of the value of our cotton exports at that time. If the Herald's figure for total funded indebtedness included all the small industrial corporations whose shares rarely appeared on the market, it may have been nearer the truth than the Treasury estimates. Few of such shares would have been exported to England, however, and the figure of 500 millions of American securities held abroad, is almost certainly too large. *New York Times,* March 19, 1857. *Herald,* March 18, 1857. Secretary of Treasury, *Report on the Finances,* 1856, p. 35.

[69] See p. 113 below.

[70] Hunt's *Merchants' Magazine,* Vol. 59, 1868, p. 242. Bullock, Williams and Tucker, "The Balance of Trade in the United States," *Review of Economic Statistics,* 1919.

Board of Brokers had provided that unless otherwise stated in the contract of sale, all settlements were to be made on the following day, which was known as settlement the "regular way." The contract might set any period desired for the settlement, and either the buyer or the seller might be given the privilege of postponing it for six or more months. Jacob Little made such striking use of a twelve months' option in an Erie stock coup in 1840, that the Board set a limit of sixty days to sellers' options thereafter.[71] In 1857, there was an attempt to limit buyers' as well as seller's options to sixty days, but it was not until the wave of good resolutions which followed the panic of 1857, that the rule was able to muster a majority. In the same year sales on time were restricted to thirty days' settlement but the rule had been in force for only two weeks when it was repealed.

The actual practice of the brokers in regard to settlement varied widely, with an increasing use of cash settlements, and a decrease in use of the longer periods permitted. During times of business crisis there was a tendency on the Stock Exchange, as in the commercial credit market, to shorten the terms of sale. In 1837, at the height of the panic, nearly half of all the stock sales were made for cash.[72] A few years later the proportion of cash sales had sunk again to one-fourth or one-fifth. There were two factors, however, which tended to make immediate settlement the more popular; improvement in telegraphic communications, which made it possible to settle for sales made to out-of-town customers as quickly as to those in the city, and the growth of the call loan market, which made it possible for buyers to borrow with their stock as collateral, and settle the account with the seller at once.[73]

The fact that most stock sales during these early years were made on time relieved the broker from the responsibility which he carries today, of financing the sale. If a broker did find it necessary to arrange a loan for a customer, it was often possible

[71] Clews, *Fifty Years in Wall Street*, p. 10. New York *Times*, May 5, Sept. 15, 1857. *New York Evening Post*, Sept. 14, 28, 1857.

[72] *New York Evening Post*, April 11, 1837.

[73] The far-reaching effect of the call loan upon security trading will be more fully discussed in a later chapter.

for him to borrow from a fellow broker for a short period without collateral.[74] As the membership of the Board grew larger and the sales on time grew smaller, the practice of lending without collateral passed, and the banks took over the bulk of loans on stock collateral. At first many of these loans were on time, but with the growth in bankers' balances stimulating the development of the call loan market, the proportion of time loans on stock collateral fell off, and many private lenders and financial

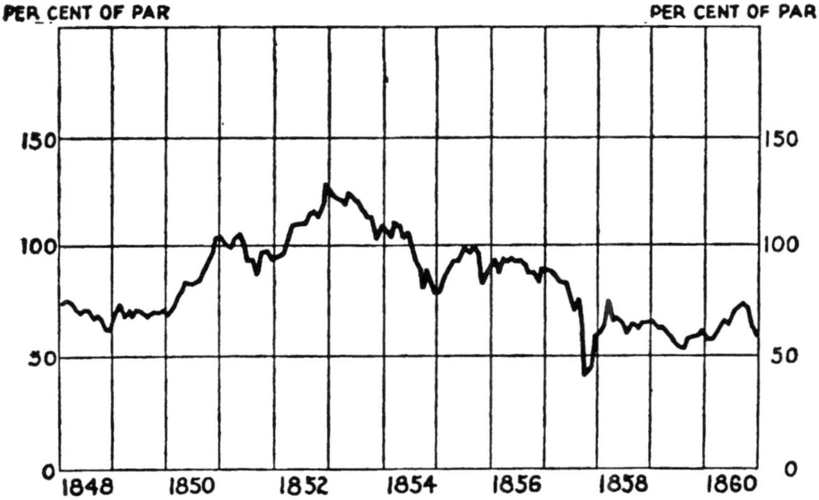

MONTHLY VARIATIONS IN PRICES OF TEN RAILROAD STOCKS

SOURCE: INDEX NUMBER COMPILED BY FREDERICK R. MACAULAY

houses as well as banks began to put their temporary surpluses into call loans with stock as security.[75]

In the years before 1863, railroad stocks were the speculative element in the money market and, in comparison with bank and gas company stocks, showed a wide range of variation, reflecting every change in economic conditions. Index numbers of railroad stock prices[76] confirm the impression that the most important factor in the security market at this early date was the importation of foreign capital, and that when this source of supply

[74] Stedman, op. cit., pp. 445, 448.

[75] For further discussion of this point, see Chap. VII.

[76] These index numbers have been computed for the period 1848 to 1860 by Frederick R. Macaulay, to whom we are indebted for their use.

failed, the fact that there was prosperity at home did not avail to keep up stock prices. In many cases, of course, foreign investors ceased to buy American securities because they were experiencing the same sort of depression that was felt in the United States, and at such times the stock prices were a faithful picture of conditions at home. But an example of the other sort may be found in the course of stock prices from 1855 to 1857 when, in spite of rapid expansion at home, the return of securities from Europe incident to the Crimean War kept prices of stocks from rising proportionately. The rise of prices during the Civil War, in spite of the withdrawal of foreign capital, was due to the general inflation of monetary values, in which stock prices participated less than commodities.

The long major swings of stock prices in this period were pronounced. From a high point in the middle of 1835 prices fell off with only minor recoveries until 1842, a period of seven years. A sharp rise for two years and a slowly increasing level for eight years more failed to recover all the ground that had been lost in the drop after 1834. Another period of declining prices, from 1853 to 1857 carried the market back to another low point, although not to the extremes of 1842. After 1857 prices rose again, with recessions in 1859 and 1861, until the gust of speculation during the War carried them rapidly upward to new high levels.

It is difficult to say whether or not the prices of stocks ran up and down a wider scale in the years before 1863 than in more recent years. Certainly the average of railroad stocks has fluctuated less and less, but this is due to the fact that railroads have become less speculative enterprises. The growth of the country has steadied earnings and the declining volume of new mileage each year has reduced uncertainty. The wide fluctuations in early rail shares are comparable to those in the early industrial securities.

Other institutions which affected the investment market

Among the institutions which were becoming powerful factors in the investment market of New York were the savings banks and the insurance companies. The first savings banks had been organized in New York State in 1817 as an incentive to the "industrious poor." The deposits of these banks grew rapidly; and by 1846 the total was 112 millions; in the one year 1857, the growth amounted to nearly 25 millions. The laws of New York state regarding the investments of such funds were more lax than in many other states. Frequently the total deposits of a savings bank would be redeposited with a single commercial bank. But more often the money was put into securities, and savings banks exercised a growing power in the investment market.[77]

Marine and fire insurance companies were formed almost as soon as banks, and the amount of capital represented by the insurance companies doing business in New York City grew rapidly. In 1827, the capital of the insurance companies of the state amounted to 16 millions. By 1860 the total capital of insurance companies of all kinds doing business in New York state was about 75 millions, a sum slightly above the capital of all the banks in New York City at that time.[78] The law of 1853 permitted a wide range of stocks to be used as investments by fire insurance companies, though limiting the life and health insurance companies to the stocks acceptable by the bank commissioner, *i.e.*, to Federal and state bonds and certain types of mortgages.[79] Besides the sums available for genuine investment, these companies put large sums also into the security loan market. A group of joint stock fire insurance companies in New York state, for example, had practically the whole amount of their capital stock loaned on bonds and mortgages.[80]

Summary

The outstanding features of the New York investment market before the Civil War were its comparative lack of industrial

[77] New York State Superintendent of Banks, *Report on Savings Banks*, 1858. Keyes, *History of Savings Banks in the State of New York*, pp. 75, 88.

[78] *New York State Assembly Journal*, January, 1822, p. 441. *Report* of the New York State Superintendent of Insurance, 1860, p. 369.

[79] Angell, *Treatise on the Law of Fire and Life Insurance.*

[80] New York State Comptroller, *Report on Fire Insurance Companies*, 1853, Table A.

securities, and its dependence upon the importation of capital funds from abroad. It was only in time of war, when the interests of industry were subordinated to those of the government, that the domestic market was called upon to absorb the securities offered without the aid of the foreign investor. During the rapid extension of internal improvements, financed largely by the issue of stocks of the states, as later during the rapid development of the railroads under private companies, it was foreign capital which provided the greater part of the necessary funds. The United States was an importer of capital until well into the twentieth century, and the market at New York was often in the position of poor country cousin, dependent upon every change of mood in its rich relative, the London market—a position which it did not relish, but from which it was impossible to escape. The Stock Exchange developed early in New York as a mechanism for handling the first issues of government securities, and was a highly developed organization before the call loan market had grown up, so that the technique of trading in the period before the existence of call loans differed materially from that of the later period.

CHAPTER III

THE COMMERCIAL CREDIT MARKET BEFORE 1863

The small volume of domestic commerce in the early years of the nation's existence postponed the development of commercial credit. Much of the domestic trade was carried on by barter and much of it by cash payments, neither of which required the creation of credit instruments. Foreign trade was a more important factor in the commercial life of the country than domestic trade until the Embargo of 1807 cut it short. Nearly all manufactured goods had to be imported from abroad, and they were paid for by agricultural produce and raw materials for which the turmoil created by the Napoleonic wars kept up a heavy demand.[1] This foreign trade did not rely for its financing upon American credit and did not give rise to dollar bills of exchange. As the frontier extended, the business of distributing goods imported from abroad, and of collecting and transporting to the seaboard the goods to be exported, became an increasingly important share of the internal commerce of the country, linking together inseparably the two branches of commerce, so that the domestic trade shared also in the benefits of the credit which was extended by London to foreign traders.

The demand for credit in the United States was conditioned by the direction of the internal commerce. Before the advent of canals and railroads, trade was carried on in a triangular course. Farmers of the western states sent much of their produce down the Mississippi River to New Orleans, where it was sold for cash which was carried back home. From New Orleans cotton and other agricultural products were shipped to the northeastern states, to the ports of New York, Philadelphia, and Baltimore, and from those cities in turn the manufactured goods which were imported from abroad were shipped to New Orleans.

[1] Johnson, *History of the Domestic and Foreign Commerce of the United States*, I, pp. 202-3; II, p. 14.

The western states sent to the East the coin which had been brought up from New Orleans, in return for foreign imports, thus forming the third side of the triangle. After 1830, improvements in transportation brought a change from this simple trade structure to a far more complicated one. The states farther west, which had formerly had no market for their produce but the South, now were able to send shipments to the East. A growing volume of manufactures was exchanged among the northern states, and sent also to the South. The shipments of imported goods from New York to New Orleans were always larger than those in the opposite direction, because much of the cotton which paid for the imports was shipped directly to Europe from the southern port.

Although the increasing volume of domestic trade brought about a demand for commercial credit, the banking facilities of the country were slow in developing. Before there could be commercial banks in the modern sense, a standard of banking technique had to be developed out of American experience, for there was in this country no family or professional group within which the traditions of banking were handed down. Any prosperous merchant who had surplus funds, any retired farmer who had accumulated a small capital, any group of enterprising business men who saw an opportunity for profit, might establish a bank and proceed to issue bank notes and dispense bank credit.

Development of loan practices

Another difficulty lay in the fact that although the early banks of the United States were modeled upon those of Great Britain as to charter provisions, it was impossible for them to adopt the rules laid down in England for the safe conduct of banks, which would have confined the loans and discounts to self-liquidating paper based upon an exchange of goods. The place of trade in the economy of Great Britain was far more important than in America; in this country there was a very large demand for long-term credit for the development of new lands and new industries, and a comparatively small demand for short-term credits with which to finance the exchange of products.[2] It was only in the larger cities, in the earlier part of the century, that banks were able to find enough paper of the strictly commercial type to fill their portfolios. In the smaller towns and country districts, they were obliged to lend on whatever collateral was available, which was largely upon mortgage security or personal signatures. Perhaps the first form of security to come into common use was the mortgage on land. William Gouge, in 1831, bemoaned among other things the fact that the honest mechanic of Philadelphia could no longer secure funds with which to set himself up in business, no matter how good his reputation, unless he could offer real estate as collateral.[3] The State Bank of Indiana, one of the strongest and most carefully conducted of the state banks, made the bulk of its loans during the first years of its existence (it was chartered in 1834) to farmers who were buying or improving land. The bank suffered few losses from these loans, but found them "sluggish and unreliable" during the difficult years after 1837. As soon as the volume of trade made it possible, therefore, the bank transferred its loans from real estate security to bills of domestic exchange drawn against shipments to the East or the South.[4]

Another type of security for promissory notes consisted of stocks and bonds. These time loans of varying length must not be confused with the call loans similarly collateraled, which played an important part in the money market. But neither real estate nor securities were behind most promissory notes; the usual procedure was for the borrower to secure one or two endorsers known to the bank.

Attempts on the part of a bank to confine its loans to short-term paper were often bitterly resented by the community, which felt that the bank had received valuable monopolistic privileges with its charter and that the least it could do in return was to meet the credit needs of its home community. For the same reason, banks were often forbidden by law to send their funds

[2] Edward Clibborn, *American Prosperity; in Outline of the American Debit or Banking System* (1837).

[3] William Gouge, *An Inquiry into the Principles of the American Banking System*, p. 16 (1835).

[4] McCulloch, *Men and Measures of Half a Century*, p. 116.

out of town for investment, or were required to loan a certain proportion of their assets at home before any funds were sent away. The idea was widely prevalent that a bank's first duty was to provide the community in which it was located with "circulating capital." The Newport Exchange Bank of Rhode Island, for example, was severely criticized in 1827, for keeping so large a proportion of its funds in New York, and thus "diverting the bank from the object of its creation." Connecticut passed several laws restricting the amount which banks of that state might lend "abroad," that is, outside the state. As late as 1854, the Bank Commissioner of Massachusetts deplored the discounting of outside paper as contrary to the interests of the merchants at home. Maine and New Hampshire went even further and wished to keep their people from borrowing from, as well as from lending to, outsiders. Such legislation was difficult to enforce and created constant friction between the banks and the officers to whom enforcement was entrusted, but it was adopted by many states in the years before 1860.[5]

Promissory note versus acceptance

The two principal forms of business paper upon which banks made advances were the promissory note and the acceptance. The promissory note was based upon the personal security of the maker, and it was usually secured, either by one or two endorsers, or by collateral in the form of real estate, stocks or bonds. The acceptance was at least theoretically based upon a commercial transaction, and was self-liquidating in the sense that the funds which paid for the goods involved, provided the means for repaying the advance upon them. The acceptance, or draft, or bill of domestic exchange, as it was variously termed, was the standard instrument of trade credit in England and on the Continent. But in America trade was not the chief occupation of the people, and the trade acceptance, although used, was unable to gain for itself the place which it occupied abroad. The promissory note has always played the leading role in American bank credit.

[5] Dewey, *State Banking Before the Civil War*, pp. 200-3.

In spite of its widespread use, there was much criticism of the promissory note. It was said to be mere accommodation[6] paper, a danger to the banks because it was not self-liquidating, and to the whole community because it lent itself readily to inflation.[7] The conventional attitude towards the promissory note was well summarized by an English writer in 1837:[8]

The great and essential difference between the American and our system of banking depends upon their mode of doing business; their rule is our exception; our rule is their exception. . . . They prefer accommodation paper, resting on personal security and fixed wealth, to real bills of exchange, resting on wealth, in transition from merchants and manufacturers to consumers.

On the other side, Mathew Carey estimated that the loss suffered by American banks from their loans on personal security was less than that from trade bills at the British banks during the same period. His eloquent defense of the accommodation loan presents the case as it must have appeared to many Americans:

A miserable delusion prevails on the subject of accommodation notes. Many directors of the different banks, some of whom have themselves made fortunes by credits of this description, not looking back to their early beginnings, violently declaim against them as a pernicious abuse, that ought to be eradicated altogether. And some of the banks, particularly the Bank of North America and the Farmers and Mechanics' Bank, have laid the axe to the root, in order to remove them. The Bank of Pennsylvania has recently adopted the same measure, and demanded by written notice, ten per cent. of all accommodation notes, large and small.

[6] *British Parliamentary Papers,* 1819, Vol. 3, p. 140, testimony of Mr. John Smith, gives a definition of accommodation *acceptances.* "The usual meaning of the term alluded to is, where two or more individuals agree to draw, indorse, and accept, Bills of Exchange for each other, there being no real Transaction of Business between them and the whole Operation being intended for the sole Purpose of raising money; or where, there being Transactions of Business between them they issue Paper beyond the Amount of such Transactions; and this Latter Species of Accommodation Paper is very common, because it is not very easy of Detection." In this country, such loans took the form of promissory notes as well as acceptances. The phrase "accommodation loan" is still used occasionally by country bankers.

[7] Aristides, *Letter to the Secretary of the Treasury,* etc., p. 31 (1819) and C. F. Adams, in Hunt's *Merchants' Magazine,* II, p. 197, represent the conservative American attitude.

[8] Edward Clibborn, *American Prosperity,* p. 29.

This whole train of ideas is erroneous. Its operation is highly pernicious. This will appear obvious to the most superficial observer, who considers how large a portion of the community cannot possibly have access to the Banks in any other form, than accommodation paper. For three-fourths of all the business done in the city, there are no notes received that are discountable at Bank. For the dry goods and hardware sold to the country storekeepers; for the merchandise exported to the southern states, and for a very large portion of our foreign exports, there are not ten dollars in the thousand for which notes of this description are received. Thus, at one stroke, if accommodation notes are annihilated, the whole mass of merchants, who supply the country, as respectable a body as any in the United States for their numbers, have every avenue to Bank credit closed against them.

Moreover, what is to become of the numerous and important classes of tradesmen, the carpenters, masons, shoemakers, tailors, smiths, printers, bookbinders, saddlers, curriers, &. &. &. They rarely receive notes for their work. When they do receive them, they are at such distant dates, as to be inadmissible at Bank. To meet their current engagements, they would be obligated to have all of them discounted by usurers, unless they could avail themselves of accommodation notes at Bank, whereby they would be enabled to await the arrival at maturity of their business notes.

Can a system be sound, which goes to dispense all the advantages of bank credit to a small portion of the community, and entirely to debar from it the most numerous and industrious portion of our citizens?[9]

The few bank returns still in existence from that early date throw little light on the subject, for they do not give separate totals for "loans on personal security" and "domestic bills of exchange," but include both under "total loans and discounts." Early discussions of bank credit indicate that the promissory note was the usual form of business paper discounted by banks during the first quarter of the nineteenth century. In describing the rapid increase of business during the expansion of 1815, for example, Matthew Carey says:[10] "As this . . . was principally carried on upon credit, it may readily be conceived that it must have created an inordinate quantity of promissory notes." He did not mention acceptances.

[9] Matthew Carey, *Essays on Banking, pp.* 130-32 (1816).
[10] Gouge, *A Short History, etc.*, p. 23 (1835).

Influence of second Bank of the United States

The use of trade acceptances seems to have been relatively infrequent until after the second Bank of the United States came into existence.[11] In 1817, the Board of Directors voted that the Bank should engage in the purchase and sale of bills of exchange. Very little progress in the use of the acceptance was made during the next few years; the item "bills of domestic exchange" first appeared on the balance sheet of the Bank in 1819. It was not until Nicholas Biddle became president of the Bank in 1823 that the full possibilities of such paper were realized. Mr. Biddle had made a thorough study of the British political economists and of the banking technique of Great Britain, and it was to this training that his emphasis upon the use of the trade acceptance and his efforts to encourage it must be ascribed. The rapid growth in the item, *bills of domestic exchange,* as compared with *loans on personal security,* which were the discounts of promissory notes, may be seen in the table on page 50.[12]

A large part of this growth in the use of the trade acceptance was the result of the financing of cotton exports, which created in the South a great volume of drafts upon New York.[13] These possessed obvious advantages over the promissory notes formerly used, in the fact that the Bank of the United States, with its numerous branches, would discount them, and that other banks also were beginning to advance against them. Biddle's testimony before the investigating committee of 1832 thus describes the process:

[11] In the notebook of Duncan P. Campbell of New York (Manuscript Division of the New York Public Library) we find the following entries:

> "Feb. 1, 1827 I accepted Mary Macomb's Note, 4 Mo. $500
> "Sept. 4, 1829 Accepted for W. Bayard, W. Corbier's draft $193.36 and also $156.40
> "Nov. 15, 1831 Accepted Vanderhemp's draft at 6 mo. $1087.37 I drew on Vanderhemp at sight $1055.70
> "May 10, 1831 Wm. Bayard drew on me for expenses at salt works. I did not accept."

These are the only acceptances noted during four years.

[12] Monthly reports of the Bank of the United States, in 23 Congress, 2 Session, Senate Document 17, pp. 204-224. The original resolution authorizing the Bank to do an exchange business is given on page 49.

[13] Report of the committee . . . to examine into the proceedings of the Bank of the United States, April 30, 1832. 23 Congress, 1 Session, House Report 460, p. 357.

A single example will make it intelligible. The crop of Tennessee is purchased by merchants who ship it to New Orleans, giving their bills founded on it to the branch at Nashville, which furnishes them with notes. These notes are in time brought to New York for purchasing supplies for Tennessee. They are paid in New York, and the Nashville bank becomes the debtor of the branch at New York. The Nashville branch repays them by drafts given to the branch at New York on the branch at New Orleans, where its bills have been sent, and the branch in New York brings home the amount by selling its drafts on the branch at New Orleans; or the New Orleans branch remits. Such an operation so far from "disturbing the regular course of trade," is its best auxiliary.

CHANGES IN THE TYPE OF LOANS AT THE BANK OF THE UNITED STATES

(In thousands of dollars, at date nearest to January 1 each year)

Year	*"Bills discounted on personal security" (Loans on promissory notes)*	*"Domestic Bills of Exchange" (Discounts of trade acceptances)*
1820	20,981	1,487
1821	20,598	1,509
1822	20,343	1,573
1823	22,597	1,940
1824	24,324	2,324
1825	23,170	2,728
1826	27,105	3,119
1827	24,331	3,347
1828	26,452	5,022
1829	29,855	7,689
1830	30,655	8,691
1831	32,827	10,457
1832	48,853	16,691
1833	40,086	18,069
1834	33,703	16,302

The Bank of the United States did more than purchase large amounts of acceptances on its own account. It encouraged other banks to make such purchases by maintaining a market for this type of paper, and through its branch offices it also provided a convenient method of collecting the acceptance upon maturity.[14]

When the Bank of the United States dropped from the field there was no bank or group of banks which had a strong interest in pushing the acceptance. The New York Assembly committee on bank reform, in 1835, felt obliged to urge that it was not only the right, but the duty, of banks, to take trade acceptances, since they were drawn against goods in transit and were more truly "business paper" than many promissory notes, which were actually accommodation paper of a reprehensible sort.[15] But the promissory note was widely used in domestic trade at that time. The dealers from all sections of the country made purchases in New York by giving their notes payable at the home banks. A merchant of long experience in the wholesale dry goods trade about the time of the Civil War, was unable to recall a single instance in which an acceptance had been used to finance a sale of dry goods in the West.[16] Merchants in the South made similar statements. Just a few years before the Civil War, Gibbons, in writing of the banking system in New York City, almost ignored the acceptance, stating that "commerce in its broadest sense, is carried on by promissory notes." And Stephen Colwell in the same year, in the best book on banking theory written before the War, mentioned acceptances only indirectly in discussing the extension of commercial credit. "The real basis of our paper currency," he wrote, "is the individual promissory notes, and other evidences of debt, in exchange for which it is issued."[17]

The failure of the trade acceptance to win for itself in America a place similar to that which it held abroad must be ascribed primarily to the different economic conditions and the lower place held by trade in the activities of the country. The lack of a central bank after 1837 was a further serious handicap, for the history of the second Bank of the United States showed what

[14] 23 Congress, 1 Session, House Report 460, p. 357. *United States Democratic Review*, Vol. 11, p. 433.

[15] New York Assembly Document 229, 1835, p. 6.

[16] *Journal of Accountancy*, Vol. 12, pp. 527, 529.

[17] Gibbons, *The Banks of New York*, p. 214 (1859). Colwell, *Ways and Means of Payment*, p. 472 (1859).

a determined effort to push the acceptance could accomplish. The central bank was essential to the development of an acceptance market, not only for the influence which it could exert in its favor, but for the discounting facilities which it could provide. With no real economic need for the acceptance, and without a central bank, it is not surprising that the promissory note was able to retain its preeminence. And it will be seen that the unsettled conditions after the Civil War presented still another obstacle to the development of an acceptance market.[18]

The trade acceptance did not keep its reputation unsullied. The experience of the United States followed closely that of England, in discovering that the acceptance could be used for other purposes than the financing of trade, and that it was often extremely difficult to determine whether a bill was founded upon a sale of produce, or was merely camouflage for an unsecured loan. Railroad acceptances made their appearance in the market during the period when the expenses of construction were putting a heavy strain upon the railroad companies. This type of paper was obviously nothing but finance or accommodation paper, and the fact that there was behind it no self-liquidating transaction caused the rates of discount to be higher than for true commercial paper. Mercantile houses abetted this use of the acceptance on occasion, by permitting themselves to be drawn on, and then discounting their own acceptance, in order to dispose of temporary funds. Thus the trade acceptance was turned aside from its original function and became no safer than the promissory note. Both might be used for "finance bills" as well as to provide credit for trade, or for justifiable loans upon personal security.[19]

Credit terms

The extension of commercial credit at this early period was a far more personal matter than today. Until quite late in the century it was customary for the full board of directors to pass on every piece of paper offered for discount. Many banks dis-

[18] See p. 315 below.

[19] *New York Evening Post,* November 26, 1849; August 11, September 6, 1851; March 26, 1853; July 24, 1854.

counted only once each week; in 1853, only the New York Exchange Bank and the Chemical Bank directors met twice a week for that purpose.[20]

During each of the successive periods of prosperity, the banks tended to grow lax in the extension of credit, extending the time and lowering the standards of the paper accepted for discount. As interest rates rose the banks became more eager to lend. After each crisis they again became conservative and cautious, shortening the time of their loans and scrutinizing more severely the standing of the borrower. After the panic of 1825, the New York banks became so strict that many protests were heard.[21] From 1830 on, money again became plentiful, the banks expanded their loans and discounts rapidly, and with the exception of 1834, the movement proceeded steadily to its culmination in the crisis of 1837. Open-book accounts and "easy credit" played a large part in the history of those years, and the volume of credit outstanding reached enormous proportions. Not only was the total credit issued of larger amount than ever before, but the terms upon which it was issued were longer than usual. According to one critic they had been increased from 2 or 3 months to 4 and 6, and on imported goods and manufactures, to 9 and 12 months.[22]

The panic of 1837 and the prolonged depression which followed brought about a tightening of credit conditions, as panics are wont to do. Commercial paper was looked upon with suspicion, and dealers demanded cash whenever possible. So marked was the change that in 1841 the *Democratic Review* could speak of the "old system" under which purchases had been made with promissory notes. The necessity for obtaining cash with which to meet their bills led merchants to discount their own unendorsed promissory notes—one of the first uses on record of the single-name paper which was to become the outstanding feature of post-bellum credit. When ordinary notes or acceptances were admitted, they had to be short and well secured.

[20] An amusing account of a meeting of the Board of Directors is given in Gibbons, *Banks of New York*, pp. 26 ff., (1859). *Bankers' Magazine*, Vol. 8, p. 590.
[21] *Remarks upon the Auction System* (1828) pp. 16, 17. Gouge, *A Short History, etc.*, p. 50 (1835).
[22] *Financial Register*, II, p. 7.

Where formerly commission merchants had been willing to take the drafts of farmers and produce dealers secured by produce not yet arrived, they now insisted that the goods be on hand, and even then cut down the credit to three-quarters of its market value.[23] Cotton as well as western produce was affected by the general suspicion, and was sold only for specie by many of the cotton factors.[24] So scarce was commercial paper in the market of New York in 1843 that the *Evening Post*, in discussing the possible fields of investments for funds, spoke of mercantile paper as non-existent from the investment point of view.[25]

This commercial stagnation was finally overcome by the revival of trade after 1845, and again there was the familiar spectacle of gradually lengthening credit terms as confidence was restored. The plethora of money made banks eager to lend, and merchants eager to sell. By 1850 it was customary in many lines of trade to give notes at 6 to 8 months in payment for goods. Debts incurred in the spring would not mature until November, and might then be renewed for several months more. In 1853 there was complaint that the kinds of bills which had formerly been dated at 6 months were becoming bills for 8, 10 and 12 months. The banks of New York blamed the merchants[26] for this state of affairs, but nothing was done about it until the panic of 1857 brought back to the money market the cautious state of mind which had prevailed in 1837. Then the 8- and 10-month bills were again reduced to 3 and 6 months, and in 1859, we find the banks of New York refusing altogether to discount notes longer than 4 to 8 months, and requiring instead, that, the dealer substitute his own note at 60 days, with the longer note held by the bank as collateral.[27]

The spasm of virtue which passed over the banking community after each crisis made the banks more careful as to the type of paper, as well as to its length. Although it was difficult to

[23] Hunt's *Merchants' Magazine*, Vol. 43, pp. 80, 178, 272. *United States Democratic Review*, Vol. IX, p. 205; Vol. XI, p. 210.

[24] *United States Democratic Review*, Vol. XI, pp. 433, 437.

[25] *New York Evening Post*, December 22, 1843.

[26] *Journal of Commerce*, November 27, 1850; Silex, *Letters on Banks and Banking* (1853).

[27] Gibbons, *Banks of New York*, p. 60 (1859). *Bankers' Magazine*, Vol. 12, p. 510. Evans, *History of the Commercial Crisis, etc.*, pp. 122-24.

distinguish between true commercial paper and the accommodation variety, some of the larger city banks tried to protect themselves against it by taking paper for short dates only, and refusing renewals. The Bank of Massachusetts, for example, gave public notice that it would take no notes on personal obligations for more than 30 days, and no notes for more than 60 days even when secured by articles of merchandise or other security. The Bank of New York demanded that notes be payable in 30 days, but this was later changed to 45 days, with no renewals. About 1815, the banks of Philadelphia made it a general practice to discount only notes of 60 days or less although they later became more lax.[28] But the banks in the country could not be argued out of accepting such notes, and in 1833 it was estimated that more than half of the loans and discounts of the country banks of New York state were accommodation loans.[29] Even the Bank Commissioners, usually the most conservative of advisers, could not condemn these loans unreservedly, as is shown in this nicely balanced official judgment from Connecticut in 1841: "The practice of some Banks to confine their discounts exclusively to business paper or paper that is subject to no renewal, is a great innovation, and denies to a worthy class of borrowers those facilities and advantages to which they are entitled;" but on the other hand, "We are totally averse to dead loans . . . and did not mean to be understood to encourage discounting accommodation paper except to a limited extent."[30] The attempt to distinguish between accommodation and trade paper was futile. Although accommodation paper was not directly concerned with a specific transaction, the proceeds from it came more and more to be applied to the liquidation of such transactions. With the development of single-name paper after the War, the term "accommodation" ceased to be an invidious one.

The note broker

The independent commercial paper house as it exists today, a buyer and seller of notes on its own account, is a recent de-

[28] Stone, *A Century of Boston Banking*. *Financial Register*, Vol. II, p. 7. Domett, *History of the Bank of New York*.

[29] New York State Bank Commissioner, *Annual Report*, 1833.

[30] State Bank Commissioners of Connecticut, *Annual Report*, 1841, p. 6.

velopment and nothing comparable to it was to be found in the early part of the nineteenth century. The earliest dealers in commercial paper were commission men who acted merely as agents. Their activity in buying and selling notes and bills on commission was often only one phase of a general "Negotiating Business," to quote from an advertisement of 1799, and often included the purchase of out-of-town bank notes at a heavy discount, as well as the handling of commercial paper. These "money-shavers" were the object of great opprobrium, and they were often accused of usurious charges. Niles' *Register*, in the year 1818 and 1819, is full of references to their nefarious activities.

During the 1830's the status of note brokers became more respectable, and financial journals carried frequent matter-of-fact references to their activities. Quotations were given for paper "at the Banks or in the Street." The usual procedure was for the broker to take the customer's paper and peddle it about until he found a bank which would discount it; the broker's commission was then deducted, and the remainder of the proceeds given to the customer. It was only on exceptional occasions that the banks took the initiative in the buying of paper from the broker. In May, 1850, for example, the demand for funds was so small that a number of the New York City banks were forced to buy "in the street," in order to keep their resources employed.

The development of the broker beyond the status of agent, to the point where he bought the paper outright from the customer and then sold it on his own account, did not come until after the panic of 1857. Credit for this innovation was claimed by Mr. Henry Clews,[31] who speaks with scorn of the old-fogy methods of his two chief predecessors. The new method gained popularity at once, and forced other dealers to change their methods in order to offer the same advantages to their customers.

This progress in the evolution of the commercial paper house

[31] Clews, *Fifty Years in Wall Street*, pp. 78-79. The two firms were probably, Prime, Ward, and King, and John Ward and Company. See Barrett, *The Old Merchants of New York City*, II, p. 167.

inevitably affected the relations which existed between the merchant and his banker. Until this time it had been usual for each merchant to look upon his banker as one of his closest advisers, as well as his sole source of credit. A firm which kept accounts at two banks was looked upon with suspicion and disfavor. When business men began to sell their paper directly to note brokers it became less essential for them to maintain such close contact with their bankers as formerly, and the tie between them was weakened. Much of the commercial paper in which the bank invested its funds was now purchased from a note broker, instead of directly from the drawer of the bill, and the necessity of exercising close supervision over the credit condition of the firm behind the bill was transferred from the bank to the broker. Although the note broker of 1860 had to undergo many more changes before he evolved into the commercial-paper dealer of today, a long step in that direction had been taken by Mr. Clews and the dealers who followed his example.

Summary

The commercial paper market as it exists today was almost unknown before the Civil War. Its late development is explained by the history of American trade. The demand for commercial credit which is the basis of the commercial-paper market, was comparatively slight through the first quarter of the century, and the heavy demand for credit in the foreign trade of the country was met by extensions of credit from London. When the domestic trade of the nation did reach larger proportions the commercial banks extended credit to an extent which, if not adequate, was at least sufficient to make unnecessary the development of a separate group of dealers in commercial paper. After 1837 and the passing of the Bank of the United States, special note brokers came into existence in New York City, acting merely as agents in selling among the banks the notes of their customers. About 1857 these agents began to deal in the paper on their own account, buying it outright from the customer, and selling it in a separate transaction to the banks.

CHAPTER IV

FOREIGN CREDIT AND THE FOREIGN EXCHANGE MARKET BEFORE 1863

Foreign trade based on foreign credits

The shortage of capital funds which kept the American investment market dependent upon foreign capital had its counterpart in a shortage of commercial credit which forced the American merchant to rely upon foreign bankers for a large part of his short-term funds. The greater part of American trade before 1807 consisted of the importation and distribution of foreign goods, and the credit which was necessary during the lengthy process of distribution was furnished almost entirely by the seller. The long-credit terms offered by British merchants to American importers brought about a renewal of the intimate relations which had existed between them before the Revolution.[1] Neither the difficulties experienced on the English side in collecting the pre-Revolutionary debts due from American traders,[2] nor the hostility to England which had not entirely died down among American patriots, was able to prevent the merchants of the two countries from resuming commercial intercourse. Madison declared in 1785 that the trade of Virginia had never been more monopolized by the English,[3] and in 1805 Talleyrand found it necessary to explain to a puzzled French public that the Americans were trading with their erstwhile

[1] A discussion of foreign exchange prior to the Revolution may be found in Arthur H. Cole, Evolution of the Foreign Exchange Market of the United States," *Journal of Economic and Business History,* Vol. I, pp. 384 ff.

[2] *Case of the British Merchants who traded to America previous to the late War,* (1787). *American State Papers on Foreign Relations,* Vol. I, p. 188, (Mr. Hammond to Mr. Jefferson).

[3] Between 1793 and 1800, the United States imported from Great Britain a greater amount of manufactured goods than all Europe together. More than one-third of the American imports came from Great Britain, and nearly one-third of the American exports went to that country. Seybert, *Statistical Annals,* pp. 285-88, and Pitkin, *Statistical View of the Commerce of the United States,* pp. 169-74.

enemies, the English, rather than with their friends, the French, because they could buy in England more cheaply and pay more slowly.[4]

The credit terms which the American merchant found so attractive permitted him to pay for his imported goods with bills dated from 6 to 12 months, many of which were renewed so that the actual payment was postponed for as many as 18 months after goods were shipped.[5] New York, with limited banking facilities, could not hope to compete with London for the financing of this trade.

There were only two important branches of the foreign trade of the United States which were practically independent of London credit. These were the trade with the West Indies in one hemisphere, and with China and the East Indies in the other. Their independence of London was due less to their ability to secure credit at home than to the fact that the large and quick profits in this trade made credit almost unnecessary.

At its beginning the trade with the West Indies, like that with Europe and England, had been financed by British capital, but by 1808 it had become almost self-supporting.

> The West India trade requires in America less capital than any other, and . . . can be undertaken almost without any actual disbursement beyond the value of the ships; provisions, lumber, etc., can be purchased on short credit; the British manufacturers (and it is for that reason that they principally are British) on a very long one . . . and the cargo of sugar or coffee may return before he is called upon to pay for his outward investment.[6]

A merchant who could finance one voyage to the West Indies could thereafter finance himself from his initial profits. Moreover, the United States government permitted payment of the heavy duties on imports from those islands to be deferred from

[4] Callendar, *State Enterprise and Corporations*, p. 137. Talleyrand, *Memoir concerning the Commercial Relation of the United States with England* (1806).

[5] *British Parliamentary Papers*, 1808, (119) X, 81, evidence of Mr. Wood, p. 2; Chalmers, *Considerations, etc.*, p. 49, ". . . the merchants give credit for twelve or eighteen months and he deemed those happy who get payment so soon."

[6] "Like the effect of European emigrations on her population, what was once a principal agent is now scarcely felt," said Sir Francis Baring of British credit in the West Indies trade. *Inquiries into the effects of the Orders in Council* (1808).

3 to 12 months. The importing merchant had ample time to dispose of his goods and was able to pay the customs from the proceeds of their sale.

The other American-financed branch of the foreign trade of the United States was the Oriental trade, which began with the sending out of the "Empress of China" from New York in 1784, and grew rapidly thereafter. By 1821 the American trade with Canton was larger even than that of the British East India Company.[7] The problem of financing this trade in the years before 1819 was a simple one, for the actual exchange of goods was conducted by a combination of barter and cash payments. As in the trade with the West Indies, the long time permitted for the payment of duties, (tea duties might be postponed for 24 months), and the large profits, made it necessary to secure only enough capital for the initial voyage in order to get a start in the China trade. Fur was the only article of American production acceptable to Chinese taste in the early days, so that most of the ships went to Canton loaded with bullion, where the silver was exchanged for teas and silk, to be taken directly back to America.[8] The trade was carried on chiefly by the great "China houses," such as N. L. and G. Griswold, and Archibald Gracie, and by wealthy individuals like John Jacob Astor in New York, Stephen Girard in Philadelphia, and Elias Haskett Derby in Salem, each of whom was more than able to provide capital for his own ventures.[9] The actual specie, however, had to be obtained from the banks and regularly recurring demand at the banks of New York for silver to be carried to the East always caused a pressure in the money market.

About 1819 the method of conducting this trade began to change. Instead of sailing directly to the East with a cargo of bullion or silver dollars, the American ships began to make the trip by way of England, where they furnished themselves with

[7] For details of this exciting era in the history of American trade, see Barrett, *The Old Merchants of New York City*, I, pp. 23, 45. *British Parliamentary Papers*, 1821, Vol. 7, p. 9. Canton was the only port open to western trade before 1842.

[8] *British Parliamentary Papers*, 1821, 6, pp. 228, 289; 7, p. 10.

[9] Johnson, *History of Commerce*, I, 186. Forbes, *China and the China Trade* (1844). Barrett, *The Old Merchants of New York City*, I, 18, 31, 418. Gouge, *A Short History, etc.*, p. 18.

woolen and cotton goods for which a demand had arisen in the Chinese market. Bills on London were as good as bullion for the purchase of goods in England, and it was no longer necessary for ships following this route to carry the cargo of specie which had formerly been essential to the China trade.[10] American exports of silver, which had sometimes amounted to 7 millions of dollars in one year, dropped to much lower figures.

The Bank of the United States was the principal seller of the sterling drafts used in the China trade, as of other sterling bills. Nearly 5 million dollars' worth of such bills were sent to Canton in the year ending June 30, 1833 as compared with little more than half a million of coin and bullion, and 3 million dollars' worth of goods. After 1842, when the opening of five treaty ports for trade in China brought in a great number of western merchants and familiarized the Chinese merchant with Occidental business methods, even the direct trade could be financed by letter of credit on London.[11]

In the import trade the same dependence upon the London money market was apparent. During the first decade of the century the bulk of imports from the continent and from Great Britain were brought in by merchant importers, men of large wealth and of high standing in the community. They sold their goods to regular customers from all over the country, particularly to jobbers who came to the city twice each year to make up an attractive assortment for the retailers at home. Occasionally a number of the larger retailers joined together to buy directly of the importer, in order to obtain advantage of the lower prices accorded the jobbers. To the jobbers whom they knew personally and with whom they had been trading for years, the merchants could afford to give comfortably long credits, for they bought the goods on equally long credit from abroad.[12]

In those days the name "merchant" was applied only to the

[10] *British Parliamentary Papers*, 1821, Vol. 6, pp. 221, 225, 289, 313; Vol. 7, pp. 10, 37, 122, 139.

[11] Pitkin, *Statistical Annals*, p. 253 (1835). Catterall, *The Second Bank of United States*, p. 112.

[12] *British Parliamentary Papers*, 1810-11, Vol. 2. Clark, *History of Manufactures*, p. 365.

large wholesale dealers who traded in all parts of the world and amassed fortunes in supplying America with the goods which she was not yet able to make for herself. As they grew richer they began to establish partners in England to take advantage of the bargains to be obtained on the spot. The goods were paid for in short-dated notes which the English manufacturer had no difficulty in discounting; while the American agent was able to borrow, with the invoices and bills of lading as security, until his firm remitted funds from America. The distribution of goods on the American side was not affected by the establishment of American purchasing agents abroad, and until the War of 1812, nine-tenths of the imports were sold through the usual channels to jobbers at private sale.[13]

At the end of the War of 1812, when the British manufacturers were eager to sell their accumulated stocks as quickly as possible in the reopened markets of America, they followed the example of their American customers and began to send agents to New York with consignments of goods. These agents had no trade connections, and the only way to dispose of their stocks rapidly was the auction.[14] Auctioneering at once became the most promising profession for the ambitious young New Yorker. The number of auctioneers in the City of New York increased from 2 or 3 in 1812 to 36 in 1817 and 59 in 1830, all duly licensed by the city council.[15] The imports sold under their auspices also increased steadily; in 1817 half of the dutiable goods at the port of New York were entered on foreign consignment for sale at auction and by 1820, three-fourths of the total. The greater part of the retail dry goods in New York City were said to be purchased at auction piece sales.[16]

[13] Brown, *One Hundred Years of Merchant Banking*, pp. 73, 75. *Facts, etc., Relating to Auctions* (1828).

[14] *The Beneficial Tendency of Auctioneering*, p. 13 (1817).

[15] *Facts, etc., Relating to Auctions*, (1831). *The Beneficial Tendency of Auctioneering*, (1817).

[16] Westerfield, *Early History of American Auctions*, pp. 181, 184. Practically all of the goods destined to be sold at auction were consigned to New York, after 1817, rather than to Boston or Philadelphia, because the State tax on auction sales had been reduced at New York to 1 per cent on East Indian goods and 1½ per cent on European goods. In Boston and Philadelphia the tax remained high in a vain effort to discourage the auction system; the effect was to drive it to New York. McGregor, *Commercial Statistics of America*, p. 187.

The American merchants with their old-fashioned methods of selling in small lots could not compete with this new rapid-fire system of sale by auction. One by one they were forced out and only those who adopted the methods of their English competitors were able to avoid business extinction. The great importing house of Champlin and Minturn, for example, failed in 1815, and Jonas Minturn went into the auction business; John Haggerty, one of the large dry-goods merchants from 1801 to 1822, became an auctioneer in the latter year, and by 1833 had the largest auction house in the city.[17] The wholesale merchants were not the only ones who suffered from the auction system, for as it spread it lost its exclusively wholesale character and auction goods began to be sold to the retailer by the piece, as well as to the jobber by the package. This brought the auctioneer into competition with the jobbers and increased the chorus of opposition to the system.[18] After 1835 the system of selling imported goods in this manner declined, owing not only to the increasing volume of domestic manufactured goods, but also to warehousing provisions of the tariff laws which permitted goods to be drawn out gradually, and the duties paid in the same way, over a long period of time.

The decline of the auction system gave the American importer an opportunity to resume his former prominent place in the trade of the country. As in the years before the War of 1812, much of the actual purchase of goods was carried on by agents of American firms resident in England, who bought outright the merchandise to be shipped to the home office in New York. This mercantile organization was supported by an English credit organization, consisting of a banker in London or Liverpool, and his agent in America, who financed the shipment of goods. The merchant in New York applied to the English bank agent in New York for a letter of credit; upon investigation, it was granted, and the British banking house notified. The English manufacturer from whom the goods were

[17] Barrett, *The Old Merchants of New York City*, I, pp. 99, 113; II, pp. 128, 196, 240.

[18] *Remarks on the Auction System*, (1831) pp. 4, 11.

purchased then drew upon the banker, who accepted the bill and sent the documents (invoices and bills of lading) to the bank in America, where they were held as security for the payment by the importer.[19]

The system was more highly organized than the earlier one of buying bills of sterling exchange which happened to be available in the market, and remitting them from New York to London to pay for imports. It was also more concentrated, for the bulk of the American trade was carried on by seven "houses" in London and one in Liverpool whose resources were very large.[20] The financing of American importations from England, and also from Europe, continued throughout the nineteenth century to be conducted by branches of foreign firms.[21]

Foreign credits before 1837

The climax to the great flood of short-term British funds into the United States was reached in 1837. The manner in which British credit was used to finance the export of goods from America, as well as the import of goods into America, has already been indicated. After 1830 the credit obtained in this way was greatly increased by the English eagerness to absorb American securities. The United States was thus enabled to import from abroad, not only the amount of goods for which the American exports would pay, but in addition a great amount which was paid for by the export of securities. The annual imports increased from 63 millions in 1830 to 177 millions of dollars worth in 1836. The total excess of imports over exports, from 1821 to 1837, was 185 millions of dollars, an amount very close to the estimated sale of American securities abroad.[22]

Competition among British manufacturers brought about in

[19] Buck, *Anglo-American Trade*, pp. 153-55.

[20] Among them were the three houses whose suspension in 1837 had such disastrous results for the United States—Thomas Wilson and Company, Timothy Wiggin and Company, George Wilde and Company, as well as Morrison and Company, Lizardi and Company, the Rothschilds, the Barings, and the Browns. Jenks, *Migration of British Capital to* 1875, p. 68, and p. 359 (Note 59).

[21] Colwell, *Ways and Means of Payment*, p. 229. Clews, *Fifty Years in Wall Street*, p. 584.

[22] Bullock, Williams and Tucker, "The Balance of Trade in the United States," *Review of Economic Statistics*, 1919, p. 218. See p. 30 above.

this period a relaxing of the credit conditions upon which the English had built up a sound foreign trade. It had been customary for the British manufacturer to send invoices to the American agent as security against the acceptance but it now became the rule to send the documents direct to the importer, enabling him to obtain the goods whether his bank had been paid or not.[23]

The credit thus generously extended by London filtered down through various levels of tradesmen until it finally reached the consumer. The process was described by an observer who had witnessed it:

> The great London houses were then so liberal in their facilities, that almost any person of fair standing in the States could make large purchases of goods in the manufacturing districts, and draw upon the London banker in his favor. The houses granting these credits usually fixed a specific day for payment; but these payments were proverbially irregular. The facility of buying goods would not have operated well without corresponding facilities here to sell. These facilities were found in the constant multiplication of banks, and their competition for business. The importer, who purchased goods in England on an open credit, sold them at long dates to the jobber, whose note the banks readily discounted, with the importer's endorsement. The jobber, in his turn, sent agents, drummers, and salesmen, in all directions over the country, and offered almost unlimited time to the country dealers. These latter bought largely, giving their notes at eight, twelve, and eighteen months; which notes were discounted on the Atlantic border, with the jobber's endorsement, and made payable at the bank in the interior nearest the dealer's place of residence. The country dealer, possessing such facilities of purchasing, in his turn sold to the consumers on credit, waiting "another crop" for his pay. In this way, very soon, a whole year's crop had been consumed in advance. The farmer owed the storekeeper, the storekeeper the jobber, the jobber the importer, and the latter the London house. This whole chain of indebtedness was sustained only by the renewal of notes, and was continued as long as the banks were able to do this, or until the London houses demanded payment.[24]

The total amount of credit which was outstanding in the first part of 1837, just before the crash, is in some dispute, varying

[23] *Financial Register,* Vol. I, p. 274. Buck, op. cit., pp. 156-57.
[24] Hunt's *Merchants' Magazine,* Vol. 10, pp. 76-77.

from an estimate of 100 millions in the *Democratic Review*,[25] which was anxious for political reasons to magnify the amount and discredit the Bank of the United States, down to 30 millions in a report which was equally anxious to clear the banks of blame.[26] In either case, it is evident that American bankers and merchants were heavily in debt to British bankers and exporters. If it was also true, as another estimate would indicate, that much of the debt had behind it no security, the situation was even more serious than the figures alone would indicate.[27] Moreover this amount included only the short-term credits, and did not include credits already funded into long-term securities, which would eventually fall due.

Upon this perilous foundation the American banks had erected a lofty superstructure of domestic credit. The number of banks had increased rapidly between 1834 and 1837, and their nominal capital had grown from a total of 200 millions of dollars to 290 millions. Their total loans and discounts in the same period of time had increased still more rapidly from 324 to 525 millions.

A great part of this inflation was in the form of credit advanced to cotton dealers, which amounted to speculation for a rise. The price of cotton rose between 1830 and 1837 from nine cents per pound to nearly double that figure.[28] At the same time its production had increased from 100 million pounds in 1833 to 540 million pounds in 1837.[29] The increasing value of cotton led to an increasing value of the land upon which it was raised, and another large part of the inflation in bank credit was accounted for by speculation in public lands in the cotton states.[30] To these economic factors must also be added the unrest occasioned by political events: Jackson's hostility to the Bank of the United States, which had resulted in the refusal to recharter it; the specie circular which attempted too late to

[25] *Ibid.*, Vol. 9, p. 103.

[26] 25 Congress, 2d Session, House Report 634, p. 35.

[27] *Financial Register*, Vol. I, p. 147.

[28] *Financial Register*, Vol. I, p. 299. Secretary of the Treasury, *Annual Report on Finances*, 1863, pp. 294-308.

[29] Secretary of Treasury, *Annual Report on Finances*, 1837, p. 374.

[30] Arthur H. Cole, "Variations in the Sale of Public Lands, 1816-60," *Review of Economic Statistics*, 1927, p. 44.

check the speculation in public lands by permitting purchases to be made only for coin; and the distribution of the surplus revenue among the states under conditions which turned it into added fuel on the flames of inflation.[31]

The trouble began in the cotton trade, and on the English side. Three of the "American houses," Wiggin, Wilde, and Wilson, had been discounting American cotton paper at the Bank of England. But the Bank became alarmed at the heavy export of specie to America, and in order to discourage further extensions of credit to that country, gave notice that it would no longer take that type of paper. Many of the notes drawn by southern cotton brokers and commission men against the crop of 1836 were returned protested. The price of cotton broke sharply and in March, 1837, one of the largest houses in New Orleans failed, followed ten days later by its New York correspondent.[32] Failures continued throughout April at an alarming rate, and the panic extended all over the country. On May 10, the banks of New York suspended specie payments in order to save the little specie which yet remained in their vaults. At the same time they began to carry out the policy which was considered the correct procedure for banks in distress—the contraction of their loans and discounts.[33]

In spite of this contraction, the banks of New York would have been unable to resume without a shipment of gold from London. Prime, Ward, and King, whose position in the market of that day was comparable to that of J. P. Morgan and Company among the latter-day financial powers, sent a representa-

[31] See p. 170 below.

[32] Brown, *One Hundred Years of Merchant Banking*, p. 79.

[33] Statement of 21 New York City banks, from *Financial Register*, Vol. 1, p. 143.

(*In millions of dollars*)

1837	*Loans and discounts*	*Specie*	*Circulation*	*Deposits*
Jan. 1	39.7	4.0	8.8	12.5
June 1	38.4	1.7	5.3	11.3
July 1	37.7	1.7	5.6	10.9
Aug. 1	37.0	1.8	6.1	11.5
Sept. 1	35.3	1.8	5.5	11.9
Oct. 1	33.7	2.0	5.5	13.4

tive abroad in the autumn of 1837. On the responsibility of his firm, and the guarantee of Barings, he secured a consignment of a million pounds in gold, which arrived in New York during the next spring. The chartered banks of the city, which would have forfeited their charters had they not resumed within a year of suspension, thereupon went back to specie payments and were followed by the Boston banks. Those of Philadelphia, led by the Bank of the United States (now operating under a Pennsylvania charter) persisted in their course and refused to resume until 1839.[34]

But the resumption of specie payments was only one step in the difficult process of recovery from the crisis. By November, 1837, it was estimated that one-fourth of the American debt had been paid in securities and another fourth in merchandise and cotton. The liquidation of the remainder was a long and difficult process, accompanied by the usual incidents of deflation—falling prices, lowered production, and unemployment. Both imports and exports declined.

In no other panic did foreign credits play so large a part; nor was the superstructure of American credit ever again based so entirely on a foreign foundation. It was not only that foreign trade was becoming relatively less important, and that the domestic trade was becoming more independent. It was rather that speculation took on new forms, so that the next great crisis, in 1857, involved the stock market and call loans more than the short-term credit market. The disturbances in the foreign exchange and commercial-paper market in 1857 were the result rather than the cause of the crisis.

Rôle of the sterling bill in foreign trade

During the first quarter of the nineteenth century the chief source of sterling bills was the large mercantile houses who began by drawing bills against goods shipped in the course of their own business transactions and found, as their credit abroad became secure, that there was a demand from less well-known

[34] Gallatin, *Suggestions*, etc., p. 29 (1841). Report of New York Bank Convention, Nov., 1837. Brown, *One Hundred Years of Merchant Banking*, p. 80. *Financial Register*, Vol. 1, pp. 35, 142.

dealers for paper which bore their names. When the Secretary of the Treasury inquired for the sterling rates at Baltimore between 1791 and 1829, he was given those which had been compiled from the "actual sales effected by two highly respectable mercantile houses." The same situation prevailed in Philadelphia and New York.[35] Between 1824 and 1833 these private dealers in sterling exchange found a rival in the Bank of the United States. The board of directors had voted, as early as 1817, that the bank should enter this field,[36] but it was not until Nicholas Biddle became president that active efforts were made to do so. Under his guidance the bank secured a virtual monopoly of foreign exchange dealings, and through its correspondents, Baring Brothers and Company of London, and Hope and Company of Amsterdam, kept the market supplied with first-class bills. They were sold principally at the offices in Philadelphia and New York.[37]

When the Bank of the United States was forced to leave the field, its place was taken by the large private bankers in New York, notably Prime, Ward, and King, Brown Brothers, and Fitch Brothers and Company. They bought good bills on Paris and London in the open market, sent them to their correspondents in those cities, and against the balances thus created drew their own bills, which were of such undoubted standing that they commanded a premium of one per cent. Brown Brothers and Company acquired their position in the New York market through their relations with the Browns in Liverpool, which enabled them to obtain accurate knowledge of the standing of mercantile firms in England, and through the ability of the firms on either side of the Atlantic to accept each other's bills.[38] Fitch Brothers and Company, which held in the French trade a position similar to that of Brown Brothers in the English

[35] Brown, *One Hundred Years of Merchant Banking*, p. 19. Barrett, *The Old Merchants of New York City*, I, p. 126. 45 Congress, Executive Document 58, p. 634.

[36] *American State Papers on Finance*, Vol. III, p. 333.

[37] Few sterling bills were drawn in New Orleans, in spite of the fact that most of the cotton was shipped from that port. Instead, bills were drawn on the commission house in New York, which in turn drew on London. Catterall, *Second Bank of United States*, p. 112.

[38] Barrett, op. cit., I, p. 16. Brown, op. cit., pp. 19-20.

trade, also had strong connections abroad. If the exporting merchant would consign his goods to the office of the firm in Marseilles, the office in New York would advance him seven-eighths of its invoice value. The French office was willing to perform the same service for the French exporter, and with such inducements a large part of the French trade was conducted through that one firm.[39] With the exception of these few American firms which were engaged in the sale of foreign bills of exchange, the financing of our external trade was dependent upon agents of foreign houses in New York. These agents were authorized to accept for the merchant or banker in London, the bills drawn upon them by the American shipper. The credit issued by these foreign houses was the most important factor in the financing of our import and export trade until long after the Civil War.[40]

The export of cotton, by far the most important single commodity produced in this country before the Civil War, furnishes an excellent illustration of how this distribution of credit was effected. Most of the actual shipments were made from New Orleans, but the financing was effected through New York commission houses, or through the agents of British firms in New York. Brown Brothers, for example, who opened an office in New York in 1825, offered to act as commission brokers for prospective customers, either in selling produce in this country, or in consigning it to their own or another house in Liverpool. For the negotiation of the sale they charged the usual rate of 2½ per cent, and for the guaranteeing of the drafts of their customers, an additional 2½ per cent. Besides the regular commission houses like Brown Brothers there were also cotton brokers who exported cotton on commission.[41]

The southern planter did not, in most cases, deal with these commission houses and brokers directly. Between them usually stood a sort of jobber, the cotton factor, who from his office in

[39] Barrett, op. cit., I, p. 126.

[40] Clews, *Twenty-Eight Years in Wall Street*, p. 584. Curtis, "Debts of the States," *North American Review*, 1844, Vol. 58.

[41] Barrett, *The Old Merchants of New York City*, I, p. 318. Buck, *Anglo-American Trade before 1850*, pp. 67-73.

a town near the plantations, made arrangements with the commission houses for the shipment of the crop on the one hand, and on the other advanced to the planter food and clothing for the laborers whose maintenance was the chief expense of the crop-growing season. The factor provided credit for the planter; the commission house provided credit for the factor; the English importer provided credit for the commission merchants by permitting him to draw for two-thirds or three-fourths of the face value of the invoice as soon as it was received.[42]

Variations in foreign exchange rates

The commercial banks carried on little foreign exchange business at this time.[43] But the fact that the banker himself did not deal in exchange did not lessen the importance which he attached to the movements of the exchanges as a guide to banking policy. Particularly before 1853, (when the New York City banks began to publish weekly reports), the rate on sterling bills was one of the few quantitative measures available for judging conditions in the money market. "That had always been the barometer by which the banker sailed his bark," said the New York State Bank Commissioner. Sterling bills were the best paper available, and the rate at which they could be discounted represented the lowest and most stable element in the various rates of interest which reflected the state of the market. The rate on sterling bills also reflected changes in the international balance of payments and gave warning of impending movements of specie upon which the credit policies of the New York City banks were greatly dependent. It was imperative that the city banks, as the holders of the reserves of the country, should maintain their own specie at a high level. A heavy shipment of specie out of the country was viewed with justifiable alarm, and if long continued, forced the banks to curtail. An export of specie often indicated the point at which banks must

[42] Buck, op. cit., pp. 37-44.

[43] Raguet, *Treatise* (1840), p. 120, in which he expressed the curious fear that if the banks were to enter the foreign exchange market, they might interfere with the normal balancing effect of trade. *Bankers' Magazine*, Vol. 15, p. 360. "The foreign exchange business in New York is confined to the private bankers." Twenty-two of them are named as drawers of bills in 1860; ibid., p. 368.

begin to curtail their loans and discounts in order to protect their reserves. In 1860 the *Bankers' Magazine* recommended that the city banks pay more attention to the "financial barometer termed foreign exchange" in conducting their business.[44]

As the new states of the West were opened to trade, the domestic commerce of the country became relatively greater in volume and in importance than the foreign trade, and the domestic commercial paper began to play a greater part in the money market. Inevitably the bills of foreign exchange declined in proportion to the domestic bills. There was, however, one form of foreign exchange which was becoming more important, and that was the finance bill. Differences in credit conditions and in interest rates on the two sides of the Atlantic frequently made it advisable for the investor to shift his funds. The increasing opportunities for profit in New York, as the field of investment widened, and the improving means of communication, tended to make New York a part of the world market. The drawing of finance bills became therefore a recognized practice, and was frequently employed in the years before the Civil War.[45]

It is extremely difficult to follow the course of sterling exchange rates in the early years of the century. England was upon a paper standard from 1797 until 1821, and specie payments were suspended on this side from 1813 to about 1817. In addition, there was the constant legal fiction that the pound was worth only $4.44, when actually under the coinage laws before 1830, it was worth 2.73 per cent more, and after 1830, 9.45⅝ per cent more. The result of using the legal rather than the true par made exchange on London seem always to be at a high premium, even though it might actually be at a discount. A rate of $4.8665 to the pound, which after 1834 was just par, was listed in the quotations as 9½ per cent premium because it was that much above $4.44, the rate set for the purpose of import valuation. Even a quotation as far below par as $4.71 appeared in the papers as a 7 per cent premium. This

[44] New York Commissioner, *Annual Report*, 1837. State Superintendent of Banks, *Annual Report*, 1858, p. 13. *Bankers' Magazine*, Vol. 14, p. 131.

[45] Colwell, *Ways and Means of Payment*, p. 229 (1859).

system was not only inconvenient, but "led the community into the mistaken notion that this country is always sadly in debt to England." There was very little attempt to bring the legal definition of the pound sterling into line with the facts. Several attempts were made to meet the situation in the only other way possible, by quoting bills at their dollar value, instead of at their variations from par. The *Journal of Commerce* made a brave attempt to introduce the new method of quotation in 1832, and in 1839 the New York Chamber of Commerce recommended the same plan,[46] but neither of these efforts was successful and the old method remained in use until January 1, 1874, when the legal par was established at $4.8665, the true mint par.

There was moreover a changing ratio of silver to gold which introduced another element of uncertainty. A sudden rise in the exchange rate during 1821 from 3½ per cent premium in January, to 8½ per cent in April, was due to the appearance of a premium on gold of 5 per cent over silver.[47] This premium disappeared with the law of 1834, but a new premium appeared in 1837 after the suspension of specie payments by the banks. In September, 1837, sterling was quoted at 21 per cent premium, a figure which seemed absurd until it appeared that 9.5 per cent of the premium was the difference between the nominal and the real par, 9.5 per cent represented the premium on gold, and the real premium on sterling was thus reduced to 2.0 per cent. Other foreign currencies were affected in the same way, for the premium on silver coin was as high as upon gold.[48] The confusion on the subject was so great that Secretary of the Treasury Ingham, reporting to Congress on the relative value of gold and silver in 1830, remarked despondently: "There are remarkable discrepancies in the tables of the rates of exchange and prices current of bullion, which cannot be reconciled, at least with any information now in possession."[49]

The improvements in ocean transportation brought many

[46] *Journal of Commerce*, August 29, 1832. Brown, *One Hundred Years of Merchant Banking*, p. 283.

[47] 21 Congress, 1 Session, House Document 117, Table I. 22 Congress, 2 Session, House Document 38, p. 2.

[48] *Financial Register*, Vol. II, p. 48.

[49] 21 Congress, 1 Session, House Document 117, p. 7.

changes to the foreign exchange market. Sailings had been irregular until after the establishment of the packet lines in the 1840's, and quotations remained in force from the departure of one vessel until the imminent departure of another. The time required for the crossing of the Atlantic in the early days had made it possible for the goods imported from abroad to be disposed of and the proceeds made available, by 60 days after the bill was received in London. When the use of steam shortened the time necessary for the ocean voyage there was some complaint from the American side that bills should still be drawn at 60 days without interest, as had been necessary during the early part of the century in order to give them time to distribute the goods and receive payment. But the 60-day sight bill remained the standard, although the sailing time between London and New York had been reduced to 10 or 15 days by 1860.[50]

The length of time required for remittances between New York and London was reflected in the specie points, the price at which it was less expensive to ship specie than to purchase bankers' bills. In 1811 the expense of sending coin was said to be 5 per cent, which would have meant that gold exports were not profitable until sterling bills had reached a premium of 5 per cent, or $5.10, and that gold imports would not be made until it had fallen to $4.62.[51] By 1829 the specie points had moved somewhat closer together because of the smaller expense of shipment. At that time the cost of sending gold to London was between 2½ and 3 per cent, freight charges accounting for ½ per cent; insurance for ⅝ per cent; commission and loss of interest for the rest.[52] When bills on London were at an actual premium in New York of 2½ per cent, it was more profitable to send specie to London than to remit sterling bills. As the improvements in shipping shortened the time in transit and the laying of the Atlantic cable reduced the risk factor by increas-

[50] *Financial Register,* Vol. II, p. 29. Colwell, *Ways and Means of Payment,* (1859), p. 229.

[51] *An Appeal to the Public on the Conduct of the Banks in the City of New York* (1815), p. 15.

[52] *British Parliamentary Papers,* 1847-1848; Committee on Commercial Dis-

ing the frequency of quotations, the specie points moved still nearer together. In 1848 the export point was said to be about \$4.93½, the cost of shipping gold having fallen to about 1½ per cent.[53]

Like the import and export points, the seasonal variation of sterling bills showed a wide range in the early years as compared with the later.[54] The improvement in transportation and communication had the same effect on seasonal variations as on gold points. The direction in which exchange rates moved during the year in the ante-bellum period was different from that which is typical today. The high point then was in the fall—September, October, or November—and the low point in March, April, or May. Since the Civil War the high has moved forward to June or July, and the low point of the year is now where the high used to be—September, October, or November. The explanation seems to lie in changes in the export trade.[55] Before the War, cotton and tobacco made up about two-thirds of the total domestic exports from the United States. These two products of southern agriculture were shipped late in the year, and since about two-thirds of the foreign bills were based upon them, the rates of exchange reflected the seasonal variations of exports. December, January, February, and March, the months when cotton went forward in greatest amount, were those in which the greatest amount of sterling drafts came on the market.

The Civil War period brought a change in these conditions. The interruption to southern production which was the direct result of the War reduced by one-half the proportion of southern crops in the total export. Sterling rates were less dependent upon cotton than formerly, and cotton export itself was under-

---

tress, Part I, p. 193; Part III, p. 261. Minutes of Evidence before the Bullion Committee, p. 148. 21 Congress, 1 Session, House Report 117, p. 49.

[53] Hunts' *Merchants' Magazine*, 1845, Vol. 13, p. 177; 1848, Vol. 19, p. 303.

[54] No attempt has been made to compute an index of seasonal variation by the usual link-relative or deviation-from-moving-average method. A simple average of exchange rates represents the seasonal variation with fair accuracy.

[55] An article by Professor Cole, published since the above was written, confirms this conclusion. See "Seasonal Variation in Sterling Exchange," *Journal of Economics and Business History*, Vol. II, p. 207.

going a marked change. The laying of the Atlantic cable in 1866 made it possible for English manufacturers to order by cable from samples, so that consignment of great shipments of cotton to Liverpool merchants, to be sold by them after its arrival, practically ceased, and the export of cotton was spread out over a longer period.[56] The northern products, wheat and pork, were shipped earlier in the autumn, and explain the low sterling rates in September and October which are characteristic at present.

Comparison of the sterling-exchange rate with the rate on domestic drafts between New York and New Orleans gives further evidence of the controlling influences which cotton bills exercised in the exchange market. The cotton drafts drawn in New Orleans against New York began to come into the New York market in the winter months, and raised the exchange between the two cities to an "export point" which inaugurated a southward movement of specie. At the same time, sterling exchange was working towards an import point, thus repaying New York for the advances made to New Orleans.[57] Interest rates on commercial paper moved with domestic-exchange rates, not with foreign. Evidently the severe autumnal pressure in New York was accentuated by the position of the foreign exchanges, and the mere fact of higher interest rates in the New York market was not sufficient to bring in gold. After the Civil War high interest rates in the autumn were ordinarily accompanied by specie imports.

One other reason for the comparatively wide variation in sterling rates was the one-sidedness of the market. All bills were drawn on London, none on American importers. When the supply of drafts became low in New York, there was no alternative except the export of gold. If it had been possible to purchase American drafts in London, actual shipment of specie might often have been avoided and the exchange rates would less often have moved as far as specie point.[58]

[56] Brown, *One Hundred Years of Merchant Banking*, p. 123.

[57] Arthur Cole, "Statistical Background of the Crisis Period, 1837-42," *Review of Economic Statistics*, 1928.

Other currencies

Although sterling exchange was by far the most important of the foreign currencies in which dealings were carried on in this country, several others were quoted quite regularly. Dutch guilders, French francs, the Hamburg mark, and the "rix dollar" of Bremen appeared in all the foreign exchange articles. The confusion with regard to these coins was almost as great as in the case of the pound sterling. The French franc, for example, had a mint par of 5.34 to the dollar, but since foreign coins were not a legal tender in France, and there was a seigniorage of 1½ per cent at the French mint, the American dollar in France was actually worth only about 5.26 francs. This figure was taken as par by some writers, while others used 5.34. The Dutch guilder was in equally ambiguous position. The mint par was 39.97 cents per guilder, but the par usually assumed was 40 cents. The Dutch quotations were given in terms of United States money, as were also the Hamburg mark, which had a par value of 35.14 cents, and the Bremen "rix dollar," a money of account worth slightly over 80 cents.[59] With greater facility of communication between New York, London, and the Continent, arbitrage operations became more frequent, and exercised an important steadying effect upon the market.[60] They had the same sort of influence as that wielded by the finance bills on London, and to these factors may be ascribed at least part of the lessening in seasonal fluctuations of the rate of exchange.

Summary

Bills of foreign exchange played an important role in the early history of the New York money market. They were the immediate instruments through which extensions of foreign credit were made. Especially before the panic of 1837 American trade, both domestic and foreign, was dependent upon such extensions, and the crisis of that year was first felt in that part of the money market. Sterling bills were the most important foreign bills in

[58] Colwell, *Ways and Means of Payment*, p. 229 (1859).
[59] 25 Congress, 2 Session, Senate Document 457, p. 3.
[60] Hunt's *Merchants' Magazine*, 1845, Vol. 13, p. 177.

the market. They were drawn at first by the large mercantile houses, later by the private bankers, with commercial banks taking littlė part. The rates of exchange showed a seasonal variation which was both wider and differently timed than that of the present. The specie points drew steadily nearer to par.

Courtesy New York Historical Society

WALL STREET ABOUT 1845

CHAPTER V

THE BANKS OF NEW YORK

The development of commercial banking made no headway in the United States until the Revolutionary War cut off the credit upon which the trade of the colonies had been wont to depend, and at the same time undermined the paper money which the Colonial governments had issued. The new states relinquished the right to emit bills of credit, and the vacuum which was thus created brought about a demand for bank facilities.[1] The limited services of the Bank of North America in Philadelphia[2] were not sufficient to meet the needs of the whole country, and within a few years banks had been organized in Boston, Baltimore, and New York, as well as in Philadelphia.

Organization of first bank

The first bank in the city of New York was the Bank of New York, which was sponsored by Alexander Hamilton and other members of the Federalist party. It had been proposed originally that the capital stock of the new bank should be based upon landed security for two-thirds of its value, and upon specie for only one-third, following in part the plan upon which land banks had been organized before the Revolution in Massachusetts. The influence of Hamilton in the direction of "sound" banking, according to the more sophisticated European notion, saved the bank from this error, and all of its million dollars of capital was required to be subscribed in specie. The future cashier was sent to Philadelphia to study the methods in use at the bank there, and the Bank of New York opened its doors for business on June 9, 1784. At that time, owing to the opposition of political enemies, it was still without a charter and it was not until 1791, after it had acted as fiscal agent for the state, that it obtained

[1] Eliason, *The Rise of Commercial Banking Institutions in the United States.*
[2] See p. 3.

one. In spite of this lack, the bank was a financial success from the start, declaring its first dividend on May 1, 1786, and conducting an increasing volume of business. In six months of 1787 the bank discounted more than 10 million dollars' worth of paper, and took in more than 40 millions of cash deposits.[3]

In 1791 the Bank of the United States opened a branch office in New York, which inevitably was looked upon as a rival by the Bank of New York. Other rivals made their appearance, but the increasing commerce of the city made it possible for all of them to profit. The Manhattan Company, organized ostensibly to supply the city with water, in 1799 tricked a hostile legislature into granting it a charter which included banking privileges and became the Bank of the Manhattan Company, with a capital of 2 millions of dollars. The organization of other banks followed rapidly; the Mechanics', the Union, the Merchants', the Bank of America, the City, and the Manufacturing, brought the total number to eight in 1815. The growth of the city's banking capital in the early part of the century may be seen in the following table:

AUTHORIZED CAPITAL OF BANKS IN NEW YORK CITY*

1800	$3,420,000
1805	5,430,000
1810	7,430,000
1815	18,215,000
1820	21,105,000
1825	25,105,000

* Secretary of Treasury, *Annual Report on State Banks*, 1837, p. 102.

The growth of banking soon attracted the attention of the state legislature, for of all the institutions of the money market, the banks were the most numerous and the most directly in contact with the public. Much of the blame for the alternations between prosperity and depression was laid upon the banks; and their inability to maintain their note circulation upon a stable basis, the large number of bank failures, and the frequent suspension of specie payments, were cited as sufficient evidence for

[3] Domett, *History of the Bank of New York.*

the need of regulatory legislation, as indeed it was. It is characteristic of this early period that no attempt was made to undertake such regulation by means of national laws. The state authorities were assumed to be the proper instruments for this purpose,[4] and there was no general national bank law passed until 1863. Wide variation existed among the states in the matter of their bank laws, but those of New York are the only ones which need to be considered here.

New York state laws regarding banking

The first important act of the New York state legislature in regard to banking was a statute of 1804 requiring that every banking corporation, in order to have a legal existence, must possess a state charter, although individuals might still carry on a private banking business without that formality. The legislature thus reserved for itself the power to enforce banking standards by granting only those charters which met its requirements. The Act probably saved the state from a flood of wildcat institutions, but it had also the less fortunate effect of turning the obtaining of bank charters into occasions for political bargaining.

Once a bank had succeeded in obtaining a charter, it was little hampered in its activities by state regulation. The general laws on banking during this period were of the most superficial kind, like the law of 1813, which prohibited the issue of notes of denominations of less than one dollar,[5] or that of 1824, which required that bank notes be redeemed only in lawful money of the United States. There was no legal requirement for reserve against either notes or deposits, no limitation on the amount of loans which could be made, or of notes which could be issued. The only restrictions on complete freedom of action lay in the particular provisions of the individual charters, modeled generally upon that of the first Bank of the United States. These

[4] President Buchanan, in his Annual Message to Congress on December 7, 1857, for example, said that "After all, we must mainly rely upon the patriotism and wisdom of the States for the prevention and redress of the evil" of banking.

[5] The issuance of bank notes of small denomination was prohibited rather generally in order to make redemption more frequent and to make a place for specie circulation.

usually fixed the name, the location, the amount of capital, and the length of life of the bank, and contained sometimes in addition, a requirement that its total debt should not exceed three times the paid-up capital—provisions which were quite inadequate to keep banks within the path of financial probity. The banking powers conferred by these general charters were not even defined until after 1825. In that year, the charters granted to the Commercial Bank of Albany and to the Dutchess County Bank specified that each should "have and possess all incidental and necessary powers to carry on the business of banking—by discounting bills, notes, and other evidences of debt; by receiving deposits; by buying gold and silver bullion, and foreign coins; by buying and selling bills of exchange, and by issuing bills, notes, and other evidence of debt; but the said company shall have and possess no other powers whatever, except such as are expressly granted by this act."[6]

This era of unregulated banking in New York state was brought to an end by the exposure of the corruption with which the whole banking structure was saturated. Grand jury investigations in New York City in 1826, and the conspiracy cases in which they resulted, brought about a general demand for reform which was augmented by the business depression. The result was the passage of the Statute Regulations of 1827. These laws limited the action of all banks chartered thereafter by forbidding the declaration of dividends except from actual surplus profits, by making stockholders doubly liable for debts of the corporation, by requiring annual reports to the Comptroller, and by stipulating that the total loans and discounts were not to exceed three times the paid-up capital. Instead of resulting in reform, the provisions were so severe that they simply prevented the formation of any new banks. Not a single charter was applied for during the two years that these laws were in force.[7]

When Governor Van Buren came into office, he seized the opportunity to bring about a more effective bank reformation,

[6] Cleaveland, *The Banking System of the State of New York* (1857).

[7] Buchanan, *Report and Observations on the Banks* (1828). Cleaveland, op. cit., pp. xxiv, xxix (1857). Jacob Barker, *Disclosure of the Real Parties to the Purchase and Sale of the Tradesmen's Bank* (1827).

through the scheme which had been proposed by Joshua Forman, and which has attained considerable fame as the Safety Fund Act. Van Buren's zeal for the plan was not diminished by the fact that in it he saw also a means of punishing the Federalist banks which had strongly opposed his election.[8] The Act was passed in 1829, and in spite of the political motives behind it, exercised for some years a large and on the whole beneficial influence upon banking and the money market. It made no effort to limit the number of charters granted to banks, nor did it remove the granting of charters from the sphere of politics,

GROWTH OF THE BANKS IN NEW YORK CITY*

(Report for January of each year, in millions of dollars)

Year	*Capital*	*Circulation*	*Loans and discounts*	*Deposits*	*Due to other banks and corporations*
1836	18.4	7.8	43.2	14.8	14.0
1837	20.4	9.7	46.2	14.9	14.3
1838	20.2	3.6	34.1	12.5	11.3
1839	20.2	5.5	35.9	13.2	11.1
1840	20.2	4.0	26.9	12.5	4.2
1841	20.2	4.9	26.9	12.2	5.8

* Annual Reports of the New York State Bank Commissioners. Quarterly bank reports for New York City compiled from the available official sources for the years 1843 to 1863 are given in a diagram in Arthur H. Cole, "The New York Money Market of 1843 to 1862," *Review of Economic Statistics*, 1929.

but it did bring the banks so chartered under the control of a government agency, by subjecting them to regular examination and requiring periodic reports.

Another very important feature of the law was that for the first time protection of the creditors of a bank was recognized to be properly a governmental function. The "Safety" feature of the Act was the requirement that each bank chartered under its terms should pay into a state-administered fund an annual tax of ½ per cent upon its capital, up to a total of 3 per cent. From this sum, all the debts of insolvent banks were to be

[8] Van Buren, *Autobiography*, pp. 36, 221.

paid, except capital liabilities, and the fund was then to be replenished by further instalments of ½ per cent annually until it had again reached the required total. Thus depositors as well as note holders were protected by a fund beyond the control of the banks.[9] Moreover, the issue of bank notes was restricted to twice a bank's paid-up capital, and loans and discounts were not to exceed two and one-half times the paid-up capital.

For one other provision of this law the state had reason to be particularly grateful—the prohibition of post-dated notes. These had been a fruitful source of difficulty for years, and continued to be so in other states where the law did not forbid their use. Post notes were issued by a bank which found itself in need of funds, in the form of promises to pay at a definite date in the future. But the future date usually found the bank even less able to meet its obligations than before, and many a bank was completely undone by the debts thus indiscreetly piled up. This practice was an important factor in the final suspension of the Bank of the United States of Pennsylvania, in 1841, and it played a conspicuous part in state bank failures until 1863.[10]

The number of banks organized under the Safety Fund Act increased rapidly during the general expansion in business prior to the crisis of 1837. By that year, 90 of 98 banks in the state and 18 of the 23 banks in New York City were included in the system. In spite of its rapid growth it had aroused much opposition.[11] Country bankers objected to the law because it was still necessary for each bank to receive an individual charter from the legislature, with all the political evils attendant on that situation. City bankers objected to it because, with their large capital in proportion to circulation, the tax provisions bore more heavily on them than upon the country banks with smaller capital. New York bankers had an additional reason for wishing a change, in their desire, after it became apparent that the

[9] The safety feature broke down badly after the bank failures following the crisis of 1837. See Chaddock, *Safety Fund Banking System in New York*, Chapter III.

[10] Cleaveland, op. cit., p. 29 (1857). Dewey, *State Banking Before the Civil War*, p. 104.

[11] New York Bank Commissioner, *Report*, 1837, pp. 1, 5.

second Bank of the United States was not to be rechartered, to organize a large bank in the city of New York to take its place. Under the Safety Fund Act, with its tax based upon the amount of capital, such a bank by reason of its very size would be heavily penalized.[12]

The plan of James Hamilton of New York, originally submitted to Van Buren as an alternative to the Safety Fund Act, was therefore revived, and its main feature incorporated into the Free Banking Act of 1838.[13] This law opened the business of banking to any one meeting the requirements of the Act, removing the chartering of banks from the legislature, and putting it under the control of an administrative officer. The business of banking thereupon ceased to be a monopoly privilege granted by the legislature and took the status of any other corporate business activity. The second important provision of the law required bank notes to be secured by stock of New York state,[14] which had to be deposited with the Comptroller to the full amount of the issue. Representatives of the agricultural districts in the legislature insisted upon the use of mortgages also as security, the mortgage to be equal to half of the value of the land against which it was held. So much loss resulted from attempts to dispose of these mortgages during various crises that the law was amended in 1853 to prohibit any one mortgage from securing more than five thousand dollars' worth of notes; and it was frequently recommended by the Superintendent of Banks that mortgage security be altogether eliminated. Besides this security against the ultimate redemption of bank notes, a specie reserve of 12½ per cent of circulation was required to be held by every bank, in order to insure the prompt redemption of notes presented at their counters. This establishment of a legal minimum specie reserve against notes, although it was repealed several years later, was copied by many states and was incorporated into the National Bank Act. No bank organized under this law could have a capital of less than $100,000; semi-annual reports

[12] Flagg, *Banks and Banking in the State of New York*, Par. 1829, Par. 1838 (1868).

[13] James Hamilton, *Reminiscences*, p. 82.

[14] Until 1840 stocks of several other approved states might also be used.

were required, and shareholders were exempt from liability for the debts of the bank whose stock they held.[15]

A great variety of laws was enacted in New York between 1838 and 1863. Country banks after 1840 were required to redeem their notes in New York City or in Albany at not more than ½ per cent discount, and after 1851, at ¼ of one per cent. In order to protect the country bankers from a sudden large demand for specie from the city, to which this law might have subjected them, a further enactment of 1857 made it compulsory for any bank which held as much as $10,000 in notes of any other bank, to send them home for redemption.

New York was the outstanding example of that group of states in which the redemption facilities were adequate, but in which the issue of notes was closely and artificially tied to some factor, like the specie reserve or security collateral, which made it difficult if not impossible to increase the note circulation in time of stringency in the money market. Indeed the experience of New York indicated that the time of stringency usually saw a decrease rather than an increase in the circulation. As the Free Banking Act was copied by state after state between 1840 and 1860, inelasticity in currency due to the bond-secured feature became more widespread. Whether or not the redemption system in those states was effective, was a question of less importance, since the notes by their very nature were prevented from adjusting in amount to the business situation.

Regular reports were also a matter of increasing concern to the legislature and a law of 1843 required quarterly reports instead of semi-annual to be made to the Comptroller. In 1851 the office of Superintendent of Banking was established, to take over the functions which before 1838 had been exercised by the Bank Commissioner. The Superintendent instituted regular inspection of the banks, and demanded reports which were far more complete and informative than those with which the Comptroller had been satisfied. In 1853 a further step in the direction of adequate publicity was taken, in the law requiring weekly reports of loans, circulation, and specie and deposits, from all

[15] Cleaveland, op. cit., (1857).

banks in New York City. The principle items in these weekly reports may be followed in the diagram on page 91.

Development of banking theory

One of the most significant facts brought out by the diagram was the small amount of circulating notes issued by the New York banks in proportion to the other items of their reports. When the first banks were organized, it was taken for granted that their chief function would be the issue of a circulating medium for the communities in which they were located, and that their real value would arise from this service. Confusion of note issue functions with banking was widespread. In spite of the clarity with which Alexander Hamilton explained the nature of deposit credit in his report on the Bank of the United States in 1800, there was such confusion in the public mind that the Professor of Political Economy at the University of Pennsylvania could write, as late as 1838, that "the furnishing of a paper circulation was the essential feature of the banking system."[16] In 1833, the New York State Bank Commissioner declared: "The legitimate use of banks is not for the purpose of loaning capital, but for the purpose of furnishing a currency to be used instead of specie." The fact that the notes were issued in response to the need for bank credit was usually overlooked, and public attention was concentrated on the paper currency of the banks and methods of safeguarding it, instead of on the more fundamental matter of loan restriction and control. Writers of the type of William Gouge and Thomas Benton directed their fulminations against paper money as if the elimination of that one form of credit would set the whole banking structure to rights. Banks were scarce and only a small portion of the population was served by them; only a very few persons were so situated that they could have had checking accounts if they had wished them. "Bank paper" was the only form of currency available in many places, and it was inevitable that it should become a symbol for the whole of banking.

[16] Vethake, *The Principles of Political Economy* (1838). Miller, *Theories of Banking in the United States before 1860*, pp. 12 ff. New York State Bank Commissioner. *Report*, 1833, p. 5.

This attitude was reflected in the state laws regarding banking. It is true that the safety fund established in 1829 was to be used to meet all the debts of insolvent banks, but it was taken for granted in the discussions which preceded the passage of the Act that the note issues would be the larger part of the liabilities. The issue of bank notes was restricted to twice the paid-up capital in order to limit the liabilities and prevent too great a strain upon the safety fund. In 1837, an amendment to the law gave belated recognition to deposits by requiring that one-third of the safety fund be reserved for other debts than notes. This was not sufficient provision, and the actual breakdown of the system was brought about by bank deposits. When a number of bank failures followed the panic of 1837, the safety fund was ample to meet the liabilities due to note holders, but it could not in addition pay the depositors.[17] The general banking law of 1838, which made it unnecessary for each new bank separately to petition the legislature for a charter, likewise failed to recognize the importance of deposits. As a substitute for the safety fund, the law required that banks keep a reserve of 12½ per cent in specie against notes in circulation, and the possibility of a reserve against deposits as well as notes was not mentioned in the debates.[18] The danger in unprotected deposits had not yet impinged upon the consciousness of legislators, nor indeed upon that of the New York bankers themselves. In a series of articles in the New York *Evening Post,* in 1835, the standard specie reserve for "well managed and prudent institutions" was set at 20 to 30 per cent of *circulation.* Most criticism of inflationary tendencies also stressed the proportion of note circulation to specie, or to total banking capital, and ignored deposits.[19]

It is remarkable that the similarity of notes and deposits as parallel forms of bank credit was so long unrecognized in New York, for the banks in that city seem always to have had a larger proportion of deposit currency than of circulating notes.

[17] Chaddock, *The Safety Fund Banking System in New York.*

[18] This reserve requirement for notes was soon repealed.

[19] New York State Bank Commissioner, *Annual Report,* 1835. Sedgwick, *What is a Monopoly?* (1835).

The Bank of New York in 1791, when it was still the only bank in the city, reported nearly 50 per cent more deposits than notes outstanding. Only estimates of these items are available until the period of regular bank reports began. After that there was a fairly steady decline in the ratio of notes to deposits.

CHANGES IN NOTE ISSUES OF NEW YORK CITY BANKS

Date nearest January 1	*(In millions of dollars)*			*(In per cent)*
	Loans and discounts	*Notes*	*Individual deposits*	*Ratio of notes to deposits*
1839	35.9	5.5	13.2	41.7
1849	37.5	5.8	21.4	27.1
1859	125.0	7.6	81.5	9.3

The volume of business in New York City was too large to be transacted by the clumsy method of cash payments, and the size and prestige of the banks made their checks acceptable to merchants. In these respects New York was of course far ahead of the rest of the country, and the country banks, although showing the same trend, were always more concerned with note circulation than the city banks. The contrast between them may be illustrated by the figures for the banks of the country districts of the state, at the same dates as those above for the city banks.[20]

CHANGES IN THE NOTE ISSUES
OF NEW YORK STATE COUNTRY BANKS

Date nearest January 1	*(In millions of dollars)*			*(In per cent)*
	Loans and discounts	*Notes*	*Individual deposits*	*Ratio of notes to deposits*
1839	32.3	16.6	5.2	319.0
1849	32.2	17.4	7.8	223.0
1859	67.2	20.9	26.7	78.3

[20] These tables were prepared from the *Annual Reports* of the New York State Bank Commissioners.

Country banks in other states, especially in the less industrial sections of the country, were even slower to follow the lead of New York. The banking frontier moved westward at a slow pace, lagging well behind the agricultural frontier. The banking statistics which were published by Albert Gallatin, the former Secretary of the Treasury, for 1829 make it possible to compare the city and country banks of other states with those of New York. It is plain that New York City was ahead of her rival, Philadelphia, in the use of deposits, and that Boston and Salem were behind both.[21]

RATIO OF NOTES TO DEPOSITS
IN DIFFERENT PARTS OF THE UNITED STATES

	(In millions of dollars)		*(In per cent)*
	Notes	*Deposits*	*Ratio of notes to deposits*
MASSACHUSETTS:			
City (Boston and Salem)	2.4	2.2	109
Country	2.2	0.7	315
PENNSYLVANIA:			
City (Philadelphia) . .	3.6	5.0	72
Country	3.7	1.8	206
NEW YORK:			
City (New York City) .	3.4	6.7	51
Country	4.6	3.7	124
UNITED STATES:			
7 Cities	17.1	23.1	74
Country	31.1	17.6	177

Associated with the change in the ratio of circulation to deposits was a change in the ratio of loans to deposits. As a larger proportion of the credit issued by banks was used in the form of checking accounts, the volume of deposits rose faster than the volume of loans. This explains the difference in the trends

[21] Gallatin, *Considerations*, (1831) p. 67. The Bank of the United States and its branches were not included in the table above; throughout its history the bank had more notes in circulation than individual deposits, owing to the countrywide demand for its notes.

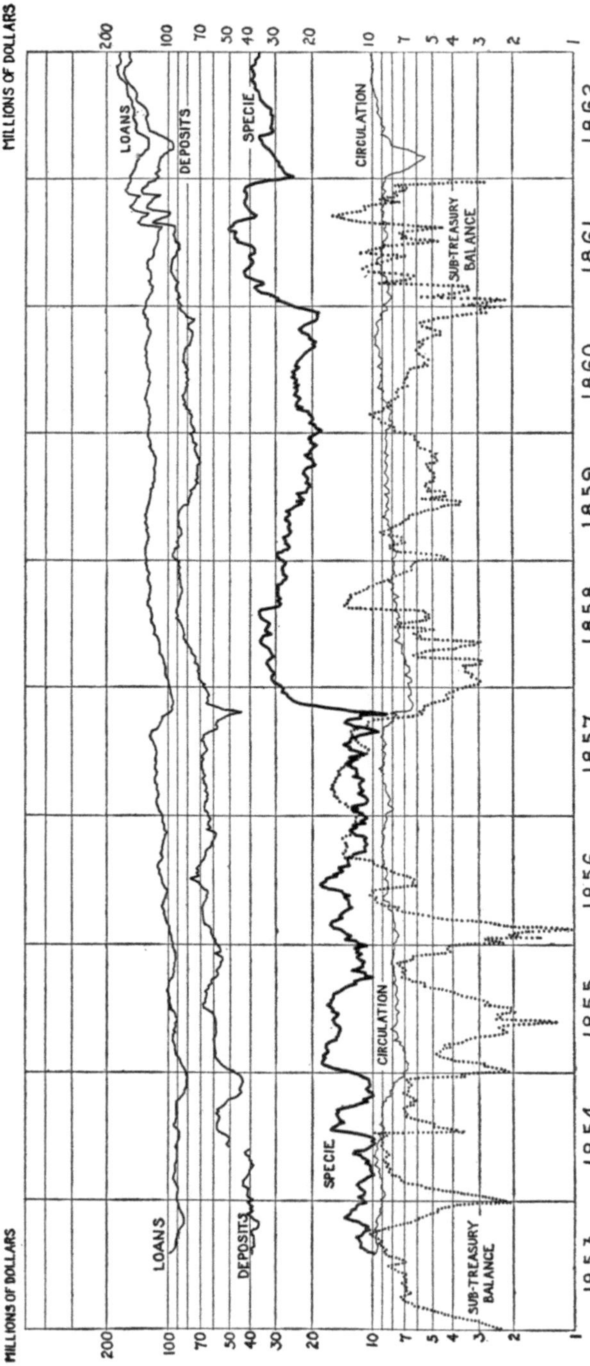

WEEKLY REPORTS OF NEW YORK CLEARING HOUSE BANKS
AND WEEKLY BALANCE IN NEW YORK SUBTREASURY

SOURCE: GIBBONS, BANKS OF NEW YORK; BANKERS' MAGAZINE

of the two series,[22] which are apparent in the diagram of New York bank statistics.

The diagram brings out also another feature of the situation, the less rapid increase in specie than in deposits between 1853 and 1857. Again it was the emphasis upon notes which caused the danger to be overlooked; because the ratio of specie to an almost stationary circulation was rising in those years, there was little apprehension. Through the whole history of American banking, there has been a tendency towards the more economical use of reserves evidenced by the smaller ratios of cash to deposits.[23] But such a change had to be accomplished gradually in order to give the banking system time for adjustment, and when it proceeded too rapidly, it usually ended in disaster which forcibly reduced deposits and re-established equilibrium on a more moderate level.

There were, of course, individual exceptions to the general blindness regarding such facts as have just been cited. Albert Gallatin, writing in 1831, pointed out that:

> The credits in account current or "deposits" of our banks are also, in their origin and effect, perfectly assimiliated to bank notes. Any person depositing money in the bank, or having any demand whatever upon it, may at his option be paid in notes, or have the amount entered to his credit on the books of the bank. The bank notes and the deposits rest precisely on the same basis. . . . We can in no respect whatever perceive the slightest difference between the two.[24]

Nathan Appleton of Boston, who published his *Remarks on Currency and Banking* in the year 1841, was even more explicit.

> Bank credits, commonly called deposits, are of precisely the same general character as bank notes; they arise from the deposit of coin or bank notes, from the collection of individual notes, or bills of exchange, or from discounts made by the bank for the parties to whose credit they are placed. However originating, the bank admits them to be a debt payable in gold and silver on demand.

[22] Cole, "The New York Money Market of 1843, to 1862," *Review of Economic Statistics*, 1929, p. 169, gives the ratio of loans to deposits from 1843 to 1863.

[23] See Chapter XII below for evidence of this tendency after 1863. The same generalization may be applied to the history of world banking.

[24] Albert Gallatin, *Considerations on the Currency and Banking System of the United States*, p. 31 (1831).

The most elaborate and well-reasoned statement of the true position of deposits in the banking system was made by Stephen Colwell, in his 600-page volume, *The Ways and Means of Payment: A Full Analysis of the Credit System, with its Various Modes of Adjustment*. He thus summarized the popular idea of bank notes:

> To very many, a bank is looked upon only as an institution enjoying, by charter, the privilege of issuing and lending bank-notes as a currency.

His own point of view emphasized deposits rather than circulation, and insisted that the real banking problem of the day was the regulation of deposits rather than of note issues.

Such sporadic contributions to banking theory as these made little impression upon the public. It was not until the decade of the fifties that New York banks began to realize they must follow rules stricter than those of the rest of the country, if they were to be protected adequately against the dangers of suspension. Their deposits needed to be guarded by a specie reserve just as well as, if not more than, their notes, for the first strain upon the banks during a crisis was felt in a withdrawal of deposit balances, rather than in a return of notes for redemption. The New York banks were set apart from those of other parts of the country, not only by the smaller proportionate note circulation which they issued, but also in the kind of deposits which they carried. The bankers' balances which made up so large a part of their total deposits[25] were quite different in kind from the individual deposits which arose largely from loans and discounts. They were in the first place less subject to the usual forms of banking control, for they could not be curtailed by reducing loans, as could the ordinary deposits. In the second place, they were more subject to violent fluctuations since they represented in a sense the margin above the basic specie reserves which had to be kept in the vaults of country banks. It is doubtful if the full implication of these differences was realized by New York bankers, but their experience during the decade between 1850 and 1860 forced them to set certain standards of banking practice.

[25] See Chapter VI below.

Liquidity of assets is of course almost as valuable as a specie reserve for the protection of notes and deposits, but American bankers had never learned to manage their investments from that point of view as did European and Canadian bankers. The specie reserve was therefore of primary importance.

The New York Clearing House

The most important achievement of the New York City banks before the Civil War was the organization of the Clearing House, and the development through it of a technique for coöperation. The suggestion that the banks of New York City should cancel their mutual indebtedness by bookkeeping entries, rather than by the clumsy and hazardous exchange of actual coin, has been traditionally credited to Albert Gallatin, who put forth the idea during the suspension of specie payments in 1841 when the need for coöperation between the city banks was particularly evident.[26] Such a clearing technique had existed in London since 1775, and it was this plan which Gallatin proposed as a model for New York. But the small volume of business, banking as well as commercial, in the years after 1841, made it possible for the banks to continue their old, cumbersome methods.

It had gradually come about that during the week inter-bank balances were permitted to accumulate and that settlements between the banks of the city were called for only on Friday. On that day bedlam reigned in the money market; porters with bags of gold dashed from one bank to another, settling accounts; and paying tellers spent the day in waiting upon the porters of the other banks, to receive from or pay to them the difference which had arisen during the week. Loans were called in order to build up specie reserves, interest rates rose, and loans and discounts had to be curtailed until the position of the lending banks had been adjusted to the others.[27] An unfortunate by-product of this system was the possibility of running up large balances due to other banks, and lending on the basis of funds belonging to those banks, until the end of the week, when the

[26] Gallatin, *Suggestions on the Banks and Currency of the Several United States*, p. 64 (1841).

[27] Gibbons, *Banks of New York*, pp. 292-93 (1859).

necessity of building up reserves forced the calling of demand loans and sent the rates soaring. In times of unusual stringency this Friday settlement became a factor of serious import to the market.[28]

The rapid growth of banking operations in New York City after the Mexican War forced the problem of mutual settlement upon the attention of the bankers, and after a series of discussions and meetings, a plan was informally agreed upon, to go into effect in October, 1853, just two months after the banks had begun to publish weekly statements.[29] Banks which had profited most from the advantages of the old system were of course those most opposed to the plan for change, but the leadership of five of the strongest banks of the city forced the others into line. The organization of the Clearing House had a stabilizing effect in forcing banks to make daily, rather than weekly, settlements, and in preventing the accumulation of large adverse balances, with the consequent dangerous lowering of reserves and scramble for funds in the call market. Indeed its success in that regard was so great that a few weeks after its organization four of the more reckless of the city banks were obliged to close their doors.[30]

In August, 1854, after nearly a year's trial of the informal arrangement had demonstrated the need for more definite rules, a formal constitution was adopted. The five banks—the Bank of America, the Merchants, the American Exchange, the Metropolitan (which was the leading bank in the redemption of country bankers' notes in New York City) and the Mechanics' Bank—made up a sum of one million dollars in specie, and

[28] It is interesting to compare the effect of the Friday settlement with the situation arising in New York City in 1927, from the then existing requirement of the Reserve Bank that member banks must so adjust their reserves by Friday of each week, that the arithmetic average for the week would be equal to the legal requirements. Certain of the banks took advantage of this privilege of averaging but once a week, and let their reserves in the early part of the week fall far below the minimum, borrowing heavily from the Reserve Bank in the later part of the week in order to recover their position. On January 9, 1928, the Reserve Bank at New York therefore announced that after that date member banks must average their reserves twice a week, thus making it impossible for the actual reserve to fall below the average for more than a day or two at a time. *New York Times*, January 10, 1928, p. 44.

[29] Gibbons, op. cit., pp. 295-96 (1859).

[30] Squire, *New York Clearing House*, p. 6.

issued against it certificates signed by the Mechanics' Bank. These certificates were issued in large denominations, and were to be used only in settlements between the member banks. At a later date, the Bank of America was nominated by the Association in place of the five banks, and became the holder of specie deposits for all the members, issuing in its own name the certificates which were used in settlement. By 1857 the special deposits of the Clearing House banks in the Bank of America amounted to 6.5 millions, and the daily exchanges to about 20 millions of dollars.[31]

The fact that at the beginning all of the banks in the city belonged to the Clearing House and that in every period all of the large banks belonged to it, permitted it to exercise a genuine regulatory function, in part through its power to admit or expel members, and in part through the almost unlimited power of the five bank officers who comprised the Clearing House committee. In spite of this potential ability to control the banking situation, the Clearing House was slow to make use of its opportunities. The crisis of 1854 occurred when the Clearing House had just completed its organization under a permanent charter, and it was quite unprepared to take a firm grip upon the situation. One reason for this hesitation was the lack of a definite policy; the banks of New York had yet to work out a technique for handling unusual pressures in the money market. Indeed, they did not yet realize that collectively they must carry that kind of responsibility.

The experience of the Bank of England during the first half of the nineteenth century[32] had amply demonstrated that the only way to stop a panic was for the central bank to loan freely, at rising rates. Advanced banking opinion in the United States was cognizant of this principle, but the difficulty arose in applying it to this country, where there were many small, widely-scattered banks, unregulated by any controlling central bank. The position of the New York banks among the banks of the United States was comparable neither to that of the commercial

[31] Gibbons, op. cit., pp. 296, 316, 341 (1859). Cleaveland, op. cit., p. 274 (1857).

[32] Beckhart, *The Discount Policy of the Federal Reserve System*, p. 29.

banks, private and joint-stock, of London, nor to that of the Bank of England. The kind of action which had been worked out in London with the aid of the Bank of England was impossible in New York, and a very different procedure had to be developed. If the banks were to loan freely but at higher rates, some substitute for the central bank would have to be found.

Action of Clearing House in panic of 1857

The panic of 1857 was so severe and so prolonged that the Clearing House was practically forced into action, and it began timidly to feel its way towards an emergency technique. The reserves of the banks had been declining steadily during August of that year, and near the end of the month, when the failure of the Ohio Life and Trust Company was announced, call and commercial-paper rates approached panic heights. On September 2, the Mechanics' Bank was suspended from the Clearing House, owing to its inability to meet the daily settlements, and other banks began to feel alarmed about their own reserves. The instinct of each one was to curtail its loans in order to protect its reserves, yet nothing was more certain to intensify the panic. The banks, therefore, on September 20, agreed that all would increase their loans so that the Clearing House balances of all of them would be increased proportionately and would cancel each other without reducing their slender stock of specie. Thus 5 millions of additional credit was provided, but it was not sufficient to stem the panic. A month later the banks again agreed to increase their loans, and jointly took 1.5 millions of short paper.[33]

This method of extending credit by voluntary agreement was not a powerful weapon for fighting a panic. There was needed some more positive plan for protecting reserves while an extension of credit was taking place, so that a bank which refused to assist the others would not be in a position to drain away their reserves. The question of redeeming country-bank notes was also a pressing one, for the country banks had been obliged to draw down the balances in New York with which their notes

[33] *Journal of Commerce*, September 2, 3, 30. *New York Times*, October 2, 21.

were ordinarily redeemed, and the city banks were refusing to honor them. The business depression had materially reduced the amount of money needed in circulation and so the country notes accumulated in New York. What to do with them under these circumstances became something of a problem.

Both of these difficulties were met by an extension of the Clearing House certificate. New York banks had been in the habit of using specie certificates in their daily settlement of balances at the Clearing House, and now that specie was scarce and the amount of specie certificates proportionately reduced, the Clearing House committee decided to issue certificates also against notes of New York state banks. This group of banks agreed to pay 6 per cent interest on the notes which they could not redeem, and the city banks were willing to hold them on those terms, since under the new plan they could be converted into Clearing House certificates and became equivalent to specie in the settlement of Clearing House balances. The issue of these certificates did not save the market from suspension of specie payments, but it enabled the city banks to continue to loan, and they saved the country banks from insolvency. In November, the city banks began again to redeem country-bank notes, sending them home for redemption at the rate of one-fifth of the total each month. The certificates were retired as the collateral bank notes were redeemed, but the city banks held them as long as possible, for they bore interest at 6 per cent and were a safe investment. It finally took a resolution of the Clearing House association to persuade the holding banks to part with them.[34] The importance of these certificates was not only in their immediate service to the banks, but in the fact that they pointed the way towards the Clearing House loan certificates secured by stock and other collateral which were first used in 1860 and appeared after that in every major crisis to 1913.

The *Times* carried in December a bitter editorial on the conduct of the Clearing House, accusing it of complete failure as a "regulator" during the panic. The allegations were true in part, but the editorial failed to recognize all the difficulties: the

[34] *Journal of Commerce*, December 8, 1857.

uncertainty caused by treasury activity,[35] the resentment that would have been felt all over the country if the New York banks had succeeded in regulating the situation, and the inexperience of the New York banks.

The Clearing House was not unaware of its own limitations. When the panic had subsided, it appointed a committee of bank officers to make recommendations for improvement in the management of the banks.[36] Their proposals regarding the payment of interest on deposits have been given elsewhere.[37] More effective than these, was the decision that the banks should keep a 20 per cent reserve of specie against deposits as well as against circulation. The diagram of weekly reports indicates that the banks as a whole lived up closely to their agreement.[38]

Issue of loan certificates in 1860

The technique which had been developed during 1857 was carried a step further during 1860. The crisis began in November, when the rumor of war brought the collapse of the cotton export trade and demoralized the foreign exchange market. Sixteen of the larger banks entered into an agreement to purchase 2½ million dollars' worth of sterling bills, paying for them in proportion to their capital, in order to support the exchanges. The Bank of Commerce was chosen to act as agent for the other banks in this transaction. These banks also followed the precedent set in 1857 of expanding their loans in the face of stringency, and agreed to increase their discounts during that week. The same course was to be urged upon the other banks of the city.[39] When the Chemical Bank refused to follow their

[35] See p. 191 below.

[36] *Bankers' Magazine*, Vol. 12, p. 822.

[37] See p. 119 below.

[38] *Bankers' Magazine*, Vol. 12, p. 429. *Journal of Commerce*, October 15, 28; November 17; December 1, 3, 8, 11, 12, 1857. *New York Evening Post*, October 16, 1857.

[39] *Bankers' Magazine*, Vol. 15, pp. 494, 580. Mr. Swanson points out that the low rate of sterling exchange made shipments of specie from New York improbable, and that the demand for specie in the South had also ceased. With a specie reserve of 22 per cent, the New York banks were therefore in a strong position, and quite able to extend their loans. Swanson, "The Crisis of 1860," *Journal of Political Economy*, Vol. 16, p. 218.

lead, the large banks boldly took matters into their own hands and continued to increase their loans.

On the twenty-first of November the Clearing House Association took a further step towards the centralization of reserves. A committee of five members was appointed to receive United States or New York state stock, treasury notes, or bills receivable from any bank, and to issue against that security loan certificates amounting to 75 per cent of its value, in denominations of $5,000 and $10,000. These certificates were to be used in the settlements of the daily balances at the Clearing House, and might be issued up to a total of 5 millions of dollars. The limit was raised two weeks later to 10 millions, although only 7 millions were actually issued. The governing committee had extraordinary powers conferred upon it. Not only could it demand an exchange of the collateral security behind the certificates whenever it considered that change desirable, but it might also equalize the specie among the banks "by assessment or otherwise," treating it as a "common fund to be used for mutual aid and protection."[40] In order to guide it, the committee was also to receive daily reports from each bank of its loans and discounts, deposits, specie, and loan certificates. Any loss caused by the non-payment of a loan certificate was to be assessed among the banks in proportion to their capital, and all the certificates were to be redeemed by the first day of February, 1861. A higher degree of centralization would have been hard to obtain even with the aid of a strong central bank.

Hardly had the Loan Committee completed its work in clearing up the results of 1860's crisis, when the outbreak of the War brought it into existence again. It was reorganized on April 25, 1861, and met weekly until the middle of July for the purpose of issuing loan certificates to any bank which required them. None were taken out during this period, for the reserves of the banks were ample to cover their balances in the existing dullness of trade. When the banks began to loan to the treasury during August, this condition was immediately changed, and the loss of their specie forced them to resort to loan certificates.

[40] *Bankers' Magazine*, 1860, Vol. 15, p. 500.

One of the conditions of the contract between the banks and the government had been that the securities should be received by the loan committee at 90 per cent of their market value[41] as a basis for loan certificates. The first certificates were issued on September 19, and the total issue to February 7 was $22,585,000. After that date the certificates were gradually retired. Thirty-nine of the fifty banks had made use of them during the winter. Only one bank, and that for only eight days, had used any other collateral security for its loan certificates than the government stock.[42]

The issue of loan certificates was only one of the duties of the Loan Committee. It was required also to apportion the government loan among the city banks in proportion to their capital. Altogether, 105 millions were taken by the banks of New York through the Loan Committee, which had not only to handle the securities, but also to receive the interest upon them and distribute it among the banks.

The arrangement by which specie reserves of all the banks were pooled during 1860 was somewhat altered by the Loan Committee during 1861. The banks had agreed, after February 1, 1861,[43] to keep their reserves at 25 per cent of net liabilities, excluding circulation and government deposits. This ratio was slightly higher than the 20 per cent of deposits and circulation which had been agreed upon by the Clearing House banks after the panic of 1857. Payments to the treasury on account of the loan depleted the reserves of certain banks in September, and the Loan Committee directed that interest should be charged daily upon the amount of the deficiency, and paid to the banks which held an excess reserve. After September 21 this ruling was no longer enforced, but banks showing a deficit of specie were required to exchange loan certificates for specie.[44]

The war crisis and the needs of the treasury had served as a

[41] This ratio was later changed to 80 per cent of their par value, in order to provide an increased margin.

[42] Before the bonds were actually printed and issued, receipts which indicated that they had been paid for were accepted by the Loan Committee.

[43] Hunt's *Merchants' Magazine*, Vol. 44, p. 91.

[44] The report of the Loan Committee was printed in the *Bankers' Magazine*, Vol. 17, pp. 136 ff.

powerful stimulus to the Clearing House. Without such an incentive it is doubtful if it would have been permitted to assume such extensive powers, or if the banks could have been driven so far in the direction of coöperative action. The principles of the loan certificate, evolved during the difficult years of the Civil War, were carried over into the post-bellum period and applied to later crises, but it is noteworthy that the more stringent rule of equalization of reserves was applied only once again during the crisis of 1873, and then abandoned.

Summary

Before the passage of the National Bank Act, the banks of New York were regulated by state laws. These became gradually more severe, reaching a climax in the statute of 1853 which required city banks to make weekly reports of loans, deposits, circulation, and specie. There was no legal reserve requirement, but notes were secured, first by the safety fund, and later under the Free Banking Law, by collateral securities deposited with the State Comptroller.

Outside of the legislative field, the most important development in the history of New York banks was the organization in 1853 of the Clearing House. This gave them a basis for developing coöperative action in emergency; and under the stimulus of the War, the Clearing House became an important regulative factor among the banks. The technique which it developed at that time was carried over into the post-bellum period.

CHAPTER VI

BANKERS' BALANCES IN NEW YORK

As New York City became the commercial and financial center of the country with a well-defined investment market and a rudimentary commercial-credit market, there developed also the practice which was the most important feature in the history of the New York money market—the sending of bankers' balances to the city in large volume. The call loan market could not have developed had there not been this surplus of funds at hand, and the whole complicated relationship between bank reserves and demand loans to brokers was the outgrowth of the movement of bankers' balances towards New York.

Building up of deposits in New York by bankers of interior

The growth of this type of deposit in the banks of New York rested upon the basic fact that the volume of goods flowing out of New York towards the interior necessitated an almost constant flow of funds into New York from the interior. It was only during the crop-moving period in the autumn that the direction of the flow was reversed, for country bankers at that time drew against the balances which had been building up during the spring and summer. During most of the year the New York banks held large sums subject to the demand of country banks. The rate of domestic exchange was almost constantly in favor of New York and commercial paper made payable in that city could be sold at a higher rate than paper maturing in the city where the loan was made. Even in Philadelphia, as early as 1825, New York funds bore a slight premium, and in cities farther away it was proportionately higher.[1] Balances in New York were therefore more valuable than balances at home, and it was to the advantage of the banker to keep funds in New

[1] 25 Congress, 2 Session, Senate Document 457.

York as long as possible, recalling them only when real need developed at home. Before the heavy buying seasons in spring and fall the deposits of interior bankers in New York were regularly allowed to accumulate.

The advantage of New York in the matter of exchange rates was much resented by other parts of the country. Frequent charges were made that the exchange rate was merely a cover for evading the usury laws and several state legislatures attempted to fix exchange rates by law, as they had already fixed interest rates. Their success in the former case was no greater than that achieved in the latter and since the rate of exchange was usually higher than the cost of shipping funds, the difference continued to operate as an incentive to the building up of balances in New York.

Another reason for building up bankers' balances in New York was that commercial paper bearing New York names was more desirable than that of small local merchants, from the standpoint both of strength and marketability. The great importing houses were known all over the country, and drafts accepted by them were of unquestioned credit. The attractiveness of this type of paper frequently made it difficult for merchants in the interior to find purchasers for their own bills, and we find the state legislatures attempting to counteract the drawing-power of New York in this respect, as well as in the matter of exchange rates.[2] In 1854 Connecticut forbade any bank to loan to a "foreigner," that is, to a person outside of the state, a sum greater than one-fourth of its combined capital and deposits. When this law proved ineffective, the problem was attacked from a new angle; a bank was required to lend up to the amount of its capital to persons within the state, before it

[2] *Report* of investigating committee, New York State, 1835; 1837, p. 25. *Reports* of Bank Commissioners of Connecticut, 1841, p. 55; 1849, p. 7; 1851, p. 5. *Reports* of Bank Commissioners of Massachusetts, 1853, p. 33; 1854, p. 84; 1855, p. 73; 1860, p. 135. Ohio Public Documents, 1854, XVIII No. 9, p. 559. President Jones, of the Bank of the United States, testified before a Congressional Committee in 1819, "that he believes it to be the general practice of the state banks, to deal in exchange whenever they can operate to advantage, and he believes the purchase of bills, payable in the cities on the sea-board, to be one of the principal sources of profit to the banks in the western country"; 15 Congress, 2 Session, House Document 92, p. xvi. For the dealings of the Bank itself in domestic exchange, see p. 50 above.

might make any loans to a person outside. The law did little to change the situation, and even the Bank Commissioners were obliged to confess that one of the safest and most reliable investments for country bankers was good New York paper. The country banks therefore continued to invest in New York paper, and thus accumulate balances in that city, as they had been doing.[3]

The current of trade which flowed steadily through New York City brought with it bank notes from all parts of the country. In order to keep them in circulation, it was essential to keep them near their par value, and in order to keep them at par, it was necessary to provide for their redemption in New York, usually by making arrangements with a city correspondent, and keeping a balance there for the purpose of redemption. The country banks of New York were the first to undertake the redemption of their notes in the city on a large scale. During the decade of the thirties, the balances thus kept in the city increased rapidly. The process was described in a report by the Dutchess County Bank, in 1828:

> Since the last annual return, as before, the bank has kept an account in the North River Bank, in the City of New York, in order to have its bills receivable and current in New-York, so that such bills might pass in the state and elsewhere, without discount; and the directors have accordingly ordered such surplus funds, as were not needed at the bank for its ordinary business, to be sent to the said North River Bank, to redeem the paper there, and the sum above stated as being in that bank are the funds of this bank, placed there for the aforesaid purpose, with the ordinary means of the bank; and these deponents also say, that they have used such means whenever requested by their customers and persons holding their bills, by giving drafts on New York at sight, and without premium.

In 1837 an attempt was made to put into operation a voluntary system of centralized redemption for the notes of New York state banks, but it broke down during the suspension of

[3] *Report* of Connecticut Bank Commissioners, 1857, p. 7. *Report* of Massachusetts Bank Commissioners, 1852, p. 8. Secretary of Treasury, *Report on State Banks,* 1855, p. 94; 1862, p. 80. *Bankers' Magazine,* Vol. 5, p. 694. For further discussion of types of paper, see p. 46 above.

specie payments. It was not until the law of 1840 went into effect that the redemption was organized. Every country bank was required to name an agent in New York, Albany, or Troy, to redeem its notes at the fixed rate of ½ per cent. Since Albany and Troy drew funds from New York when the demands for redemption became heavy, New York City continued to bear the burden of note redemption for the state, and the balances of country bankers had to be kept at a high level in the city to enable the New York banks to perform this service.[4] After 1840 banks of other states also began to provide for the redemption of their notes in New York, and until the passage of the National Bank Act put an end to state bank issues, redemption was a strong incentive to the keeping of bankers' balances in New York.

Another direct advantage from balances in New York appeared as country bankers became more experienced. This was the possibility of keeping smaller reserves at home when large balances were kept in New York. Such balances served as reserve equally against notes or deposits, for bank notes were often redeemed in greater amount in the city than at home, while depositors frequently preferred a draft on New York to cash payments over the counter. The country banker who had a substantial account to his credit with a city correspondent therefore found it possible to get along with a very small amount of cash in his till. In New York state where there was no legal minimum cash reserve requirement and country bankers were permitted to use their own discretion in the matter of reserves, reserve balances were always large in proportion to cash, and the percentage of cash reserve held against deposits by country banks was far smaller than that held by city banks.

The immediate availability of New York balances as reserves was early recognized by the banks of Connecticut also, and in 1836 the banks of that state held 2/5 of their total reserve funds in the form of deposits with city bankers. By 1849 the practice of substituting balances for cash had gone so far that a legal

[4] *Niles' Register*, Vol. XXV, p. 212; Vol. XXIX, p. 179. New York Bank Commissioner, *Report*, 1840, p. 5. Comptroller of the Currency, *Report*, 1876, p. 25. Johnson, *Treatise on Banking*, p. 39 (1850).

minimum was set for the cash reserve, requiring thereafter actual specie in vault to equal 10 per cent of circulation. In several other states the banking law gave explicit recognition to New York balances; in Ohio after 1851, one-half of the 30 per cent reserve against circulation might be kept on deposit in New York or another eastern city, and in Massachusetts after 1858, New York balances could be included in reserve computations.[5]

It will be noted, in reviewing the factors which drew this large volume of bankers' balances to New York City, that a number of them were seasonal in operation, and that only a part of them were effective throughout the year in comparatively unvarying intensity. The possibility of profiting by the premium on New York exchange was greater at the periods when heavy shipments of imported goods were being distributed to the interior merchants, during the spring and fall buying seasons. It was during the same periods that there was the greatest opportunity to invest in bills payable at New York, for many of these bills which formed such desirable material for bank portfolios were drawn during the crop-moving season against exporters in New York by the producers of the interior. On the other hand, the necessity for the maintenance of New York deposits for the redemption of country-bank notes was of course not seasonal in nature, for although a greater volume of notes found its way to the city during the spring and fall buying than at other times, notes were constantly drifting to New York, and the redemption deposits had always to be kept at an adequate figure. The advantage of lower specie reserves at home, because of balances in New York, was also operative throughout the year. To think of the bankers' balances as purely seasonal surpluses is consequently to ignore the permanent elements among the forces which brought funds to New York, and to underestimate both their amount and their importance.[6]

[5] Secretary of Treasury, *Report on State Banks*, 1836, p. 170. Connecticut Bank Commissioner, *Report*, 1848, p. 5. *Bankers' Magazine*, Vol. 5, p. 863. *Journal of Commerce*, November 11, 1858. *Report* of the Bank Commissioners of Massachusetts, 1858, p. 95. See also p. 222 below, for reserve changes made by the National Bank Act.

[6] See p. 206 below for discussion of seasonal factors affecting the money market.

Source of bankers' balances

The economic forces which directed streams of funds to New York from all parts of the country reacted with varying intensity on different states and cities. The regions about those cities which had been early centers of trade, and which had therefore highly developed credit institutions and commercial credit methods, were later in sending funds to New York than the more recently opened sections. But the necessities of trade eventually brought to New York balances from the districts near Boston, Philadelphia, and Baltimore, as well as from the newer states of the West and the South.

The banks of its own state were the first to send large balances to New York City. The rich agricultural country served by the Erie Canal furnished a large part of the products shipped from the port of New York, and absorbed a large part of the imports brought in there, so that there was a strong movement of trade and funds between the city banks and the country. By 1835 the balances of New York country bankers in the city had reached the sum of 4 millions, equal to 1/8 of their total resources. In this early period, the country banks of New York sent about 1/3 of the total bankers' deposits in the city banks. As New York's trade with the interior increased, the proportion furnished by New York state banks fell off, dropping to 1/4 of the total by 1850, and to an even smaller proportion by 1860.

The new states of the Middle West, which were linked to New York first by the canals and then by the railroads, seem to have been the next to send bankers' balances to New York. Ohio had a number of banks by 1820, and the eastern balances credited to them were modest in amount but steadily increasing. They had banking connections with Boston and Philadelphia, but these were quite unimportant in comparison with those between Ohio banks and New York, and in the prosperous years preceding 1837 New York held nearly 2 millions of Ohio funds. Indiana and Illinois were later in developing than Ohio, and were far behind it in trade and banking. But the State Bank of Indiana, organized in 1834 with a network of branches, had balances constantly in New York. The State Bank of Illinois, which, like that of Indiana, had a practical monopoly of banking in its state, also kept a portion of its funds on deposit in New York after 1836.[7]

The proximity of the New England banks to Boston, and the excellence of the Suffolk Bank's system for note redemption, kept their balances in New York down to a very small amount, when compared with those from other parts of the country. New Hampshire banks began to keep small balances in New York about 1845, and by 1857 at least one of the banks had transferred its note redemption from Boston to New York. After 1860 many banks in Maine as well as in New Hampshire sent balances to New York in order to find profitable investment for their funds.

Vermont, as a neighbor of New York on the east, was more easily tempted away from her banking relations with Boston than either Maine or New Hampshire. There were Vermont balances in New York in 1834, and by 1839 1/5 of the bankers' deposits of Vermont were in New York City. When the state banking law was amended to permit deposits in New York as well as in Boston to count as part of the required reserve, the movement of funds towards New York was accelerated, and by 1852 nearly all the banks in western Vermont kept their accounts in that city. By 1860 the total of their New York balances had reached nearly one million dollars.[8]

Connecticut was another of the New England states whose proximity to New York caused a divided allegiance in financial matters. During the early part of the century, her trade was chiefly through Boston, and it was there that she kept her balances. But her bankers soon began to send funds to the New York market. About 1810 the Bridgeport Bank arranged to have its notes redeemed at the Mechanics' Bank in New York. In 1817 the New Haven Bank was commended as a con-

[7] Huntington, *History of Banking and Currency in Ohio before the Civil War*, p. 302. Secretary of the Treasury, *Report on State Banks*, 1838, p. 627. *Bankers' Magazine*, Vol. 4, p. 297. Knox, *History of Banking in the United States*, pp. 691 ff. Report to Illinois Legislature, 11th Assembly, 2d Session, January 21, 1840.

[8] Reports of Bank Commissioners of New Hampshire, 1844-1864. *Reports of* Bank Commissioners of Vermont, 1843-1864. Secretary of the Treasury, *Report on State Banks*, 1837, p. 13; 1839, p. 44. *Bankers' Magazine*, Vol. 7, p. 338.

servative institution because it loaned most of its money at home and had recourse to New York loans only when the business situation in New Haven was "rather heavy." Most of the Connecticut banks joined the Suffolk system about 1825, but by 1835 the influence of New York had become stronger than that of the New England metropolis. Connecticut balances in the hands of New York banks and brokers during 1836 and 1837 were estimated to vary from 1 to 1½ million dollars, part of which was in the city primarily to redeem bank notes. From this time the balances in New York increased and although in 1850 many of the banks were still redeeming their notes in Boston, little banking business was done with Boston, except by small country banks in the northern part of the state. Hartford, New Haven, and Bridgeport banks kept their accounts in New York as did also those of Providence, Rhode Island. Many Rhode Island banks did a heavy discount business in New York.[9]

For Massachusetts banks, of course, there was less reason to place funds in New York, since Boston was a considerable banking center and the seat of a large southern trade. The larger banks had accounts with correspondents in New York but there seems to have been little depositing in New York by the banks of Massachusetts in the period before 1860.[10] With the breakdown of Boston's southern trade at the onset of war, the heavy exchange rates against Boston forced many New England bankers to redeem their notes in New York rather than in Boston, so that the volume of Massachusetts bank balances in New York grew to large proportions.

In the Middle Atlantic states the relations of bankers with New York were similar to those in New England. Like the Suffolk Bank, the Bank of the United States provided a redemption service for state bank notes until about 1840. The large banks in Philadelphia, like those in Boston, carried some reserve

[9] *An Appeal to the Public on the Conduct of the Banks in the City of New York* (1815). Reports of Bank Commissioners of Massachusetts, 1839-1864.

[10] J. G. Woodward, *Currency and Banking in Connecticut, 1635-1838*, pp. 41-55. *"Corrector" on Banking*, 1817, No. II. Connecticut Bank Commissioner, *Report*, 1844, p. 6. Secretary of Treasury, *Report on State Banks*, 1837, p. 847; 1848, p. 172; 1850, p. 109. *Bankers' Magazine*, Vol. 7, p. 338.

accounts of country banks. The Girard Bank in 1833 held about $250,000 of the deposits of southern and western banks, and the Bank of the United States, although not a great holder of country bankers' balances, had small redemption balances belonging to state banks. Between 1840 and 1850 few Pennsylvania banks except those in Philadelphia and Pittsburgh reported New York accounts; between 1850 and 1860 it seems to have become quite common for banks in the eastern part of the state to carry balances in New York. The invasion of Pennsylvania by the southern armies during the War accelerated the movement of balances towards New York, and caused many country banks to send directly to the city funds which had formerly gone to a Philadelphia banker.[11]

The New Jersey banks were in a position very similar to that of the Connecticut banks, midway between New York and another large city. The larger towns in the state were nearer to New York, however, and kept the greater part of their balances in that city after 1840, and perhaps earlier. By 1850 the balances in Philadelphia had sunk to small correspondent accounts, and the deposits in New York were well over half a million dollars. Most of the New Jersey banks at that time redeemed their notes in New York, rather than, as formerly, in Philadelphia.[12]

Not until after 1840 did the banks in the South send large amounts of deposits to New York City. South Carolina had established an agency of her State Bank there in 1831 and other banks kept small balances, but about 1840 the movement gained real momentum and the greater part of the balances were kept in New York instead of in Philadelphia. The Phenix Bank, the Merchants' Bank, and the Mechanics' Bank seem to have been particularly popular with southern depositors. The deposits ran at times into large amounts; a single bank in Louisiana or Alabama sometimes had New York credits of a million dollars.

[11] Pennsylvania Auditor General, *Reports of the Banks*, 1843-1864.

[12] New Jersey Department of Banking and Insurance, 1842-1852. New Jersey Department of Banking, 1853-1864. *Bankers' Magazine*, Vol. 5, p. 779. 22 Congress, 1 Session, House Report 147; Letter from the Secretary of the Treasury, November 1, 1832.

Banks in Tennessee and in North and South Carolina also had deposits in New York, in smaller amounts as befitted their smaller banking capital and smaller volume of trade. The growing trade of New Orleans after 1850 made it worth while for many of the southern and southwestern banks to keep balances there, but the effect upon New York deposits was to increase rather than to diminish them, for it enabled the banks of New Orleans to maintain larger balances in New York than formerly. Missouri, which lay between the southern and the western states, had close relations with New York through the Bank of Missouri, whose deposits in the Bank of Commerce and with Nevins, Townsend, and Company were large, even in 1840.[13]

Banking development in other states was too meager, or records too scanty, to permit more than the most general statement regarding their relations with New York. In general, it may be said of them, as of the older states, that as their trade developed, their bank balances were certain to go to New York City in ever-increasing amounts.[14]

Foreign balances in New York

Although outside the United States proper, Canada was as dependent upon New York City in financial affairs as any of the states, keeping large balances in that city, and calling upon it for specie when her own supply was low.[15] The seasonal movements of trade in Canada coincided with those of the United States; it was an agricultural country, and shipped the greatest part of its produce in the fall. This added strain which Canadian demands at times put upon the money market of New

[13] Cable, *The Bank of the State of Missouri.* Report of Committee to examine into . . . the Bank of Missouri, November 28, 1840. Reports of State banks and branches, Alabama, 1837, 1843, 1846. Bank of Tennessee, Reports to Senate, 1858. Bank Statement of North Carolina, 1855, 1856. Reports of President and Directors of Bank of State of South Carolina, 1848-1862. Report of Joint Committee on banks and banking of the Senate and House of Representatives of the State of Louisiana, 1857. Bryan: *History of State Banking in Maryland.* Royall, *History of Virginia Banks and Banking Prior to Civil War.*

[14] Felch, *Early Banks and Banking in Michigan.* Hinchman, *Banks and Banking in Michigan.* Reports of Secretary of Treasury respecting the Banks of Wisconsin, 1854, 1856, 1867. Sherman, *Early Banking in Iowa.* Knox, *History of Banking in the United States,* pp. 740, 761.

[15] This intimacy of relationship is equally marked today and Canada is frequently referred to as the thirteenth Federal Reserve district.

York was felt at least as early as 1827. In the days of the Second Bank of the United States, Nicholas Biddle tried to effect an arrangement by which the British Treasury in Canada should dispose of its bills of exchange directly to the New York branch of the Bank of the United States, instead of permitting them to trickle in irregularly through correspondent banks and merchants. In return, the New York branch was to supply the government with specie whenever it was needed. Popular Canadian prejudice against Americans made this plan impracticable, and the movements of funds between New York and Canada continued to be unregulated. Canadian banks continued to keep deposits with New York correspondent banks and later the Canadian banks established their own branches here.[16]

More erratic in their movements than the Canadian funds, and less to be counted upon because they were only slightly influenced by seasonal factors, were the occasional funds left in or sent to the city by European bankers, for investment in the New York call-loan and the commercial-paper market. The principal cause for the accumulation of such balances was the difference in interest rates between European countries and New York.[17] During the decade of the 1840's, there were large amounts of foreign capital in the city, owing to high exchange rates, and interest rates at 2 per cent in London and at 6 per cent in New York. The favored form of investment for such funds was "temporary loans on negotiable security," although good, short business paper was also employed. During 1853 and 1854 the Crimean War caused large amounts of the foreign balances to be withdrawn, but by 1855 the usual flow of funds between America and Europe had been resumed. The funds fluctuated between New York, London, and Paris on the tides of the changing interest and exchange rates.[18] In the summer of 1860 over 30 millions of dollars are supposed to have been on deposit in New York on European account. It seems improbable that

[16] *Journal Canadian Bankers Association*, VIII, p. 10. Ross, *Canadian Bank of Commerce*, p. 196. Buchanan, *Report and Observations on the Bank*, p. 17 (1828).

[17] *New York Evening Post*, April 21, 1850.

[18] Bigelow, *The Tariff Question*, Appendix 112, (1862) gives monthly interest rates in England, France, and the United States, 1831 to 1860.

this could have been the normal amount of such balances; it represents more probably the foreign funds put into easily shiftable form because of the threat of civil war.[19]

Total amount of bankers' balances in New York

The sum of all these currents of funds flowing towards New York made a total which grew steadily. Our only basis for estimating the amounts of bankers' balances in the early years of this period is data contained in the annual reports of certain New York banks. On January 1, 1828, reports were rendered to the state legislature by eight banks in New York City, four of which later ranked high as holders of country bank deposits. The total bank balances held by the 8 banks amounted to $500,000, and the net balances to $100,000. The expansion of bank loans and the increase in prices after 1830 brought about a substantial increase in the volume of bankers' balances. By the autumn of 1833, when reports for 3 of the largest banks were published (2 of them had been among the 8 reporting in 1828), the total balances in those 3 banks alone were between $1,000,000 and $1,500,000, and the net balances, about $1,250,000. The Mechanics' Bank held deposits for 45 banks in 14 states, besides 3 branches of the Bank of the United States, and the Bank of America held balances belonging to 19 banks outside New York City.[20]

After 1836, the amount of country balances with Safety Fund banks in New York City was reported annually to the Bank Commissioners. In the beginning of that year the net bankers' balances amounted to slightly less than 3 millions and during the next five years, it varied between 1 and 4 millions. What amount was deposited with other banks and brokers it is of course impossible to estimate. In 1841, however, the total bankers' balances in the city were said to be 8 millions, and

[19] *New York Evening Post*, October 9, November 6, 1849; October 26, 1850; November 3, 1853; April 7, 8, 11, 1854; January 29, 1855. *Bankers' Magazine*, Vol. 12, p. 509; Vol. 15, p. 77. *New York Times*, December 29, 1852.

[20] 23 Congress, 1 Session, Senate Document 16; Report from Secretary of the Treasury . . . December 30, 1833. New York State Assembly Journal, January, 1828, pp. 646, 757.

in 1848 the incorporated banks alone had almost 8 millions of dollars of gross balances.

By 1850 there were about 700 incorporated banks in the United States and nearly 600 of them kept balances regularly in New York, ranging in size from $15,000 to $100,000, and amounting in the aggregate to 17 millions of dollars. Probably an equal sum was due by New York banks to brokers, and to individuals out of town, so that the total amount of demand deposits subject to instant withdrawal to the interior was nearly 35 millions of dollars. By 1860, 900 private bankers and 1,600 banks kept balances in New York City more or less regularly, and the aggregate of their deposits with banks, private bankers, and brokers was set at 25 millions.[21]

The bankers' balances deposited in the incorporated banks of the city represented only a part of the total country balances in New York. Nearly the same amount was on deposit with the private bankers and brokers of the city. The deposits with brokers were not only less safe from the point of view of the depositor bank (as was often pointed out by the Bank Commissioners in their efforts to persuade the state banks to more conservative policies), but they were also a greater danger to the stability of the money market. The law of Ohio permitted only the deposits with solvent banks to be counted as part of the reserve of Ohio banks, but in most states there were no requirements, either as to the amount of bank reserves, or their placement. The balances with brokers were not reported, so that it was impossible to tell, except by changes in money rates, how they were fluctuating.[22]

Concentration of balances in a small group of banks

So far, in discussing bankers' balances with New York banks, they have been treated as if the banks of the city were a unit.

[21] *Journal of Commerce*, July 9, 1841. *Bankers' Magazine*, Vol. 1, p. 518; Vol. 5, p. 178; Vol. 14, p. 971. Secretary of the Treasury, *Report on State Banks*, 1850, p. 416. The net bankers' balances were only half as large as the total. Between 1850 and 1860 the net balances in New York City banks varied between 16 and 30 millions.

[22] New York State Bank Commissioner, *Report* for 1833, p. 14. *Bankers' Magazine*, XIV, p. 971. Secretary of the Treasury, *Report on State Banks*, 1837, pp. 13, 847; 1852, p. 28.

As a matter of fact, the individual banks of the city showed great variation, as far back as the records go, in the proportion of their total deposits which originated with banks rather than with individuals.

The first year in which all the incorporated banks of New York City are included in published reports is 1837. In that year there were 23 banks in the city, with a total paid-in capital of $20,361,000. Nine of these banks, with individual capital ranging from $200,000 to $2,050,000 and with joint capital aggregating 68 per cent of the total, held 78 per cent of the total bankers' deposit in the city banks.[23]

The average bankers' balances for the 9 banks were $1,-233,000, and for the 14 others, $225,000, or about 1/5 as much, but between the 9 banks which carried the largest bankers' balances at this time, and the 14 other banks of the city, there was not a distinct gap. The lowest of the 9 banks held bankers' deposits to the amount of $545,000, while the highest of the 14 held $467,000 and the next highest, $419,000. The banks of New York City, in other words, were distributed fairly evenly over the scale representative of the size of bankers' balances, instead of being divided sharply into two groups, one at the higher and the other at the lower end. There was even at this early date a certain degree of concentration of balances within the city,[24] but it was much less marked then than later.

Eleven years later, on November 1, 1846, the process of concentration had proceeded somewhat further. This date, like that of the report for 1837, preceded a depression, and conditions at the two dates may therefore be considered comparable. There were at this time 25 incorporated banks in New York City, 20

[23] Professor Sprague, in his *History of Crises under the National Banking System*, (p. 17) prefers net balances as an indication of concentration. A serious objection to net balances in this connection is that they result from two independently varying series, *Balances Due To*, and *Balances Due From*, other banks. In order to interpret changes in net balances, therefore, it is necessary to refer back to the two series from which they are derived, and so the series must eventually be studied separately. Only the total balances can be compared at this date, for three of the banks had larger balances due from other banks, than they owed to other banks, because of their note redemption service. The net balances of these banks would therefore be quite misleading.

[24] New York State Bank Commissioners, *Annual Report*, 1837. The material in the report for 1836 confirms the results given above, but is less complete.

of which had been in existence in 1836. Nine of the 25 banks stood out as the largest holders of bankers' balances, carrying 82 per cent of all. Between these banks with their large bankers' balances and the 16 other banks, there was a wide gap. The average amount of bankers' balances in the 9 banks was $715,000, and in the 16 banks, $92,000. Moreover between the lowest bank in the first group, and the highest bank in the second group, there was a drop from $391,000 to $275,000. There was also a wide difference in the proportion which bankers' balances bore to individual demand deposits. For the 9 banks, the ratio of bankers' to individual deposits was 44 per cent while in the other banks of the city, bankers' deposits were only 15 per cent of individual deposits.

Although the 9 banks which held the bulk of the bankers' balances represented 60 per cent of the bank capital of the city, they were not the largest banks in the city from the point of view of size of capital. The Bank of the Manhattan Company, which had the second largest capital stock, was not included among the heavy holders of bankers' deposits at this time, although it had figured in the similar list for 1836. Nor did the Bank of New York have an amount of bankers' balances proportionate to its million dollar capital. These two banks, the oldest in the city, were exceptional among the larger banks of the city in their indifference to such balances after 1837.

The contrast between the two groups of banks in New York City seems sufficient to warrant the assumption that there was an underlying difference in policy. Although it is impossible, with our present information, to verify the assumption, the later history of the New York City banks points strongly to the payment of interest on deposits by the 9 banks as the reason for their undue share of the bankers' balances. It is clear that a few years later such payment was a factor in influencing the choice of its New York correspondent by the country bank, and the same factor may well have been operative in this earlier period.[25]

A study of the bank reports in New York City for June 14,

[25] The material for the foregoing analysis is to be found in the *Report* of the New York State Superintendent of Banks for 1847.

1856 (another pre-panic period), indicates that in the preceding years the process of concentration of deposits in a few New York City banks had gone on despite a rapid increase in the number of banks in the city and the consequent increase in bank capital. The total number of incorporated banks which reported regularly to the State Superintendent of Banking was 54 and their combined capital stock was nearly 53 millions of dollars. Eight of them had 2 millions or more, and 13 of them from 1 to 2 millions, of capital stock paid in.

But the number of banks which were the outstanding holders of bankers' balances had declined to 6 since the year 1847. These 6 banks were among the largest, but were not the very largest, of the 54. Their combined capital was about 16 millions, or 30 per cent of the total for the city, and their individual deposits were also 30 per cent of the city's total. The bankers' balances in these 6 banks, however, were 63 per cent of the total. The average amount of the bankers' balances in the 6 banks was $2,440,000; of the other banks in the city 7 had from ½ to 1 million of such deposits (averaging $675,000 each); the next 13 banks averaged $250,000 each and 28 banks carried no bankers' deposits, or such small amounts as to be negligible.

The spread between the share of the regular banking business (represented by deposits and by loans and discounts) of certain large banks in New York City, and the share of bankers' balances in those same banks, grew wider with each decade. It is evident from these facts that the concentration of bankers' balances in a few banks in New York City, which Professor Sprague pointed out in his study of the panic of 1873,[26] was not a new phenomenon, but the result of a process which had been going on for thirty or forty years. The table on page 119 presents in summary form the successive stages of this concentration.

When the names of the banks which carried the bulk of the bankers' balances at each period are set down in order, it is

[26] Sprague, *History of Crises under the National Banking System*, p. 17. New York State Superintendent of Banking, *Annual Report* for 1857, Table D.

apparent that many of the same banks continued the policy of holding large out-of-town balances year after year.

INCREASING CONCENTRATION OF BANKERS' BALANCES IN NEW YORK CITY

Year	Total number of banks in New York City	Number with large balances	In banks with large balances				
			Per cent of total capital	Per cent of total individual deposits	Per cent of total bankers' deposits	Per cent of total loans and discounts	Ratio of bankers' deposits to individual deposits
1837 . .	23	9	57	68	78	61	110
1846 . .	25	9	60	60	82	45	44
1856 . .	54	6	30	30	63	31	69
1872 . .	50	7	20	18	72	32	152

RANK OF NEW YORK BANKS AS TO AMOUNT OF TOTAL BANKERS' BALANCES AT DIFFERENT PERIODS

Rank	1837	1846	1856
First . .	Merchants'	State of New York	Bank of America*
Second .	Phenix	American Exchange	Metropolitan
Third . .	Bank of America	Bank of America	Bank of Commerce
Fourth .	Mechanics'	Merchants'	American Exchange
Fifth . .	Manhattan	Bank of Commerce	Merchants'
Sixth . .	Union	Union	Bank of Republic
Seventh .	Merchants' Exchange	Phenix	
Eighth .	City	Mechanics'	
Ninth .	Dry Dock	Merchants' Exchange	

* The Bank of America held also the deposits of New York City banks used in the settlement of Clearing House balances, but these deposits were held in trust and did not enter into the "balances due to banks" item of the bank's balance sheet. Gibbons, *Banks of New York*, p. 316.

Interest on deposits as a factor in bankers' balances

A banking practice inextricably bound up with that of bankers' balances and one which bore an unjust share of blame for their existence, was the payment of interest on deposits by the city banks. This subject has been agitated for almost a century through practically every discussion of banking policy or financial reform up to the present time. It is generally taken for granted in such inquiries that the interest which was paid on many of the bankers' balances was the chief factor in inducing their deposit in New York. Closer scrutiny of the facts indicates that the payment of interest was instrumental rather in determining in which particular bank the deposits were to be kept when they came to New York. The actual flow of funds to the city was brought about by much more fundamental causes related to the trade of the country.[27]

The practice of paying interest on customers' deposits had been unknown in the early days of banking in this country. To loan "borrowed funds," as deposits were considered, would have been looked upon as pernicious, if not immoral, and popular opinion expected the banker to do business on his own capital and not on that of his customers. The Farmers' Bank of Maryland claims the distinction of having been the first to pay interest on deposits in this country, in 1804, and the practice made rapid headway. A New York investigation of 1820 found several witnesses who knew of instances, but were unwilling to give details, and another witness who thought that the Bank of America had paid interest to the Planters' Bank of Georgia. By 1831, when the first report of the New York State Bank Commissioner appeared, the payment of interest was sufficiently common to warrant an expression of his disapproval.[28] As long as deposits were made almost entirely by individual depositors, there was little danger in the practice, and it was encouraged by several of the early American writers as conducive to the development of banking.

It is evident that payment of interest on deposits arose at the same time that bankers' balances began to be kept in New

[27] New York State Bank Commissioner, *Report*, 1831, p. 5. *Merchants' Magazine*, Vol. 38, p. 715. Miller, *Theories of Banking in the United States before 1860*, p. 217.

[28] Bryan, *History of State Banking in Maryland*, p. 16. Dewey, *State Banking Before the Civil War*, p. 215.

York. But the payment of interest on deposits was not general among all bankers at any time; it was used by them rather as a competitive device than as a routine measure. Some bankers refused to pay interest at all, even before there was any general opposition to it. Even the bankers who paid interest did not pay it on all deposits, offering it as an inducement to obtain new accounts, or to draw an account from a rival bank, and paying it more frequently to an out-of-town depositor than to one at home.[29] Trust companies and private bankers seem to have indulged in it more frequently than the incorporated banks. Brokers were nearly always obliged to pay interest, since they had little else to offer depositors.

In 1854 a legislative committee in Ohio made a special investigation of the eastern deposits of Ohio banks and the interest received for them, since such deposits with city banks were counted as part of the legal reserve in Ohio. Of 21 banks visited by the examiner, only 6 kept deposits with incorporated banks, and 4 of these 6 had also accounts with brokers or private bankers. Seven of the Ohio banks kept their eastern deposits with the New York branch of the Ohio Life Insurance and Trust Company, which paid interest, and 10 of them had deposits with one or more brokers and private bankers, all of whom, but 2, paid interest on bankers' balances. Of the latter, those which appear most frequently in the account, were Winslow, Lanier and Company; Kent, Lowber and Company; Atwood, Dunlevy and Company; Adams and Buckingham, and Clark, Dodge and Company. The only New York banks which are mentioned by name in the report are the Continental, and the Bank of the Republic, which appears in the list of the New York banks carry-

[29] Pitkin asserts that trust companies paid such interest in 1835; *Statistical View* (p. 438) and *Bankers' Magazine*, Vol. 15, p. 77; Barrett, op. cit., I, p. 16, for such payment by Prime, Ward, and King. Ross, *Canadian Bank of Commerce*, (p. 266) quotes a London banker who wrote, in 1863, that it was the private, and not the joint-stock banks, in America, who paid interest on current accounts. Secretary of Treasury, *Report on State Banks*, 1837, p. 13, and 1852, p. 28, discusses high rates paid by brokers. The Ohio report is in Ohio Public Documents 1854, XVIII, No. 9. The Connecticut Bank Commissioner in 1844 (p. 7) and the Vermont Bank Commissioner in 1852 (Secretary of Treasury, *Report on State Banks*, 1852, p. 28) note that most of the banks in their respective states received no interest on New York balances.

ing the largest gross bankers' balances in that period.[30] Their device of paying interest on deposits in order to attract balances from other banks was evidently successful.

The rate of interest paid, if and when any was offered, fluctuated. It seems to have varied with the call loan rate to a certain extent, but it varied also with the business reputation of the depositary firm; brokers usually paid a higher rate than conservative banks. The lowest rate of interest mentioned in the published discussions of the subject was 3 per cent and the highest, 6 per cent. A bank president, writing against the system in 1858, took 4 per cent as a representative figure. The interest paid to the banks of Ohio in 1854, on their eastern balances, varied from 4 to 6 per cent. The incorporated banks paid 4 and 5 per cent, when they paid interest at all; the single trust company mentioned paid 5 per cent, and brokers and private bankers paid from 4 to 6 per cent.

Whether the payment of interest on country bankers' balances was profitable to the city bank was a much disputed question. It must have been so to those banks which continued in their course in spite of all the objurgations of their fellow-bankers, yet the impossibility of keeping such deposits constantly loaned out at a profitable rate frequently reduced the net gain to a negligible figure. Indeed it could be demonstrated that a banker paying 4 per cent and loaning again at 7 per cent, would actually lose about ½ per cent on the transaction, when the additional expenses of the increased volume of business were considered. As a matter of fact many of the loans were made at rates far above the legal 7 per cent and were consequently profitable.[31]

While the practice was of doubtful value from the point of view of the city bankers, to the isolated country banker it represented almost pure gain. He would lose, of course, if the interest paid on his deposits forced the city banker into dangerous investments which might involve eventually the whole banking system, but this danger seemed remote. The usual attitude of the country banker is typified by the state legislature

[30] Ohio Public Documents, 1854, Vol. XVIII, No. 9.

[31] Secretary of the Treasury, *Report on State Banks*, 1837, p. 847, and 1852 p. 28. *Bankers' Magazine*, Vol. 12, p. 677.

of Illinois which was concerned in 1840, not about the evils of the system, but in making certain that the state's funds in New York were receiving the highest interest rates obtainable.[32]

When the panic of 1857 had demonstrated again, and more forcibly than before, the urgent necessity of some improvement in the financial system, the attacks upon the payment of this interest were redoubled. The New York State Superintendent of Banks devoted several pages to the subject in his report for 1857, complaining first, that the practice of paying interest on deposits "forces up bank liabilities and . . . curtails the circulation of bank notes" (an argument obviously intended to win the attention of the country bankers whose chief source of profit lay in their circulation), and secondly that it put upon the city banks the necessity of lending out the deposits again, and thus inflating bank credit "beyond the requirements of healthy trade and commerce."[33]

The committee of the New York Clearing House banks which considered the matter in 1858, was more specific in its objections and adopted the following resolutions:

> That the practice of the payment of interest on deposits by our city banks is:
>
> Inherently unsound.
>
> That it tends to weaken the legitimate commerce of the country, and to disturb the regularity of the business of the city.
>
> That no banks can safely and profitably practice it.
>
> That it tends to interfere with the efficiency and stability of our banks and with the harmony of their intercourse with each other.
>
> That its discontinuance will not divert any substantial deposits from the city.
>
> That the reasons for its discontinuance are daily increasing.
>
> That it has, under like conditions, no fair precedent in older countries.
>
> That as it exists here, it has been unjustly applied.

These strong opinions were supported by a vast amount of detailed material and the argument was enough to convince 40

[32] Illinois Joint Committee of Investigation, 11th Assembly, 2d Session, January 21, 1840.

[33] New York State Superintendent of Banks, *Report*, 1857, pp. 11, 20. *Bankers' Magazine*, Vol. 12, p. 822.

of the 46 banking members of the association that they should abolish the practice at once, if they had not already done so. The 6 recalcitrant members who refused to sign the agreement of renunciation presumably continued to pay interest on the country balances. Unfortunately, the names of these 6 banks were not given, and the only clue to their identity is the size of the bankers' balances appearing in their quarterly reports.[34]

While the abolition of the payment of interest on deposits may have been admirable from the point of view of the individual bank, as a measure of reform, it was completely ineffective. A few conservative country bankers continued to keep their balances with the safer incorporated banks, but most of the funds went to the 6 banks which still paid interest, or to brokers or private bankers who had always done so. The situation, in other words, was just what it had been for years previously except that the 6 non-signing banks had been publicly rebuked by the 40 good banks, and that the consciences of the 40 banks were clear.[35]

Summary

Bankers' balances were directed toward New York City in ever-increasing volume by the course of trade, which put a premium on New York funds. The necessity of providing for note redemption in the city, and the greater variety and superior quality of New York commercial paper were subsidiary factors in this movement. The payment of interest on balances had less to do with bringing funds to New York than with determining in which of the banks in New York they were deposited.

These funds came to New York from all parts of the country, varying in amount according to the economic development and

[34] See pp. 118-19 above for further discussion.

[35] *Bankers' Magazine*, Vol. 12, p. 822; Vol. 15, p. 77. Hunt's *Merchants' Magazine*, Vol. 38, pp. 326, 715. Connecticut Bank Commissioner, *Report*, 1856, p. 7. Miller, *Theories of Banking in the United States before 1860*, p. 217. In no other part of the country was this problem so acutely felt as in New York City, but opposition to the practice was strong enough to bring about adverse legislation in Connecticut in 1854, in a limitation of the rate to 4 per cent., and in complete abolition of such payments in Massachusetts in 1837. The Connecticut law was soon repealed, but the Massachusetts statute was still on the books in 1858.

the banking facilities of the state in which they originated. They were deposited with private bankers and with brokers, as well as with incorporated banks, but tended more and more to be held by a few large banks. Their presence in the banks of the city made possible the development of the call loan market.

CHAPTER VII

THE ORIGIN OF THE CALL LOAN MARKET

The most distinctive feature of the present-day money market in New York is the call loan. In none of the European money centers has a similar type of loan reached such predominance, or been utilized in the same degree. The demand loan secured by stocks and bonds is a peculiarly American product, and it is important not only by reason of that fact, but also because it has always been closely linked with other parts of the money market. Upon the supply side it has been intimately connected with the reserves upon which the entire banking structure of the nation rested, so that banks were dependent upon the call loan market for funds in time of crisis. On the demand side, it formed the basis for the investment market, securing the funds with which it operated through the medium of call loans and building up the technique of stock trading around them. The call market has been subject to attack upon both flanks, therefore, and for three-quarters of a century has been a favorite objective of financial reformers. Yet its relation to bank reserves was not assailed until the passage of the Federal Reserve Act in 1913, and its position in the speculative transactions of the Stock Exchange is still untouched.

The call loan made its appearance in New York in close association with bankers' balances, and would never have become important if there had not existed these great reservoirs of funds available for just such a use. A call loan market never developed in Philadelphia while that city was the financial center of the country because it was never the holder of bankers' balances to an extent which made such loans possible. Philadelphia lost its position as a center of trade so early that balances did not flow there as they later went to New York. Even the location in Philadelphia of the head office of the Bank of the United States did not attract balances to that city. During the years of its greatest prestige, the net bankers' balances were almost always in favor of the bank, due to its activity in sending the notes of the state banks home for redemption.

Early loans on collateral security

Loans on collateral security had frequently been made in Philadelphia, as in other cities, but they had been time and not demand loans. Ordinarily they seem to have been used in connection with the establishment of a new bank, the shareholder who had made a small cash payment being permitted to borrow on his shares, often from the new bank itself, in order to meet the balance of the payments.[1] The odium which attached to such loans had much justification for it prevented the bank from securing enough specie to insure a sound reserve, but it was carried over to other loans on security collateral. The second Bank of the United States had been specifically authorized to make loans upon government bonds and stock of the bank by a resolution of its Board of Directors in 1817, yet fear that such loans might lead the bank into a speculative interest in the stock market produced a Congressional inquiry two years later. The wording of the report which provided a vindication for the bank indicates how new such loans still were, and how unaccustomed to them was the banking community:

> they [the Committee] do not perceive in the words or principles of the law incorporating the bank any reason to object to the practice which they understand to prevail, of admitting as a substitute for personal security that which results from a deposit of stock, with a power to sell it when it may be necessary to enforce payment of a debt. . . . On the whole, the committee do not understand the practice to be one which gives to the bank an interest in the price of stock, or an opportunity of speculating in its rise or fall.[2]

Relation between bankers' balances and call loans

These early loans on Stock Exchange collateral did not develop into call loans until the banks of New York began to hold deposits of bankers in large amount. It is difficult to obtain

[1] Gouge, *Inquiry*, pp. 19, 20 (1835).

[2] *American State Papers on Finance*, Vol. III, pp. 261, 340. 15 Congress, 2 Session, House Document 92, pp. 76-77.

definite reports about the association of these two items in the early statements of the New York banks, for the statements were not only very infrequent, but very incomplete when they did appear. Demand loans on securities were often included in the total of loans and discounts, or even in the "cash on hand."[3] In 1828 eight of the larger city banks made reports to the Legislature in some detail.[4] All reported loans on collateral security, but only one specified that these were demand loans. The Union Bank included among its assets, $70,600 of loans "payable on demand, with interest, on hypothecation of stock, foreign gold, and other good security" compared with a total of other loans and discounts of $1,184,740. It is significant that this bank reported at the same time deposits by bankers outside of the state of $66,000.

The eight banks reporting in that year had altogether about half a million dollars of loans against collateral security,[5] an amount almost identical with the total bankers' deposits reported by the same banks. No indication is given, however, as to which of these loans were on time, and which demand. The Bank of America reported $24,500 of loans against stocks, out of total loans of $2,352,574. The Tradesmen's Bank had only $1,625 loaned against stock collateral; and only one loan of this kind was reported by the Merchants' Bank, for $8,600, against a total of other loans and discounts of $2,083,289. The City Bank did not think it worth while to give the collateral loans in a separate figure, remarking only that "a few shares of different stocks are sometimes held as collateral security, but usually with a power of attorney to transfer; and as they are perpetually varying the precise kinds held on the 1st of January, cannot be ascertained, not having been registered." The Phenix Bank had made only one small loan on stock collateral, and that on its own stock.

The Mechanics' Bank had the largest volume of loans on stock collateral; $139,074, against other loans and discounts of $2,848,898. The collateral included an unusually long list of

[3] *United States Democratic Review*, Vol. XVIII, p. 468.
[4] *New York Assembly Journal*, 51st Session, 1828, pp. 646-757.
[5] Their total loans and discounts were about 15 millions of dollars.

securities; seventeen different issues, with a par value of $211,580. It is a great lack that the loans are not classified as time or demand, but unless the management of the Bank changed radically, the probability is that they were demand loans, for in 1837 we find the Bank being sharply criticized by a committee of the Legislature for putting so large a share of its funds into this form. The committee reported:

that the bank has loaned a considerable amount as temporary loans, having stocks hypothecated as security, to be called in on short notice; which stocks have fallen in price, from the present extreme depressed state of the money market, and are not now more available than loans would have been, if made on regular business paper, but which your committee are of opinion will not eventuate in very great loss to the bank. The officers of the bank informed your committee that this was done with the view of at all times being enabled to meet any government drafts upon them without being under the necessity of curtailing their regular dealers, which would endanger the interest of the bank and its dealers. Your committee are of the opinion that the officers of the bank, when temporary loans have been made, have generally been actuated by pure motives, and in so doing, have endeavored to protect the general interests of the institution and its dealers, and have also, by these means been prepared to meet the government drafts upon them without any serious embarrassment or curtailment to their regular dealers; yet your committee are of opinion that this species of loan has been quite too large, and one great cause of the clamor against the banks of the city, as it has enabled brokers and others, who held a large amount of stocks, both of our own and other States, to procure means by which to buy paper at a large discount, which means they could not have obtained upon their personal security. Your committee are, however, of opinion that the banks were bound, as the agents of the government, to keep themselves at all times in readiness to meet any drafts made on them by government; and that if a portion of these funds were not put out in this way, they must have remained idle in the vaults of the bank. They have a right, by their several charters, to take stock in hypothecation, and they have not, in any wise violated their charters by this course of procedure; yet your committee are of opinion that it would be more conducive to the interests of these institutions, and vastly better for the public, if no bank in the State was permitted to take stocks in hypothecation, as it tends more to the abstraction than the introduction of capital into our State, inasmuch as these stocks take the place of individual liability, while the money they originally cost goes to furnish other States with capital. The committee are of opinion that this is one of the leading causes of difficulty in our banking institutions in the city of New York—that if banks were prohibited from taking stocks in hypothecation, the large amount of capital absorbed by the fancy stocks of our own and other States, would soon find its way into legitimate and productive business, and thereby effectually cure the avaricious appetite for an increase of incorporations of this kind; as it is evident these stocks, under the present system, serve as a capital on which a large amount of business is done, principally in the purchase of paper and which is generally abstracted from our banking institutions, while the money expended in their purchase is used in other places.[6]

The Mechanics' Bank at this period was one of the three banks in New York City in which the government deposited its funds, and the uncertainty of the political situation was ample warrant for the bank's use of demand loans. Treasury money had been deposited with banks and withdrawn from them in the most arbitrary fashion under the Jackson régime, and the depositary banks had reason to feel they must be prepared for sudden changes. But the tone in which the committee discusses "temporary loans, having stock hypothecated as security" indicates that their use was not confined to the government depositary banks, and that they were not a new element in the money market in 1837.

The Manhattan Company was another of the city banks which held government deposits from 1834 to 1837 and it, too, made extensive use of the call loan market. In 1834 this bank, which had a capital of more than 2 millions, individual deposits of 1½ millions, and the same amount of government deposits, was lending from $600,000 to $1,000,000 on "stocks and other securities payable on demand." The ordinary commercial bills discounted ranged from 2½ to 3 millions, so that demand loans were from one-third to one-fourth as large as the others.[7]

The individual banks which carried the largest bankers' balances were also the largest lenders to brokers in the call loan market. For the early dates such an inquiry reveals, as one might expect, that the loans to brokers were concentrated in a

[6] New York State Assembly Documents, 60th Session, 1837, No. 328, pp. 15-17.
[7] 23 Congress, 2 Session, Senate Document 8.

few banks of the city, closely paralleling the concentration of bankers' balances. In 1843, for example, the banks of the city together had loaned to brokers a total of $3,700,000, of which sum 7 banks had loaned $3,268,000. Five of these 7 banks ranked in 1846 among the 9 largest holders of bankers' balances.[8] In 1846, nine-tenths of the loans to brokers reported by city banks had been made by two of the larger holders of bankers' balances.[9] In 1856, however, the 6 banks which were in that year the largest holders of such deposits, with 78 per cent of all the bankers' balances, had made only 37 per cent of the brokers' loans reported by the banks of the city.[10] In the four quarterly reports during 1858, the reported brokers' loans averaged about $4,400,000 for all the banks in the city, but for the 6 chief receivers of out-of-town balances, only $1,520,000, or 35 per cent. It seems probable that brokers' loans had once been made almost exclusively from deposits which originated as out-of-town balances. As their familiarity with the call loan market increased, bankers began to use it as a method of investing their own funds as well as their out-of-town balances.

Quoting of rates in New York papers

The call loan market began to be discussed in the newspapers at an early date. The *New York Daily Express*, in its financial article for October 14, 1837, mentions that "on Stocks temporary loans can be had without the least difficulty." On August 4, 1838, call loans are again singled out for comment: "Our banks have lent largely to brokers on stocks at 6 per cent. . . . Business notes have become quite scarce." During the early part of 1839, the references to call loans became more frequent: on January 26, "Money easy. Temporary loans on stocks at 5 per cent." On March 2: "Banks have called in freely, their temporary loans on stocks . . . there is therefore a little squeeze among stock jobbers." On April 13: "Banks

[8] *New York Evening Post*, December 6, 1843. The amount of bankers' balances in these seven banks is not given.

[9] These two were the American Exchange and the Union banks, and they had made $581,000 of the $655,000 total loans to brokers reported by New York City banks.

[10] *Report* of New York State Superintendent of Banks, 1856.

doing short paper for regular customers, but for large operations or for stock transactions it is difficult to negotiate outdoors."

A few years later the *Journal of Commerce* began to quote rates on call loans at irregular intervals. On July 3, 1843, it observed that "loans have been made at 3 per cent, and some at 2½ per cent though at this rate to be called back on demand." In the same year, Hunt's *Merchants' Magazine* began to discuss call loans in its "Monthly Commercial Chronicle." The article for July cites as evidence of the abundance of money, the fact that "Trust funds, and other large amounts of money, have been freely offered to the large brokers' houses at call at less than 4 per cent per annum, and in some cases loans have been made at rates as low at 2½ per cent." This was "the cause of the very rapid rise in stocks which has taken place within the last ninety days."

The more compact phrase, "call loans" did not become popular until about 1845, and by 1850 it was the customary term used in discussing them. Call rates were frequently given as early as 1845, and by 1857 they were usually included in any account of the state of the market. The call loan was firmly entrenched in the New York money market by that time.[11]

Effect of call loans on the security market

The development of this system of short-term loans with stock collateral, which grew out of the surplus of funds ordinarily present in New York, had important repercussions upon other institutions of the money market. The most striking were in connection with the investment market. The increase in call loans brought about a new technique for financing the purchase of securities and carrying the burden of marginal sales of stock. Until call loans were established as a part of the financial mechanism in New York, the greater part of stock transactions were settled on time. The first by-laws of the Board of Brokers, adopted in 1817, had provided that in the absence of a different agreement, all sales should be settled on the following day, but since most of the sales at the New York Board were made with

[11] N. Appleton, *Remarks on Currency and Banking*, p. 57 (1841). Gibbons, *The Banks of New York*, p. 58 (1859).

a definite arrangement as to the time of settlement, the "regular way" was at first infrequently employed. As the growth of bankers' balances made larger sums available for call loans, the proportion of stocks sold on time declined, and by 1857 daily settlements were more frequent than time settlements on the New York Stock Exchange.

It is largely due to the existence of a call loan market in New York, therefore, that there was never established a system of term settlements comparable to the fortnightly period of the London market. The fact that in New York there was a well-developed market for short loans on stock collateral which was exactly what a system of daily settlements required in order to function smoothly, gave an impetus to that device which made it impossible to secure the adoption of term settlements in the New York market.

There were several features of the call loan which made them attractive to speculators engaged in buying stocks on margin. They were in ordinary times obtainable at a lower rate than time loans on similar security, the margin between the two widening sometimes to 2 or 2½ per cent. In times of stringency the call rates did rise above the time rates, but call loans were nearly always obtainable at a price, while time loans were frequently unobtainable during a panic even though the nominal rate for them was comparatively low.

The existence of a growing call loan market was the most important factor in the growth of cash settlements for stock sales, but there were other influences also at work in the same direction. It is unlikely that the system of daily settlement could have gained prominence had there not accompanied it a change in the technique of transferring registered shares by which they were assigned in blank, so that it was possible for them to change hands almost as quickly as bearer shares. In London, where time settlement is the rule, such transfer is made by formal deed, a process far too time-consuming for use with daily settlements.[12] Another aid to the growth of daily settlements was the introduction of the telegraph, which came into

[12] Meeker, *The Work of the Stock Exchange.*

use in the eastern part of the country in 1847, and made daily settlement possible between cities which had formerly, because of their distance from New York, been required to rely upon time settlements in their security transactions.[13]

An interesting problem in connection with the rise of the call loan market is the question of margin trading. Stock speculation in New York has been carried on by that method to a greater degree than in any other country. There is very little exact information as to the extent of margin trading, but the diatribes against speculation and stockjobbing frequently mention buying stocks on margin as one of the worst features of the system. It was certainly a factor in the extreme variation of stock prices to which the New York market was subject. The origin of margin trading may have been the practice, already alluded to, of permitting subscribers to bank stocks to put in only a small portion of actual cash, and to borrow from the bank, deposit credits with which to complete the payment.[14] If that was the beginning, the growth was steady, for margin trading soon became a complement to the call loan system.

Although the call loan market had considerable influence upon the development of the investment market, it was in its turn influenced by it. Indeed, call loans upon collateral security could never have become widespread had there not existed a security market of sufficient range to offer diversified collateral, and of sufficient size to assure the marketability of collateral securities under ordinary conditions. As the security market grew and broadened, the call loan market grew with it, improving its technique and tightening its hold upon security transactions.

The complaint that call loans absorbed funds which should have been invested in commercial paper was frequently heard before the passage of the National Bank Act, as after the passage of the Federal Reserve Act. The two markets attracted

[13] It was the opinion of some contemporary observers that the use of call loans in stock trading made the prices of stocks in New York fluctuate more violently than those abroad. Such an opinion is difficult to verify in the absence of adequate stock price indexes for foreign countries. New York State Senate Report No. 58, February 28, 1856.

[14] See p. 127 above.

different types of funds; banks invested in commercial paper, which usually bore a higher rate of interest than call loans, all the funds which they dared to tie up for a considerable length of time. Into the call loan market they put only those funds which they were holding against the possibility of momentary withdrawal. That the call loan was not entirely satisfactory for the investment of such funds is not evidence that the commercial paper market would have been a more suitable receptacle for them. Except for times of crisis, the call loan was quite safe, and bank reserves invested in that way were promptly realizable. Interest rates on commercial paper were usually higher than those on call loans secured by United States and good state bonds. In normal times the differential was 1 or 2 per cent. Both rates were affected by seasonal causes, and tended to reach a minor peak in March or April, and a major peak in September or October, moving generally in unison. At the beginning of a crisis, however, call rates rose more sharply than commercial, reaching fabulous heights as the panic approached. At such a time, the call market served in a way as a buffer to the commercial paper market, since it bore the first force of credit contraction; in later stages of the pressure, banks became unwilling to tie up their funds in time loans and used the call market instead.

Effect of call loans on banking

Because of this relationship the consequences of the call loan system which were of widest import were to be observed in the field of banking. For the call loan market, as it developed, gradually became the final reservoir for the banking reserves of the nation, and upon it, in emergency, fell the final responsibility for providing banks with funds. The banks had no governmental agency to which they could resort in emergency, for the "Independent Treasury" had not as yet freed itself from the literal interpretation of the law which created it.[15] In later years the treasury came regularly to their rescue when they

[15] See Chapter IX below.

needed help, but at this time no such plan of coöperation had been worked out.

Nor did the banks have a central bank to which they could apply for aid. The New York Clearing House eventually developed a technique for turning itself into an emergency central bank and issuing Clearing House loan certificates during a panic. But the Clearing House was not organized until 1853, and did not discover its own capacity to act in this way until 1860. The New York banks, therefore, were left to blunder along as best they could, with the result that most of the banks took the line of least resistance and invested their idle funds in call loans, from which they could presumably be withdrawn more easily than from any other type of loans.

If the balances in New York had been merely surplus funds, with no relation to bank reserves, the connection between bankers' balances in New York and the call loan market there would have had little significance. But as a matter of fact a large share of the bankers' deposits in New York City was made up of funds upon which the country banker relied for cash reserves. And the call loans in which these bankers' balances were largely invested were not liquid in the sense in which that adjective applies to bills of exchange arising from actual commercial transactions. They were not utilized in transactions which would automatically, in a given length of time, provide funds with which to close the transaction. Call loans were shiftable, rather than self-liquidating, investments. The demand for the return of its deposit by a country bank forced upon the New York bank which was holding it the necessity of lowering its loans and discounts by that sum, thus shifting the burden to another party or inducing a sharp decline of stock prices. Since the original deposit might have been loaned by one bank to another and by it in turn to a broker to carry his customer, it is apparent that the demand set in motion by the country banker might have considerable effect upon the money market. And the New York banker upon whom the first demand had fallen might find himself with lowered assets for several days before these were

Courtesy New York Historical Society

WALL STREET ABOUT 1845

compensated for by increasing Clearing House balances in his favor.[16]

The experience of the New York banks with call loans from 1850 to 1860

How this call loan mechanism would function in an emergency was clearly demonstrated for the first time in the decade between 1850 and 1860. During the life of the Second Bank of the United States that institution had always stood ready to lend assistance during a crisis and the call loan market, then in its infancy, had played a minor rôle. During the panic of 1837, which came after the Second Bank of the United States had ceased to feel responsibility for other banks, there were so many other factors of stress that it is practically impossible to separate the difficulties which arose in the call loan market from those which arose out of foreign financial connections, the indiscreet expenditures of the state governments, treasury policies, and half a dozen other disruptive forces. The short depressions of 1846 and 1848, following on the war with Mexico, were more influenced by government financing and the inauguration of the subtreasury system than by financial or business conditions. In the depressions or panics which occurred between 1850 and 1860, however, the difficulties were more directly related to strains within the financial and banking system. They offer, therefore, excellent opportunities for studying the call loan market in relation to the financial structure, and the dangers for the banking system which were inherent in it.

In every one of these depressions it was the seasonal drain of funds from New York in the autumn which brought on the pressure and stopped the machinery of the money market. New York could stand one stress at a time; an export of gold to London, a large bankruptcy or fraud, could be endured; but when to such a strain the seasonal stress was added, the market was unable to brace itself for the double shock. Interest rates rose regularly in September and October as bank reserves, loans, and deposits fell. In those months of every year the New York

[16] Gibbons, *The Banks of New York*, p. 316 (1859).

market was characterized by "tight money," and it was in those months that every one of the crises of the decade before 1860 took its origin.

The depression of 1851

The first of the depressions of this decade was the shortest and the least severe of all. The year had opened propitiously. Prices were rising; the trend of loans and discounts of the New York City banks was still upward as it had been since 1848; demand deposits were also increasing, closely related as they were to loans and discounts. The total bankers' balances in the banks of New York were at a high point of more than 18 millions of dollars in February, an amount equal to nearly half the total individual deposits of the city banks. The only disquieting factor was the course of stock prices which, after advancing steadily for two years to a new high level in January, 1851, began to decline sharply during the next two months, recovered for several months, and began in May a precipitate downward course.[17] In spite of the stock decline there was an increase of 6 millions in loans and discounts during the six months preceding August, 1851. This was no greater than the increase which had taken place during the same months of the two preceding years, but a greater proportion was in call loans which were being undermined by the decline in stocks. Deposits, both bankers' and individual, began to be drawn down, and specie in city banks declined from 11 to 7 millions of dollars between February and August.

The low state of the specie reserves in August finally forced the banks to start the contraction in loans and discounts; demand loans were called in, and further commercial loans refused. Call rates jumped to 10 per cent at times during the month, and good 60- 90-day paper ruled even higher, going to 17 per cent. During the three months from the quarterly bank report of August to that of November, 1851, loans and discounts were reduced from 66 to 60 millions; individual deposits fell from 41 to 37 millions, and bankers' deposits, from 18 to 11

[17] See diagram on p. 39 above.

millions. The decline in the latter item was both absolutely and relatively greater than that of individual deposits, and was more than sufficient to account for the total decline in loans. The loss in bankers' balances also explains the fact that the specie of the banks fell to 6 millions of dollars, and for a while the banks were unpleasantly close to suspension.

Further shipments of gold from California brought some relief during October, and heavy purchases of government securities by the treasury gave aid.[18] By the end of the year interest rates were almost down to normal levels, and the prices of securities on the stock market were rising again. Just how narrow the escape from a real panic was, is difficult to decide in the absence of weekly reports for the New York banks. The underlying business conditions seem to have been favorable, and apart from temporary difficulties experienced by merchants in securing credit during September, they were little affected by the financial flurry. Foreign trade had increased rapidly, and exports had grown faster than imports. The chief danger arose from the rapid decline in deposits which forced banks to contract their loans. The deposits would not have fallen so rapidly had not a large part of them represented the reserve balances of country bankers. It was on the call loan market that the brunt of this withdrawal of country balances fell, and bankers had a practical illustration of what bank commissioners and banking reformers had been trying to point out—that the call loan market was not a safe place for bank loans and that, in a time of stringency, call loans would be undeserving of their name.[19]

The depression of 1854

Three years later, in the fall of 1854, there was another depression in the New York money market. Though it did not have the widespread disastrous results of the panic of 1857, it was far more serious than the short period of financial distress in 1851. There had been two important developments in the

[18] See p. 189 below.

[19] Hunt's *Merchants' Magazine*, Vol. 25, p. 338; Vol. 38, p. 157. *Journal of Commerce*, 1851, passim. New York State Superintendent of Banks, *Report*, 1851.

field of banking. The state legislature of New York required, after August, 1853, that every bank in the city should report weekly the amount of its loans, deposits, specie, and circulation.[20] This law made much more difficult than under the old system of quarterly reports, the "window-dressing" by which a bank could cover up for the period of the report the inflated condition of its loan portfolio, and it undoubtedly forced a number of the banks to curtail their operations. A month after the weekly reports began to be published, the Clearing House was organized, thus forcing upon the city banks a daily settlement of accounts with each other and making impossible a great overextension of loans by any one bank. These new requirements tended to produce a feeling of nervousness among the city bankers, and in order to make their funds more readily available in a possible emergency, many time loans were transferred to the call market.[21]

In addition to these banking changes, there had been a heavy falling off in the foreign demand for American securities in 1853, due to the Crimean War. Both state and railroad shares were involved. Because of the reduced sale of rail shares several of the state banks drew down their balances in New York in order to lend to half-finished railroads which could no longer borrow abroad. The declining prices of state securities, which were used in many western states, as in New York, to secure bank note circulation, involved the banks of the West in difficulties. During May, 1854, banks in Indiana were forced to suspend, followed by those in Ohio and Illinois.[22] In July came the news that fraudulent stock of the New York, New Haven and Hartford Railroad had been issued to the amount of nearly 2 millions of dollars, and that 3,000 shares of the New York and Harlem Railroad stock had been forged. There were also reputed irregularities in Illinois Central. It became impossible to borrow on call with railroad securities as collateral, and since railroad shares made the bulk of the transactions on the New York Ex-

[20] See diagram on p. 91 above.

[21] *Bankers' Magazine*, Vol. 8, pp. 274, 442, 579. Hunt's *Merchants' Magazine*, Vol. 38, p. 157; Vol. 39, pp. 340, 721. *New York Times*, Sept. 26, Oct. 10, 1853.

[22] Secretary of Treasury, *Report on State Banks*, 1854, pp. 204, 236.

change, stock and loan brokers were hard hit. Call rates went to 8 per cent, and good short paper to 12 per cent. When an attempt was made to call in these demand loans, they were found to be as difficult to collect as time loans, and in many cases it was impossible to dispose of the collateral. The treasury again put funds into the market,[23] and a crisis was averted for the time.

The panic of 1857

The depression of 1857 was more serious than either of its immediate predecessors. During the early part of 1857 prices on the stock market, which usually move in advance of other money market indicators, began to decline. This was due in part to the difficulty in borrowing on railroad stock collateral; call rates had gone to 12 per cent during February and March, which was far more than the seasonal rise. Commercial paper rates which usually ruled above call rates did not increase proportionately, and fluctuated between 8 and 10 per cent. In May, when bank deposits were lowered by spring buying in New York, total loans and discounts continued to increase, and the specie of the banks remained about the same, between 11 and 13 millions of dollars. With deposits at 69 millions and circulation at 9 millions, the high point reached in August, this amount of specie was a reserve of little more than 15 per cent against notes and deposits. The balances of country bankers in the city banks at the beginning of August were about 15 millions, one-fourth of the total deposits in New York banks. It was inevitable that these balances should be withdrawn during the next three months, and the banks of the city should have had sufficient experience with the seasonal demand of previous years to prepare themselves for it. Deposits began to decline in the first week of August, and fell rapidly throughout the month, but bank loans did not begin to be reduced until the second week, and even then they fell less rapidly than deposits. The proceeds of new loans were taken out in specie, so that specie was being drawn down more rapidly than deposits.

[23] See p. 190 below.

The crisis was precipitated by the failure of one of the largest banks in the country. The New York branch of the Ohio Life Insurance and Trust Company carried nearly one-half million dollars in balances of many western banks, on which it paid 5 per cent interest. These funds it had loaned out on the call market, with railroad stocks as collateral. When falling prices in the stock market lowered the value of this collateral and made it impossible for some of the borrowers to repay their loans, the company was unable to send back the country balances which were now being demanded from it as from the incorporated banks of the city. The obligations of the New York office were so great that there was nothing for the Company to do but to suspend payment. The announcement came on August 24, 1857,[24] and conditions in the money market rapidly approached a state of panic.

The reports of the Clearing House banks reflect the course of events during the weeks which followed.[25] Country banks in fright called for their balances more rapidly, and deposits which had already dropped from 69 to 64 millions, kept on downward until they reached 43 millions by October 17. On the same date specie in the New York banks was less than 8 millions. Loans fell less in proportion, although more in total amount, than the other items, from 120 millions on August 22, to 97 millions on October 17. Call loan rates went to 3, 4, and 5 per cent per month during September, and ranged so widely that the *Journal of Commerce*, which customarily gave quotations each week, made no attempt to publish interest rates from October until the following February. Loans on commercial paper, either promissory notes or bills of exchange, were almost unobtainable at any price during September and October, and efforts of the Clearing House to increase credit, described in an earlier chapter,[26] gave little relief. Commercial houses which found themselves unable to obtain credit were forced into bankruptcy, and their failure reacted upon banks which had formerly loaned to them. During September banks in Philadelphia and Baltimore began to fail,

[24] *Bankers' Magazine*, Vol. 12, pp. 140, 322.
[25] See diagram on p. 91 above.
[26] See p. 97 above.

and in the West all but the Bank of the State of Indiana and the banks of Kentucky were forced to suspend. New York banks suspended specie payments in October in order to save what little coin was left.[27]

The suspension of specie payments in New York put an end to the panic by giving the banks and the merchants a breathing spell. It was no longer necessary for the banks to continue the policy of loan contraction, and there was no further decline. Throughout November loans remained practically stationary at 95 millions, and in December they began slowly to rise again. Deposits came pouring back into the banks also, and by the end of the year were almost at the level of August. But the most remarkable recovery was in specie, which jumped from 8 millions in October to 28 millions at the end of the year, and made possible the resumption of specie payments on December 14, after two months of suspension.

The panic of 1857, like the other depressions of that decade, was brought about by the autumnal strain being superimposed upon a market for which the drain of specie and the difficulties of the stock market had ill prepared it, and which was forced to rely entirely upon the call loan market. The *Times*, in summing up the causes of the panic, felt that they were less severe than those which had preceded the depression of 1854. In 1857, as in 1854 and 1851, the drawing down of the balances of country bankers marked the beginning of the strain. The recalling of the deposits necessitated the calling of loans in New York, forcing the call loan market to give up large amounts of funds, and the New York banks to contract their loans. Three-fourths of the deposits withdrawn from the New York banks between August 22 and September 26 went to out-of-town banks; while during October, when the danger of bank suspension was obvious, country balances were called for even more rapidly, frequently by telegraph. When the country balances began to leave there was nothing the city banks could do except to reduce their loans and discounts. There was no central bank to which

[27] The Chemical Bank was the only one which did not suspend, and was rewarded for its action by being debarred from the use of the Clearing House.

they could resort for aid, for the New York City banks themselves were the center of the American banking system. And they did not keep, as a central bank would have kept, a reserve of specie in their own vaults sufficient to tide them over such a crisis. They had trusted instead to the call loan market to provide them with funds, and this it had been unable to do.

During November, after most of the damage had been done, the treasury bought more government securities, but the funds thus put into the market could not take the place of the specie reserves which the banks lacked. They could not be put into the most effective position for giving assistance, and probably accomplished little good except to satisfy the popular clamor that the government "do something."[28]

Contemporary criticism of the call loan market

The dangers of the call loan system were pointed out by contemporary observers even before the panic of 1857 which set its faults in such clear relief. Much of the early comment on the increase in the funds devoted to call loans had its source in resentment of the fact that loanable funds tended to drift to New York, while in many places outside of the city loans were difficult to obtain. This was the same objection which had been raised to the deposit of bankers' balances in New York[29] and indeed the two were logically connected. This line of criticism came from the borrowers, and since the point of view which it represented was always present in the money market, this type of objection continued to be raised even after other and more vital arguments against call loans had been found.

Another, and perhaps the most frequent, of the early complaints was that call loans encouraged speculation, stockgambling, or stockjobbing as it was variously called. Theophilus Fisk, in a heated pamphlet entitled "The Banking Bubble Burst," published in 1837, and Edward Kellogg, who wrote under the alliterative nom de plume of Godek Goodwell in 1845, made much of this aspect of call loans. Since the evils of specu-

[28] Hunt's *Merchants' Magazine,* Vol. 37, p. 582; Secretary of the Treasury, *Report on the Finances,* 1857, p. 19. See p. 191 below.

[29] See p. 104 above.

lation were taken to be self-evident, such a charge against these loans was considered sufficient proof of their danger. Related to this type of criticism was one which pointed out that from the lenders' point of view the call loan, being made usually to a broker engaged in speculative transactions, was a much less safe form of investment than commercial paper. In 1841 the Bank Commissioner of Connecticut deplored the fact that so large an amount of funds from his state was employed in call loans, because the collateral security was generally quite inadequate, frequently consisting of speculative shares of doubtful value.

There was a strong feeling that the proper business of banks was the discounting of commercial paper, and that they should avoid other types of loan, particularly those which were tainted with the speculative element. The *Journal of Commerce,* in an article on banking reform in 1856 recommended, among the four changes essential to improvement, the elimination of all demand loans in bank portfolios, and the limitation of bank credit to paper having a certain fixed time to run. The *Bankers' Magazine* agreed that the interests of business as well as of the banks would be better served if loans on call were reduced in favor of discounts of commercial paper.[30]

This early line of attack, although it recognized the danger of the call loan to the individual bank, failed to perceive what is now considered to have been the really vital point. That was the connection between the call loan market and the bank reserves of the country, due to the "pyramiding" of such funds in New York City, and the lending of them in a form which did not always safeguard the interests of the lender. It was not until after the panic of 1857 that recognition of this serious danger became general. The concentration of banking reserves in New York had been going on for many years before 1857, and the use of the call loan by the banks of New York City had been increasing with the out-of-town balances. Instead of futile protests against the centralizing of bank reserves in New York, which they saw to be almost inevitable with the existing trade

[30] *Journal of Commerce,* February 2, 1856. *Bankers' Magazine,* Vol. 7, p. 362.

situation, the reformers after 1857 wisely centered their efforts upon the task of breaking the connection between bank reserves and call loans.

Gibbons, writing just after the panic of 1857, was so impressed with the danger of call loans that he felt it might be wiser for banks to let any excess balance "remain as a dead weight, until the activity of trade shall again call it into use. Such in fact has been the experience of several of our city banks which have repudiated stock loans altogether." This plan was equivalent to the keeping of a very high specie reserve during the slack seasons of business, in order that there might be no doubt of the bank's ability to retain a moderate reserve in times of pressure. The reform offered by Samuel Hooper of Boston was a moderately high specie reserve at all times, with a legal requirement of 33-1/3 to 50 per cent of circulation and deposits as the minimum. If the banks of New Orleans could withstand suspension of specie payments in 1857, on their legal 30 per cent reserve against notes and deposits, the New York banks with a higher reserve to meet their peculiar responsibility would also be saved from suspension and would always be in a position to meet the demands made upon them by the country bankers whose funds they held. Mr. Nathan Appleton, another Boston critic of the New York system of banking, suggested that the banks, rather than loan at call, should extend their loans on long-term paper, both for the safety of the bank and the convenience of the borrower. He added that if real business paper at six months' maturity was not available, the bank might take short-dated accommodation paper with the long business paper as collateral, since it would be difficult for a bank with large capital to find sufficient business paper at short dates to fill its portfolio. As a matter of fact, this is just what some of the New York banks were doing.[31]

In spite of the large amount of controversy over call loans, the proposals for specific reforms made little headway. Early

[31] Gibbons, *Banks of New York*, pp. 58, 350 (1859). N. Appleton, *Remarks on Currency and Banking*, p. 57 (1857). Samuel Hooper, *An Examination of the Theory and the Effect of Laws Regulating the Amount of Specie in Banks* (1860). *Bankers' Magazine*, Vol. 15, p. 760.

efforts at legislation were based upon a realization of the close relationship between call loans and the speculative movements of stocks, and the feeling that since all speculation was wrong, loans to brokers must also be wrong. An example of this type of reform was the state law of 1812 aimed against short selling; it made void a contract of sale made by a seller not actually in possession of the shares. The law was never enforced and was repealed in 1860. Another was the proposed law of 1836, to require public reports of all sales of stock. This one was never passed.[32] In 1856 the governor of New York devoted a paragraph in his annual message to the subject of reforming Wall Street, and as a result of this stimulus a committee of the state legislature was appointed to investigate. After rejecting the legal abolition of interest on deposits and restrictions on the total amount of loans as liable to be no more effective for their purpose than the usury laws had been in controlling interest rates, it recommended that the banks be restrained from loaning upon the hypothecation of stocks and bonds, more than 15 per cent of the amount of their capital stock, and that they be required to report the amount of deposits upon which interest was allowed.[33] The committee, while not defending the practice, felt that the payment of interest on deposits was the result of the facilities afforded by the call loan market, rather than the cause for its existence, and that forbidding the payment of interest would not affect the larger evil behind it.

No action was taken on the recommendation in 1856, and the unfortunate experience with call loans during the panic of 1857 produced a decided halt in the growth of call loans, probably due as much to the low rates prevailing during the depression as to the fact that bankers and brokers were unwilling to put a great amount of funds into a form of investment which had so recently proved disastrous. In June, 1859, the *Bankers' Magazine* called attention to the difficulty of placing loans on call because of the surplus of funds in that market, due to the fact

[32] Stedman, *New York Stock Exchange*, p. 78. New York State Assembly Document 291, 1836.

[33] New York State Senate Report No. 58, February 29, 1856. *Journal of Commerce*, February 2, 1856, editorial. *New York Times*, March 5, 1856.

that "so many brokers suffered loss and inconvenience from the late sharp turn in the money market that they are now refusing again to try the 'call loan' system." And in March, 1861, it reported that several of the leading banks had decided to make no further loans on call, because they had found such loans to be "a fruitful source of trouble." But like the attempt to do away with interest on deposits, this reform movement did not last long, and the call loan recovered its former position as it again became profitable. It was even more of a problem in the years following 1863 than it had been before.

Summary

The call loan market developed out of the necessity of investing for short intervals, in easily liquidated loans, the large sums which found their way to New York. They were usually in the form of balances due to country bankers, and they represented not only temporarily "surplus" funds, but also part of the actual reserves of these banks. It was the latter factor which introduced the element of danger. These funds were concentrated in the hands of a few powerful banks in the city, but there was no effective system of coöperation between them and each in a crisis was constrained to guard the interests of its stockholders before the interests of the banks whose reserves it held. In spite of constant opposition, and in the face of specific proposals for reform, the call loan became an increasingly important factor in the New York money market.

CHAPTER VIII

THE GOVERNMENT AND THE MONEY MARKET BEFORE 1840

From its very beginning the government of the United States has been an important, and on occasion the most important, factor in the New York money market. Not only have its expenditures exceeded those of any other person or corporation, but it has from time to time been the largest single borrower in the country. Both of these activities affected New York. The chief source of revenue of the United States treasury before the Civil War consisted of import duties; in half of the years between 1791 and 1860, customs duties alone were sufficient to meet the whole of governmental disbursements. Since two-thirds of the goods imported into the country entered through the port of New York, the treasury received a great part of its income there and was dependent upon banks of that city for its transfer to other parts of the country in order to meet disbursements. In the second place, government loans were increasingly dependent upon New York and the issues and open-market supply of securities were so few in the early history of New York that government shares were relatively far more important than today. Yet in spite of their inevitably close relations, the attitude of government officials toward the money market has varied greatly, from the cordial and canny coöperation of Alexander Hamilton to the undisguised hostility of Roger Taney and the Jackson administration. This changing point of view has affected the tranquillity of the relationship between the treasury and the market, but it has not been able to minimize its importance.

Early assistance rendered to the government by the banks

During its earliest years, the lack of a well-developed money market at home obliged the government to borrow largely from abroad. One of the first acts of the Continental Congress in 1776 was to authorize a loan in France at 5 per cent interest, but only $182,000 of the authorized issue of 10 millions could be sold. Other foreign loans were more successful, and by 1789 the total amount of foreign indebtedness was nearly 10 millions of dollars, most of which was owed to France and Holland.[1] The growth of American banking and the beginnings of an investment market made foreign loans unnecessary after 1795 and Europe's preoccupation with her own difficulties made them impossible. Between 1795 and 1801 nearly three millions of dollars were borrowed at home through the Bank of the United States and the Bank of New York, as loans repayable in one to four years. Two loans at 8 per cent, which brought more than 6 millions, were also subscribed directly by individuals.[2]

The New York market was of assistance to the government not alone in the borrowing of funds, but also in the difficult process of repaying the loans which had been negotiated abroad. To make these payments by shipments of specie would have been very expensive, and the absence of a broad market in the foreign exchanges made remittance by bills difficult. Secretary Wolcott therefore converted the French debt into a domestic one by giving to the French holders of United States obligations credits in New York which were used for the purchase of supplies. Only the Dutch loan still remained to be paid abroad, and it was found impossible to fund this into a domestic debt. In order to make the payments due, the sinking fund commissioners drew bills of exchange upon the American agents in Amsterdam, Rotterdam, Hamburg, and London, and sold them through the banks. Up to April, 1792, the Bank of New York and the Bank of North America sold nearly a million dollars' worth of such bills. Thereafter the Bank of the United States, through its New York and Philadelphia offices, took over this task, and sold another million dollars' worth of exchange for the government. Another plan of remittance was the purchase from the banks of half a million dollars' worth of the 6 per cent stock of the United States, and its subsequent sale in Europe to provide funds with which to pay interest and principal of the Dutch

[1] Stedman, *History of the New York Stock Exchange*, p. 35. *American State Papers on Finance*, Vol. I, pp. 26, 181.

[2] 28 Congress, 1 Session, Executive Document 15, pp. 445, 448.

debt. This method was only partially successful, for the stock could not be sold abroad except at a heavy discount.

The Bank of the United States was the chief reliance of the treasury in the repayment of the debt until 1802, when it refused to contract for making the remittance then due. The Bank of the Manhattan Company in New York thereupon offered to do so at the rate of 43 cents per guilder but an offer of Baring Brothers of London at 41 cents per guilder was accepted. The foreign debt, which in 1795 had stood at 12 millions, had been reduced by 1801 to 10 millions and by 1807 to less than 2 millions. This was such a small amount that special services on the part of banks in the remittance of funds abroad were no longer necessary.[3]

The treasury was also dependent upon the banks for the safe keeping of its funds. During the first years of the Confederation, Robert Morris, the Superintendent of Finances, utilized for this purpose the Bank of North America in Philadelphia. As other banks were organized, government deposits were left with them at the convenience of the treasury. The Bank of New York, the Bank of Maryland, and the Bank of Massachusetts had all received such deposits before 1791. When Hamilton had finally succeeded in establishing the Bank of the United States, with branches in some cities where state banks were already holding deposits of the government, he promised that he would make the transfer from the state bank to the branch in a way that would "precipitate nothing," in order not to disturb by any abrupt change the good relations existing between the treasury and the banks.[4]

Hamilton's attitude toward the money market

It has often been pointed out that one of Hamilton's chief objects in sponsoring the Bank of the United States was to strengthen the hands of the Federal government by binding to it the wealth and commercial interests of the country. It was

[3] 28 Congress, 1 Session, Executive Document 15, pp. 418, 423, 445, 473, 502. *American State Papers on Finance*, Vol. I, p. 183.

[4] 23 Congress, 2 Session, House Report 27, p. 2. 28 Congress, 1 Session, Executive Document 15, p. 213.

to be expected therefore that his attitude toward the money market should be one of solicitude. Even his political opponents were impressed with the sagacity of this plan and Jefferson himself later followed a similar course, advocating a "judicious distribution" of government favors among the branches of the Bank of the United States and the state banks in order to ally them with his administration.[5] But it must not be supposed that Hamilton's policy of maintaining friendly relations with the banks led to any such excesses of favoritism as characterized the relations of the "pet banks" with Jackson's administration.[6] In addition to the carefully graduated transfer of deposits from the state banks to the Bank of the United States, the only other tangible evidence of Hamilton's solicitude is to be found in the relief which he gave to the banks and the business community during several crises. In March, 1792, for example, when heavy duty payments were maturing in the Philadelphia district, the president of the Bank of the United States was informed that post notes of the bank, if not issued for a period longer than 30 days, would be acceptable by the collector. This was a broad hint to the bank that the government expected it to make loans to importers, but would not try to collect the proceeds of the loans from the bank for a month. The Bank of Maryland was advised at the same time that if it should "incline to make discounts for the importers," the Secretary would leave a sum of money equal to the amount of the loans, on deposit with the bank for 60 days after the dates of the notes. The Bank of New York, in April, was offered the same plan as the Bank of the United States in Philadelphia, the notes to be received by the bank as cash but the government to treat them as 30-day notes which were not to be drawn against until the expiration of that time.[7]

For several years following the establishment of the Bank of the United States regular deposits of government funds in state banks were discontinued, and the bank and its branches

[5] *Hamilton's Works*, Vol. V, p. 486. *Jefferson's Writings*, Ford Edition, VIII, p. 172.

[6] See pp. 164 ff. below.

[7] 17 Congress, 2 Session, House Report 105, pp. 173-74.

alone were used as depositaries. As time went on the treasury needed depositaries in some cities in which there were no branches of the bank, and began again to make use of state banks. By 1806 10 state banks held United States funds, and by 1811 the number had grown to 22.[8] Following Hamilton's policy, some of these deposits were made as much for the benefit of the bank as to satisfy a need of the treasury. In 1801 the Secretary of the Treasury ordered $50,000 of government money to be placed in the Bank of Columbia, in Washington, D. C., in order to protect the bank against a threatened run.

Nearly one-fourth of the total 5 millions of government deposits in 1806 was in the New York branch of the Bank of the United States. Since the total banking capital of New York City at that time was only 5 millions, the government deposits were an item of considerable importance to the banking interests of the city, and continued to be so after the dissolution of the Bank of the United States in 1811. The amount which the government found it necessary to keep on deposit in New York was large, and arrangements were made with the Mechanics' Bank and the Bank of the Manhattan Company by which the former was to receive 1/3 of the customs receipts of the port of the New York and the latter 2/3, and each bank was to receive in addition an initial deposit of about ½ million dollars. Similar plans for government deposits were made in other cities where there had been branches of the Bank of the United States, and the transition was made without any great difficulty owing to Secretary Gallatin's precautions. In New York City, where the danger from rapid liquidation of the bank was great, the state legislature also aided by granting it a temporary charter in order to spread the curtailment of commercial credits over a longer period, and thus render it less violent.[9]

The solicitude of Hamilton and the precautions of Gallatin set a precedent which was followed by their successors during the next twenty years. Throughout this period, the Secretaries of the Treasury showed the greatest concern for the safety of

[8] *American State Papers on Finance,* Vol. II, p. 218. 17 Congress, 2 Session, House Report 105.

[9] *American State Papers on Finance,* Vol. II, pp. 218, 516.

the banks upon which the government depended for the keeping of its deposits. Secretary Crawford's report in 1823 gives two examples of this policy:[10]

> . . . On the 4th of March, 1814, the Cashier of the Bank of Pennsylvania, by letter of that date, informed the Secretary of the Treasury, that the great and unprecedented demands upon that institution for specie, principally from the eastward, induced him to request, that if consistent with the interests of the government, he would give him drafts either on New York or Boston, to an amount that would counteract those demands, stating that the amount of specie in the vaults but little exceeded $200,000, and that the demands of the bank, upon those to the southward of Philadelphia, if called for, might put them to serious inconvenience. Upon the representation, a draft was, on the 8th of the month, drawn by the Treasurer, in favor of the bank, for $150,000, upon the Bank of New York. Upon the 28th of February preceding this transaction, there was in the bank a deposit of $755,000, and on the 31st of March, $799,000. . . .
>
> In the letter of the acting Secretary of the Treasury, of the 27th May, 1813, to Stephen Girard, he is informed, that the "arrangement made by Mr. Gallatin relative to the deposit of the public moneys drawn from your bank, in favor of the public agents, was to shield you against the attacks of the incorporated banks, to whom such moneys would otherwise have been transferred; and the magnitude of your contract might thus have been rendered highly prejudicial to your institution. It is the particular province, and it has been the practice, of the Department of the Treasury of the United States, to direct the moneyed operations of the public to the preservation of credit, by maintaining the equilibrium between the moneyed institutions of the country; and as it has protected your institution, by the arrangement alluded to, so it will guard those institutions against any undue pressure which the public funds in your vaults may enable you to direct against them. I am informed that you have made some very heavy and unnecessary drafts of specie from several banks, particularly from the Pennsylvania and Farmers and Mechanic's Banks, with indications of a disposition to persevere, which has excited considerable apprehension. I therefore deem it necessary to inform you, that a continuance of that system will induce the prompt application of a specific remedy."
>
> From my personal intercourse with Mr. Gallatin, I know he entertained the sentiments communicated in this letter; and I presume they have been entertained by all of his predecessors and successors in office.

[10] 17 Congress, 2 Session, House Report 105, pp. 175-76.

Financing the War of 1812

Besides serving as government depositaries, the state banks, after the downfall of the Bank of the United States, had the additional task of assisting the treasury in war financing. War was declared against Great Britian in June, 1812, and the depleted treasury made plans at once to borrow from the banks, rather than to increase taxation.[11] By the end of 1812 it had borrowed nearly 13 millions of dollars, of which 10 millions were in the form of long-term loans or special contracts, and the rest in treasury notes. The treasury notes were particularly sought by banks, which found them excellent substitutes for the commercial paper which the War's interference with trade had rendered scarce. The financial importance of New York at this early date is demonstrated by the fact that the banks of New York City subscribed a larger share of the loans and treasury notes than those of any other city in the country, taking nearly one-third of the total sum.

During 1813 and 1814 the government continued its policy of financing the War by borrowing, but at an increasing cost.[12] The policy of inflation, the absence of a courageous, well-reasoned fiscal program, the opposition of New England to the conflict, and the lack of military success, all combined to make the offerings of the treasury less attractive to the public. A loan of 16 millions in 1813 was subscribed only after three public offerings of the stock and the agreement of Girard and Parish in Philadelphia and John Jacob Astor and his associates in New York to take the remainder at a discount of 13 per cent. During 1814 the treasury was forced to sell 13 millions of stock at a discount of 15 to 20 per cent, and an effort to sell another 6 millions in Europe proved unsuccessful. It was during this period that the government, in order to get the money at all,[13] was reduced to pledging that $200,000 borrowed from Phila-

[11] 17 Congress, 2 Session, House Report 105, p. 601. 28 Congress, 1 Session, Executive Document 15, p. 548. *Niles' Register*, Vol. III, No. 22.

[12] The War ended in December, 1814.

[13] *American State Papers on Finance*, Vol. II, p. 624; Vol. V, p. 32. *Niles' Register*, Vol. IV, pp. 54, 65, 81, 131.

delphia, and $1,000,000 borrowed from New York, should be applied only to the defence of those cities.

The inflationary policy of the treasury was directly reflected in the banking system. During the period from 1811 to 1815 the number of banks increased from 88 to 208, their paid-in capital from $42,610,000 to $82,259,600, and their note circulation from $22,700,000 to $45,500,000. But as the liabilities of the banks increased, the specie in their vaults was drawn down. There was a heavy export of specie to England during the War,[14] and much also found its way to the banks of New England in payment for the imported goods which were entering the country only through those ports in the war years. The banks of New England were the only ones in the country which increased their specie holdings and by January 1, 1815, they held half of all the specie in the country. They were also in a more favorable situation than other sections in regard to their investments, for while banks in the middle states had been investing heavily in the long-term issues of the government, the banks of New England had taken only a few such securities, and kept their assets consequently in a more liquid state.[15]

The banks of New York and Philadelphia found themselves obliged to suspend specie payments in August, 1814, and this action was shortly followed by all other banks except those of New England. With this check upon expansion removed, monetary inflation went forward even more rapidly than before. It was estimated that the circulation of the banks increased by 50 per cent during the next two years. Popular discontent with the depreciated paper was forgotten as unemployment ceased and business grew more brisk. Particularly in Philadelphia was

[14] This export of specie from the United States to England, through the ports of New England where there was little sympathy with the war and the Embargo, is thus described by Gallatin in *Considerations on the Currency and Banking System*, p. 43 (1831): "From the moment when the rigorous blockade of the ports of the United States prevented the exportation of our produce, foreign supplies could be paid for in specie only, and as the importation of foreign goods in the Eastern States has been very large, it has for many months past occasioned a continual drain from the banks. This drain has been much increased by a trade in British Government Bills of Exchange, which has been extensively carried on, and has caused very large sums to be exported from the United States." The British bills were sent to the United States from Canada.

[15] Annals of Congress, 14 Congress, 1 Session, p. 1611.

the boom apparent; "this," said Mathew Carey in sorrowful reminiscence, "was the golden age of Philadelphia."[16] But even banks which had suspended specie payments could not lend indefinitely. By September, 1815, seven Philadelphia banks which had invested half of their capital in long-term government obligations found themselves obliged to curtail their commercial loans, and the golden age began to look tarnished. The depreciated bank notes, worth from 20 to 50 per cent less than face value, were the only means of payment which most of the country possessed. The banks were faced with the problem of curtailing their loans and discounts, reducing their note circulation, and building up their specie reserves to a point at which resumption was possible.

For all their difficulties, the government policy of encouraging, and even demanding, bank expansion was primarily responsible.[17] Congress had permitted the Bank of the United States, which had always exercised a restraining influence upon the note issues of the state banks, to fail of recharter for lack of one vote. Then the government, faced by a war for which it could not pay, floated enormous loans paid for from "manufactured" credit—the surest road to inflation in 1813, as in 1918. The banks which supported the war program of the treasury most enthusiastically were precisely those which first found themselves in difficulties. It was hardly fair to say of them, as many of their opponents did, that the suspension would not have occurred if the banks in the middle states had exercised as much caution as those in New England.

If the government was the cause of most of the financial difficulties of the country, it was also one of the chief sufferers from them. The depreciation of bank notes paid to the treasury for government securities cost the treasury at least 10 per cent of the proceeds from their sale. The treasury was embarrassed also by its inability to transfer its funds from the place of deposit to the place of expenditure, because notes of banks in one part of the country were not acceptable in other parts except

16 Carey, *Essays on Banking*, p. 19 (1816).

17 Gallatin, *Considerations*, p. 43 (1831). Gouge, *A Short History*, etc., pp. 21, 23 (1835). *American State Papers on Finance*, Vol. III, pp. 10, 141.

at a heavy discount which the treasury had no legal right to pay. The government had on deposit nearly 2½ millions with 45 banks throughout the country, but could not use these funds until specie payments were resumed. It was equally unable to accept the depreciated notes of the banks in payment of government dues, and finally the practice of receiving them on special deposit was begun.[18]

The second Bank of the United States

The tentative offer of friendship to the state banks by Secretary Dallas in 1815, in return for the immediate resumption of specie payments, was not cordially received. The banks refused to resume, and there was apparently no method by which the treasury could force them to resume against their will. In this emergency, when the government found itself reduced to borrowing small sums in a hand-to-mouth fashion, even the party which had formerly been most bitterly opposed to the formation of another national bank found itself obliged to accede to it. For the seventh time since 1811 Congress took the plan under consideration and finally drafted a measure which received the support of enough members of both parties to be enacted into law in March, 1816. One-fifth of the stock was to be owned by the government, and one-fifth of the directors to be appointed by the President of the United States. Loans to the government and purchases of public stock were closely limited and certain duties were imposed upon the bank, but in most respects it functioned as a commercial bank. Its power to control the state banks lay in its size and in its prestige, rather than in its form of organization. Subscriptions to the bank stock were opened in July and, after some hesitation, all of the 35 millions was subscribed. New York subscribers took less of the stock than those of Philadelphia and Baltimore, but the interest of New York in the new bank was keen.[19]

The organization of the bank gave the treasury a lever with which to force the recalcitrant state banks to a resumption of

[18] *Life and Writings of A. J. Dallas*, p. 255. 21 Congress, 1 Session, House Report 358, p. 10.

[17] *Life and Writings of A. J. Dallas*, p. 285. See also p. 6 above.

their specie obligations. On the first of February, 1817, the representatives of the Bank of the United States met bankers from New York, Philadelphia, Baltimore, and Richmond, for the purpose of coming to an agreement regarding the resumption of specie payments. The most important points decided by the conference were that the government would not remove its deposits from the state banks until July 1, and that the Bank of the United States would discount for individuals in the cities represented at the conference, to the amount of 2 millions of dollars each in New York and Philadelphia, and another 2 millions in Baltimore and Richmond together, before it began to collect the balances accumulated against the state banks. With these precautions to make the deflation process a gradual one, the state banks felt able to undertake resumption, and the government saw the end of the chief source of its embarrassment.

The establishment of the bank also relieved the treasury of much of its responsibility for the safe keeping of the government funds. The number of state banks which held government deposits declined from 1817 to 1834, and the Bank of the United States held by far the greater amount of treasury funds. On January 1, 1817, just before the Bank of the United States went into operation, the treasury had had credits of about 15 millions of dollars in 94 different banks throughout the country.[20] Of this sum, however, more than 3 millions were bank notes held as special deposits because they were not negotiable at their face value, and another 3 millions were treasury notes which had depreciated below their face value and were therefore equally unavailable. Three millions of cash assets in the Mechanics' Bank, the City Bank, and the Bank of the Manhattan Company of New York City, comprised the only large amounts of usable funds at the command of the treasury. After the resumption of specie payments and the consequent government improvement in the value of state bank notes, the government was able to recall these deposits, transferring most of them to the different branches of the Bank of the United States.[21]

[20] 17 Congress, 2 Session, House Report 105, p. 170.

[21] 25 Congress, 2 Session, Senate Document 128.

The location of the main office of the Bank of the United States in Philadelphia had little effect upon the distribution of treasury funds among the branches of the bank in different cities. The heavy receipts of customs and other revenues in New York made it inevitable that government deposits there should be larger than elsewhere, and the necessity of transferring those funds from New York to the points at which the government expenditures were made constituted the heaviest problem which the Bank of the United States as fiscal agent was forced to solve. The treasury coöperated with the bank in furthering this solution, and took great care to order transfers in such a way as to avoid disturbing the money market.

Besides its active coöperation with the Bank of the United States, the treasury maintained a paternalistic attitude toward the state banks of the country. In March, 1817, the Farmers and Mechanics' Bank of Georgetown received a deposit of $75,000 in order to assist it in the resumption of specie payments, and earlier deposits made in the banks of that city and of Washington were permitted to remain until July, 1817, instead of being transferred to the Bank of the United States in January. Moreover the state banks did not hesitate to call upon the treasury for aid when they became involved in difficulties during the depression of 1819. "Believing that a failure of one or more of those banks would produce a general run upon all," deposits totalling $287,000 were placed by the Secretary of the Treasury in the Union Bank of Alexandria, Virginia, and in the Mechanics' Bank and the Franklin Bank of the same city, in the Union and Central Banks of Georgetown, in the Bank of Columbia, and in the Patriotic Bank and the Bank of Washington.[22]

The treasury also showed itself mindful of the welfare of the money market as a whole in its endeavors to avoid a heavy accumulation of surplus revenue in the banks. This was a period when, in sharp contrast with a decade earlier, the government's income was rising so rapidly that it far exceeded expenditures. The public deposits in all offices of the Bank of the

[22] 17 Congress, 2 Session, House Report 105, pp. 4, 170, 177.

United States increased by nearly 2 millions of dollars during each six months' period from December, 1821, to December, 1823, and the estimated surplus for 1824 was nearly 10 millions of dollars. The Secretary of the Treasury therefore petitioned Congress for permission to pay off gradually during 1824, that part of the public debt which matured on January 1, 1825, in order to release these funds.[23]

Although the Bank of the United States aroused the bitter hostility of many of the state banks by its unpleasant habit of sending their notes home for redemption, there is no doubt that it was of benefit to the banks in many ways, and that it was of great assistance to the treasury in its endeavor to mitigate the various shocks to which the money market was subject. Its services were summed up by one Secretary of the Treasury as follows: First, that it enabled the treasury to apply the public funds at the proper moment to every part of the country; second, that its stock served as a remittance abroad; third, that by discounting government stock it enabled the public debt to be reduced gradually; and fourth, that the public funds were safer than they had been before. There could hardly be better evidence that under the presidency of Nicholas Biddle the second Bank of the United States was a valuable adjunct to the treasury.

Changing attitude of the government toward the Bank

During the administration of President Andrew Jackson there was a complete reversal of the traditional policy of friendliness between the treasury and the banks, and a complete change in the official attitude of the treasury towards the money market. This antagonism was directed at first only against the Bank of the United States, but it turned eventually against all banks. In the first message to Congress after his accession to the Presidency in 1829, Jackson evinced a distrust of the bank, but for the next three years, in spite of his increasing hostility, no active measures were taken against it. During this time the officers of the bank wavered between hope and fear, guiding their policies

[23] Secretary of the Treasury, *Annual Report*, 1824, p. 16; 1829, p. 9.

first by one and then the other.[24] In spite of the fact that there was much jealousy of the bank in New York there were many persons in Jackson's own party in the latter city who did not favor the taking of strong measures against it. Isaac Bronson, Albert Gallatin and Martin Van Buren were the most important of these. Moreover, Jackson's Cabinet was not unanimous in opposition to the bank, and two successive Secretaries of the Treasury resigned rather than carry out his wishes in regard to it. But Jackson was nothing if not pertinacious. He succeeded in 1832 in preventing it from obtaining a renewal of its charter, which expired in 1836, but that alone did not satisfy him. The pressure in the money market during the year 1833 gave him the opportunity for which he seemed to have been waiting.

Removal of the deposits

The pressure of 1833 developed from a deflated boom in the stock market, synchronizing with a change in the tariff law which doubled the demand for bank credit by importers just at the time when a large amount of funds was tied up in securities. Added to these factors was a restlessness engendered throughout the country by the doubt regarding the government's attitude toward the Bank of the United States.[25] Anxiety on this account was proved to be justifiable when the announcement of the order for the removal of the deposits appeared, as a notice in the Washington *Globe* for September 20, 1833.[26] The government deposits were not actually removed from the bank and its branches, except for five drafts of a somewhat shady history which amounted to about $1,300,000 and were cashed in Philadelphia, Baltimore, and New York.[27] The remainder of the $9,868,000 was drawn out gradually, in the normal course of

[24] Catterall, *Second Bank of the United States*, Chapters IX and X.

[25] *Report of Union Committee*, pp. 5, 7 (1834). James Hamilton, *Reminiscences*, pp. 253, 258.

[26] Duane, *Narrative and Correspondence concerning the Removal of the Deposits and Occurrences Connected Therewith*, Chapter X (1838). 23 Congress, 2 Session, House Report 27.

[27] Catterall, *Second Bank of United States*, pp. 302-5. The proceeds of these drafts were used by the banks which cashed them, in speculation and expansion of loans.

government expenditure, and the income of the government, instead of replacing these withdrawals, went into the newly appointed state depositary banks.

The bank felt obliged to embark at once upon a policy of contraction, and began by reducing discounts and purchases of bills. New York suffered less than any other part of the country throughout this period. The following table shows the reduction in domestic exchange by months and illustrates the difference in favor of the city:[28]

DISCOUNTS ON DOMESTIC BILLS OF EXCHANGE
BY BANK OF UNITED STATES

(In thousands of dollars)

Month	1833		1834	
	New York City	*Total*	*New York City*	*Total*
January	$1,096	$19,987	$849	$17,299
February	994	21,515	902	18,787
March	1,002	22,750	940	18,677
April	952	23,147	960	18,544
May	790	22,428	926	17,462
June	798	21,677	903	16,601
July	752	20,923	957	13,932
August	760	19,287	1,138	12,196
September	886	17,868	1,291	10,884
October	817	16,148	1,503	11,086
November	746	15,673	1,798	13,608
December	693	16,302	2,083	17,183

The depression of 1833, which had been blamed upon the contraction policy of the Bank of the United States and made the excuse for the removal of the government deposits from its keeping, was short-lived, and a new period of expansion soon got under way. The government funds served as additional incentive to expansion by the newly-chosen depositary banks. These, in New York City, were three: the Bank of the Manhattan Company, the Mechanics' Bank, and the Bank of

[28] 25 Congress, 2 Session, Senate Document 128.

America. The effect of the deposits by the treasury upon their loans and discounts, at a time of year when they would normally have been contracting, and when the other banks in the city actually were contracting, may be seen in the following table:

REPORTS OF THREE DEPOSITARY BANKS IN NEW YORK CITY

(000 omitted)

1833	*Due to government*	*Loans and discounts*
October 1		$8,186
November 1	$1,407	9,109
December 1	3,574	9,964

By the end of March, the increase in the loans and discounts of these banks amounted to more than 4 millions of dollars, and expansion was well under way. The next three years were marked by unprecedented activity, as business rushed on towards the crisis of 1837.[29]

The relations between the treasury and the money market, which had been comparatively orderly and stable during the régime of the Bank of the United States, became confused and disordered when the connection between the bank and the treasury ceased. But the government did not at once abandon its traditional paternalistic attitude towards the money market, and wished it to be clearly understood that its opposition was to *the bank* and not to *banks*. It was still using state banks as depositaries for its funds and these institutions were utilized also in transferring funds and making payments for the treasury, but no group of uncoördinated banks could be as successful in this field as the Bank of the United States and its branches had been. The officials of the treasury would not admit that this was the case, and moreover they were very anxious to escape blame for the difficulties of the money market in 1833, at the time of

[29] 23 Congress, 2 Session, House Report 27, p. 10. Moulton, *Legislative and Documentary History of Banks*, p. 199 (1834).

the removal of the deposits. Secretary of the Treasury Roger B. Taney, under whom the operation had been carried out, devoted much space in his special report on the removal to a justification of the act and the manner in which it had been executed. "The change was always designed to be gradual," he pointed out, and the Bank of the United States had had no reason for contracting its loans so early. He intimated that the public deposits had been placed with the state banks in order to protect them from the unnecessary and unreasonable demands of the bank for specie.[30]

The report of the secretary on the keeping and distributing of the public money for 1834 drew a very optimistic picture of the results of the new system. The depositary banks, according to this report, were so distributed over the country that a minimum of transfers was required to meet the needs of government expenditures, and not more than 3 millions, out of a total government income of 21 millions of dollars, had to be transported any great distance. The only states in which collections were greatly at variance with expenditures were in the eastern and middle parts of the country, and by utilizing the favorable course of trade the necessary transfers had been made by treasury warrants, without cost to the government. Collections and disbursements in the different sections of the country were as follows:[31]

GOVERNMENT EXPENDITURES AND COLLECTIONS
FOR THE FISCAL YEAR 1834

(000 omitted)

Sections of the country	*Expenditures*	*Collections*
New England states	$2,920	$2,949
New York	3,650	9,021
Other middle states	7,498	3,254
South and southwestern states	4,235	3,278
Western states	2,990	2,123
TOTAL	$21,293	$20,625

30 23 Congress, 1 Session, Senate Document 2, pp. 8, 9.

31 23 Congress, 2 Session, House Report 27. *Report,* Secretary of Treasury 1835, pp. 20, 22; 1836, pp. 13-15.

The three New York City depositaries did the greater part of this work of transferring funds for the treasury. From June, 1834, to May, 1835, inclusive, they transferred more than 6 millions, and paid out for the government as much more. During the next fiscal year they transferred 5 millions, and paid out 3 millions. These transfers had been made with such care that the secretary believed they had tended "to obviate rather than to create" any pressure in the money market. The report of 1836 spoke in even more glowing terms of the success of the new policy, and boasted that "the latest returns to the Department from those banks show that the domestic exchanges generally were never conducted with more regularity or at a cheaper rate, than at present."[32]

But the report of the Secretary of the Treasury for 1837 was somewhat less buoyant in tone. Although there was no admission that the removal of the deposits from the Bank of the United States had been a mistake or that the services of the bank were missed, the secretary felt it necessary to remind the public that the treasury had always kept in mind the exigencies of the money market in ordering the transfers, and that all the transfers had likewise been "so modified in respect to time, place, and business, as to produce the least inconvenience and expense possible to the banks or the community." Further, it had "required great caution not to create more embarrassment than has really occurred from this source, and a greater derangement in exchange than actually exists." At the same time he pointed out that the Act of June 23, 1836, providing that in no case could the deposit of public funds in any bank amount to a sum greater than three-fourths of its capital, had materially reduced the scope of the secretary's discretion in the matter of apportioning the deposits, as well as his responsibility for the effects of such apportionment.[33]

[32] The Bank of the United States had made transfers of funds for the government to the amount of ten to fifteen millions annually between 1820 and 1829; twelve millions in 1830, and sixteen millions in 1832. 24 Congress, 1 Session, Senate Document 356, p. 4.

[33] *Report*, Secretary of Treasury, 1837, pp. 13-15.

The specie circular

The victory of Jackson over the bank[34] had put an end both to its ability and to its desire to control the note issues of the state banks. Just as in the years immediately following the end of the first Bank of the United States, so the years following the end of the effectiveness of the second bank were characterized by a rapid increase in the number of state banks and of their notes. From 329 banks in January, 1830, with a capital of 110 millions and note circulation of 48 millions, they had increased to 677 banks in January, 1837, with a capital of 378 millions, and circulation of 120 millions.[35]

One of the most striking accompaniments to this increase in bank credit was its effect upon sales of the public lands. They rose rapidly from one million dollars in 1828 to 25 millions in 1836.[36] Jackson, who had formerly taken pride in this, as evidence of "real abundance of capital and ease in the money market," became alarmed.[37] His first step, taken as early as September, 1835, was to forbid the acceptance of notes of a denomination of less than five dollars in payment of the public dues. This was a logical outgrowth of his growing hostility to the use of bank credit, but it had little effect in controlling the issues of the banks. On July 11, 1836, came the more drastic measure, the "Circular to Receivers of Public Money, and to the Deposit Banks," forbidding any government officer to accept "for land sold, any draft, certificate, or other evidence of money or deposit . . . unless signed by the Treasurer of the United States."[38]

The immediate effect of this circular upon the treasury was, of course, to increase its holdings of specie. That, however, was not the purpose Jackson had in mind, for he was particularly

[34] Its Federal charter expired in 1836; after the removal of the deposits it had been foreseen that there was no hope of a re-charter.

[35] Gallatin, *Considerations*, p. 53 (1831). Secretary of Treasury Report 1837, p. 18. These figures do not include the 35 million capital and 13 million circulation, of the Bank of the United States in 1830.

[36] Cole, "Cyclical and Sectional Variations in the Sale of Public Land, 1816-60," *Review of Economic Statistics*, 1927.

[37] 24 Congress, 1 Session, Senate Document 356, p. 13.

[38] Secretary of Treasury Annual Report, 1837, p. 96. The Circular was an administrative order, not a law.

concerned to increase the specie in circulation and in the banks. The course of these items, as given by the Secretary of the Treasury, partly from returns and partly from estimates, is given in the table below.[39]

(In millions of dollars)

Month and Year	*Paper in circulation*	*Specie in circulation*	*Specie in banks*
October, 1833	80	4	25
January, 1834	76	12	27
January, 1835	82	18	43
January, 1836	108	23	40
December, 1836	120	28	45

As the table indicates, paper in circulation increased less rapidly during the year 1836 (during half of which the specie circular had been in effect) than during 1835, and specie in banks increased instead of declining as in the previous year. Specie in circulation had, however, increased by the same amount as during the two years preceding. The figures show the change during the whole of the year 1836 without dividing it into the six months before the circular and the six months which followed its promulgation, so that the evidence at best is inconclusive that the circular had any effect in the changes which appear to have taken place. Since there were large increases in the specie of the country during 1834 and 1835, due to the monetary law of 1834 which reduced the content of gold coins and tended to keep them at home, the stock of gold would probably have risen during 1836 whether the specie circular had been issued or not.[40]

If the specie circular can not be given credit for the increase of specie, it must bear at least part of the blame for the difficulties which now began to beset the money market. The

[39] Secretary of Treasury Annual Report, 1837, p. 18. This table was the estimate of an official who desired to put the best possible face on Jackson's policy, and it undoubtedly erred on the side of optimism.

[40] The Act of 1792 had fixed the legal ratio between gold and silver at 15 to 1. Since gold was worth more than this in the market abroad, there was a continual export of gold coin from the United States until the law of 1834, by altering their fineness, reversed the situation.

result of the ban on bank paper was to reverse the normal course of funds across the country. The western banks had been accustomed to keep deposits in the banks of the Atlantic cities, upon which they could draw for the redemption of their notes and the accommodation of merchants. Suddenly these banks found their paper discredited by the government. They were forced to curtail their loans and discounts and reduce their circulation, in order to get their specie back for the use of prospective purchasers of public lands.[41] It was impossible for them to pay out specie continually unless the treasury should redeposit with the banks the coin which it had received in payment for the public lands.[42] This the treasury would not do, for it had moved rapidly from the position of consideration for the banks which had marked other administrations and even the early part of the Jackson régime, to an attitude of hostility towards all credit institutions and a determination to keep the government from coöperating with them. This attitude is clearly reflected in a law passed just a few weeks before the specie circular was issued. Among other things it provided: "That all warrants, or orders for the purpose of transferring the public funds from the banks in which they now are, or may hereafter be deposited, to other banks whether of deposit or not, for the purpose of accommodating the banks to which the transfer may be made, or to sustain their credit, or for any other purpose whatever, except it be to facilitate the public disbursements and to comply with the provision of this act, be and the same are hereby prohibited and declared to be illegal."[43] There was to be no more aid rushed to a wavering bank to enable it to withstand a run, no more treasury funds sent to a bank which found the demands for its specie beyond its power to meet. The treasury would insist upon receiving specie for itself, but how the banks were to get it was none of its concern. The movement towards an independent treasury was already well under way.

[41] Gallatin, *Suggestions*, p. 31: "The only effect of that measure . . . was to cause a drain of specie on the banks of New York, at a time when it was important that that point should have been strengthened" (1841).

[42] Secretary of Treasury, *Report on State Banks*, 1837, p. 417.

[43] Act of June 23, 1836, Sec. 12; Statutes at Large, Vol. V, p. 55.

The distribution of the surplus

The third of the major political measures, from the point of view of the money market, was the distribution of the surplus revenue of the government among the states of the Union. The margin between income and expenditure had frequently in the past been a source of embarrassment to the treasury, at times because income failed to meet disbursements, and occasionally because it exceeded them. Especially since the high tariff of 1828 had the latter circumstance been a matter of concern. After the removal of the deposits from the Bank of the United States, and particularly after the law of 1836 which made it unlawful for any banks to hold public funds to an amount greater than three-fourths of its capital, the problem of finding a safe place in which to keep this growing surplus was pressing. More than 18 millions of dollars had to be transferred upon the passage of the law, and a still larger amount was transferred in the ensuing year. It was frequently necessary to find new banks in which deposits could be placed up to the legal maximum, and this necessitated a great many transfers of funds from the points at which the collections were made to the newly chosen depositaries.[44] The Secretary of the Treasury used as a guiding principle in these transfers, the distribution of deposits among the several states according to their population, but found it extremely difficult to attain this ideal in practice.

To the administration party the surplus was a nuisance; and to the opposition party it was a political menace, because a possible source of political power to the administration.[45] Some members of both parties were therefore eager to dispose of the sum, and the most plausible scheme seemed to be its distribution among the states as a non-interest bearing loan. In July, 1836, very soon after the specie circular, came the Act of Congress which divided the surplus into four equal quarterly installments, to be paid to the state treasuries during 1837. The total sum to be thus distributed was about 37 millions of dollars, or more than 9 millions each quarter.

[44] *Financial Register*, Vol. I, p. 41.

[45] *Niles' Register*, Vol. XLIX, p. 209; Vol. L, p. 145. Benton, *Thirty Years View*, pp. 649, 657.

The plan devised by the Secretary of the Treasury to carry out these provisions, which constituted a major operation on the money market, was transmitted to the deposit banks in November, 1836, in order to give them time to prepare. Each bank had a list of the drafts which would probably be drawn against it on each quarter-day in 1837. The total amount to be transferred from the thirteen New York depositary banks was more than 1½ millions at each date. The drafts were to be drawn in favor of New York, Vermont, New Jersey, Delaware, and North Carolina, showing a praiseworthy desire on the part of the Treasury to transfer the funds over as short distances as possible. The first installment was paid according to schedule; the banks of New York had more than 7 millions of government funds on deposit on January 1, and the loss of 1.5 millions did not create any serious shortage.[46] Ten days before the second payment became due, however, the Mechanics' Bank wrote to the secretary that during the preceding week it had paid out nearly ½ million dollars on government account, and that it was therefore ill-prepared for the large draft of $200,000 due on April 1. The secretary replied that he was sorry, but could do nothing, as the bank still held more than the sum to which it was legally entitled by the act of June, 1836. The second payments were made in spite of their protests, by all of the New York depositary banks. But in a few weeks they were again complaining in unison that the payment of more than 6 millions in government drafts during three and one-half months, one-fourth of which was in specie, had forced them to curtail their loans by nearly 5 millions, and was producing a distinct pressure in the city. Their specie reserve had fallen from 4 to 1.7 millions of dollars by June 1, and the payment of the third

[46] Government Deposits in Banks of New York City, 1837.

(In millions of dollars)

Jan. 1	7.2
June 1	3.2
July 1	3.2
Aug. 1	.7
Sept. 1	.6
Oct. 1	.4

From *Financial Register*, Vol. I, p. 143.

installment on July 1 would be a severe test.[47] Banks in other parts of the country were also experiencing difficulty in meeting the drafts of the treasury. They had been encouraged to loan the deposits made with them during 1836, and now a large part of these deposits were being withdrawn in favor of the states. Many of the states planned to use the funds for permanent improvements, and some had already spent their shares.[48]

Difficulties of the treasury during the panic of 1837

A double drain of specie, foreign and domestic, combined with the commercial troubles of the cotton export trade of the time, were too much to be borne and the New York banks suspended specie payment on May 10, 1837. The government found itself in an embarrassing dilemma. The banks in which the public deposits had been placed suspended with their fellows and it was no longer lawful for the deposits to remain with them. It was almost impossible, however, to remove the deposits for, as in 1816, the government could not accept depreciated paper currency, and there was no specie. Fortunately the treasury had sufficient deposits in banks whose paper was still good, to meet the third payment on the surplus on July 1, with the exception of $650,000 of drafts which were protested.

The fourth payment, which fell due on October 1, 1837, five months after the suspension of specie payments by the banks, could not be met at all. The sum due to banks in the fifteen northern states was about $6,500,000, and the treasury had to its credit in those states little more than $3,000,000. In the southern and western states, where the balance in the "pet banks" was $9,000,000, only $3,000,000 of the surplus was due. The transfer of more than 3 millions from the South to the North, which would have been necessary to make the distribution of the last installment of the surplus, was quite impossible during the bank suspension, and would have been difficult under the most favorable circumstances. The result of this impasse was that the northern banks felt they had been discrimi-

[47] Report of New York Investigating Committee, 1837, p. 17. *Financial Register,* Vol. I, p. 36.

[48] Bourne, *History of the Surplus Revenue.*

nated against, since the treasury had known for more than a year that the payments would fall due in the amounts detailed above.[49] The suspension of specie payments by the banks brought the operations of the treasury almost to a standstill. Its revenue was reduced by the general stagnation of business which followed, and the balances to its credit in the banks could not be withdrawn because the treasury was unable to accept the depreciated paper in which alone the banks were able to make payment.

The obvious conclusion to be drawn from events was that the treasury was helpless when the financial mechanism of the country was not functioning fully. Instead of returning to the policy of close and harmonious coöperation between the treasury and the money market which had successfully prevailed for forty years before Jackson, the party in power rushed on in the course which had already proved so disastrous, towards a completely independent treasury. The period in which it was the open and avowed policy of the government to work in harmony with the money market and to assist it when possible was brought to an end.

[49] *Congressional Globe*, Vol. 5; Appendix, pp. 265-68. Secretary of Treasury, *Report*, October 4, 1837.

CHAPTER IX

THE INDEPENDENT TREASURY FROM 1840 TO 1863

The plan for an independent treasury, towards which the government had been moving steadily since the failure to re-charter the second Bank of the United States, took definite form and became a political issue with the opening of the first Congress under President Van Buren. Congress had been called to meet in special session to consider measures for the relief of the country in the crisis of 1837.[1] President Jackson's term of office had expired at just the right moment for him, and to his successor fell the task of solving the problems which had been bequeathed by the preceding administration. Of the four proposals presented to Congress by President Van Buren, the first was the establishment of an independent treasury. The measure was the logical outcome of Jackson's policy towards the Bank of the United States and his growing antipathy to all banks.

First subtreasury law

In presenting the case for the independent treasury, Van Buren minimized the services which had been rendered by the Bank of the United States and the commercial banks of the country, exaggerated the ease with which such problems as a large government surplus and the transfers of treasury funds could be met, and insisted that there was no alternative to the scheme, since the creation of a new national bank had been twice "solemnly and unequivocally condemned" by the results of elections.[2]

[1] All that legally could be done for the importers and merchants of the country, without the sanction of Congress, had already been done in the postponement for 60 to 90 days of the bonds of customs duties.

[2] There were three other proposals in the complete plan of Van Buren presented to Congress. Postponement of the fourth instalment of the Treasury surplus was the first; it was essential because the surplus had already turned into a deficit, but it was passed only after the most bitter debate. An issue of ten millions of Treasury notes was equally necessary, to save the Treasury from admitting bankruptcy. The third would have made suspension of specie payments by a bank

The twenty months' of debate in Congress and throughout the country which followed Van Buren's proposal gives an excellent picture of the attitude toward the money market taken by leaders of the two parties. Much of the time was, of course, spent in political recrimination, for each party blamed the other for the crisis. But emerging from the floods of political oratory which nearly engulfed the subject can be detected certain underlying differences of opinion and different assumptions upon which each side rested its case. The speech of Senator Allen of Ohio[3] is typical of the hostility to banks which was part of the Democratic dogma. His point of view was that banks were monopolies of political origin, with power to corrupt the officers of the government, and that it was therefore safer to place the government funds with officers directly responsible to the government. The banks had betrayed the public by suspending specie payments, and should the government relinquish its insistence upon specie and accept the notes of the banks, it would be tantamount to the legalizing of the suspension. This was, of course, a reversal of the former Democratic position, that the funds of the treasury would be quite safe if moved from the Bank of the United States to state banks. Senator Benton, the doughty hard-money Democrat from Missouri, took up the problem of the amount of specie that would be required as a minimum base for the operations of an independent treasury.[4] Representative Cambreleng of New York undertook to refute the objection that the bill would "make New York the grand market for specie and all the rest of the states tributary," by pointing out that in all the great operations of the treasury actual specie would not be transferred but treasury warrants would be sent by mail and the money drawn from the subtreasury office at the point of expenditure by the bank or merchant who had bought the warrant from the creditor of the government.[5] This matter of the issue of treasury warrants was

equivalent to bankruptcy and would have destroyed practically every bank in the country. It was not passed. Congressional Globe, 25 Congress, 1 Session, Vol. III, pp. 11-29. Benton, *Thirty Years View*, Vol. II, p. 27.

[3] Congressional Globe, Vol. 6, Appendix, p. 250.

[4] Congressional Globe, Vol. 5, Appendix, p. 53.

[5] Ibid., p. 149.

of great importance and caused many difficulties when the independent treasury had gone into actual operation.

William Gouge, a close adviser of the administration, although never a member of Congress, made out the best case for the new scheme in his pamphlet, "An Inquiry into the expediency of Dispensing with Bank Agency and Bank Paper in the Fiscal Concerns of the United States," which was published in 1837. He first cited the difficulties arising from the use of banks as depositaries of the government, because of the resultant credit expansion. At that time, expansion of bank credit more often took the form of increased note issues than of deposits, and Gouge's contention that the note-issue privilege of the banks was one of the chief sources of overexpansion was correct. But his conclusions based on that premise, that a purely specie currency was to be desired and that the problem of elasticity in the use of such currency would be met by an automatic alternation between hoarding and spending on the part of individual holders of coin, was hardly worthy of consideration although he deserved some credit for recognizing that an elastic currency was necessary.

The opponents of the bill were not silent in the face of these charges. They made much of the disasters which had resulted from the policies of Jackson's administration, and of the possibilities for corruption latent in a government-administered repository for the public funds. Daniel Webster, one of the leaders of the party, used the general economic argument that the credit system was a great improvement over the money economy, and that it was quite absurd for the government to return to primitive cash methods when the rest of the country would inevitably continue to use credit to a large and increasing extent. He opposed any artificial separation of the government from the people in this respect and pointed out that the immediate result of the establishment of a subtreasury would be to penalize those very banks which should first resume specie payments, since they would be subjected to a heavy drain of specie in order to provide the funds for government dues which other banks could not or would not furnish.

Other reasons advanced against the bill emphasized the difficulty in the way of carrying out its specie clause. Senator Smith of Indiana, speaking from the western point of view, protested that the effect of the measure must inevitably be to drain all the specie from the West to the East, since the government's abandonment of internal improvements on a large scale in the West had shifted the heaviest disbursements of the government back to the eastern states. And Senator Tallmadge[6] of New York, representing the East, was equally opposed to the bill because it would be quite impossible for the banks of New York City to furnish enough specie for customs dues. The average balance of the treasury in the deposit banks of New York City in 1834 had been 5 millions, or twice as much as the specie in all the city banks put together; the total collections of the government during that year had amounted in New York to 12 millions, of which only 1.65 millions were spent in New York State, and a still smaller amount in New York City. The transfer of such huge amounts would be a continuous strain upon the treasury, as its collection would be a strain upon the money market of New York.

The most convincing of the opponents, Albert Gallatin, like the most convincing of the advocates, was outside of Congress, but prominent in political affairs. His experience as Secretary of the Treasury, and later as a New York banker, put him into an unusually favorable position for judging the merits of the proposition. Although he was a Democrat he was opposed to an independent treasury on two main grounds: first, that the plan was unfair to the specie-paying banks, and favored those which had not resumed; and second, that the danger of an accumulation of specie was so great that the whole plan should be abandoned. This danger would become an actuality whenever the income of the government exceeded its expenditure, for the difference would remain as a surplus in the treasury with no channel for distribution to the country since it could not be deposited in banks.[7]

[6] Congressional Globe, Vol. 5, Appendix, pp. 167, 234.
[7] Gallatin, *Suggestions*, p. 88 (1841).

There was one underlying assumption in all the speeches of the advocates of the plan, and even in those of many of its opponents—that a separation of government finance from the financial existence of the rest of the country was possible, whether or not desirable. This was contrary to the experience of both parties. Even Secretary Woodbury, of Van Buren's own Democratic cabinet, in making his report to Congress in December, 1837, recommended the inclusion in the law of provisions which recognized the intimate relations of government and private finance, and indicated that he had a lively notion of the importance of adjusting treasury operations to the exigencies of the money market. He proposed, in order to make the system more flexible:[8]

1. That contingent authority be granted to some public officer to invest any government surplus which might arise;
2. That limited power to issue treasury notes, in case of deficiency, be granted to the Secretary of the Treasury;
3. That receivers and collectors of the public money, and mints, be named government depositaries, whether banks were used or not;
4. That the treasury be given permission to receive in advance payments for public lands;
5. That the warehousing system for imported goods be extended, duties to be paid when the goods were taken out of warehouse.

The first two of these proposals, and the fourth, would be necessary because there was no longer a national debt to absorb and regulate government surpluses, and no central banking institution to maintain a sound currency. It was unfortunate that none of these provisions was included in the original law.[9] But the members of the Secretary's own party were at that moment in Congress asserting in all seriousness that the subtreasury plan would protect the government in case of another bank suspension, because the government would accept only specie and refuse bank paper. The fact that specie for the government came from the banks, and circulated through them, was completely ignored.

[8] Secretary of Treasury, *Annual Report on Finances*, p. 18.

[9] Most of them were eventually adopted either into the law or the practice of the subtreasury.

The majority and minority reports of the Committee of Ways and Means were given to the House of Representatives in March, 1838. The majority of the Committee was in favor of the subtreasury, but the bill missed passage by a narrow margin in June, 1838, and was introduced again into the regular session of Congress six months later. It was finally passed in June, 1839, and went into effect on July 4, 1840.[10]

While Congress had been exercising its prerogative of talking, the Secretary of the Treasury had been struggling to keep the government from involuntary bankruptcy.[11] The banks of New York resumed specie payments in August, 1838, because under the law of the state they would have forfeited their charters had suspension continued longer than a year. It was not until July, 1839, that the Philadelphia banks resumed, and still later that the banks of the South and West followed their example. In October, moreover, all the banks except those in New York, New Jersey, and New England, suspended again. Since the Act of June, 1836, made it illegal to keep public funds in non-specie-paying banks, the treasury could find few depositaries which met the law's requirements. About 20 per cent of the funds had to be kept on special deposit with suspended banks, and the remaining 80 per cent left in the hands of the collecting officers of the government. For a period of three years, from the middle of 1837 to the middle of 1840, the government was left without a definite plan for keeping its money. Fortunately, perhaps, the income of the government during that time was small[12] and it did not have at any one time a great amount of specie on hand. Although 20 millions of dollars were paid out during the fiscal year 1839, the amount of specie in the hands of collectors and receivers at any one time was seldom more than 1.5 millions. At New York City the specie on hand did not average half a million dollars. So promptly did the treasury draw out funds collected in that city that at the end

[10] 25 Congress, 2 Session, House Report 634.

[11] Secretary of Treasury, *Annual Report on Finances*, 1839, pp. 14, 19, 20.

[12] Between 1837 and 1841, the Treasury was forced to issue short-term notes to the amount of 32.8 millions of dollars, in order to meet current expenses. Knox, *United States Notes*, p. 62.

of the week there was usually not more than $50,000 left in its vaults.

The new plan went into operation in July, 1840. In his report of December, which covered only half a year of the subtreasury's history, the Secretary criticized the details of the Act and the manner in which it was working, and recommended again his proposals of 1837 as essential to its proper functioning. It was too soon for him to judge the effect of the new system as a whole, however,[13] and the Democratic party which had enacted the law went out of office in March, 1841, leaving the infant subtreasury in the none-too-gentle hands of its opponents. It was only to be expected, therefore, that the report for 1841 upon the first full year of its operation should be extremely pessimistic in tone. It detailed a long list of particulars in which the law was deficient, many of them, such as the liability to loss by fire and theft and the expenses of salaries and rents, being too petty to warrant serious consideration. Of far more significance was the objection that the system concentrated disbursements in New York City, where funds were at a premium and where, therefore, public creditors insisted upon receiving payment. The Secretary complained also that the system resulted in the locking up of large quantities of the precious metals, to the detriment of trade and commerce. As a matter of fact, owing to the unusual condition of the banks of the country and to the depleted state of the government's resources, the subtreasury seems to have been neither the conspicuous failure asserted by its enemies nor the success predicted by its friends. So little change had been produced by the much-heralded plan that Henry Clay, in moving for the repeal of the Act in December, 1840, said he understood there was not the slightest difference prevailing at that time from the system in operation before July, 1840. The challenge was immediately taken up by the Democrats, and the Secretary of the Treasury was called upon to make a report as to the facts. In the main, they substantiated Clay's charges. Banks were still in use,

[13] Secretary of Treasury, *Annual Report on Finances*, 1837, p. 18; 1840, p. 12.

though to a limited extent, as depositaries,[14] and since the law required only one-fourth of the government dues to be paid in specie during the first year of operation, bank notes were still being received by the government. The relations between the banks and the government were in some respects even closer than those which had existed before the removal of the deposits from the Bank of the United States. In New York City particularly the agent of the subtreasury had his office in the Bank of America, the government funds were kept in a vault in that bank, although separate from other bank funds, and the bank made temporary loans to the government and acted as its agent in the sale of treasury notes. Moreover a merchant who had payment to make to the treasury could secure a certified check from his own bank, exchange it at the Bank of America for a check drawn against that bank, and use that check in payment of government dues. The whole situation was so contrary to the spirit of the law that Senator Benton, who had been one of the chief sponsors of the bill in Congress, characterized its actual operation as "humbug."[15]

The essential features of the Act were repealed by the Whigs in August, 1841. Bank notes were again fully acceptable by the treasury and the deposits of the government went to the banks on terms similar to those under which the transfer from the Bank of the United States to the state banks had been made in 1834. A depositary bank was required to give collateral security if the public funds amounted to more than one-half of its paid-in capital, to make transfers of funds for the government without charge, both domestic and foreign, and to receive the notes of specie-paying banks as well as coin. By July, 1842, 26 banks were being used as public depositaries in addition to the United States mints and four receivers of public money.

[14] Approximately $200,000 was still in 27 banks on special deposit subject to the drafts of the Treasury, besides of course a large part of the "surplus" funds which had been deposited with the states, and redeposited by them in banks. Secretary of Treasury Annual Report on Finances, 1841, p. 15.

[15] Congressional Globe, Vol. 16, pp. 9, 16, 19; Appendix, p. 820. 27 Congress, 1 Session, House Report 35. 27 Congress, 2 Session, Senate Document 386. New York *Daily Express,* August 10, September 9, 1840. Secretary of Treasury, *Annual Report on Finances,* 1854, p. 266.

The state banks had been reduced in number and chastened in spirit by the events of the preceding four years, and the redeposit of the public funds with them had little effect upon the amount of their loans and discounts. Government revenues were so small that the temptation to inflation which had been offered by the huge deposits of 1835-1836 no longer existed. In New York City the Bank of America continued to hold treasury funds, but they were shared with the Bank of Commerce and the Merchants Bank, each institution in turn receiving the customs receipts for one month. The funds were loaned on the call market in order to keep them readily available against a treasury draft. By 1844 the American Exchange Bank in New York was also holding government deposits, and the four banks together had in September of that year $5,600,000 of such funds. The total number of depositary banks throughout the country had increased to 39. The New York City banks during this period were the chief support of the treasury in all its financial operations.[16]

The Independent Treasury Act of 1846

After a decade of stormy relations between the treasury and the money market, this five years of comparative peace and quiet, from 1841 to 1846, provided a grateful interlude. It was all too brief, and again the question of national bank or independent treasury began to agitate the country. Two Whig plans for the establishment of a new national bank were unfortunately vetoed by President Tyler and when the Democrats returned to office, in 1845, they introduced a new subtreasury law.

The debates which preceded the passing of this law brought out no new evidence in the controversy which had now been raging since 1830, and no new argument except that provided by the imminence of the Mexican War, which made a radical change in treasury operations undesirable.[17] The party which was pushing the bill contained some members bitterly hostile to all forms of banking and credit, but the majority denied hostility

[16] Hunt's *Merchants' Magazine*, Vol. 10, p. 369. *United States Democratic Review*, Vol. 14, p. 432. 28 Congress, 2 Session, Senate Document 88.

[17] Congressional Globe, Vol. 15, p. 1172.

to banks, and expressed a desire merely to regulate their issue of notes. This result they expected to achieve through the specie clause in the act, which would force the banks to redeem their notes in specie in order to provide money for the payment of government dues.

They differed among themselves also in the matter of the use of bank notes by the government. Representative Dromgoole of Virginia, one of the die-hards of the party, looked with equanimity upon the prospect of the actual transportation of specie by the treasury whenever a transfer of funds was necessary,[18] while Senator Lewis, at the instance of the Secretary of the Treasury, made a strong plea for an amendment which would permit a disbursing officer, if he could not obtain gold and silver for the government draft, to be allowed to sell it for what it would bring and make the necessary payments in the money received. But Senator Benton, who had spent his life in fighting the hard-money battle, centered all his powers of invective against it.[19]

In the main the Act was a victory for the hard-money Democrats. The principal clause, Section 6, required all officers of the government "to keep safely, without loaning, using, depositing in banks, or exchanging for other funds than as allowed by this act, all the public money collected by them, or otherwise at any time placed in their possession and custody, till the same is ordered . . . to be transferred or paid out." It was passed in August, 1846, but was not to go into effect until January 1, 1847, in order to give the country time to prepare for the resumption of specie payments. One other act of the same Congress was an important adjunct to the working of the subtreasury act. This was the establishment of government warehouses, where imported goods might be stored until they were required by the importer. The duty was paid on the goods as they were withdrawn, and the specie with which the customs were met was thus collected in a number of small payments instead of in one large sum.

[18] Congressional Globe, Vol. 14, p. 591, ff.

[19] Congressional Globe, Vol. 15, p. 1164; Vol. 14, Appendix, p. 820.

The constitutional treasury, as its sponsors liked to call it, was placed in full operation on January 1, 1847. From that date until the Civil War the government system of finance underwent no change of importance and the subtreasury had an opportunity to demonstrate its worth. But no matter how sternly the Secretary of the Treasury at the moment might interpret the law or struggle to keep the skirts of the government free of the contamination, there was an inevitable drift towards coöperation between the treasury and the money market.

Difficulty of literal interpretation

One of the first difficulties arising from the literal interpretation of the law was in connection with the transfer of funds belonging to the government. The surplus of government income over expenditures in New York necessitated a steady flow of funds from that city to points in the South and West. The actual shipment of specie was both expensive and hazardous and the obvious method of transfer, to save the government both time and expense, would have been the sale of treasury drafts to merchants and bankers in the cities where New York funds were needed. This method, as proved by its later trial, would have made the transfers an actual source of profit, but Secretary of the Treasury Walker was, as became a member of his party, a strict constructionist. The treasury circular issued to receiving and collecting officers stated explicitly that government drafts were always to be made payable to order, and not to bearer, and that they could be assigned to a third party only on special endorsement.[20] During 1846 and 1847, when the war in Mexico made heavy transfers between New York and New Orleans necessary, the treasury delegated the task of transfer to the bankers because of these stringent rules. The bankers sold drafts at the point of destination, as was forbidden to the treasury, and obtained, besides a profit on this transaction, the interest on the money during the period when it was ostensibly in transit. In 28 months after October, 1850, about 16 million dollars of transfers, or one-fourth of the total, were performed

[20] Secretary of Treasury, *Annual Report on Finances*, 1846, pp. 30, 31.

in this way. Under this system, the transportation time between cities increased amazingly. It became customary for a bank to take from 100 to 135 days to transfer funds from New York to Washington, and one company in Ohio required the record length of time of 604 days for a transfer from Boston to New Orleans. At one time in 1853 the total amount of government money actually outside the treasury was nearly 5 millions.[21]

Banking houses which made loans to the treasury during the War also found possibilities for profiting by the system. Secretary Walker had arranged that the funds might be deposited at any subtreasury office. A Philadelphia bank which had a branch office in St. Louis sold exchange on New York and Philadelphia at 2½ per cent premium, and deposited the proceeds to the account of the government in the St. Louis subtreasury. Since the mails took ten or fifteen days to carry the draft to the eastern city upon which it had been drawn, the bank had the interest for this time, plus the premium, plus the profit on the loan. Secretary Walker did not want the funds so far West, but did not know how to get them to the East without violating the law. He therefore arranged with the bankers that instead of depositing the funds at St. Louis, they should draw bonds and get them certified by the United States judge, or the collector of the port, as good for the amount on their face. These bonds were then mailed to Washington; by return mail the banking company received a treasury draft on a subtreasury in the West or South, and within four months the company was to deposit that amount in the subtreasury at New York or Philadelphia. Finally Secretary Walker abandoned the attempt to equalize exchanges between the subtreasury offices, and required the proceeds of all further loans to be deposited in an eastern office, which enabled the treasury instead of the bankers to profit by the difference in exchange rates.[22]

[21] *New York Daily Express,* December 19, 1846; February 6, May 17, 1847. *New York Times,* February 20, 1851, March 28, 1852. Secretary of Treasury, *Annual Report on Finances,* 1854, p. 262.

[22] Oberholtzer, *Jay Cooke,* p. 81. No hint of the way in which the bankers made the subtreasury system ridiculous is to be found in the reports of the Secretary.

The absurdity of these maneuvers brought about several changes in the practical operation of the subtreasury system so that the necessary transfers of coin could be reduced. An act of March 3, 1853, authorized the issue of sixty-day certificates against deposits of bullion for coinage at the Mint, instead of payment in gold coin as formerly, and saved the government several hundreds of thousands of dollars annually. Several years later, purchasers of public land were permitted to make their payments at any government depositary and receive in exchange a certificate which could be used at the frontier land office in place of gold. In addition to these measures, treasury drafts were used whenever possible, and found to be both more profitable and more expeditious than bankers' transfers or shipment of specie.[23]

Still another means of reducing the actual transportation of coin lay in the strengthening of the depositary offices in the places where considerable collections were made, so that the funds need not be sent away to the nearest treasury strongbox. The provisions which had been made by some of the government offices for the safety of the funds in their keeping were ludicrously inadequate. One strong room in Indiana, a wooden barricade opening off of a tavern barroom, was compared by a government investigator to Robinson Crusoe's fortification. The disbursing officers were no better provided for in the original act than were the collecting officers. The law required them to draw out in large sums from the depositaries the amount needed for expenditure and to keep this on hand as best they might while it was being disbursed in small sums to many creditors. Many of them redeposited the money, if not regularly in banks, at least with officers of banks, or with private bankers or brokers who had convenient vaults. This condition was remedied in 1853 by a treasury order which permitted disbursing officers to redeposit the amount not immediately needed for expenditure

[23] *Bankers' Magazine,* Vol. 13, p. 23. Secretary of Treasury Annual Report on Finances, 1852, p. 12; 1853, p. 13; 1854, p. 261; 1855, p. 21. A special report by William Gouge on the operations of the subtreasury system was included in the report for 1854.

with the government depositary, so that the funds could be kept in safety without the aid of banks.[24]

All these problems which confronted the subtreasury, in its attempt to give a literal interpretation to the law, illustrated the difficulty of separating the functions of a bank of deposit, which alone were supposed to be exercised under the act, from the functions of a bank of exchange, which the subtreasury gradually assumed under the pressure of necessity. The day had gone by when those two functions could be carried on independently.

The problem of a treasury surplus

During the decade before the Civil War the relations between the treasury and the money market were further complicated by the growth of a surplus. There was danger that under the subtreasury system the government would become the involuntary hoarder of a large amount of coin for lack of which the rest of the country would suffer. The more optimistic even claimed this feature of the plan as an advantage, since they believed that it would force a downward revision of the tariff as a means of reducing income, an event which the Democrats had long desired.[25] The attitude of the various secretaries during the decade of the 1850's, when this problem of a surplus loomed large upon the financial horizon, was almost invariably one of sympathy and coöperation with the institutions of the money market in respect to the difficulties which the surplus involved. Some of them were more conscientious than others in carrying out the letter of the law, but none of them acted according to its spirit by enforcing independence. Treasury practice became more and more widely divergent from treasury law.

At this time there was only one method by which the Secretary of the Treasury could release funds when the surplus revenue threatened to produce stringency in the money market. That was the redemption of the public debt in sufficient amount to restore the funds to the banks. It had long been the practice

[24] Secretary of Treasury, *Annual Report on Finances,* 1849, p. 19; 1853, p. 14; 1854, pp. 16, 257.

[25] *New York Daily Express,* June 19, 1849.

of the government to buy up its own stock with whatever sums were unexpended at the end of the year, and by 1835 the public debt had been almost extinguished. Lowered revenues after 1837 and the Mexican War of 1847 created a new debt, and by 1850 it amounted to about 50 millions. This would have been sufficient to absorb a large surplus, had not the law authorizing redemptions of the public debt required that they be made at par. When market prices of the government stocks rose above par, the hands of the Secretary were tied. Fortunately for the market, the several secretaries under this administration were aware of its difficulties and the *New York Express* was correct when it predicted[26] that "under the present administration of the treasury department it is safe to presume that no accumulation of coin will be allowed that will cripple our general business." When the surplus began to accumulate again, the secretary immediately asked Congress for permission to buy bonds at the market price. This request was granted in acts passed in March, 1848 and March, 1849, and during the next years large amounts of the public debt were repaid before maturity.[27]

The principle of prepayment was then applied to other government obligations. In February, 1849, the *Daily Express* carried a notice that the secretary was willing to redeem treasury notes as well as bonds, in order to relieve the plethora of funds arising from heavy duty payments. The duties continued to pour into the treasury during February and March at a rapid rate and the banks of the city found themselves hard put to it to provide specie for their payment. In March the payment of one million dollars of the Mexican indemnity also was anticipated, in order to reduce government funds in New York, and nothing further was heard of the danger of a surplus for some months. But in the next year it rose steadily to 5 millions by May, and was a source of concern to the market until June, when payment of the Mexican indemnity and falling customs receipts reduced the balance to the more manageable figure of 2 millions. During the autumn of 1851, when a stringency arose

[26] March 9, 1851.

[27] Secretary of Treasury, *Annual Report on Finances*, 1848, p. 28.

which threatened to be more serious than the usual seasonal demand, the treasury again resorted to the expedient of buying bonds in order to aid the market, and in October released 1.2 millions of dollars in that way, which materially relieved the situation.[28]

A definite stringency in the market during 1853[29] forced the treasury to adopt a more aggressive policy in its bond purchases. Heavy imports had so increased the payment of customs duties that by April, 1853, the balance in the New York subtreasury amounted to nearly 7.5 millions. There was as yet no stringency in the money market, but the surplus was so alarmingly large that Secretary Guthrie felt obliged to buy government stock in New York; about half of all the purchases in the city during May went to agents to whom the secretary had made advances for the purpose. Their buying of securities continued through July, but ceased in August, just as the autumn pressure for funds was beginning. The customs duties were still accumulating rapidly and banks in New York began to find it inconvenient to meet the drafts in favor of the treasury. Near the end of the month a delegation was sent to Washington to ask the secretary for a more effective form of relief, but the secretary replied that he could do nothing more than continue the purchase of bonds. He offered to redeem 7 million dollars' worth at the market price before December 1, but in spite of this the balance had reached a new high point of 10 millions by the middle of September. In October and November the usual seasonal disbursements brought relief, and the government made an additional purchase of nearly a million of United States stocks. By the end of the year the balance was down to 5 millions, a reduction of 50 per cent in three months,[30] and the tension in New York had passed.

The financial history of the subtreasury in New York City for 1854 was a repetition almost verbatim of its course during

[28] *Journal of Commerce,* January 21, 28; March 18; April 1; June 10, 1850. December 1, 1851. *New York Daily Express,* June 19, 1849. See p. 138 above.

[29] See p. 140 above.

[30] *New York Times,* May 25, August 22, September 18, October 22, November 3, 1853. Secretary of Treasury, *Annual Report on Finances,* 1853, pp. 6, 13.

1853. The balance increased steadily during the spring, in spite of treasury redemptions of $625,000 of government stock in May, $250,000 in June, and an extension of the period of government repurchase, from January to July 1, with an additional redemption of $500,000 on July 1. The largest single draft ever presented at the New York office, 7 millions, for payment of the Mexican indemnity, did not lower the balance for more than a few weeks in July and in the fall of that year, as in the preceding year, there was a strong demand that the Secretary of the Treasury come to the rescue of the community, which was confronted by a panic. The secretary promised to buy 3.8 millions of stocks between September 1 and November 20, and was as good as his word, even moving gold from Boston to New York that it might be put into the market in the latter city. By December there was more confidence and the balance had dropped to 2 millions, the point at which it had stood in December, 1853.[31]

The next two years were marked by prosperity and a subtreasury balance that rose almost steadily,[32] with slight swells before the two dates of heavy interest disbursements in each year, January 1 and July 1. The reductions in the public debt were continued, and in December, 1856, the *Times* suggested the paying of the fourth installment of the surplus of 1837 as a means of reducing the accumulation of 1855. The suggestion was not taken seriously and by March, 1857, the balance was at 15.5 millions of dollars. Throughout this period before the panic, the uneasiness in the money market was enhanced by the amount of coin held by the government, but the Secretary of the Treasury made no plans for actions in an emergency. The report issued in the middle of 1856 contains a pious hope that "such a disaster will rarely occur,"[33] based on the belief that the large balance in the government vaults would act as a check

[31] *New York Times,* August 30, 1854; January 5, 1855. Secretary of Treasury Annual Report on Finances, 1854, p. 272. *Journal of Commerce,* December 11, 1854.

[32] The average annual customs receipts from 1850 to 1860, were 54 millions.

[33] Secretary of Treasury, *Annual Report on Finances,* 1856, p. 32.

to the overexpansion of the banks by reducing their reserves and so preventing a crisis.

The hope of the secretary was not justified, and one reason is made clear by the diagram of New York City bank statistics on page 91 above. Throughout 1855, 1856, up to August, 1857, the amount of specie in the city banks fell steadily, from about 17 millions in 1855 to about 8 millions in 1857. Yet because it was very large in proportion to circulation, there was no fear and the loans and discounts of the banks, instead of being curtailed, rose steadily, with a total increase of 50 per cent in less than three years. The holdings of the subtreasury in New York during the same period rose from 2 millions to a high point of 15.5 millions in March of that year. This rise occurred in spite of the fact that more than 45 millions of government stock had been redeemed between March, 1853, and June, 1856. At such a rate the public debt would not last long and the subtreasury would lose the only outlet for its surplus. By March, 1857, the subtreasury balance had reached a high point of 21 millions and there was distinct uneasiness in the money market. The government increased its purchases of bonds during the summer, but the surplus was not materially reduced even by the dividend payments of July 1.

The treasury in the panic of 1857

The period of crisis began in August, and at once the revenues of the treasury were cut down. Not only was the amount of the imports greatly reduced during the business depression, but tariff rates had been finally reduced by about 20 per cent beginning with July, 1857, and the warehousing provisions of the new law permitted importers to postpone payment of duties until the goods were removed from the warehouses. This circumstance lightened the task of the New York banks in conserving their specie, but it rapidly depleted the treasury, and left it unable to come to the aid of the market if it had desired to do so. When the banks were finally obliged to suspend specie payments, on October 13, the treasury balance had sunk so low that it felt obliged to issue 20 millions of short-term notes.

Since the total purchase of bonds during the last six months of the year was less than 5 millions, it is evident that the treasury withdrew more funds from the market than it put in.[34] Several apologists for the subtreasury during this period emphasized the aid which the regular disbursements of the government, made in specie according to the law, rendered to the financial community. There was little justification for this claim; most of the funds which were disbursed had but recently been collected, or even borrowed, and the two operations canceled each other, as far as benefit to those outside the treasury was concerned.

Throughout the suspension which lasted for two months, from October 13 to December 13, the subtreasury did continue to collect and disburse specie, and for this it took great credit. Invidious comparisons were drawn between the condition of the treasury during the suspension of 1837, when the government funds were in banks, and that during the suspension of 1857, when the subtreasury was handling the money.[35] In several respects the two periods were not comparable, however. In the first place, the suspension of 1837 was of much longer duration than that twenty years later, and if the banks had not resumed so promptly in 1857, the treasury would have found itself as embarrassed as during 1837. Its balances in New York fell rapidly during the two months when the banks were not paying specie, from 12.5 millions of dollars just before the panic, to 3 millions at the close of the year. A rapid decline in the last month of the year was not unusual, but during the first three months of the next year, the balances remained at 3 million instead of rising as usual to a much larger figure. In the second place, the gold production of California made resumption in 1857 much less difficult than in 1837, when gold had had to be imported from abroad. The net export of specie, which

[34] Knox, *United States Notes*, p. 70. *New York Times*, September 4, 1857. Secretary of Treasury Annual Report on Finances, 1857, pp. 7, 42; 1858, p. 34. During the panic the suggestion was made that the treasury lend directly to the banks. This was not only illegal, but was by that time almost impossible.

[35] Secretary of the Treasury, *Annual Report on Finances*, 1857. President Buchanan, Message to Congress, December 7, 1857.

amounted to 57 millions in the year ending June, 1857, sank to 33 millions in the year ending June, 1858, in which the panic occurred. In the next year they rose again to 57 millions, and it is plain that the source of the 20 millions of gold which enabled the banks to resume was the smaller export, and not the subtreasury. The blame for the crisis of 1857 cannot of course be placed upon the subtreasury, but it cannot be doubted by anyone who has read the contemporary accounts of the months preceding the crisis, that the subtreasury system furnished one more element of uncertainty and dread, and that its lack of flexibility made possible a state of affairs which could hardly have arisen under the régime of the United States Bank.[36]

The independent treasury during the Civil War

The panic of 1857 put an end to the treasury surplus for the time and it soon became apparent that although the management of a surplus created many problems for an independent treasury, the lack of a surplus made it impossible for the treasury to remain independent of the banks. The government was obliged to borrow heavily during the Civil War, and the treasury suffered a permanent impairment of its independence. In June of 1860 the public debt had amounted to 45 millions, besides nearly 20 millions of outstanding treasury notes. An attempt to fund the notes maturing before January 1, 1861, was only partially successful because of the financial crisis which had occurred in October.[37] At the same time the receipts from customs had fallen off, and the payments made consisted largely of treasury notes. More treasury notes had to be issued in December in order to meet the interest payments due on January 1, 1861, and among the last acts of the expiring administration of Buchanan was the authorization, on March 2, of 25 millions of bonds, and 10 millions of notes or bonds.[38]

When Secretary Chase took office in March, 1861, he was confronted with a heavy national debt, the prospect of an imme-

[36] *Bankers' Magazine*, Vol. 8, p. 579. Colwell, *Ways and Means of Payment*, p. 609 (1859).

[37] See p. 100 above.

[38] Secretary of Treasury, *Annual Report on Finances*, 1860, pp. 7-9.

diate increase in that debt, and an impairment of the public credit. One of his first official actions was to get in touch with the banks of New York, Philadelphia and Boston, in order to obtain their assistance in the conduct of the government's financial affairs.[39] They met in conference at New York, and agreed to make three advances of 50 millions each to the government. The terms, as described in the annual report were[40] that the banks "agreed to unite as associates in moneyed support to the government" and to subscribe at once a loan of 50 millions of dollars, of which 5 millions were to be paid immediately to the Assistant Treasurers, in coin, and the residue, also in coin, as needed for disbursement. The secretary, on his part, agreed "to issue three year 7.30 bonds or Treasury notes, bearing even date with the subscription, and of equal amount; to cause books of subscription to the National Loan to be immediately opened; to reimburse the advances of the banks, as far as practicable from this national subscription; and to deliver to them 7.30 bonds or Treasury notes from the amount not thus reimbursed." It was further understood that the Secretary of the Treasury should issue a limited amount of United States notes, payable on demand, in aid of the operations of the treasury, and that the associated institutions, when the first advance of 50 millions should be expended, would, if practicable, make another, and when that should be exhausted, still another advance to the government of the same amount, and on similar terms.

The objects of this arrangement were to place at the command of the government the large sums immediately needed for the payment of maturing treasury notes and for other disbursements and to insure, if possible, the maintenance of payments in specie.

On August 5, 1861, Congress repealed enough of the subtreasury act to permit the secretary to leave with the subscribing banks the proceeds of such loans until it was necessary to

[39] Hart, *Samuel Portland Chase*, p. 222.

[40] Secretary of Treasury, *Annual Report on Finances*, 1861, p. 8. See diagram for effect on loans and deposits of New York banks, p. 91 above.

draw against them. This repeal had originated in the House and passed the Senate almost without debate, after Senator Fessenden had assured his colleagues that it was necessary.[41] The spirit of the independent treasury act had been violated by the secretary when he went to the bankers for aid in floating the loan; the letter of the act had been altered in order to legalize the secretary in his course, and the "independence" of the treasury may properly be considered to have suffered a serious breakdown. But at this point the early Jacksonian principles of Chase suddenly asserted themselves and he refused to take advantage of the liberty offered him, insisting instead that the banks make payment to the government in specie. They protested, but eventually acceded to his demands, and the burden thus undertaken was a large factor in bringing about the suspension of specie payments in December, 1861.

The banks of New York City were in an unusually good technical condition in the autumn of 1861, for the falling off of the southern and western business and the depression of 1860 had brought about a decrease in their loans and deposits and a corresponding increase in their specie reserves. In fact the loans to the government, not only in New York but in many other parts of the country, were a welcome investment to banks which had found difficulty in keeping their portfolios filled with satisfactory paper. In spite of that the amount which the associated banks had obligated themselves to take, at the secretary's terms, put a heavy strain on their resources,[42] and required careful management. In New York City this was accomplished by giving considerable power to a central Loan Committee of the Clearing House banks.[43]

Each of the associated banks had agreed to keep a specie reserve of 25 per cent against its net liabilities during the period of this agreement, and one of the most important functions of the Loan Committee developed out of the attempt to keep the specie of the city so apportioned among the banks that none

[41] Congressional Globe, Vol. 55, pp. 383, 396-97.
[42] For amount taken by each bank, see *Bankers' Magazine*, Vol. 16, p. 237.
[43] Secretary of Treasury, *Annual Report on Finances*, 1861, p. 127.

should fall below the standard. The first installment of 35 millions was credited to the government account on August 19, and the banks began to pay specie into the subtreasury at the rate of 3.5 millions per week. By September 2, some of the banks had already fallen below the 25 per cent standard, and the Loan Committee directed that interest on the deficiency be charged daily. On September 19, the Clearing House began to issue loan certificates, and instead of paying interest the banks which lacked specie exchanged their loan certificates for gold.[44] The specie of the banks as a whole was not seriously reduced by their payment of coin to the government, for it speedily returned to them in the form of government disbursements and balances of outside bankers. On October 1 the second 35 millions of treasury notes were allotted to the New York banks, and on November 16 another loan of the same amount, half in registered stock, and half in coupon bonds. Until February the only evidence of this debt in possession of the banks was the loan certificates issued by the Clearing House Committee to 90 per cent of its value. Without the Loan Committee and the loan certificates it seems certain that the banks could not have withstood the strain of the government withdrawals for more than a few weeks.

In December however the secretary introduced a new element into the financial situation in the form of demand notes. In his annual report he spoke of this issue as a part of the scheme of treasury financing which had been discussed and approved by the meeting of banks in August. There is other evidence to indicate that the bankers, at least in New York, had understood that these notes would not be issued if the loans were taken. However the misunderstanding arose, the notes were put out, and at once produced a further drain of specie. James Gallatin pointed out, in a detailed criticism of Chase's policy, that it was now a question of whether the banks or the government suspend specie payments first, and urged the banks to do so at once in order to keep what little specie remained to them. There was a

[44] Secretary of Treasury, *Annual Report on Finances,* 1861, p. 125. See p. 101 above. *Report* of New York State Superintendent of Banks, 1862, p. 14.

rumor in Wall Street that they would take this course on December 17, but it was not until after the heavy drain of the last fortnight in the month that they finally agreed to do so.[45] The treasury was obliged at once to follow suit, and the independent treasury act became a dead letter.

The suspension of specie payments by the banks was a serious blow to the fiscal program of Secretary Chase. It had been a paramount object of his policies to maintain inviolate the specie clause of the independent treasury act. For the sake of that clause he had refused to permit the proceeds of the loans to remain on deposit with the lending banks, although the requirement that government obligations be paid for in gold made it inevitable that the banks would suspend. Now that the bank suspension had actually occurred, it was recognized that the government itself could no longer pay coin to its creditors.

Since gold was about to disappear from circulation, it became necessary for the treasury to make some new arrangement, for the specie clause of the act of 1846 made it unlawful for the government either to receive or to disburse anything but coin. The government's stock of gold had fallen by the end of the year to 4 millions in the vaults at New York. At the current rate of disbursement, that sum would soon be spent. Two days after the bank suspension, and as a consequence of it, an act to make the demand notes of the government legal tender in payment of all debts except customs duties, was introduced into Congress. Again the banker friends of the administration protested, as they had done in August in the face of the Secretary's loan policy,[46] against a measure which they felt would make more difficult the coöperation between the banks and the government. A committee representing the banks and the Boards of Trade of New York, Philadelphia, and Boston, went to Washington early in January, to confer with the Senate Committee on Finance, the House Committee on Ways and Means, and the Secretary of the Treasury.[47] Mr. James Gallatin, son of the former Secretary of the Treasury, submitted on behalf of the

[45] *Bankers' Magazine*, Vol. 16, pp. 353, 558, 625.
[46] See p. 195 above.
[47] Mitchell, *History of Greenbacks*, p. 30.

New York bankers a plan by which the War might be financed without a legal tender act. Among the means which he recom mended were:[48]

1. Taxation to the amount of 125 millions, besides customs duties;
2. The immediate cessation of the issue of demand notes by the Treasury;
3. The issue of 100 millions of 2-year Treasury notes, to be receivable for all government dues except customs;
4. The use of banks as government depositaries;
5. The issue of 20-year 6 per cent bonds at market prices;
6. The authorizing of the secretary to hypothecate funded stock for temporary loans.

These proposals received little consideration from the secretary and the Senate and House committees. Their chief objection arose from the fear that by removing the legal limitation on the price of government securities, the price would fall below par and thus the prestige and dignity of the government would suffer irreparable damage. Secretary Chase felt that the terms of all loans should be set by Congress, instead of being left to his discretion or to the state of the money market and Mr. Spaulding, the chairman of the House committee, declared that the great object of the legal tender act which he was sponsoring was to prevent the government from being forced to sell its bonds in the open market to the highest bidder. Since treasury officials were determined at any cost to keep government securities nominally at par, they could not approve the suggestions made by Mr. Gallatin, which would have left the bonds to the mercies of the fluctuations in the credit of the government. They therefore introduced a plan of their own, retaining some features of the Gallatin plan, but substituting for increased taxation, the formation of a national bank system.

The rejection of the plan for increased taxation as a method of financing the War was a matter of major importance. Any large government expenditure must be paid for either by taxation, by borrowing, or by an issue of paper money. Taxation and borrowing are painful, and apt to create discontent with

[48] Spaulding, *History of the Legal Tender Paper Money*, pp. 18-22, 127. Secretary of Treasury, *Annual Report on Finances*, 1861, p. 23.

the collecting agency, while inflation is temporarily painless and its evil results are not felt for some time. It is therefore easier to inaugurate a policy of inflation than one of taxation, and for that reason it is apt to appeal to government officials. If Gallatin's plan for taxation, supplemented by a careful plan of restricted borrowing, had been followed, the country might have been spared the serious consequences of inflation during the War and the difficult resumption of specie payments after the War.

Summary

Study of the relations between the government and the money market gives ample evidence that the separation of the financial interests of the government from those of the rest of the country was as impossible of accomplishment as it was dangerous to attempt. The danger arose from the fact that when the treasury had made what it considered adequate arrangements for its own safety, it ceased to interest itself in the rest of society and even procured its own welfare at the expense of the whole. As one reads of the results of the unregulated state bank note issues of the period before the National Bank Act, one must have considerable sympathy with the harrassed government officials who found their troubles immensely increased because of them. But to revert, because of these difficulties, to an outworn theory of government, as well as to an obsolete system of exchange, was neither wise nor courageous.

CHAPTER X

THE NEW YORK MONEY MARKET BEFORE 1863

In order to bring together the different phases of the money market, each of which had to be considered separately in the preceding chapters, it may be useful to view cross sections of the market at several important points in its history. In this way developing institutions can be pictured in their proper relation to each other, and the market as a whole can be viewed with some perspective.

The money market in 1800

At the beginning of the century Philadelphia was still the important city in all things financial, and in it was located the head office of the first Bank of the United States. The branch office in New York however carried on an almost equal volume of business. In New York there was an informal Stock Exchange which was a close rival to that of the former city, and about it was developing something of an investment market. The shares listed were government issues and those of a few banks, but when one considers that all of this growth had taken place within ten years, it appears creditable. There were only two banks in New York City. Of commercial paper and call loan markets there was yet no sign. The greater part of the trade of New York was foreign, carried on through sterling bankers' acceptances drawn by merchants and private bankers. The functions of merchant and banker were still intermingled, and more than one merchant prince, who as a side line discounted the notes of his friends, found his business turning into that of a banker until the merchandise end was altogether abandoned.

The money market in 1825

A quarter of a century later the course of trade had definitely shifted from Philadelphia to New York, and only the presence

Courtesy of the Committee of One Hundred

INTERIOR OF THE STOCK EXCHANGE IN 1853

in Philadelphia of the head office of the Bank of the United States permitted it to retain any share of its earlier prestige. The Stock Exchange of New York was the largest in the country; and although it had not acquired a formal organization until 1817, it had shown remarkable growth and was trading in government, state, bank, insurance company, and canal, shares. Not only were the daily transactions of the Stock Exchange larger than those of any other city, but New York was also the center for new issues of securities, a function essential to the development of a true investment market.

The growth of internal commerce and the activity of the Bank of the United States had established within the commercial banks something akin to a market for commercial paper. Besides the usual loan on personal security, in the form of promissory notes with or without endorsers, there was also coming slowly into use the domestic bill of exchange, or what we should now call the trade acceptance. Both types of paper were sought by the metropolitan banks. With the increasing trade of New York, interior bankers who wished to build up balances for the benefit of their customers, or of those who found it difficult to invest their funds at home, were beginning to send balances to New York.

The panic of 1819 had been almost forgotten, and there was a general feeling of confidence in the financial situation, engendered on the one hand by the comforting presence of the Bank of the United States, which kept its stock of specie large in order to have it available for an emergency and, on the other hand, to the attitude of treasury officials who often had before, and undoubtedly would again, come to the rescue of banks which found themselves in difficulties.

The money market in 1836

This was a year marked by the feverish activity of the money market which usually preceded a panic. In the securities market, the increased volume of business had brought about the organization of a second Board of Brokers, so that there were two formal Stock Exchanges besides the street market. A majority of the stock sales were made on thirty days' time, or on option, and the stocks were used as collateral security for the loan made to the buyer. Because of increased speculation in securities there had arisen a demand for loans with which to carry on this trading, some of which were payable on demand, and some at definite short dates. A large part of the bankers' deposits in New York had been put into this convenient form of loan.

The most striking feature of this period was the enormous volume of imports pouring in from Great Britain and being paid for, not by the export of goods, but by securities and short-term floating credits. The result was that bills were being drawn on London in great volume and that open-book accounts were being carried by many English exporters in favor of their American clients. As a result of the influx of manufactured goods, more American commercial paper was used to finance the distribution of the imports and the Bank of the United States, although it had lost its Federal charter and much of its prestige, was still a sponsor for the commercial-paper market. Both promissory notes and domestic bills of exchange were used in the domestic trade.

The policy of the government, which eleven years before had been one of sympathetic consideration for the money market, was a source of much uneasiness, for it seemed likely that the hostility of the party in power would vent itself on anything related to the banking system. A few of the New York banks were on such good terms with the Democrats that they had no fear, but at most of the banks, as at the stock market, the political news was anxiously awaited and was immediately reflected in the financial news.

The money market in 1846

The Independent Treasury Act had just been passed and in a money market which was still in the doldrums following the crisis of 1837, the event was of unusual interest. War was declared against Mexico in May, 1846, and a downward revision of the tariff made in July. The lowered customs receipts and the increased war expenditures, prevented the problem of a large surplus of funds in the vaults of the subtreasury from disturbing the country for the first few years of its operation, and the famine in Europe, with its demand for American agricultural products, saved the country in all probability from the effects of the depression which occurred in England and on the Continent in 1847-1848.

The stock market was not very active at this time, compared with the amount of trading in 1837. The new shares appearing on the lists were almost entirely those of railroads, except for a number of state issues to which the European markets were closed. Trading was still done largely on time, but enough was carried on the basis of immediate settlement to bring about an increased demand for call money, or "demand loans on stock collateral," as it was referred to in papers of the day. Bankers' balances, which were the funds making possible the development of the call loan market, had grown with the increasing banking resources of New York, and were to be found, not only with the incorporated banks, but also with private bankers and brokers. In the commercial paper market the trade acceptance had become very popular and was estimated by some observers to be afloat in as great amount as the older promissory note.

The money market in 1856

The chief development of the previous decade had been in the relations of the subtreasury to the money market. The ever present danger of a large surplus in the treasury and a proportionate deficit in the vaults of the city banks, tended to a feeling of disquiet and uneasiness. Treasury officials were on the whole cognizant of the danger and eager to prevent its effects, but the law gave them little scope for action. In most cases moreover the action was in the nature of attempted repair, rather than prevention.

The opening of the New York Clearing House in 1853 and the beginning of weekly reports from the city banks had produced a great improvement in the field of everyday banking relations, and made possible coöperation between the banks in emergency.

The banks were still the chief market for commercial paper; the note brokers were mere commission agents, and the volume of their business was small.

There was a strong upward movement under way on the Stock Exchange, and the list of shares was lengthened by many rails and a few industrials. Call loans were becoming a more frequent method of financing stock transactions but time sales were not yet relegated to a minority position. The problems growing out of bankers' balances were under constant discussion and suggestions for reform included the abolition of interest on bankers' deposits, the maintenance of a larger specie reserve by the New York banks, and the stricter regulation of note issues by law.

Forces working against equilibrium in the money market

In many respects the money market of New York fell short of the ideal functioning which it might have achieved. A part of the fault lay in the fact that the money market during a great part of its history, was an organism without a head, and that upon this witless monster was imposed a task requiring the most delicate cerebration. There was, in other words, no central bank to exercise effective leadership in financial affairs. The first Bank of the United States, like many of the European central banks, came into existence to aid the government and when it might have achieved a position of responsibility in the market, its charter expired. The second Bank of the United States came nearer to the ideal of a central bank than the first, but it was handicapped by location in Philadelphia at a time when New York was rapidly becoming the center of the money market's activities. It was also involved during the latter part of its existence in a political altercation which made it worse than useless as a regulator of the market.

New York was well aware of the advantage to be derived from the presence of a large bank within its boundaries. The first Bank of the United States had no sooner been dissolved than a group of New Yorkers petitioned the state legislature for a charter for a large bank which they hoped would take the place of the Bank of the United States. This was the Bank of America, which is still in existence. Following the end of the second bank, a similar desire prompted the formation of the Bank of the United States of New York. It was hoped that Mr. Biddle himself, with his associates, would take charge of the new bank, but this was found to be impossible. Another attempt to fill the gap was the organization of the North American Bank and Trust Company, in 1838, with a capital of 10 millions of dollars. But the purpose of all these efforts was rather to protect the merchants of the city from "pecuniary inconvenience" than to provide a regulatory mechanism for the money market.[1]

The need for a central bank, which could have performed for the money market of New York the services of the central banks of Europe, was felt in two directions, lack of a common reserve, and lack of a common policy. The reserve funds of the country were being concentrated in New York City, but in a number of banks rather than in one bank in which was vested responsibility for the control of these reserves. The funds were invested on the basis of maximum profit for the city bank, rather than on the needs of the banking system of the country as a whole. It was inevitable that reserve funds deposited with city banks in this way should fail to meet an emergency. Funds in the call loan market, where the reserves were placed in large amounts, were ordinarily easily recalled but at just the time when their recall was most essential, at a time of panic, these loans became frozen and the collateral security on which they were based became of less value. Had there been a central reserve bank with adequate power and resources, the keeping of the reserves might have been entrusted to it instead of to the call loan market. Under the circumstances the call loan was the best disposition for such funds, but at best it was not very good.

The lack of a common policy regarding reserves was accentuated by times of stress in the market, but it was a disadvantage at all times. Every export of specie abroad, every withdrawal to the interior, brought problems which concerned not

[1] *Financial Register*, Vol. I, p. 383; Vol. II, pp. 14, 154, 350.

only the bank from which the coin had actually been taken, but all the banks. The success with which the Clearing House banks worked together during the financing of the Civil War is ample evidence of the advantages of a uniform policy.

Dependence upon foreign funds

Another characteristic of the money market which was especially marked in the years before 1863, was its dependence upon London for capital and credit. Not only the importation of capital for purposes of long-term investment, and much of the financing of our imports, but the specie reserves of the banks, were dependent upon the flow of funds between the two countries. During periods of monetary stringency, when the specie in city bank vaults reached a low point, there was nothing the banks could do to prevent further drain of specie except curtail their loans and discounts or else give up the redemption of their notes in specie altogether. The importation of specie from abroad was expensive and slow. During the panic of 1837 it took months for an arrangement to be made whereby enough specie could be brought to New York to make it safe for the banks to resume. During the depression of 1847 London was obliged to withhold the usual credits from New York, and it was only the famine abroad, with the resulting increases in grain exports, which made it possible for the United States to absorb its usual amount of imported goods.

The consciousness of its dependence upon London often irked the financial powers of New York and they were eager to seize upon any indication that this dependence was waning. The newspapers during the crisis of 1847-1848 in England, for example, pointed out with much pride that the United States was far less affected by London's difficulties than had been the case in 1837. This public rejoicing was premature, for the history of the years after that date gives as much evidence as the years before of the close ties between London and its competitor.

Seasonal changes in the money market

Binding together all the institutions and functions of the money market in one fundamental rhythm was the seasonal ebb and flow of funds, "almost as regularly as the tides." The primary cause for this movement was the seasonal character of the principal industry, agriculture; and the secondary cause, related in part to the first, the seasonal character of mercantile business. With the first was linked the export trade, in which agricultural products held the lead, and with the second was linked the import trade.

Crops began to move towards the eastern markets and ports in the autumn, and the movement was not completed until spring. Grain and meat from the West jammed the canals until they were frozen over, and then continued to be shipped by rail, while cotton from the South came by train and coastwise steamer. Balancing this autumn shipment of goods, was a movement of funds in the opposite direction, from New York to the South and West. The first indication of this movement was the drawing down of the bankers' balances which had been accumulated in New York against this very prospect. The decline in these deposits forced a curtailment in the loans and discounts of the city banks, which was another indication that the usual seasonal movement was under way. At the same time interest rates on commercial paper began to rise and funds were drawn away from other parts of the money market to fill the need for more commercial loans. This equalizing tendency brought higher interest rates in the call loan market, and the range of rates in the latter was apt to be wider than in the former, since the relative change in volume of funds in the call market was wider than in the commercial-paper market.

The scarcity of borrowable funds also tended to lower stock prices and thus to become apparent in the investment market. This phenomenon was not confined to the latter days of the period being studied, when the call loan market supplied the major portion of the funds with which operations on the Stock Exchange were financed. In 1793, when most of the purchases were made on time and demand loans on collateral security were almost unknown, Alexander Hamilton advised that redemption of the public debt be carried on during the winter, for "it is a familiar fact that during the winter in this country, there is always a scarcity of money in the towns—a circumstance calculated to damp the price of stock."[2]

Another basic factor in the seasonal movement of funds was the fact that the purchases of imported goods, which comprised a great part of the stock in trade of merchants throughout the country, were concentrated in the spring and the fall, preparatory to the winter and summer trade. The peak of the import trade was reached in July and August but there was also a secondary peak between January and April. The shipment of imported goods in the fall to all parts of the country counteracted to a certain extent the withdrawal of money from New York and tended to mitigate the severity of the drain. Upon this movement of goods, there was set up a corresponding flow of funds towards Europe, just as the crops moving from the western states to New York set up a flow of funds towards the interior of the country. In the autumn there was thus a double drain from New York, and this fact alone is sufficient to explain the frequent occurrence of financial crises in the autumn.

There were other minor factors in the seasonal variation of the money market. In this class belongs the quarterly stringency which resulted from the general custom of paying rents and other annual fees in four installments during the year, on the first days of February, May, August, and November.[3] Here also may be mentioned the more or less regular movements of government funds, especially following the establishment of the Independent Treasury. The income of the government reached its peak at one season of the year and the expenditure at another, so that during certain months surplus funds accumulated in the treasury vaults. And there was also, if so small a matter may be dignified by such a name, the regular Friday "seasonal" in New York in the days before the establishment of the Clearing House, when the banks scrambled for funds with which to make their weekly settlements with each other. From these recurrent tides the New York money market was unable to pro-

[2] 28 Congress, 1 Session, Executive Document 15, p. 199.

[3] Hunt's *Merchants' Magazine*, Vol. 20, p. 302; Vol. 39, p. 582. *Journal of Commerce*, August 3, 1846. Bank Clearings during a week in which a quarter day fell, were 10 per cent greater than the average.

tect itself. Its institutions had grown up in a casual fashion which made them ill adapted to withstand unusual stresses. It was not until the period following the Civil War that protective devices of any consequence were developed.

PART II

THE DEVELOPMENT OF THE NEW YORK MONEY MARKET FROM 1863 TO 1913

CHAPTER XI

THE NATIONAL BANK ACT

The development of the New York money market in the half century from 1863 to 1913 proceeded along the lines which had been laid down in the earlier period. The stage was being widened but the scene was not greatly changed. Geographic expansion was still a dominating element. The settling of the states west of the Mississippi absorbed a large share of the energies of the people during the seventies and the eighties as it had done during the fifties and the sixties. It was not until 1912 that the whole area of the United States had been organized into states to meet the needs of the pressing population. The geographic development made necessary an enormous expenditure in capital equipment. Roads and railroads, factories and houses, had to be built on a large scale—a scale far beyond the ability of the country to finance for itself. Fortunately it was possible to obtain funds for these purposes from the older countries in which the age of expansion was already past, and the New York money market was the medium through which this was accomplished. The same source had been utilized in the ante-bellum period, but less extensively. As the development of the West proceeded, it began to repay these loans by pouring grain and meat into Europe. This too was accomplished with the aid of the New York money market, which found itself obliged to exert every effort in order to make possible the smooth movement of funds in the one direction, and commodities in the other. The securities market, the banks and the domestic and foreign exchange markets expanded under the pressure of this necessity and their development was directly dependent upon it.

The geographical expansion of the country resulted in a great increase in the area of production but nevertheless agriculture declined steadily from its position of first importance in the occupations of the people. The growth of cities and the spread of factory production went on with great rapidity, and this necessitated further changes in the money market. It resulted in the first place in a greater use of banking facilities, so that deposit currency more and more took the place of the bank notes which had once been the chief means of payment. There was also a greater concentration of banking reserves; as cities became larger, they were permitted to move up into the higher classifications of the national banking law, and the banks in them were permitted to keep the reserves of other banks on deposit. Nor was banking the only phase of the money market's activities affected by the increasing industrialization of the country. The stock market felt the impetus of the growing tendency to incorporate business, for the new large-scale production made it impracticable to carry on operations with the relatively small amount of capital equipment which could be provided by an individual or a partnership. There was thus thrown into the security market a great volume of shares of a new type, which were viewed at first with suspicion but became finally the mainstay of the stock market. The expansion of the country also increased the size of the domestic market. The relative importance of foreign trade continued to decline as it had been declining since the early part of the nineteenth century, although in absolute volume it had increased many times. The foreign bill of exchange was therefore overshadowed by the domestic trade paper or promissory note. Every phase of money market activity was conditioned by this economic development. The differences between the money market in 1863 and in 1913 were due very largely to the increase in mere size and the changes which had been necessitated by that increase.

There were other elements of difference introduced by the Civil War, for destruction of property on a large scale and disorganization of a great part of the country are bound to dislocate markets. The most drastic change effected by the War in the financial situation was the passage of the National Bank Act in 1863. The necessity of raising large revenues to carry on the War had forced government officials to consider every possible plan for increasing tax returns and improving the sale of government bonds. Among these plans was that of requiring banks to use United States bonds as security for circulating notes. The increase in bond sales which could be brought about by such a device was greatly exaggerated in the minds of its advocates. It could improve the credit of the government, and it could increase to a limited extent the demand for government securities; it could not provide the enormous amount of funds required to pay for the War. But the national regulation of the currency was a measure which had long appealed to Secretary Chase. As a westerner brought up in a Democratic atmosphere, he had had ample opportunity to observe and criticize the faults of state bank notes. In his inaugural address as governor of Ohio, in 1856, he had given the subject of currency a place, and declared that he considered its regulation to be a function of the Federal government.[1] A plan which would increase the demand for bonds at the same time that it reformed the currency had a double appeal for him as Secretary of the Treasury.

The Act a direct result of the Civil War

In his annual report for 1861 presented to Congress a few weeks before the suspension of specie payments in December, Secretary Chase put forth a tentative proposal for the substitution of a national currency for the existing state bank notes. He estimated the circulation of bank notes in the northern states to be about 150 millions of dollars, and expressed the hope that a similar amount of bonds might be sold as a basis for the new currency. Secretary Chase at that time was still opposed to the issue of fiat money by the government, but advocated the issue of paper money by the banks under three conditions which had been suggested to him by the successful experience of the state of New York: "That the notes should bear a common impression and be issued by a common authority; That they be redeemed by the association through which they had been issued, and That they be adequately secured by the pledge of United States stock and an adequate provision of specie."[2] The advantages of this plan over the issue of legal-

[1] Davis, *Origin of the National Banking System*, p. 3.
[2] Secretary Treasury, *Annual Report on Finances*, pp. 17-19.

tender treasury notes were that it would prevent depreciation of the currency by preventing excessive issues, and that it would give immediate aid to the treasury by creating a demand for at least 150 million dollars worth of government securities, to serve as collateral for the new notes. It was taken for granted that the national bank notes would force the state notes out of circulation.

In spite of the enthusiasm with which Secretary Chase urged the measure, Congress could not be persuaded to authorize it. Instead the legal tender act was rushed through both houses and became a law on February 25, 1862, authorizing the first issue of greenbacks. Its most zealous advocates did not claim that it was a solution for all the problems which were confronting the treasury; many of them favored the national currency plan also, but realized that it could not be passed in time to aid the government in the immediate crisis.[3] Secretary Chase finally gave his reluctant approval to the measure.

Influence of New York in framing the Act

The failure of the national currency scheme to obtain serious consideration from Congress on its first presentation did not discourage its advocates, nor prevent it from arousing intense interest throughout the country. The proposed legislation was naturally of greatest interest to New York, both because it was based upon the plan in operation in that state and because it would have an important effect upon the city banks, and through them upon the money market, should it ever be adopted. In August, 1861, just after the agreement between the bankers and the treasury regarding the 150-million dollar loan had been reached,[4] Mr. Orlando Bronson Potter of New York City had written a letter to the Secretary of the Treasury in which was outlined a plan for a national currency very similar to that advocated in the secretary's report for December. In November of the same year Mr. Eleazar Lord, the former president of the New York and Erie Railroad, had also written to the secretary

[3] Spaulding, *History of the Legal Tender Paper Money.*
[4] See p. 197 above.

with the proposal that banks be permitted to invest their capital in United States bonds and receive in return notes for circulation. His suggestion did not go as far as the organization of a new group of banks to issue these notes but utilized the existing state banks for the purpose.[5] Mr. Silas Stilwell, who had written a number of pamphlets on financial subjects, was another of the New York men instrumental in giving form to the new banks. He went to Washington in the late fall of 1861, and spent some weeks in drafting a plan which should combine the advantages of stimulating the demand for government bonds and of establishing a "permanent and comprehensive system of credit, exchange and currency." From this outline, according to Mr. Stilwell's account, the Attorney-General prepared the draft of the bill which was approved by Secretary Chase, and Mr. Stilwell then wrote a pamphlet explaining the proposal, which was widely distributed over the country.[6]

Not only did New York play an important rôle in the unofficial preliminaries to the passage of the act, but also in the official action which preceded the establishment of the system. Mr. Elbridge Gerry Spaulding, chairman of the Subcommittee on Ways and Means to whom Secretary Chase entrusted the drafting of a national bank act, was from New York state, as was also one other member of the committee of three, Mr. Corning of Albany. The bill drafted by Mr. Hooper, and introduced into Congress in July, 1862, did not fare well at the hands of the harried legislators, and was permitted to perish after very little discussion.

When the Secretary of the Treasury had made up his mind, he did not permit himself easily to be diverted from his object. In his second annual report, in December, 1862, he again recommended the currency bill, and persuaded President Lincoln to present a special message to Congress, urging the bill as a necessary part of the program of war finance. Even Congress could not ignore this appeal, and the bill was introduced into the Senate on January 26, 1863. The debate on it began on

[5] Davis, op. cit., pp. 45, 50.
[6] Stilwell, *Private History*, etc., pp. 4-8.

February 9 and lasted only three days. It was approved by the Senate on February 12 and went to the House, where it lay until the 19th. Discussion in that body was almost as brief as in the Senate, and by the 25th the bill had been passed by both houses and was in the hands of the President who signed it at once.[7]

In a debate of such short duration it was inevitable that many points of importance should have been ignored. Senator Sherman's speech may be taken as a convenient summary of the case for the bill. His chief argument was that the act would increase the demand for United States bonds and thus support the credit of the government. He contended also that by creating a nationally acceptable currency it would prevent the further issue of greenbacks and counteract sectional tendencies, thereby strengthening the Union.[8] The chief opposition to the bill came from defenders of the state bank circulation. Few of the speakers on either side of the question looked beyond the period of the War to discern the effect which the bill might exercise upon the banking future of the country or upon the money market. Many insisted that the measure could have little influence upon the financing of the War, but nearly all were blinded by the War to the importance of the act as a permanent peace institution. They voted for it, not because they felt any enthusiasm for it, but because the President and the Secretary of the Treasury had declared it to be necessary—the same reason which had influenced the vote for the bill making the greenbacks legal tender.[9] It seems exceedingly doubtful if the act could have passed Congress without the war emergency to serve as an excuse, for that body was neither anxious to legislate on banking nor conscious of the full significance of their action when they did legislate.

The National Bank Act as it was originally passed in 1863 bore a striking resemblance to the New York Free Banking Act. The most important feature common to both was the provision

[7] Swanson, *The Establishment of the National Banking System*, p. 82. It was the Sherman draft of the bill which was actually passed.

[8] Congressional Globe, Vol. 60, pp. 843, ff.

[9] Congressional Globe, Vol. 60, p. 581 (February 10, 1863).

for the issuance of notes only upon the basis of public securities deposited as collateral with a public officer. Though identical in principle, the National Act was more detailed in its regulation of bank-note issues than its prototype in New York. The amount to be issued by any one national bank might vary between one-third and the total of its paid-in capital. For all the banks in the system, not more than 300 million dollars of notes could be issued, one-half of which was to be apportioned among the banks according to population, and the other half according to the demands of business. To the noteholder the currency issued by the national banks had an important advantage over that of the New York free banks, in the fact that it was given first lien upon the assets of a failed bank. In New York the notes were secured only by the securities in the hands of the Comptroller, and when that collateral had to be liquidated hurriedly it usually brought far less in the market than the notes outstanding against it. The national bank notes were therefore safer than the notes of New York.

The original National Bank Act required also that a lawful money reserve of 25 per cent be held by each bank against its notes and deposits. But banks located in smaller towns had to keep only two-fifths of that amount, or 10 per cent, actually in their vaults. The rest, 15 per cent, might be deposited with a national bank in any one of the nine large cities, Boston, New York, Philadelphia, Baltimore, Cincinnati, New Orleans, Providence, Chicago, and St. Louis. Since many of the country banks already had such balances on deposit with city banks, this clause of the law merely gave legal sanction to a practice which had long existed. But upon the banks of the eight large cities this law bore with considerable severity for they also customarily kept in New York balances which could not now be counted as reserve.

In this respect the national law owed little to that of New York, for the original law in that state had included a reserve of 12½ per cent against notes only and even that scanty provision had been repealed two years after its passage. There had been other attempts to incorporate a specie-reserve requirement in the New York law, but without success. The inclusion of deposit liabilities with notes as the basis for computing reserve percentages under the national law was in line with the most advanced banking practice. In New York City after the panic of 1857 the banks in the Clearing House Association had voluntarily agreed to maintain a specie reserve of 20 per cent against notes and deposits, and in 1860 had raised it to 25 per cent. Similar provisions had been incorporated as recently as 1858 in the law of Massachusetts which required a specie reserve of 15 per cent against deposits and notes; in a requirement for 25 per cent specie reserve for the Bank of Iowa, and in the still more stringent law of Louisiana, for a reserve of 33-1/3 per cent against all liabilities. In a number of other states a reserve was required against notes only, and ranged from a negligible 5 per cent in Maine, 10 per cent in Connecticut, and 20 per cent in Virginia, to a high point of 30 per cent in Ohio.[10]

There were many minor points of similarity between the national and the New York laws. Both contained provisions for regular reports from banks organized under their requirements; both contained detailed regulations for the sale of the collateral security of the notes issued and the subsequent reimbursement of note holders.[11]

The new law became at once the center of acrimonious controversy. But like that which had preceded its passage in Congress, the discussion of the law by the public showed little conception of the place the system would occupy in the future development of the money market. The report of the New York Clearing House Committee, for example, although it might have been expected to display more financial wisdom, expressed an opposition to the system which was based upon the most trivial grounds. The fact that most of the national banks organized in the first months after the law had gone into effect were small banks, was taken as evidence that the larger and more important banks of the country would never enter the system. The national

[10] Knox, *History of Banking in the United States*. Dewey, *State Banking before the Civl War*, pp. 217-24.

[11] Bonnefoux, *Vindication of the Free Banking System* (1848). Dunbar, *Economic Essays*, p. 338.

bank notes were criticized because they were not legal tender, a fact certainly not to their discredit, and they were accused also of producing inflation.

Gradually the attitude of New York City became one ot resignation to the new plan and the opposition grew less. New York state could not but commend the national government for adopting a currency principle which she had inaugurated, and which had proved on the whole satisfactory during a trial of nearly fifteen years. If the city banks saw little advantage for themselves in the change from state to national charter, they at least had little to fear from the competition of the new currency. They derived little profit from circulation, and two of the largest banks, the Bank of Commerce and the City Bank, had abandoned the issue of notes altogether because they found the trouble and expense greater than the return.[12]

The small country bankers suffered most from the new law. The steady trend away from bank notes to deposit currency, which was so marked a feature of city banking, had affected small-town bankers to a much less degree. When the tax of 10 per cent was imposed on state bank notes in 1866, they were practically forced into the new system, and they had considerable reason to feel that the law discriminated against them. It was for them and not for the large city institutions that the New York state bank superintendent spoke when he protested against the tax upon state bank notes.[13] By 1864 however the superintendent felt that it was useless to plead the cause of the state banks against the national system, and he recommended that the legislature pass a law to expedite the change from state to national charter for banks which wished to make it. The legislature had its own grievance against the national banks, for they were not subject to state taxation, and if state banks in large numbers should reorganize under the National Bank Act a considerable source of revenue would be lost. Moreover the state banks of New York held large amounts of state stock which would be thrown upon the market when the reorganization

[12] *New York State Chamber of Commerce Report*, 1860-1861, p. 290; New York State Superintendent of Banks Report, 1854, pp. 12, 16.

[13] New York State Superintendent of Banks, *Report*, 1863.

took place. The first report upon the law to legalize the change was therefore adverse, but eventually on March 9, 1865, the legislature succumbed to the combination of prudential and patriotic reasons and the act was passed which enabled a state bank to make the transition to a national charter without first going through a lengthy process of liquidation.[14]

The Act of 1863 and the reserve situation

Outside banks had been in the habit of keeping part of their reserves in the form of deposits in New York City for many years before the National Banking Act recognized and legalized that practice.[15] How did the actual reserves which the state banks had been accustomed to keep compare with the requirements laid down for the new national banks? The act as it was passed in February, 1863, required a reserve of 25 per cent of lawful money to be kept against both notes and deposits, with the provision that banks outside of nine large cities might keep three-fifths of that reserve on deposit with a national bank in any one of the nine cities. The term "deposits" was not defined, either in this act or in the revisions during 1864 and 1865. The practice of the comptroller's office, however, in computing the total deposits for reserve purposes, was to add together the government deposits and the time and demand individual deposits. To this sum was also added the net balance due to other banks, if there were such a balance. If the sum due from banks was greater than the sum due to banks, those items in the balance sheet were ignored.[16]

In order to determine what changes were introduced into the reserve situation by the National Banking Act, the state bank reports for 1859 and 1860 have been studied. These dates avoid the panic of 1857 on the one side and the abnormal conditions of the War on the other. The reports published by the Secretary of the Treasury cover 27 of the 33 states in the Union at that

[14] *Bankers' Magazine*, Vol. 18, p. 964. New York State Superintendent of Banks, *Report*, 1861, p. XV; 1864, p. X.

[15] See p. 103 above.

[16] Letter to the author from Deputy Comptroller of the Currency, March 30, 1928.

time and include practically the whole banking area of the country. The cash funds and principal liabilities reported by state banks in these cities in 1859 and 1860 are presented in the table below.

RESERVES HELD BY STATE BANKS IN THE NINE REDEMPTION CITIES NAMED IN THE ACT OF 1863*

(In thousands of dollars)

	1859	*1860*
Liabilities:		
Notes	$36,445	$30,248
Individual deposits	143,610	142,901
Net balance due to banks	24,008	25,983
TOTAL	$204,063	$199,132
Specie reserve	$46,293	$49,272
Per cent of reserve to liabilities	22.7	24.7

* These cities were Boston, New York, Philadelphia, Baltimore, Cincinnati, New Orleans, Providence, Chicago and St. Louis. All figures are for the end of the year.

It is evident from the figures given that the requirement of 25 per cent reserve against notes and deposits was not greatly in excess of that which the state banks of the larger cities had been accustomed to keep. There was of course considerable variation among the cities of the group. In 1860, for example, Providence stood lowest with a specie reserve of only 6 per cent, while New Orleans was at the other end of the scale with a reserve of nearly 40 per cent. New York was close to the average of the group, with a specie reserve of 24 per cent of deposits and circulation.

Outside of the nine cities, the reserve required for national banks was the same in amount, but only 10 per cent had to be kept in specie in the banks' own vaults; the remaining 15 per cent might be kept in the alternative form of balances in national banks in the nine cities. The actual reserve of these country banks for 1859 and 1860 is given for comparison with what they would have been under the national law of 1863.

The average reserves of the country banks in 1859 and 1860, like those of the larger cities, came very close to the requirements of the National Bank Act of 1863. Banks in many states were well above this average. Missouri, Ohio, Iowa, Illinois, among the western states; Kentucky, Tennessee, North Carolina, and Maryland, among the southern; Vermont among the

RESERVES HELD BY COUNTRY BANKS AS DEFINED BY THE ACT OF 1863

(*In thousands of dollars*)

	1859	*1860*
Liabilities		
Notes	$170,757	$153,379
Individual deposits	108,558	105,272
TOTAL	$279,315	$258,651
Reserve:		
Specie	$37,330	$35,276
Net balances due from banks	27,931	25,318
TOTAL	$65,261	$60,594
Per cent of reserve to liabilities:		
Specie	13.4	13.6
Balances	10.0	9.8
TOTAL	23.4	23.4

New England states, had reserves ranging from 30 to 50 per cent. At the other extreme, with low reserves, must be placed New York state country banks, with cash reserves against notes and deposits of only 3 per cent, and with reserve balances of only 2 per cent.[17] The New England banks showed a tendency to keep very low reserves of actual cash, but brought up their total reserves by large balances in Boston, a situation for which the Suffolk bank system of note redemption in Boston was probably responsible.

[17] The notes of New York banks were covered also by securities to the full amount of their issue.

The 1864 revision of the National Bank Act

The many criticisms to which the new act had been subjected by friends as well as by opponents had demonstrated the necessity for a thorough revision. In March, 1864, therefore, Representative Hooper of Massachusetts, who had had a large share in the passage of the original act, introduced into the House a new bill whose purpose was to strengthen and clarify the law, and to make it more advantageous for state banks to join the system. The first act had suffered from hasty drafting and insufficient debate, but this revised version was the subject of prolonged discussion. The most serious controversy arose over the right of states and municipalities to tax the stock of national banks, and the place of redemption for the notes.

In the original act the notes had been made redeemable only at the counters of the issuing bank. In order to make the currency truly national, it was obvious that the notes should be redeemable also at some central place or places. Many of the western members favored New York as the best city for the purpose;[18] while members from other large cities wished to have those points made redemption cities also. The debate centered around the question whether New York alone, or New York and other cities, should be selected. Seventeen different places were finally named in any one of which, with the approval of the comptroller, a bank might redeem its bills. Exhausted by the labor of arriving at this decision, the House voted to lay the bill on the table.[19] The indefatigable Mr. Hooper at once introduced another bill, similar in all important respects to its predecessor. This passed the House and went to the Senate on April 26. Again the debate centered around taxation and redemption. After a letter from Secretary Chase it was finally agreed that taxation of national banks should be restricted to the national government. With regard to the cities in which banks might re-

[18] Since one of the purposes in revising the Act was to make it more palatable to the state banks, Mr. Brooks asked that representatives of the New York banks who had been outspoken opponents, be permitted to appear. He was told that a committee from that city had submitted their amendments but that all of them had already been incorporated in the bill except that one which removed the office of the Comptroller to New York.

[19] Congressional Globe, 38 Congress, 1 Session, Part 2, Vol. 62, p. 1378.

deem their notes, the Senate overruled the House and selected only New York, Philadelphia and Boston, where a charge of ¼ per cent might be made for redemption. In the conference committee, however, the redemption privilege was given to eighten cities besides New York, and banks in those cities were required to redeem their notes at par in a national bank in New York City. Banks in other cities and towns could redeem at a national bank in New York or in one of the other redemption cities.[20]

The reserve requirements were also changed; a bank in New York City or one of the eighteen redemption cities was compelled to keep "on hand, in lawful money of the United States, an amount equal to at least 25 per cent of the aggregate amount of its notes in circulation and its deposits." But half of the reserve of banks in the eighteen redemption cities might be kept in cash deposits in New York City. For banks in other cities and towns, a reserve of 15 per cent was considered large enough, three-fifths of which might consist of balances with a national bank in one of the redemption cities.[21] Unfortunately the decision to make this change was formed in conference committee of which no minutes were published. Since the purpose of the revision as a whole however was to attract state banks into the national system, we may be fairly certain that the lower reserves for country banks were intended as an inducement to them to exchange their state, for national, charters.

The Act of 1864 and the reserve situation

The legal standards for reserves in the law of 1863 were slightly above the actual practice of the banks in 1859-1860; the revised requirements established in 1864 were somewhat lower. The new law set New York City apart from all others as a central reserve city whose national banks were obliged to keep a reserve of 25 per cent. It is evident from the table that the

[20] The redemption cities named were St. Louis, Louisville, Chicago, Detroit, Milwaukee, New Orleans, Cincinnati, Cleveland, Pittsburgh, Baltimore, Philadelphia, Boston, New York, Albany, Leavenworth, San Francisco, and Washington; and Charleston and Richmond might be added to the list when the war was over. Sections 31, 32, 45, of revised law of June 6, 1864.

[21] Congressional Globe, 38 Congress, 1 Session, Part 3, Vol. 63; p. 2143.

banks of New York City in 1859 fell short of the 20 per cent reserve which they had set as a standard in 1857; and that in 1860 they failed to attain the 25 per cent standard adopted in the same year. The new national requirements were therefore slightly above the practice of the banks, although not above their own aim.

RESERVES HELD BY BANKS IN NEW YORK CITY

(*In thousands of dollars*)

	1859	*1860*
Liabilities:		
Notes	$8,251	$8,000
Individual deposits	73,542	78,792
Net balances due to banks	22,694	17,206
TOTAL	$104,487	$103,998
Specie reserve	$19,566	$24,706
Per cent of reserve to liabilities	18.7	23.8

The Act of 1864 retained the 25 per cent reserve for large cities (increasing their number from nine to eighteen) but permitted them to redeposit half of that amount in the national banks of New York City. Reports are not available for all of the eighteen cities named as redemption centers in the 1864 amendments. San Francisco, Leavenworth, and Washington are not included in the total for 1859 and 1860, and the following table includes only fifteen cities: Boston, Philadelphia, Baltimore, Cincinnati, New Orleans, Chicago, and St. Louis of the earlier list, and the additional cities, Louisville, Detroit, Milwaukee, Cleveland, Pittsburgh, Albany, Charleston and Richmond. Providence, which had been named in the Act of 1863, was left out of the list in 1864.

The reserves actually held in the redemption cities in 1860 appear to be larger than those which these cities would have been required to hold if the National Bank Act had then been in force. When they are considered individually instead of as a group, part of this excess is seen to be the effect of the high reserves of the banks of New Orleans, which carried a cash reserve of nearly 40 per cent, but the average specie reserve of the others was still almost 20 per cent. What additional reserves. in the form of deposits in New York, were kept by the banks of these cities is impossible to tell from the material available in the published reports.

RESERVES HELD BY FIFTEEN OF THE EIGHTEEN REDEMPTION CITIES NAMED IN THE AMENDED ACT OF 1864

(In thousands of dollars)

	1859	*1860*
Liabilities:		
Notes	$43,529	$34,697
Individual deposits	85,304	77,036
Net balances due to banks	7,360	8,774
TOTAL	$136,193	$120,507
Specie reserve	$31,958	$28,873
Per cent of specie reserve to liabilities	23.4	24.0

For the country banks, as well as for those in large cities, the new law made important concessions. In place of the 10 per cent in cash and 15 per cent in balances which had been required in 1863, the law of 1864 set 6 per cent in cash and 9 per cent in balances. This was a substantial reduction, and brought the reserve requirements to a figure well below the average reserves actually maintained by country banks in 1859 and 1860 (see page 224). It was a change in conformity with the policy which had governed much of the revision—the desire to make the national charter attractive to existing state banks.

The conclusion to which these figures lead is that the National Bank Act did not greatly raise the existing standards in regard to reserves. This conclusion is confirmed by the opinion of a contemporary observer, who wrote in 1868:

The provisions of the National Currency Act do not as is popularly supposed, much increase the aggregate bank reserves of specie of the whole country, beyond what has been the customary holding. Assuming that the required reserve will average, as between the city and country banks, 20 per cent for all, it will not much exceed the average holding for seven years (1856-1862) prior to the passage of the law, which was 18-6/10 per cent. But it will equalize the distribution of a fund, which has hitherto been very unequally distributed; and as the strong banks will probably not keep less specie than before, while the weak ones will be compelled to keep much more, the aggregate reserve should be considerably increased.[22]

The most important change in the reserve requirements of the revised law was the permission accorded to national banks in the redemption cities to keep half of their reserves in the form of balances with national banks in New York City, and half in lawful money in the bank's own vault. Did this also accord with conditions existing under the state bank régime?

The bankers' deposits which might have been kept in the banks of New York City if the revised National Bank Act of 1864 had been in force in December, 1860, may be computed as follows:

The total of country bank notes and deposits was	$253,383,000
A reserve of 15 per cent on this sum was	38,000,000
Assuming that three-fifths of this was kept on deposit in redemption cities	22,800,000
And adding the notes and individual deposits of those cities	117,712,000
The total of demand liabilities at banks in redemption cities was	140,512,000
Upon which a reserve of 25 per cent amounted to	35,128,000
Of this sum, one-half might be on deposit in New York, producing bankers' balances in that city of	17,564,000
Which compares very closely with the actual net bankers' balances of	17,287,000

The figures just given are particularly interesting because they prove that there was concentration of reserves in New York

22 George Walker in *Bankers' Magazine*, Vol. XXII, March, 1868, p. 699.

before the passage of the National Bank Act. The "pyramiding" of reserve funds, for which the act has so often been blamed, was not a creature of the act, but the reason for many of its provisions. Since the temper of the people and the history of American banking made the establishment of a genuine central bank an impossibility, legal recognition of the New York City banks as holders of the ultimate banking reserve of the nation was the only alternative, for the course of trade inevitably drove funds to that center.

The importance of the national banking law should not be minimized because it introduced no drastic innovation in respect to reserves. It determined the general plan of development which banking in the next fifty years was to follow, and the whole course of the money market was inextricably bound up with that of the banks. One of its contributions was the simplification of the currency by the elimination of state bank notes. It was of particular helpfulness to have one form of bank note, issued under one law for the whole country, substituted for the multitudinous bits of paper which had formerly been circulated by authority of the most various laws. It is true that the state bank notes had possessed a certain amount of elasticity, from the fact that every bank was eager to send home the notes of its rivals for redemption, and issue in their place its own, but the heavy discount to which many of these notes were subject, the frequency and the ease with which they were counterfeited, and the danger of failure of the bank issuing them, more than offset the elasticity with which they were endowed.

Branch banking under the Act

A feature of the National Bank Act which had important consequences for the economic development of the country was its failure to authorize the establishment of branches. The prejudice which prevented the growth of a branch-banking system was part of the ancient hatred of "monopoly" which was characteristically American and which had been the undoing of the First and Second Banks of the United States. State-chartered banks with branches, like the State Bank of Indiana and the

State Bank of Missouri, had for the most part come to grief in the panic of 1837 or that of 1857, and after 1865 the fact that they could not issue notes prevented the establishment of any others. In the New York Free Banking Act, upon which many of the other states based their own bank laws, branch banks were definitely prohibited.

The National Bank Act of 1863 did not follow the New York law in its definite prohibition of branches. Indeed in that first draft of the Act there was an implied permission for branches, since national banks were empowered, among other things, to carry on their business in "offices." When the law was revised in 1864, the plural form of the word was changed to the singular, and a national bank was thereafter able to operate only in a "banking house or office." In both cases however the actual phrasing of the law seems to have been accidental rather than the result of a conscious policy towards branch banking, and the change from "offices" to "office" was probably an inadvertence. The subject of branches seems never to have been mentioned in the Congressional debates which preceded the passage of the two laws. In the case of the first Act, the speed with which the bill was rushed through may explain the omission. But in the revision of 1864 there was long and animated discussions of many provisions of the law. Special attention was paid to the plight of small towns, and the minimum capital was reduced from $100,000 to $50,000 in order to give them banking facilities, but not once was the possibility mentioned of meeting their needs with branch banks.

In 1865 the subject of branches was brought up in an amendment to the Revenue Act, permitting state banks already in possession of branches to keep them when they came under national charter. It was sponsored by Representative Van Winkle of West Virginia, in order to save the branch banks of several small towns in his state which would otherwise have been deprived of banking facilities.[23] The amendment was passed almost without comment, and no one suggested that branches be allowed to all national banks. Very few state banks availed

[23] Congressional Globe, 38 Congress, 2 Session, p. 1281.

themselves of the privilege, and there was little demand for similar rights from banks organized originally under national charter.

Gradually the lack of the branch-banking privilege made itself felt. Even the Comptroller of the Currency joined in the plea for an amendment to the National Bank Act, and in 1895 and 1896 included in his annual report a recommendation that branches be permitted where towns were so small that it would be impossible under the law for them to have a national bank. Since many state banking laws also forbade the organization of banks in small towns, they were entirely without banking facilities. The success of the Canadian system, as evidenced in the greater stability of interest rates in that country, was the strongest argument in the case for branch banks. In Canada the 37 chartered banks which were in existence in 1899 had 600 offices scattered about the country, and the competition between them for the business of the farming districts was so keen that even in the remote parts of the country the rate of discount was not more than 2 per cent above that of the largest cities. The proposal to permit branch banking in the United States made little headway, however, and it is still being debated as acrimoniously as ever.

Importance of the Act in the history of the money market

The National Bank Act was designed to meet the chief currency need of its time, that for a secure and nationally acceptable bank note. This was in complete accord with the concept of banking which had always governed American thought, that the first function of a bank was to issue paper money. The larger rôle to be played by banks in the developing credit economy was not comprehended, and would probably not have affected the act if it had been, owing to the time-honored distrust of banking "monopolies." Its primary purpose was successfully achieved, but its primary purpose was narrow. It was nevertheless the most important single piece of legislation affecting the money market in this period. By establishing the currency on a basis of unquestionable soundness, however inelastic, it permitted reformers to concentrate their attention upon other aspects of the financial situation, and until after the panic of 1893 it relegated the note-issue function of banks, which had held the center of the stage for nearly a century, to an inconspicuous position. New problems took its place as the scenes shifted.

CHAPTER XII

BANK RESERVES: THE BASIS OF THE MONEY MARKET

The reserves of the New York City banks, in the period from 1863 to 1913, were a factor of primary importance to every phase of money market activity. The call loan market, the commercial paper market, the security market, were all subject to their influence. A declining reserve ratio had been considered a warning signal by prudent bankers and business men even before 1863, but it had not then attained full legal recognition as a controlling element in the amount of bank credit to be issued. Before 1863 the reserve ratio was a slip leash which loosely held together the cash reserve and the total of bank credit outstanding; from 1863 to 1913 it was a rope of limited length which jerked the banks up sharply if they ventured too far in the direction of expansion.

New York reserves the central reserve of the nation

The responsibilities of the New York banks in the matter of reserves were increased by the changing conception of the function of bank reserves in the financial life of the community. At the beginning of the national bank period there was still a survival of the feeling which had long been prevalent in the United States that the privilege of organizing a bank was a kind of monopoly of the profitable privilege of note issue, and that the first duty of a bank was to keep these notes redeemable in specie. This attitude was reflected in the original requirement of the National Bank Act that a specie reserve be held against notes in addition to the bond collateral which more than covered them.

While the financial organization was still so primitive that proceeds of bank loans were taken out largely in the form of notes, and the ratio of deposits to notes was relatively small, protection of bank creditors was sufficiently assured by the certainty of note redemption. But as deposits increased in importance among bank liabilities and notes declined, protection of the note holder ceased to be enough and it became of equal, and then of greater, importance to protect the depositor. As the issue of bank credit came to take the form of deposits more frequently than of notes, the deposit of actual cash in banks was diminished and deposit credits arising from extensions of bank credit became more important. The banks' responsibility for these deposits was asserted by the provision of the National Bank Act requiring a definite reserve to be held against them, and by similar provisions in many state banking laws. Just as public opinion had come to demand that banks protect depositors as well as holders of notes, it began to insist upon a still larger measure of responsibility from banks and to demand that the reserve be sufficient not only to prevent loss to note holder and depositor but also to prevent any breakdown in the banking system. In other words, the general public was now dependent upon bank credit and was entitled to protection. These demands fell with particular gravity upon the banks of New York, which carried the reserve burden of the country.

Declining reserves of national banks

The National Bank Act had set a standard for reserves which was close to the prevailing practice of state banks of that time.[1] During the first years of the new system actual reserves were kept well above the legal figure, due perhaps to the high standards of banking practice enforced by the comptroller and by the necessity of making reports at frequent intervals. In 1868, for example, the reserves of the country banks averaged 24 per cent as compared with the legal minimum of 15, and nearly half of the reserve, or 12 per cent, was kept in actual cash, although under the law cash need have been only 6 per cent. But by 1873 the margin between the actual and the required reserve had grown narrower. In that year the average reserves of country national banks stood at 21 per cent of deposits and circulation.

The reserves of banks in redemption cities showed the same

[1] See p. 226 above.

tendency to creep downward to the minimum. In 1868 the average reserve of the national banks in these fifteen cities was 31 per cent as compared with the legal minimum of 25. The proportion of cash was also above that required, 23 per cent against

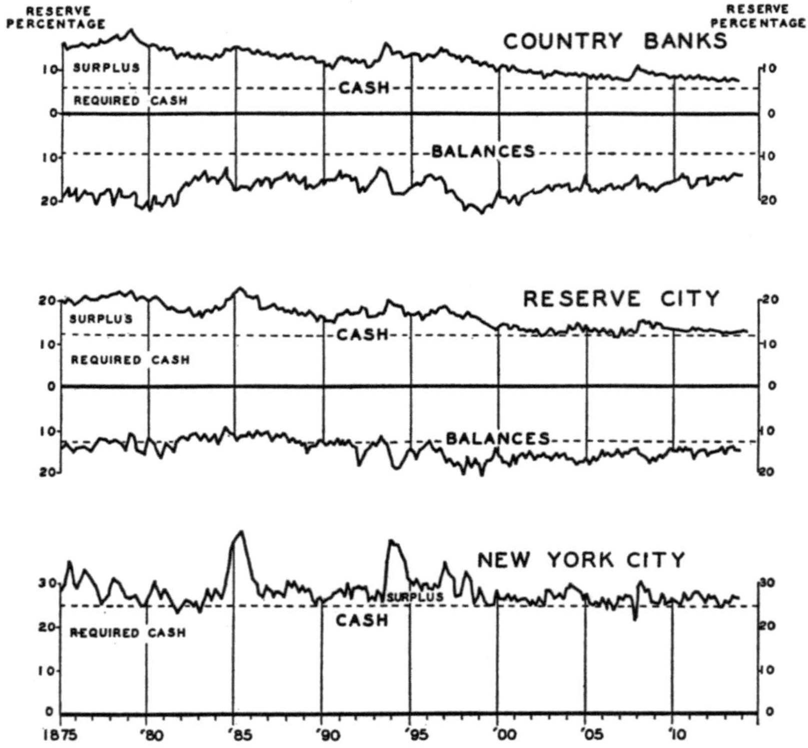

CASH RESERVES AND RESERVE BALANCES OF THREE GROUPS OF NATIONAL BANKS, BY CALLS.

SOURCE: ANNUAL REPORTS OF THE COMPTROLLER OF THE CURRENCY.

the permissible 12½. By 1873 these averages had fallen to 27 per cent for total reserves, and 20 for the cash portion; the margin above the legal minimum had been reduced from 6 points to 2.

Following the panic of 1873, which gave ample evidence of inherent defects in the banking system, popular demand centered upon an increase in the amount of money in circulation rather than upon a reform of the reserve requirements. It was for the purpose of releasing greenbacks rather than to increase the surplus reserve that the Act of June 20, 1874, altered the reserve provisions by requiring the reserve percentage to be computed thereafter only against deposits; notes, which were already secured by government bonds, were no longer to be included in the computation. This change released about 44 millions of greenbacks which had been locked up in bank vaults as reserve against notes in circulation, and temporarily satisfied the demand for more money.[2] Its effect upon the banks was to put them in possession of excess reserves and increase the reserve margins in country and reserve cities by about 12 per cent. The process of wearing down the margin thereupon began all over again, and the actual reserve crept steadily closer to the minimum. The course of this movement is shown in the diagram on page 236.

It is apparent that both country banks and banks in reserve cities tended to reduce their holdings of cash more rapidly than their reserve balances. The reasons for this were the same as those which had been instrumental in building up large bankers' balances in New York before 1863—the relative profitableness of balances as compared with till money.[3] Cash reserves in the course of the years after 1874 fell to a point much nearer the legal minimum than did the balances, so that they could fall very little more without crossing the legal line. Consequently the changes in reserve ratio were confined largely to that part of the reserve which took the form of balances, and the surplus reserves of the banks were usually in the form of balances with other banks. Variations in the cash reserves of country banks seldom amounted to more than 1 or 2 per cent about the downward trend, while variations in balances were frequently as much as 4 and 5 per cent on either side of the trend line. When these percentage changes were translated into millions of dollars they made a not inconsiderable item, and the wide fluctuations in country bank balances at New York had important consequences for the banks there.

[2] Congressional Record, 43 Congress, 1 Session, p. 5312, re House Bill 1572, June 20, 1874.
[3] See p. 103 above.

The use of actual cash in the American banking system was being steadily economized and a larger volume of credit was being based upon a shrinking ratio of specie and legal tenders. This economy was made possible by the substitution of deposit credit for cash payment in ordinary transactions so that banks were able to meet daily requirements with relatively less till money than before. New York City depositors had long shown a preference for checks rather than for specie and, as banking facilities became available, this preference made itself evident in other cities and eventually in country districts. In 1870 notes issued by national banks outside of New York were equal to their bank deposits, but by 1913 the note circulation had dropped to one-eighth of the deposits. Another measure of the same tendency is given by the ratio of deposits to total money in circulation.[4] In 1881, deposits were 2.76 times as great as the quantity of money in circulation; by 1899 the ratio had risen to 3.96, and by 1913 to 4.36. In 1922 it stood at 5.80, indicating that the tendency towards the substitution of deposit currency for cash was continuing beyond the half century being studied here, as it had begun before it.

Another reason for the ability of the banking system to carry on with a steadily declining proportion of cash reserve was the fact that the deposits of country banks, on which the lowest cash reserves were required, grew more rapidly than those of reserve and central reserve city banks on which the required reserve was higher. Whereas in 1875 the net deposits of New York City banks had been approximately equal to those of all the country national banks, by 1910 they were only half as large; New York deposits, with a 25 per cent cash reserve, had increased only five-fold, roughly speaking, while the country deposits, with a 6 per cent cash reserve, had increased ten-fold.

Still another factor was the increasing centralization of reserves, effected by the substitution of reserve balances for cash. The cash reserve of country banks tended to fall closer and closer to the legal minimum, while the excess reserve was kept

[4] Computed originally by Professor Fisher, and carried on by the Federal Reserve Bank of New York.

in the form of balances in the banks of reserve and central reserve cities. Since at most the cash reserve held by the depositary bank against such balances was 25 per cent, the proportion of cash to the original deposit of the country bank was cut to a very low figure. It is worthy of note that since the further centralization of reserves under the Federal Reserve system, the proportion of cash reserves to member bank deposits has reached still lower levels.

There was wide variation among the different sections of the Union in respect to the total amount of reserves carried, and to the apportionment of the reserves between cash and balances. In general the highly industrial sections of the country which were equipped with more adequate banking facilities tended to keep a large share of reserves as balances and a small proportion as cash, while the agricultural sections followed the reverse policy. The highest proportion of cash reserve was to be found in the western states. This was a reflection of the preference for coin money which still prevails in the West, a vestigial remnant of the days when national banks of the West refused to issue notes redeemable in paper and received special license to circulate notes payable only in gold.[5] In some of the western states the high ratio of specie reserve was accompanied by high balances with other banks as well; in others the reserve balances fell below the permissible 9 per cent.

The next highest cash reserves were held by the banks of the southern states which combined a high proportion of cash reserve—more than twice the legal minimum—with a widely varying proportion of reserve balances. During the autumn and summer the balances for this group of states sometimes fell to 9 per cent, to rise during the winter to twice that figure.

The lowest cash reserves were held by the country banks of New England and the middle Atlantic states where the population was more largely urban and the banking system more highly developed than elsewhere. The cash reserve in these states was kept close to the legal minimum of 6 per cent, and variation in reserves was confined to the balances.

[5] Act of July 12, 1870.

Concentration of reserves in New York

Until 1887 New York was the only central reserve city in the country. In that year an amendment to the law gave cities of 50,000 or above the privilege of becoming reserve cities, and cities of 200,000 or above the privilege of becoming central reserve cities, upon application of three-fourths of their national banks. Chicago and St. Louis at once took advantage of this opportunity and were raised from reserve to central reserve cities with the responsibility of maintaining cash reserves of 25 per cent and the attendant privilege of holding reserve balances for reserve city and country bankers. Although the primary aim of the legislators in passing this bill was "to relieve Congress from this contention between rival cities," in the words of Mr. Sherman, outside of Congress there was great expectation that the creation of other central reserve centers would take from New York part of the responsibility for banking reserves which she had hitherto carried. In the "rival cities" themselves there was the determination to use this means of wresting from New York the prestige and financial preëminence which caused such envy among the growing towns of the West. Although bankers' balances of those cities did increase rapidly—in Chicago five-fold between 1890 and 1910, in St. Louis eightfold, as compared with a threefold increase in individual deposits—bankers' balances in New York showed no slackening in their own rate of growth. The rapid increase in the balances at Chicago and St. Louis was due rather to the geographical expansion of the country than to a loss of position by New York. Balances in Chicago came largely from banks in contiguous states and the same was true of St. Louis. Farther to the West and South banks continued to turn to New York in selecting their city correspondents.[6] The national banking system was often discussed as if it were a complete hierarchy, with the country banks depositing their reserve balances in the banks of the reserve cities, while the banks of those cities in turn kept their balances in New York. The National Bank Act made such an organiza-

[6] *Bankers' Magazine*, Vol. 78, p. 187, 1909. Senate Federal Reserve Hearings, 1913; 63 Congress, 1 Session, Senate Document 232, pp. 224, 1671.

tion permissive, but the actual operation of the system was by no means as simple as this would indicate. Many of the country banks skipped entirely over the reserve cities and took their balances directly to the central reserve city banks.

It is true that the ratio of New York balances tended to fall off in proportion to the total deposits of the country, but not because of the competition of Chicago and St. Louis. It was the reserve cities which were more than holding their own, not only against New York but against the three central reserve cities combined, in the matter of country bankers' balances. The development of local banking centers with the possibility of securing adequate correspondent services nearer home may have been responsible, and if the movement had gone far enough it would have served as a valuable antidote to the centralization of reserves in New York. But neither the selection of two additional central reserve cities nor the increase in the balances held by the reserve cities was sufficient to take from the New York banks the burden of all unusual demands for money and credit

TOTAL BANKERS' BALANCES AND INDIVIDUAL DEPOSITS IN NATIONAL BANKS OF CENTRAL RESERVE CITIES

(Date nearest October 1 each year; in millions of dollars)

Year	*New York*			*Chicago**			*St. Louis**		
	To national banks	*To all banks*	*To individuals*	*To national banks*	*To all banks*	*To individuals*	*To national banks*	*To all banks*	*To individuals*
1870	55.9	72.2	104	2.9	5.3	13.9	0.8	1.1	3.5
1875	69.0	94.2	123	5.9	10.3	20.3	1.7	3.0	5.4
1880	105.9	137.2	147	11.6	19.9	23.5	2.3	6.1	5.3
1885	105.7	139.8	195	17.0	28.1	41.0	2.0	4.2	5.6
1890	124.3	173.4	187	26.8	46.6	59.7	5.4	10.4	21.7
1895	139.9	206.0	269	32.7	52.7	67.3	7.6	13.7	18.1
1900	260.0	431.0	345	88.3	133.5	102.9	22.5	38.4	30.8
1905	303.1	583.6	464	119.8	177.9	140.0	43.8	71.7	63.6
1910	315.0	618.0	523	136.0	218.1	191.7	51.3	80.6	71.4

* Chicago and St. Louis were not classed as central reserve cities until 1887.

and the panic of 1907 bore as heavily upon the city as had the panic of 1873.

The most significant feature shown by this compilation is the greater growth in bankers' than in individual deposits. While the latter increased nearly fivefold between 1870 and 1910, the former increased nearly eight times. In 1870 deposits of bankers in the national banks of New York City were about two-thirds as large as the deposits of individuals, but by 1900 bankers' had outstripped individual deposits, and the distance between them steadily widened. It is noteworthy also that the deposits of state banks and trust companies in the national banks of New York increased three times as rapidly as those of country national banks. The deposits due to bankers by banks in central reserve cities were therefore made up of balances owing to many different kinds of banks. Some of the state laws recognized this situation and permitted their banks to count certain types of balances as part of reserves in much the same way as national banks did. But since the large banks of New York upon which the responsibility for reserves ultimately rested were national banks, a study of their reserves will throw light upon the situation of all the banks. Moreover it was the national banks that always controlled the greater part of the individual deposits. State banks increased rapidly in number after 1879[7] and by 1913 were almost twice as numerous as national banks, but even then their deposits were only half as great as those of national banks.

Concentration of balances within New York

The pyramiding of reserves in New York had put a heavy responsibility in the hands of the city banks. This effect was heightened by a further concentration within the city, and the result was that a few large banks held virtual control of the whole credit structure whenever a hint of disaster started a withdrawal of reserves from New York.

One evidence of this increasing concentration was apparent in the changes in Clearing House membership. The smaller,

[7] Barnett, *State Banking, etc.*

weaker banks of the city had never been members, but had cleared through a member correspondent; the advantages of membership were left to the larger and stronger banks. The Clearing House enjoyed a considerable prestige, and actually exercised a large measure of power in such matters as the issue of loan certificates during panics and in relations with the treasury. In spite of the growing importance of such actions, the circle of members which shared this authority grew steadily smaller. As the table below indicates, the increase in the proportion of banking assets represented by the members was accompanied by a decrease in the number of banks owning those assets. A marked division was appearing between the large and strong member banks, and the small and relatively weak non-members.

CLEARING HOUSE MEMBERSHIP OF NATIONAL AND STATE BANKS, 1870-1910*

Year	*Number of banks*	*Capital and surplus (In millions of dollars)*
1870		
Members	68	$115
Non-members	10	6
1890		
Members	63	$123
Non-members	32	8
1910		
Members	49	$322
Non-members	29	21

* Table prepared from material in the official reports of the Comptroller of the Currency, and the New York State Superintendent of Banks. Trust companies are not included in this table.

The national banks of New York City were on the average larger than the state banks, and nearly all of them were members of the Clearing House. Only half of the state banks were members, and about the same proportion of trust companies after they were given an opportunity to join in 1911.

Within the national group of Clearing House members there was a further narrowing of power, an inner circle of big national banks which quite overshadowed the rest in total assets, in individual deposits, and most of all in bankers' balances. This tendency for bankers' balances to collect in the hands of a few banks had been apparent many years before the passage of the National Bank Act,[8] but it became more and more pronounced in the years between 1863 and 1913.

TYPES OF BANKS IN CLEARING HOUSE

Year	*All banks in New York City*			*Banks in Clearing House*		
	National	*State*	*Trust Companies*	*National*	*State*	*Trust Companies*
1870 . . .	54	24		49	19	
1890 . . .	47	48	13	43	20	
1910 . . .	39	39	35	31	18	

In 1870, when there were 54 national banks in the city, nine of them belonged to this upper group; in 1880, the number of banks had dropped to 47 but there were still 9 in the upper group. With the same total number of national banks, the top group fell to 7 in 1890, remained at that number in 1900, and stood at 6 in 1910. Changes in the number of these large banks tells only part of the story; another is made clear by the table which gives the relative position of each New York bank with respect to bankers' balances and shows the widening gap between the large holders and the small holders. By 1910 the largest amount of balances held by a bank in the smaller group was less than half as great as the smallest amount for the larger group.

The state banks in New York City fell, in respect to bankers' balances, into the lower group in each decade. Since the reports for state banks appeared on dates different from those of the national banks, and since the categories of the statement are not strictly comparable for the two classes of banks, the reports of the national banks have been made the basis for the study of concentration of balances, and the reports of the state banks,

[8] See p. 115 above.

where used at all, have been added as supplementary to the national bank figures. In many respects the reports of the Clearing House banks of the city would be best adapted to a study of concentration of balances, but in them the deposits of individuals and bankers are grouped together, and they are therefore quite useless for this study.

For 1870 and 1880 the situation with regard to the large holders of bankers' balances is given in the following table:

BANKERS' BALANCES HELD BY NEW YORK NATIONAL BANKS

(*In millions of dollars*)

Highest nine, 1870		*Highest nine, 1880*	
National Park	11.0	Importers and Traders'	18.8
Fourth	10.2	First	13.7
Importers and Traders'	7.1	Park	13.3
Central	6.8	Fourth	12.6
Ninth	4.2	Metropolitan	10.2
First	4.0	Third	5.8
Metropolitan	3.5	American Exchange	5.6
Third	3.4	Central	5.2
Republic	2.7	Hanover	5.1
Average	5.9	Average	10.0
Next highest	1.7	Next highest	4.7
Average of all except nine	0.43	Average of all except nine	1.2

It is apparent in this table that the concentration of balances in 1880 was less intense than in 1870. The amount held by the nine banks at the top had increased, but the average balance of the other banks had increased even more, and the distance between the bottom bank of the upper group and the top bank of the lower group was relatively less in 1880 than in 1870.

There was, indeed, some difficulty in deciding just where the limits of the upper group should be placed for 1880, for the boundaries are by no means so distinct as for the other years. The Chase Bank, the Merchants', and the Ninth, crowded closely on the Third and the Republic, and in the following years sometimes supplanted them. The panic of 1873, with its widespread bank failures and consequent disarrangement of existing correspondent relations between banks, seems to have brought a sharp halt to the concentration movement, and by 1874 the proportion of bankers' balances held in the 9 banks of the top group had dropped from 73 per cent to 57 per cent. Within a few years the movement had begun again, but it took three decades to recover what had been lost.

Meantime the banks which held the greater share of bankers' balances had grown in other respects and held the greater share of individual deposits and reserves also. While the banks of the top group in 1870 had owned only one-fourth of the capital and surplus of the city national banks, the 6 top banks in 1910 possessed three-fifths. The proportion of the total loans and discounts of the top group increased during the same years from three-eighths to three-fifths. The same tendency is shown for individual deposits. The proportion of bankers' to individual deposits actually fell between 1880 and 1910, although, as is indicated in the table below, it never reached so low a figure as that for the banks outside the top group.

BANKERS' BALANCES HELD BY NEW YORK NATIONAL BANKS

(In millions of dollars)

Highest, 1890		*Highest, 1900*		*Highest, 1910**	
First	18.8	City	61.4	City	102.0
Park	15.0	Commerce	41.8	Commerce	86.7
Importers and Traders'	14.2	Hanover	37.7	Chase	70.4
Hanover	12.7	Chase	33.5	Hanover	64.4
Republic	11.1	Park	30.7	First	63.5
Fourth	10.4	Western	28.2	Park	57.8
Chase	9.8	First	25.0		
Average of highest	13.1	Average of highest	36.9	Average of highest	74.1
Next highest	7.5	Next highest	19.4	Next highest	25.5
Average of all except highest	2.0	Average of all except highest	4.7	Average of all except highest	5.2

* The figures for 1910, given by the Comptroller of the Currency, are for "due to banks and all other liabilities," but since "all other liabilities" are small the relative error is not significant.

The greater concentration of bankers' balances was accompanied by a still more rapid concentration of bank reserves and banking strength. The process is clearly indicated in the table, which pictures the situation for one date in each decade. Although the figures for state banks in New York City are not comparable with those for the national banks as to date and classification, the totals are included in order to give a more complete view.[9]

This process of identifying the large banks with the large holders of bankers' balances had the result of greatly increasing the concentration of banking power in New York City. As the number of banks in the top group grew smaller, their share of the total capital and surplus, of the total volume of banking business, and of reserve funds, grew larger, so that each bank in the group held a relatively greater amount of power and of responsibility. This was one factor in the situation which aroused the attention of Congress and resulted in the famous Pujo Committee's investigation into the "Money Trust." It was unfortunate that what amounted to the management of the banking system of the country was vested in the hands of banks which were primarily profit-making institutions.

The banks of New York, with their thousands of correspondents over the country, and with the prestige which attached to their position at the head of American banks, occupied in many respects the place of a central bank, but they lacked the ability to increase their note circulation or to suspend the reserve requirement under panic conditions. They lacked also an organization among themselves which would have held the banks to a common course of action. The smaller banks in New York were as hasty in drawing down their balances with the larger banks

[9] The discrepancies between the figures for the national and the state banks given in the table arise partly from the dates which are, for the national banks, October 8, 1870; October 8, 1880; October 2, 1890; September 5, 1900; and September 1, 1910; for the state banks the corresponding dates are September 24, 1870; September 18, 1880; September 27, 1890; September 4, 1900; and August 31, 1910. For the state banks, "Due to banks" sometimes includes "Due to brokers." In 1910, for national banks, "Due to banks" includes "All other liabilities," among which are unpaid dividends, bonds borrowed, notes rediscounted, bills payable, and reserves for taxes, a total of 13 millions for all the New York City national banks.

INCREASING CONCENTRATION OF BANKING STRENGTH IN NEW YORK CITY

(In millions of dollars)

Year		*Number of banks*	*Loans and discounts*	*Reserves*	*Individual deposits*	*Bankers' deposits*
1870	Top group	9	$63.3	$22.7	$42.8	$52.9
	All national banks . .	54	$168.1	$59.3	$167.0	$72.2
	Percentage of top to national	..	*38*	*38*	*26*	*73*
	National and state . .	78	$199.1	$66.0	$202.0	$75.3
	Percentage of top to national and state .	..	*32*	*34*	*21*	*70*
1880	Top group	9	$106.1	$30.9	$66.9	$90.3
	All national banks . .	47	$238.5	$69.5	$242.0	$137.1
	Percentage of top to national	..	*45*	*45*	*28*	*66*
	National and state . .	67	$279.7	$77.4	$283.4	$144.8
	Percentage of top to national and state .	..	*38*	*40*	*24*	*62*
1890	Top group	7	$101.3	$32.7	$56.0	$92.0
	All national banks . .	47	$297.3	$90.6	$251.4	$173.4
	Percentage of top to national	..	*34*	*36*	*22*	*53*
	National and state . .	95	$391.4	$109.9	$372.6	$189.1
	Percentage of top to national and state .	..	*26*	*30*	*15*	*49*
1900	Top group	7	$297.0	$122.9	$189.7	$258.3
	All national banks . .	44	$569.6	$213.4	$420.7	$431.0
	Percentage of top to national	..	*52*	*58*	*45*	*60*
	National and state . .	76	$698.6	$248.1	$567.6	$473.4
	Percentage of top to national and state .	..	*43*	*45*	*33*	*55*
1910	Top group	6	$504.9	$189.1	$371.8	$444.8
	All national banks . .	39	$873.9	$291.6	$698.1	$618.0
	Percentage of top to national	..	*58*	*65*	*53*	*73*
	National and state . .	78	$1,106.7	$365.2	$977.1	$658.3
	Percentage of top to national and state .	..	*46*	*52*	*38*	*68*

and in hoarding their own reserves as were the out-of-town banks. The Clearing House banks might have secured a large measure of control over the reserves in New York if they had been able to act together in preparation for strain. But there was among them no leader of sufficient foresight and initiative to bring them together before the panic was upon them. Even during a panic it was often a private banker who first organized the banks into common action.

As in the earlier period,[10] the payment of interest on deposits was often held accountable for the concentration of bankers' balances in New York. It seems to have been true rather that interest on deposits was a device which banks used in their competition with each other. Not all of the banks paid interest on balances. In 1873 and again in 1886 it was publicly stated that about half of them were making such payments; other banks offered their correspondents valuable services instead. The Chemical, which had long been opposed to the practice, the Bank of America, the City, Gallatin, and the Merchants' Exchange, all refused to pay interest in 1886, but collected out-of-town items for their customers free of charge, a service which was said to be worth as much as 2 or 3 per cent interest. Other banks found other ways of making themselves valuable to their country correspondents. By 1891 however most of the banks had substituted the direct payment of interest for these indirect attractions. Only two or three of the large Clearing House institutions held out against the prevailing practice, and by 1911 the Chemical Bank was the only survivor.[11]

It was beginning to be realized that interest on deposits was only one phase of a system, and that the elimination of one phase alone would be difficult and probably futile. It was not the prospect of interest which brought balances to New York. As a matter of fact, many interior banks paid interest on deposits too.[12] If the interest had been the chief reason for the

[10] See p. 119 above.

[11] *Commercial and Financial Chronicle,* Vol. 59, Oct. 27, 1894, p. 716. Pujo Committee Hearings, 62 Congress, 3 Session, Vol. I, p. 141.

[12] Comptroller of Currency, *Annual Report,* 1870, p. *xii*. Congressional Globe, 40 Congress, 3 Session, Part I, p. 422.

concentration of balances in New York, we should find that the periods of low rates were marked by small balances; actually the reverse was true. The real evil in the situation was that, because city banks used interest as a means of competing for country balances, bank funds which were the final reserve in any crisis were concentrated in the banks whose chief claim to receive them was a willingness to pay for the privilege. The central reserve which should have been administered for the good of the system as a whole was prostituted to the private gain of a few. The complete abolition of interest payments might have caused bankers' balances to be scattered about among a larger number of banks, and there would have been less pressure on the banks to reloan the funds on the call market in order to earn at least as much as was being paid out in interest. On the other hand, although interior banks would still have kept that part of their balances which represented reserve funds with national banks, they would have increased the amounts of their "surplus" funds placed directly on the call market. This practice had been a common one for many years, and as much as 150 millions belonging to western and other interior banks was in the market during 1903. By 1912 these funds appeared whenever the call rate rose above the rate on deposits, that is above 2 per cent.[13]

Reserves of New York banks

Although a few large banks bore a disproportionate share of the cash reserves in New York, the reserves of the other banks were not unimportant, and the reserve ratio for the Clearing House banks as a group was closely watched.

The banks of New York City holding the central reserves of the country comprised three different types of banks, each one subject to a different regulatory law. National banks, state banks, and trust companies, were subject to three different sets of legal requirements as to reserves, requirements enacted by two different legislative agencies.

[13] *Commercial and Financial Chronicle,* Vol. 76, Feb. 14, 1903, p. 348. Senate Federal Reserve Hearings; 63 Congress, 1 Session, Senate Document 232, p. 510. For discussion of the relations between call rates and reserve ratios, see p. 276 below.

The National Bank Act, under which the largest of the Clearing House banks were organized, required that national banks in New York City keep on hand in specie or "lawful money," which in 1864 meant greenbacks, a reserve of 25 per cent of their circulation and net deposits. In 1874 this requirement was lightened by the omission of circulation, in 1908 by the omission of government deposits.

State banks in New York City were subject to no legal requirement for reserves until the revision of the state banking law in 1892. At that time the cash reserve against deposits for banks in cities of more than 800,000 population was fixed at 15 per cent of aggregate deposits, while the reserve in smaller cities and towns was set at 10 per cent. The plan of the National Act was followed in the permission given banks to keep half of the required reserve in banks or trust companies which had a capital of at least $200,000 and were approved by the State Superintendent of Banks. The state requirement was less stringent in every respect than the national; the reserve percentage for banks in each class of city was lower than for the corresponding classes of national banks, and the reserve balances could be kept with banks which would not have met the requirements for depositaries under the national law.

The revision of the state laws in 1909 introduced a much more drastic set of provisions and brought the state law nearer to the national law in respect to reserves. The cities of the state were divided into three groups: the first, with population of 1,800,000 or more, included only the Borough of Manhattan in New York City; the second, with population between 1,000,000 and 1,800,000, included Brooklyn; while the third included all others. Banks in Manhattan were required to keep a reserve of 25 per cent against demand deposits, of which two-fifths might be in balances in an approved bank or trust company; in Brooklyn, a reserve of 20 per cent of which one-half might be in balances; and in other cities, a reserve of 15 per cent of which three-fifths might be in balances.[14] It will be noted that

[14] New York State Statutes on Banking, ch. 689, Laws of 1892, Par. 44. Ch. 10 of 1909, Par. 67.

the provisions for the country banks were identical with those of the national banking act, while those for banks in Manhattan and Brooklyn were less drastic than the national act in so far as balances might be substituted for part of the total reserves.

The trust companies of New York produced the greatest difficulty in the matter of reserves. Organized originally to exercise functions other than those of commercial banks, they steadily encroached upon the field of the latter, and many of them became competitors of the commercial banks. It was the failure of a trust company which had precipitated the panic of 1857 and trust company failures had marked the panic of 1873. In spite of public demand for their regulation, the laws of New York gave them privileges which the banks did not possess, and with fewer restrictions, requiring them to hold a reserve of only 5 per cent of deposits.

The Clearing House at that time permitted its members to clear for non-members, and the state banks and trust companies which preferred not to subject themselves to the regulations of the association were able to obtain indirectly nearly all the advantages of membership. There were 93 of these non-members in Manhattan and neighboring boroughs, and only 63 members. The responsibilities of the Clearing House banks were greatly increased by this situation, since in any crisis they were obliged to sustain the credit of their associates in order to prevent a general suspension. The Clearing House was fully cognizant of the condition which had arisen and began to discuss possible remedies as early as 1890. With its customary conservatism, however, no action was taken until 1899, when it began to require weekly reports from clearing non-member trust companies as well as from members.[15] By 1903 the growth of the trust companies and the increase in their deposits brought about a more radical action on the part of the Clearing House banks. They unanimously decided that a trust company which desired the privilege of clearing through a member of the Association must keep a cash reserve of 10 per cent of deposits, twice the

[15] Pujo Committee Hearings, 62 Congress, 3 Session, p. 146. *Commercial and Financial Chronicle*, Vol. 69, Nov. 11, 1899, p. 991.

amount required by state law. Three months after the passage of this rule, in May, 1903, nine trust companies had withdrawn from their clearing non-member status, and at the end of a year only two of the original non-member trust companies remained associated with the Clearing House.[16] The loss of the clearing privilege of the trust companies fell more heavily upon the banks than upon the excluded non-members for banks under the new scheme were obliged to send out runners in order to cash checks drawn on the trust companies.

The Clearing House had failed in its efforts to make the trust companies bear their share of the reserve responsibility, and the State Superintendent of Banks thereupon recommended that legislation should undertake to meet the difficulty. In 1906 a law was passed which required trust companies in cities of more than 800,000 population to keep a reserve of 15 per cent against their aggregate deposits, time as well as demand; 5 per cent in cash, 5 per cent in bonds, and 5 per cent in bank balances. Trust companies in cities of less size were required to keep a reserve of only 10 per cent, one-third in cash. After the panic of 1907 the requirement for trust companies was raised; the reserve ratio was to remain at 15 per cent, but all of it was to be cash in vault. Balances with other banks and bonds were no longer to count as reserves but on the other hand, time deposits were excluded from the reserve requirement.

Once the trust companies had been forced to stand on their own feet in the matter of reserves there was no longer any reason for the Clearing House to exclude them. When early in 1911 the subject of coöperation between the banks and the trust companies was again brought up, the Clearing House voted to admit to full status any trust company with a capital of one million dollars or more which would furnish weekly reports of conditions and which would maintain, in addition to the 15 per cent cash reserve required by law, an additional 10 per cent in balances with bank members of the Clearing House. Within ten days seventeen trust companies had applied for membership, and the

[16] *Commercial and Financial Chronicle,* Vol. 76, Feb. 14, 1903, p. 348; May 30, p. 1169; Vol. 78, June 4, 1904, p. 2312.

long struggle between the banks and the trust companies was ended.[17]

The increasing stringency of legal reserve requirements was not sufficient to counteract the almost constant lowering of the reserve percentage for the New York banks as a whole. In spite of the increasing strain which the credit structure was showing, the reserve percentage of the New York banks was showing the same tendency to sink towards the legal minimum as that of the country and reserve city banks. The rate of decline was slower in New York only for the reason that the margin of reserve above the legal figure had never been as large proportionately as that held by the interior banks. The national banks of the city had held in 1868 average reserves of 33 per cent. By 1874 this figure had declined to 31 per cent. The shrinking process went on, carrying the average reserve percentage for 1883 almost to the legal minimum. There were brief periods of excess reserves in the depressions after 1884 and 1893, but from 1899 to 1910 the annual average was only once above 27 per cent.

The lowering of the reserve ratio was made more significant by reason of the composition of the reserves. Under the legal requirements for both state and national banks, these consisted of gold and "lawful money" of the United States. Both of these classes of money were comparatively inelastic,[18] and the only practical method of increasing bank reserves, when a demand from the interior made it necessary, was an importation from abroad. The specie itself was also expensive to handle, but various paper substitutes were devised which with the greenbacks reduced shipments of the metals to a minimum. Besides gold and silver coin, the reserves consisted of gold treasury certificates, gold Clearing House certificates, silver treasury certificates, greenbacks, and United States certificates of deposit.

Although gold was held by the banks before the resumption of specie payments in 1879, it was so overvalued in the market that banks would not use it in settling their balances with each

[17] *Commercial and Financial Chronicle*, Vol. 92, March 25, 1911, p. 760; May 13, p. 1289; May 20, p. 1350.

[18] See p. 399 below.

other. For all practical purposes greenbacks were the only reserve, and the proportion of legal tender notes to total reserves increased during that time until in 1872 and 1873 it was about one-half.[19] After 1879, the resumption of specie payments took from the greenbacks their peculiar value as reserve funds, although they continued to form about one-fifth of the total.

Equivalent to greenbacks were the certificates of indebtedness issued against them by the treasury, which bore interest and could be counted as part of the reserves. The New York banks agreed, during the autumn stringency of 1868, to accept the 3 per cent certificates in settlement at the Clearing House when stamped on the back "Payable on demand in Greenbacks" and they figured in the reserves until 1873, making their last appearance in the report for February of that year.[20] Six months earlier, another form of greenback certificate had been issued by the treasury without interest. These were issued to any Clearing House association in denominations of 5 and 10 thousand dollars, and were specifically given the right to be included in the lawful money reserve, and to be used in the settlement of Clearing House balances. By 1875 there were nearly 60 millions of these certificates outstanding, but by the end of 1879 most of them had been surrendered to meet the demand for circulation. In 1894 the certificates were again issued and remained outstanding in volume until the end of 1897. The currency legislation of 1900 finally put an end to their existence.

Although the greenbacks were acceptable substitutes for gold in all domestic settlements, only gold could be used in international payments, and it was therefore the most important reserve element. Since gold itself was awkward and expensive to handle, the banks of New York, even before the Civil War, had developed the use of the Clearing House gold certificate for purposes of settlement. The original National Bank Act copied this device but gave the privilege of issue to the treasury. The first gold treasury certificates appeared in November, 1865. By 1875,

[19] *Bankers' Magazine*, Vol. 28, pp. 425-37. Sprague, *History of Crises*, p. 8.
[20] *Commercial and Financial Chronicle*, Vol. 7, Nov. 7, 1868, p. 581.

nearly 22 millions of them were outstanding, about half in the hands of the national banks of New York City. The advantage of the treasury certificates over those issued by the Clearing House was that the former were available for settlements with

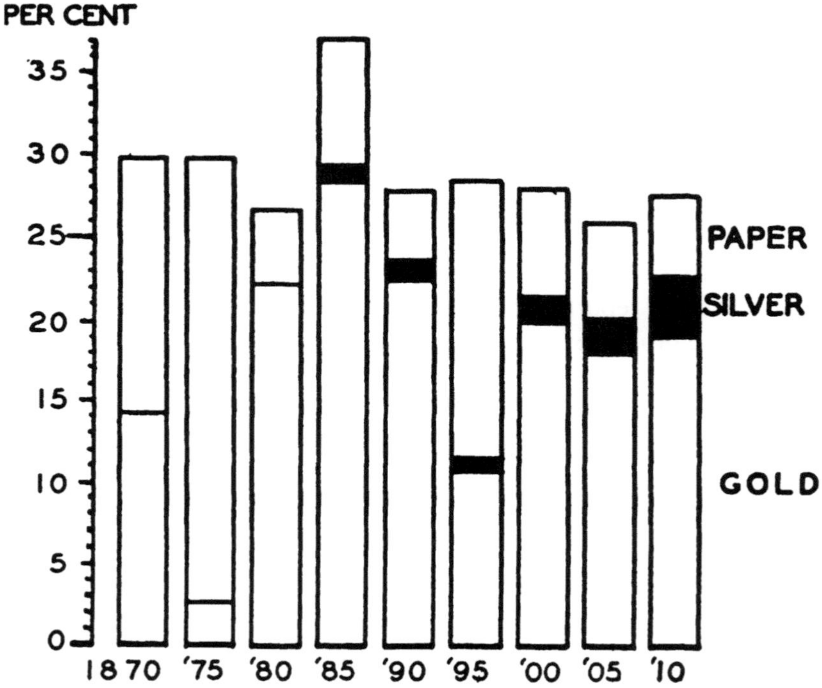

COMPOSITION OF NEW YORK NATIONAL BANK RESERVES, IN PERCENTAGE OF NET DEPOSITS.

SOURCE: ANNUAL REPORTS OF THE COMPTROLLER OF THE CURRENCY.

the subtreasury as well as for inter-bank settlements. When preparations for the resumption of specie payments caused the treasury to discontinue the issue of gold certificates the banks again took over that function, for the certificates were too great a convenience to be dispensed with. The Bank of America was appointed to receive gold for the Clearing House banks, and to issue gold certificates to take the place of the government issues.

[21] Comptroller of Currency, *Annual Report*, 1880, pp. 31-32; 1900, p. 383. *Commercial and Financial Chronicle*, Vol. 15, July 27, 1872, p. 107; Sept. 144, p. 349. See p. 363 below.

The capacity of the bank's vaults limited the total of this issue to slightly less than 40 millions of dollars.[21] Again in 1893 the Secretary of the Treasury was obliged to stop the issue of the gold certificates because of a shortage of gold reserve against the United States notes, and again the Clearing House filled the gap with an issue of its own gold certificates.[22] In 1899 the scarcity of paper currency brought about renewed demand for treasury gold certificates. The settlement of the currency difficulties permitted the Secretary of the Treasury to meet this demand and the gold certificates held by the New York banks rose steadily, forming nearly half of their specie reserve in 1910.

Although silver came under the definition of lawful money, the New York banks before 1900 never willingly used it as part of their reserves, since its fluctuations in price made it useless for international payments and held out the prospect of actual loss. When the subtreasury at New York became a member of the Clearing House, at the time of resumption, and an agreement was drawn up to cover the details of their relationship, the refusal to accept silver in settlements at the Clearing House was extended to cover settlements with the Treasury, and silver dollars and certificates were taken only on special deposit. The New York treasurer was frequently hard put to it to prevent silver from accumulating in his vaults, and to keep sufficent gold for the payment of his balances at the Clearing House.[23] In spite of the rapid coinage of silver dollars after 1878, the national banks of the city held only a few hundred thousand of them and after 1899 not more than one hundred thousand. Silver certificates were discriminated against until 1900, and made up one-tenth or less of the total holdings of cash before that year. When the gold standard was finally adopted the silver certificates were as good as gold and the amount held by New York national banks rapidly increased. By 1913 they made up one-fifth of the reserve.[24]

[22] Comptroller of Currency, *Annual Report*, 1883, pp. 37-38; 1896, p. 26.

[23] *Bankers' Magazine*, Vol. 33, pp. 450, 465. *Commercial and Financial Chronicle*, Vol. 27, December 7, 1878, p. 579. See p. 364 below.

[24] Comptroller of Currency, *Annual Report*, 1898, p. 442; 1905, p. 160; 1913, p. 276.

The American law, state or federal, has never recognized the existence of secondary reserves, those quick assets which form a part of every banker's portfolio, and upon which the solvency of the bank often depends. The Comptroller of the Currency in 1877 recommended that holdings of governments 4's in small denominations be included in the legal reserves, taking the place of balances.[25] Because of the ready market for such securities, they would have been available in emergency, although at a heavy loss, and might have prevented the deadlock in call-loan liquidation which marked a panic. English banks were accustomed to hold large amounts of their own government consols, and to look upon them as reserves in fact, although there were no legal minimum requirements in that country. A more carefully selected portfolio as secondary reserve might have helped to protect New York banks from the strain to which they were periodically subjected.

Flow of funds between New York and the interior

Since the surplus reserves of the interior banks were kept in the form of deposits with correspondents, a drain upon the resources of the interior banks resulted immediately in the drawing down of their deposits at the large centers. The greater part of this demand for interior funds fell upon the banks of New York City. With their cash reserves declining steadily in proportion to their deposits, the interior banks were more and more dependent upon their balances with other banks, and particularly upon those in New York, for relief in emergency.

The removal of the funds from New York to the interior was accomplished in one of two ways, either through the sale of exchange on New York, or through an actual shipment of currency. Data on shipments of currency for the years 1905 to 1908 were requested by the National Monetary Commission in its study of the banking system of the country in 1910. The result was a fairly complete series of figures[26] which indicated

[25] Youngman, "The Growth of Financial Banking," *Journal of Political Economy*, 1906.

[26] Kemmerer: *Seasonal Variations*, etc.

that there was a constant movement of specie and notes about the country.

When the movement of cash is analyzed by districts, it is apparent that the greatest volume of shipment in both directions was between the eastern states and New York, due partly to their geographical proximity. In striking contrast to the heavy shipments in either direction was the small net gain or loss to New York for each month. Imports so nearly balanced exports that the result for the average year was a loss of only 5 millions of dollars, leaving the eastern states next to the lowest of the districts in this respect. The eastern states were remarkable also for the comparatively slight change from month to month; like most of the other districts, they sent cash to New York in the summer and winter, and took it back in spring and autumn, but the highest average gain to New York for a month was 3.7 millions in January, and the greatest average withdrawal of funds from New York was 3.9 millions in November.

The New England states were very like those of the eastern group in the narrow range from month to month of the net movement of funds. The greatest average loss to New York was less than one million in January, while the greatest average withdrawal was 4.5 millions in November. Although the total volume of shipments was not nearly so great as that of the western states and was just about equal to that of the southern and middle western groups, the net movement in every month but one was away from New York, and the total absorption of New York funds during the year into New England was greater than that of any other group.

In the course of a year the Middle West took only half as much cash from New York as New England. Its withdrawals of funds were concentrated in the last five months of the year, and during those months, exceeded those of any other district. The range of variation from month to month was large, from an average of 4.9 millions *into* New York in January, to 8.5 millions *out* of New York in August.

The southern states were predominantly agricultural, like those of the Middle West, and showed the same sort of seasonal variation: shipments to New York during the first part of the year, withdrawals during the last, with a range from 8 millions to New York in January, to 5 millions out in September. In contrast to the Middle West, however, the net movement of funds was in favor of New York and in amount almost compensated for the net withdrawal of funds by the West.

The far western states took a small amount of cash during the last four months of the year, but it was quite insignificant in comparison with other districts. The Pacific states, which contained the gold-producing section, sent a steady stream of cash to New York which averaged more than 10 millions for the year.

For all districts, the receipts of cash at New York were high in January, fell off somewhat during February and March, rose again and remained at a moderate level until August, when they dropped sharply and remained low until December. Shipments of cash from New York to the interior moved in just the opposite fashion, remaining low during the first seven months of the year, except for a short upward swing in March and April; then rising to great heights in the last five months, with the peak in October. The average amount of cash sent from the city to the interior during a year was 180 millions and the net loss averaged 18 million dollars annually, or about one-tenth of the total amount shipped. The sum was certainly not a large one in comparison with the total banking assets of the city, nor even in comparison with the cash reserves, but during September, October, and November alone, the net withdrawal was 50 millions, and it was the concentration of the demand within a few months which caused the strain. The banks of New York usually held a very narrow margin of surplus reserves, and it was quite unequal to a demand for 50 millions in these months.

Data regarding the weekly movements of cash between the New York City and interior banks were compiled also by the *Commercial and Financial Chronicle*, beginning with June 25, 1881. These data were not divided into geographical areas as were those collected for the National Monetary Commission, but present one total for the whole country. Taking the years from 1887 to 1890—a period unmarred by panic, by inflation, or by silver legislation—we find that the net movement of funds was steadily toward New York in January. During February

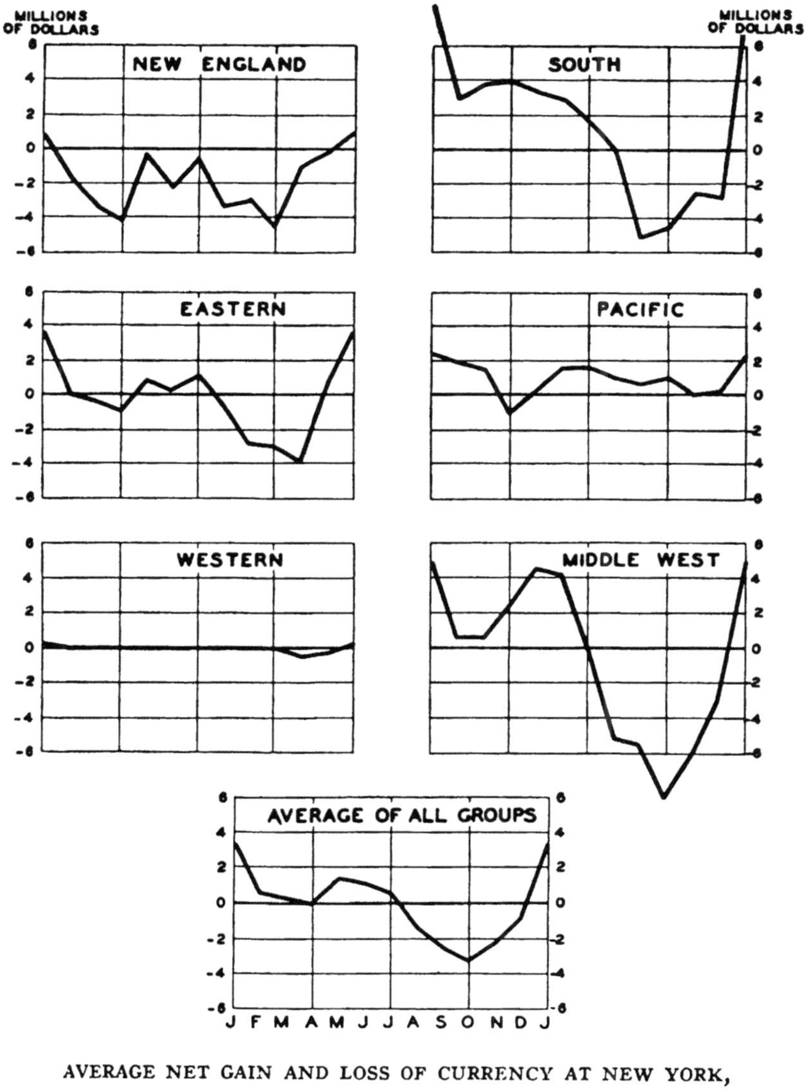

AVERAGE NET GAIN AND LOSS OF CURRENCY AT NEW YORK, MONTHLY, FROM EACH GROUP OF STATES, AND FROM ALL STATES, 1905-1908 INCLUSIVE.

SOURCE: KEMMERER, SEASONAL VARIATIONS, ETC.

and March, part or all of the weeks showed a net movement of funds away from the city; April, May, and June, again brought funds to the city; during the latter part of June or early in July the movement was reversed, and funds were taken out of the city until the close, or very near the close, of the year. There were evidently at that time two seasons of high demand for cash by the interior, the shorter in the spring and the longer in the autumn, corresponding in the former case to the temporary settlement made at that date in the country districts and in the latter, to the harvest.

Fifteen years later, in the period 1902-1905, the spring flow of funds out of the city had almost ceased; continuing for only 2 or 3 weeks where formerly it had lasted 5 or 10. This confirms the evidence of the monthly totals for the years 1905 to 1908. The autumn export had also diminished,[27] and although formerly it had gone on almost steadily for 6 months it now continued for as little as 3 or 4 months in some years. There is evident here the same tendency that has been elsewhere noted —a disposition to substitute for movements of specie the more economical transfers of bank credits. The strain on New York City was therefore alleviated, as the proportion of cash withdrawn relative to total reserves fell off. On the other hand, the margin of surplus reserves was also falling and the net shipments of cash to the interior were still large in comparison with that margin.

To a certain extent, shifts in deposit credit were substituted for movements of cash, and as the deposits of New York banks were drawn down, those of the interior increased. The indices of seasonal variation given by Professor Young[28] for the years 1901-1913 show this inverse movement clearly.

Another substitute for shipments of cash was inter-bank borrowing, which enabled banks to secure funds by rediscounting their paper with correspondents. Although a few banks had resorted to rediscounts from the very beginning of the national

[27] See also the testimony of Mr. Sherer in Pujo Committee Hearings, 62 Congress, 3 Session, Vol. I, p. 151.

[28] Young: *Analysis of Bank Statistics for the United States.* See table on opposite page.

banking system, there had always existed a prejudice against this practice, and it was not until after 1907 that it became widespread. It was chiefly used by country banks; those of the South were responsible for two-fifths of all of this type of borrowing between 1900 and 1914, and country banks elsewhere were responsible for another two-fifths. Although this relieved New York somewhat from the strain of specie shipments, the burden of rediscounting fell largely upon the shoulders of the New York national banks, which furnished one-third of all the loans on rediscounted paper before 1914. Since the demand for these loans was largely seasonal in character, occurring at the same time as the demand for cash, it increased the strain which had already been induced by the withdrawal of bankers' balances and the shipment of specie to the interior.[29]

SEASONAL VARIATION IN NET DEPOSITS OF NATIONAL BANKS

	New York City	*Outside New York City*
1st call	102.2	99.8
2d call	99.7	100.3
3d call	100.7	100.1
4th call	101.8	99.9
5th call	95.3	100.0

The gold which New York poured steadily into the interior came from the reserves of her banks, which had to be constantly replenished from abroad, and hence in the last analysis it was the imports of gold which enabled New York to meet the demands of the country for cash. Gold which came from the treasury was only once removed from the banks, and need not be considered separately. The weekly imports from abroad, and exports to the interior, show a striking correlation, especially in such years as 1906 and 1907, when both movements were exaggerated. There was, however, a lag in the importation of gold, for it was not shipped until sterling rates had reached the import point in New York, and it was not until a week or more later

29 Patterson, "New York as a Financial Center," *Journal Political Economy*, June, 1913, p. 523.

that gold actually arrived from London. Many times the gold imported from abroad was not sufficient entirely to compensate for the funds withdrawn to the interior, and it was not until the return flow set in, in late December and January, that the New York bank reserves returned to a normal level.

Summary

The reserves of the New York City banks were the foundation upon which the whole credit structure of the country rested. In the last analysis, it was the reserves of a few large banks which were the final reserve, and as the superstructure of credit increased without a proportionate strengthening of the foundation, the tension within the system, and the danger of collapse, also increased. The inability of an uncoördinated group of commercial banks, whose first motive was necessarily profit, to take over the guidance of bank policies became more and more painfully evident.

CHAPTER XIII

THE CALL LOAN MARKET FROM 1863 TO 1913

Long before 1863, the increasing concentration of banking funds in New York City had brought about a close relationship between the banks and the Stock Exchange. The technique of financing security purchases by collateral demand loans had attained a high stage of development by the time the national banking act was passed and the call loan had already become a unique feature of the New York money market. The real importance of the call loan lay, however, not in the absence of such a market in any other country, but in the fact that the funds which were so utilized were in large part those which had been sent to the New York banks from the interior to serve as reserve balances. The development of this relationship before 1863 has been traced in an earlier chapter. There was no essential change after that date; the passage of the National Bank Act did not affect the degree of independence, though the results became more and more important with the years.[1]

Source of funds employed in the call market

The Clearing House banks of New York City were the principal lenders in the call market but they were by no means the only lenders. Savings banks and trust companies, life and fire insurance companies, and the large private banks, had discovered the possibility of the call market as an outlet for funds awaiting investment. The activity of the savings banks in the call market was curbed by the state legislation of 1875, which, on the basis of the disastrous experience of the savings banks during the panic of 1873, limited their investments to state and Federal bonds.[2] Trust companies were for many years not sub-

[1] The declining ratio of reserves to deposits and total bank liabilities made the utilization of the reserves a matter of increasing moment.

[2] *Bankers' Magazine*, Vol. 30, p. 998.

ject to reserve requirements, and they were able to lend with more freedom than commercial banks. Private bankers of New York also played an important part in the call loan market. Many of them combined the functions of broker, underwriter, and banker, and found themselves in touch with the market at all three points. Very little is known about their activities, since they made no published reports, but the house of Morgan entered the market as a relief expedition in every crisis, and in 1912, witnesses before the Pujo Committee named Kuhn, Loeb and Company, Goldman Sachs, and Speyers, as the three most active lenders on call.[3]

What are now known as loans for "Others" made through banks by corporations and private lenders, were not unknown, but were comparatively small in amount, from 1863 to 1913. Information about them is very limited. What is perhaps the first mention appeared in *The Commercial and Financial Chronicle* in 1872,[4] as an explanation of the wide difference then prevailing between commercial and call rates. This was "the practice which has been growing up for several years among the merchants, of lending their money in the street directly to brokers instead of putting it in bank as a deposit without interest. . . . The brokers encourage this sort of deposits which are attended with obvious dangers." Twenty years later the abundance of money on the Street was ascribed in part to the fact that "even merchants" were offering to lend on stock collateral.[5] By 1906 the Secretary of the Treasury estimated that hundreds of millions of dollars were being loaned in New York from the interior, much of it from business rather than strictly financial institutions.[6] Part, indeed, was borrowed from the New York correspondents, and reloaned at higher rates.

A search through corporation balance sheets in Moody's *Manual* for 1907 reveals few traces of such transactions. If they did occur, they must have been covered up by inclusion

[3] Pujo Committee Hearings, 62 Congress, 3 Session, Vol. I, p. 745.

[4] Vol. 15, p. 269.

[5] *Commercial and Financial Chronicle*, Vol. 58, p. 152, Jan. 27, 1894.

[6] Hearings before House Committee on Banking and Currency, 59 Congress, 2 Session, 1906-1907, p. 193.

in "Miscellaneous" or "Cash assets" or some other term. The Union Pacific, alone among the railroads, had 34.7 million dollars of demand loans. The General Electric Company reported two-thirds of a million dollars of "Discounts," and nearly 3 millions of "Advances" and the United States Steel Company reported forthrightly, 7.6 millions of dollars loaned on collateral. But there is other evidence that corporations were accustomed to use Wall Street loans in order to keep their surplus funds employed. A writer in the *New York Times Financial Quotation Review* in 1908 said that industrial and railroad corporations holding charters from the state of New Jersey had always been "among the most conspicuous lenders of money on collateral in Wall Street." The decision of Vice-Chancellor Walker of New Jersey, that the making of loans was beyond the powers of corporations, caused some consternation but had little effect, for only the state could bring action against the corporation for this violation of its charter, and this the state of New Jersey never did.[7]

Loans for account of out-of-town banks

It is impossible to say just when the banks of the interior began the practice of placing funds directly in the call market, utilizing the banks merely as agents instead of making deposits with correspondents in New York, which would in turn place the funds on call. In 1880 the Chicago *Tribune* boasted that the banks of that city were in such strong position that they were becoming lenders instead of borrowers in New York, and that they had millions loaned on the call market there.[8] In 1903 the New York Clearing House gave as one of its reasons for requiring a cash reserve of trust company members, that the "Western and other out-of-town banks have inaugurated the practice of loaning money on call directly in this city instead of depositing surplus moneys with their New York correspondents."[9]

Three years later a St. Louis banker testified in Washington[10]

[7] *New York Times Weekly Financial Quotation Review*, Sept. 21, 1908, p. 3, also *Commercial and Financial Chronicle*, Vol. 87, p. 741, Sept. 19, 1908.

[8] *Bankers' Magazine*, Vol. 35, p. 68, July, 1880.

[9] *Commercial and Financial Chronicle*, Vol. 76, p. 348, Feb. 14, 1903.

[10] Hearings before House Committee on Banking and Currency, 1906-1907, 59 Congress, 2 Session, pp. 46-47.

that a great deal of western money was then being loaned on the call market in the East but that the interior banks were using the services of their New York correspondents in the negotiation of such loans. In the hearings leading up to the passage of the Federal Reserve Act the same condition was discussed, and it was stated by one witness that many outside banks loaned directly on call whenever rates went above 2 per cent. The same testimony was given before the Pujo Committee in 1912, by a broker who handled much of the "loans for correspondents" business of the New York banks.[11]

The only trustworthy figures regarding the amount of these loans for correspondents in relation to the total loans on securities made in New York were furnished to the Pujo Committee. About thirty city banks and trust companies, for three dates in each of the years 1908 to 1912, gave the total of deposits made with them by correspondents, the loans made for their correspondents on stock-exchange collateral, and the similar loans made for their own account. A comparison of the two series shows that there was a marked inverse relationship; when correspondent banks were investing large amounts directly in the call market, their deposits with New York correspondents were drawn down. Evidently when the call rate was sufficiently attractive banks from the interior sent their funds, or part of them, directly into the call market, using the New York bank merely as agent. When the rate was lower, the funds were sent to the correspondent for ordinary deposit.

The Canadian banks were another important source of call funds and from an early date used the New York market in much the same way as did the banks of our own western states. A number of the Canadian banks had branch offices in New York which facilitated the making of loans there, and in 1913 it was estimated that they kept from 25 to 50 millions in the call market all the time.[12] Foreign investors and bankers utilized

[11] Senate Federal Reserve Hearings, 1913, 63 Congress, 1 Session, Senate Document 232, p. 510. Pujo Committee Hearings, 62 Congress, 3 Session, Vol. I, p. 751.

[12] Hearings before House Committee on Banking and Currency, 59 Congress, 2 Session, 1906-7, p. 41. Senate Federal Reserve Hearings, 1913, p. 2167; 63 Congress, 1 Session, Senate Document 232.

the call money market also when rates were high enough to justify the transfer of funds to New York. There is even less definite evidence about foreign funds than about those from

CALL LOANS AT NEW YORK CITY BANKS

(*In millions of dollars*)

Date	*Deposits by correspondents*	*Loans for correspondents*	*Loans for own account*	*Total loans on stock-exchange collateral*
1908, Jan. 1 . . .	382.6	106.6	360.5	467.2
July 1 . . .	470.0	89.2	552.3	641.5
Nov. 1 . . .	500.5	85.0	500.7	585.8
1909, Jan. 1 . . .	504.4	103.5	586.7	690.3
July 1 . . .	567.9	121.6	628.6	750.2
Nov. 1 . . .	443.1	168.6	530.7	699.3
1910, Jan. 1 . . .	462.0	208.3	552.4	760.7
July 1 . . .	464.4	160.2	513.9	674.1
Nov. 1 . . .	455.7	125.2	495.0	620.2
1911, Jan. 1 . . .	519.2	143.9	512.2	656.1
July 1 . . .	548.6	128.8	615.4	744.2
Nov. 1 . . .	540.2	142.8	503.1	645.9
1912, Jan. 1 . . .	523.6	140.9	521.3	662.2
July 1 . . .	550.5	141.0	648.8	789.8
Nov. 1 . . .	483.4	240.5	526.3	766.8

interior banks. It is known that they increased largely in amount after 1900 and that they fluctuated widely, but as to how much there was in the market at any given moment there are only the vaguest estimates.

Loans by New York banks

Of all the lenders in the call loan market at New York, the most important were the New York City banks. In volume of loans they led all others, the national banks of the city alone supplying one-third of the call funds in 1914.[13] More important than mere volume was the fact that the New York banks comprised the only group which felt any responsibility for the

[13] *New York Times Annalist*, Vol. III, p. 299, March 9, 1914.

market, and therefore the only group which felt obliged to assume the loan burden as other lenders withdrew. Trust companies and private banks withdrew their funds on the first hint of trouble and the burden had to be taken up by the commercial banks. The shifting of loans to the New York City banks which took place in October, 1929, was not a new phenomenon; it had occurred in greater or less degree in every previous crisis.[14] The only difference was that the banks in 1929 were assisted in bearing the strain by the credit policies of the Federal Reserve Banks.

Once each year the national banks were required to report to the comptroller the amount of their demand loans on collateral security, which may be taken as an approximate measure of the volume of their call loans against Stock Exchange collateral. The absolute amount of such loans extended by national banks grew rapidly, with three distinct periods of growth. From 1868 to 1878 the rate of increase was moderate; from 1879 to 1904 the growth was much more rapid; from 1904 to 1913 the trend of call loans was slightly downward. The ratio of demand to total loans was affected by these different rates of growth. During the first period, call loans comprised about one-third of all the loans of the New York national banks; during the second, more active period of growth, call loans gained even more rapidly than other forms of loan, and comprised nearly one-half of all loans. After 1904, the proportion of call loans declined again, and by 1913 was back to one-third. The downward trend of security prices in the latter period was probably responsible for the falling ratio of call loans.[15]

The volume of the demand loans of national banks is closely related to that of bankers' balances. The upward trend in

[14] For example, see *The Commercial and Financial Chronicle*, Vol. 77, p. 273, August 8, 1903.

[15] Youngman, "Growth of Financial Banking," *Journal of Political Economy*, Vol. XIV, pp. 435-43. Up to and including 1891, the figures for call loans are given as loans "On demand, with U. S. bonds, other bonds, stocks, or collaterals, as security;" after that date, as loans "On demand secured by stocks, bonds, and other personal securities." The meaning of the last four words is somewhat vague, and since "Paper with one or more firm names" is given separately, it is probable that the other loans on personal security were negligible in amount, and did not seriously impair the total for call loans. Comptroller of Currency, *Report*, 1895, p. 387.

balances closely approximated that of call loans; only during the period 1904-1913 was there a serious divergence, when call loans turned down while balances kept on increasing, although at a slackening rate. With the exception of that period call loans amounted to about 75 per cent of bankers' balances, or just the ratio which would have existed if the banks had followed the policy of loaning out on call all of their balances except the 25 per cent required for reserve. The changes in the two series from year to year are as closely parallel as the trends; peaks and troughs nearly always coincide in time, and there are only 9 years out of 43 in which the changes are not in the same direction.

Since the total volume of demand loans was closely related to the amount of bankers' balances, it was to be expected that the individual banks which carried the greater part of the bankers' balances should be large lenders on the call market. The same six banks which in 1910 far outranked all of their competitors in regard to bankers' balances were the 6 largest bank lenders on call in the years 1908-1912. The Chase, the First, the Hanover, the Commerce, the City, and the Park, Banks, among the thirty-odd banks which gave detailed reports to the Pujo Committee, held 71 per cent of the correspondent banks' balances. The average call loans for all of the reporting banks, from 1908 to 1912, was 677 millions, and of this amount the six largest banks had 414 millions, or nearly two-thirds.

These figures corroborate the testimony from other sources, that the volume of call loans was closely related to the amount of bankers' balances. For the six largest lenders the relation between the two series was especially close, and during the five years covered by the report, "loans for own account" made by the six banks amounted to 87 per cent of the "deposits made by correspondents." An interesting contrast appears between the six banks and the others; the loans of the six banks were, at every date but one during the five-year period, below the amount of balances which they held for correspondents; while the loans for the other banks were, at every date but three, above the amount of balances of correspondents. It would seem from these

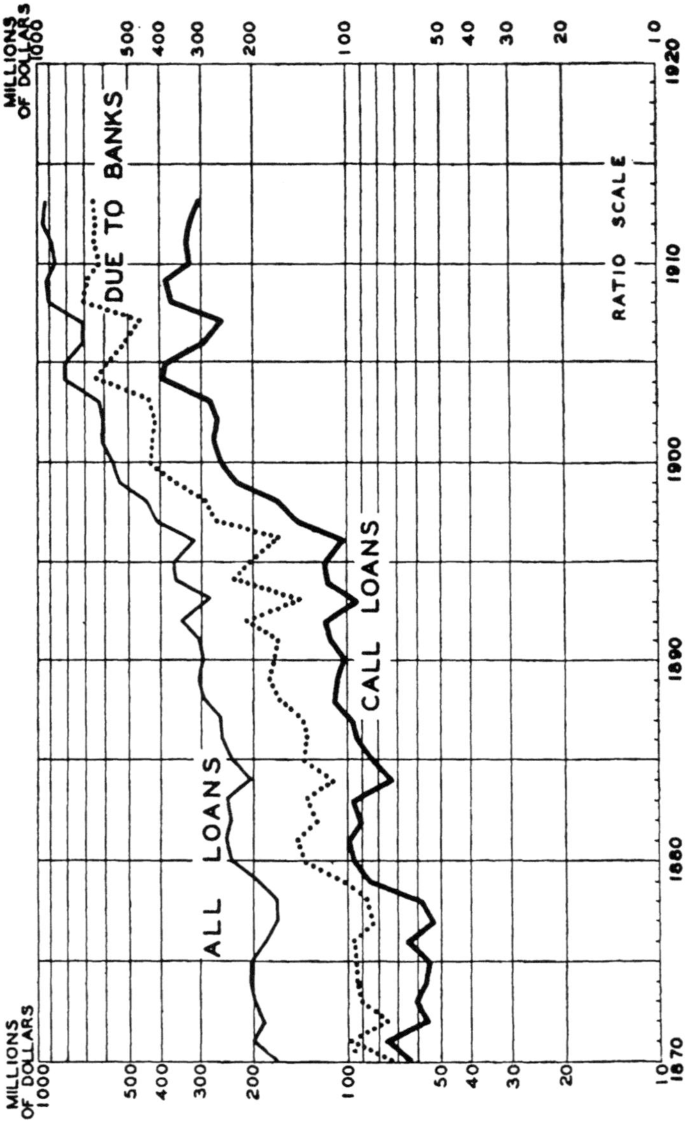

TOTAL LOANS AND INVESTMENTS, BALANCES DUE TO BANKS, AND DEMAND LOANS ON COLLATERAL SECURITY, OF NEW YORK CITY NATIONAL BANKS, ON THE FOURTH CALL EACH YEAR.

SOURCE: ANNUAL REPORTS OF THE COMPTROLLER OF THE CURRENCY.

figures that the six banks used the call loan market chiefly as an outlet for their bankers' deposits, while the other banks, which had a much smaller amount of such deposits, put other funds as well on call. For both groups of banks however the two series fluctuated together, and changed in the same direction at nearly every date.[16]

The "loans for correspondent banks" fluctuate inversely to "loans for own account" and "correspondents' balances." For the six large lending banks, which carried the bulk of country correspondent accounts, the inverse relationship was more obvious than for the others. The banks which carried the greatest amount of deposits for correspondents were also the ones to which was entrusted the task of making loans for the correspondent's own account. The following table gives the averages

CALL LOANS MADE BY THIRTY-TWO NEW YORK CITY BANKS

(*In millions of dollars*)

	Deposits by correspondents	*Loans for correspondents*	*Loans for own account*	*Total call loans*
32 banks	494	140	537	677
6 large banks . . .	353	109	305	414
Ratio of the 6 banks to the 32	71 per cent	78 per cent	57 per cent	61 per cent

for January 1, July 1, and November 1, in each of the five years from 1908-1912.[17] The amount of loans made for correspondents in proportion to their own loans was higher at the six banks than at the others, averaging 36 and 26 per cent respectively.

Call loan rates and bank reserves

The fact that bankers' balances were the source of a large

[16] Senate Federal Reserve Hearings, 1913, 63 Congress, 1 Session, Senate Document 232, p. 510. Pujo Committee Hearings, 62 Congress, 3 Session, Vol. I, pp. 654, 751.

[17] Pujo Committee Hearings, 62 Congress, 3 Session, Vol. II, pp. 1192-93.

part of the call loans made by New York banks made it inevitable that call rates should fluctuate with their reserves, or more accurately, with surplus reserves. Bankers' balances in New York were very mobile, moving back and forth between New York and the interior frequently, inducing changes in the reserves of the New York City banks. That portion of the call loans which depended upon bankers' balances was therefore a widely varying one. It represented the marginal supply of funds, and it was for that reason that the call rate was so closely linked with the reserves of New York City banks.

Since call rates were usually below the rates on time loans and commercial paper, the latter were given preference, and only so much put on call as the banks felt obliged to keep available for instant demand. It was even with a conscious air of virtue that the call loan was resorted to in some cases, since the banks felt that they were making a sacrifice of profits in order to protect their correspondents. In 1880, for example, the *Commercial and Financial Chronicle* explained the ease of the call rate by saying that "the banks have loaned on time to the extreme limit of prudence, and dare to make only call loans now, as the crop-moving season begins." Again in 1895, the same journal comments that "some banks are pursuing a cautious course, husbanding their resources as much as possible, loaning liberally on call, though they can obtain but 1 per cent."[18]

When in later years banks outside New York began to send funds directly to the call market instead of depositing them with correspondents in New York, the same feeling was expressed, that the investment of part of the bank's funds in call loans at New York was a protection to the bank customer at home. It was the "only class of paper that can be collected immediately," in the words of one western banker before the Federal Reserve Committee in 1913, and an eastern banker gave the same reason for the practice of his bank in keeping always part of their loans at call.[19] It is evident that the call loan

[18] *Commercial and Financial Chronicle*, Vol. 31, Aug. 28, 1880, p. 215; Vol. 60, Jan. 26, 1895, p. 149.

[19] Senate Committee Federal Reserve Hearings, 63 Congress, 1 Session, Senate Document 232, pp. 225, 1256.

was considered a very conservative form of investment by the banker, and the cautious bank, uncertain of the turn of events, cut down its loans on commercial paper and its investments in securities and put the money out at call, in order to have it available at need. Even though the rate of return was often, at such times, as low as one per cent, the banks felt obliged to make call loans rather than the more profitable commercial loans. It is a curious commentary on the banking system that the call loan which was looked upon by the general public as the most speculative sort of loan because it was based chiefly upon common stocks, should be considered from the banking point of view, the safest way to dispose surplus funds.

It is impossible to make a comparison between the amount of call loans extended by the New York banks and the rates for call money at the New York Stock Exchange. Even if total call loans had been reported it is doubtful whether a direct relationship would have been disclosed. There were several factors which made such a relation improbable or at least difficult to trace. For call rates may be high under two conditions: when a rapid drain of funds to the interior has reduced the surplus funds of the New York banks and caused a *reduction* in the amount of their loans on call; or when a rising movement of security prices increases the demand for call loans at a time when there is already a large volume of such loans outstanding. In the first case there would be high rates associated with low loans, in the second, high rates with a larger volume of loans. Call rates might be low under the two opposite conditions; when there is a large volume of surplus funds in the market under circumstances which make it inadvisable to invest them otherwise than at call, or when the security market is so sluggish that it does not require even the small amount of funds available. The single decade of the nineties furnished examples of each of these combinations. The year 1894 was marked by excessively low rates in every month, yet the volume of call loans in October was substantially larger than in the preceding year; in 1899 rates were very high and the volume of loans was also high. In 1893, with high rates, the volume of loans was low.

while in 1893, with unusually low rates, the volume of loans was also low.[20]

Bank reserves were undoubtedly an influential factor in the establishment of call rates. It is especially in their short-time fluctuations that the dependence becomes apparent. The indexes of seasonal variation of the two series indicate a strong inverse relation. One which covers the years 1866 to 1880[21] shows that call rates reached a secondary high in April, the month in which reserves reached a low point, and that call rates were highest during the last three months of the year when reserves were lowest. A comparison of the weekly averages for the years 1890 to 1908, prepared by the National Monetary Commission,[22] also indicates a close relationship. The diagram opposite shows that high reserve ratios were accompanied by low call rates, and that low reserve ratios of the autumn were met by high call rates. The call rates fluctuated within a somewhat wider range than reserves, since the reserve was limited on the lower side by the legal requirement, and on the upper by the high cost of money, while call rates were free to fluctuate in either direction, and there was no limit on the upper side.

What may be termed the random fluctuations in both series were not so closely related as the seasonal variations, since there were many occurrences which might affect other lenders in the call market than the banks, and thus act upon call rates more violently than the concomitant effect upon bank reserves seemed to justify. But even the random changes in the two series were often related. Another group of changes, the cyclical, were far more apparent in call rates than in bank reserves, again because the former fluctuated more violently than the latter.

Although fluctuations in bank reserves were closely related to those in call rates, fluctuations in the one were not proportioned

[20] Tables of call rates may be found in the annual *Financial Review* after 1873. Compilations of these figures have been published in Andrew, *Statistics for the United States,* and in the *Review of Economic Statistics,* 1919, p. 102, 1890-1918.

[21] Persons, Tuttle and Frickey, "Business and Financial Conditions Following the Civil War in the United States," *Review of Economic Statistics,* 1920, July Supplement, p. 40.

[22] Kemmerer, *Seasonal Variations in the Relative Demand for Money and Capital,* pp. 15, 235.

to those in the other. Call rates rose as reserves fell but when the reserve ratio approached closely to the legal minimum, the rise in call rates were greatly accelerated. A drop from 26 to 25.5 per cent in the reserve ratio had a much greater effect upon call rates than an equal drop from 28 to 27.5 per cent.

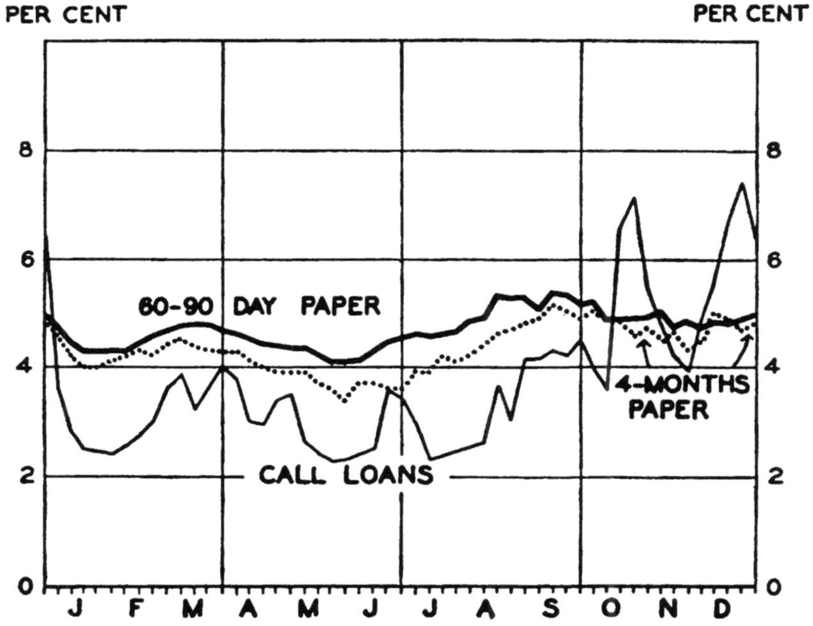

AVERAGE RATES OF INTEREST IN NEW YORK, WEEKLY, 1890-1908.

SOURCE: KEMMERER, SEASONAL VARIATIONS, ETC.

Conversely when reserve ratios were high, a further increase had less effect upon call rates than when reserves were low.[23] This change in the susceptibilty of call rates to the influence of the reserve ratio had the effect of lowering the coefficient of correlation for the two series. For the period 1885-1900, as computed by Mr. Norton, and also for the period 1901-1909, as computed by Messrs. Seltzer and Horner, it was found to be

[23] This was pointed out by John Pease Norton, in his pioneer study, *Statistical Studies in the New York Money-Market*, in 1902, p. 72. Seltzer and Horner, in "New York Bank Reserves and Loan Rates," *Journal of Political Economy*, Vol. XXX, 1922, pp. 108 ff., confirm these results.

—0.52, although there was a slight difference in the probable error of the coefficient between the two periods. In spite of the similarity of the coefficient of correlation for the two periods as wholes, there is a wide variation from year to year in the period from 1901 to 1909. It was lowest in 1901 and 1902 (—0.300 and —0.26 respectively) years of high reserves and low call rates, and highest in 1904 and 1906 (—0.75 and —0.68 respectively) when reserves were comparatively low and call rates high.

Call loan rates and commercial paper rates

The same general seasonal tendencies are to be observed in 60- to 90-day bills, and in 4- to 6-months' paper, as in call money—the secondary high point in the spring of the year and the low in the summer, followed by a new high in the autumn. The commercial paper rates do not, however, show the rise over the end of the year which is so marked in call loans. In general, the level of call loan rates is below that of commercial paper rates, and fluctuates far more widely; so widely, indeed, that it rises above the other two at the end of the year.

The extent of call rate fluctuations, in comparison with those of other rates, is still more marked when actual rates rather than averages are considered.[24] Although the call rate and the commercial rate fluctuated usually in the same direction, the call rate moved so much more rapidly and so much farther, that it was continually crossing the more even line of commercial rates, and in stringency was above, in ease below, the latter.

For the period from 1870 to 1913 as a whole, call rates showed a definite downward trend. Until 1875 the lowest point reached by call rates was 2 per cent, but in that year they fell to 1½, and in the next year, to 1 per cent. This remained the minimum until 1884, when for a time rates dropped to ½ of 1 per cent. The same low point was touched in 1894 and 1904. Maximum

[24] The rates given as "Call Loans," 1870-1889 inclusive, seem to correspond with "Call Loans at Stock Exchange" given from 1890 on. In that year rates at Banks and Trust Companies began to be quoted separately; they varied less widely than the other. Until 1910, the rates given were the weekly high and low, with the average also after 1800. In 1910 and thereafter the daily high and low was given. See annual *Financial Register*.

rates were declining as well as minimum; they had gone as high as 1½ per cent per day during the panic of 1873. Only once again did they go so high, and that was during the panic of 1884 when they once touched 3 per cent per day. After that 180 per cent, or about ½ per cent per day, reached in 1890 and 1899, was the maximum. In 1905 and in the panic of 1907 the high point was 125 per cent. Before 1877 there was no year in which rates did not at some time reach 7 per cent, but in 1894 3 was the highest; in 1895, 5 was the highest; and in 1897 and 1904, 6 was the highest.

Technique of placing call loans

The "call" market, like most of the other money markets, was centered in the financial district about Wall Street, but had no definite location within that district. The money post at the Stock Exchange was perhaps the nearest approach to an actual call loan market, but a large portion of the call loans of any day were made directly between brokers and banks. The volume of call loans which were placed on the Exchange furnished a good index of the call market as a whole. With little business there, it could be taken for granted that the outside market was also dull, but by 1912 if as much as 50 millions in a day was loaned at the money post, it was likely that several times that much was being loaned on the outside and that business was brisk.

The rates for loans made at the money post were in ordinary times very close to the outside rates. In time of stringency the Stock Exchange rate tended to be somewhat lower than that set by the banks, but it was usually a good index to market conditions. There were two call rates at the money post, the renewal rate and the new loan rate. The renewal rate is nowadays fixed by a committee of the Stock Exchange Clearing Corporation, but in this earlier period it was a very informal pronouncement; anyone who happened to be standing near the bulletin board posted the rate at which the first few millions had been loaned for the day, and the committee on arrangements did not enter into the matter at all unless a dispute arose. Since loans were not usually made until the market had been open for an hour or so, it was often eleven o'clock or later before the renewal rate was posted. Loans made later in the day might vary considerably from this first rate; during panics it was not unknown for rates to climb to great heights and drop back again in the course of a few hours. The making of loans ceased at three o'clock.[25]

In the actual placing of call loans, brokers played an increasingly prominent part. Their rôle seems to have gained in importance as the call loan gained over the time loan in the financing of security transactions. In 1869 for the first time the brokers who specialized in the lending of money and securities were given a separate post in the Stock Exchange,[26] and an element of organization was thus introduced into what had hitherto been a quite unorganized market for loans on Stock Exchange collateral. The definite localization of this business made it natural for banks to send their surplus funds to one of the brokers of this group. Private bankers were the first to overcome their conservatism and utilize the new facilities and gradually the commercial banks were won over. Four or five brokers did the bulk of the business, and each one had his regular clients—banks, trust companies, and others.

The type of security which was acceptable to the banks making call loans changed during the period. Railroad stocks and bonds seem to have been entirely satisfactory even in the period immediately after the Civil War, but the industrials, although they had figured in the trading for several decades before that time, were still viewed with suspicion. The industrial securities did fluctuate far more widely than the rails, although it is doubtful whether they were subject to more manipulation. It was many years before the industrials were admitted into the collateral portfolios at all. In 1899 some banks and a few trust companies still retained a prejudice against them and those who did accept them insisted upon larger margins. Loans against

[25] Woodlock, *Stock Exchange and Money Market*, p. 32. Pujo Committee Hearings, 62 Congress, 3 Session, Vol. I, pp. 742-54.

[26] Stedman, *History of the New York Stock Exchange*.

"good active Stock Exchange collateral," by which was meant railroad securities, were required to have a margin of only 20 per cent while loans on industrial stocks required margins of 25 and 30 per cent.[27] By 1911 the industrials had gained sufficient reputation for respectability to be admitted as collateral to about one-third of the total, the other two-thirds being rails; the margins by this time had also been lowered, and 10 to 15 per cent was the usual requirement, with a ten-point reduction in the market value of the stock.[28] It was not until 1919 that three of the largest lenders on call abandoned the practice of quoting rates on loans secured by industrials at a higher figure than for loans secured by good mixed collateral.[29] Discrimination against securities which were not listed on the "big board" still persisted.

When a customer purchased securities on margin through a broker, the title to the securities, under the laws of New York, was vested in the customer. In spite of that fact, it was the habit of brokers to take these same stocks to their banks and borrow upon them to the greatest amount possible, regardless of the amount of cash which had been actually paid by the customer. A ruling of the Appellate Division of the New York Supreme Court in 1897 proclaimed this practice illegal, but in spite of some confusion no actual change in methods was made. Brokers had only to get the permission of their customers to use the stocks as collateral in order to legalize the practice, and the matter was adjusted by an agreement between brokers and customers.[30]

A slight change in the relations between brokers and their customers was also brought about by the imposition of a state stamp tax of two dollars per hundred shares traded. If this tax had been payable every time the loan was renewed and the collateral against the loan exchanged or shifted, the cost would have been very heavy. In order to avoid this the Clearing House

[27] *Commercial and Financial Chronicle*, Vol. 68, p. 53, January 14, 1899.

[28] Pujo Committee Hearings, 62 Congress, 3 Session, Vol. I, pp. 347, 350, 495, 742; Vol. III, p. 1787.

[29] *New York Times Annalist*, Vol. XIV, p. 169, August 11, 1919.

[30] *Commercial and Financial Chronicle*, Vol. 65, p. 545, September 25, 1897. Pujo Committee Hearings, 63 Congress, 2 Sessions, Vol. III, p. 1785.

Committee developed a new form of agreement by which the banks secured effective control over the collateral while the brokers were permitted to substitute one security for another without actually renewing the loan.[31]

Over-certification

One of the most vexing questions which arose in connection with brokers' borrowings from banks was that of the over-certification of checks. In order to obtain the securities which had been purchased for his customers' account, it was necessary for the broker to pay the seller by check. But in order to obtain the deposit against which to draw such a check, the broker had first to borrow from his bank. In was impossible for both operations to be performed simultaneously, and to bridge the gap, banks were accustomed to certify the broker's check, permit him to take it to the seller and bring back the securities which were to serve as collateral, and then to deposit the proceeds of the loan to meet the draft. For several hours the bank was therefore in the position of having an unsecured loan on its books. Bank credit had been increased without a corresponding increase in deposit liabilities and reserves, for certified checks were not included in total liabilities, and were subtracted from deposits in computing the reserve ratio.

The practice of over-certification of checks had developed gradually with the growth of stock trading, and had been common for at least a quarter-century before the passage of the National Bank Act. It seems to have been an extension of the well recognized custom of extending bank credit in the form of overdrafts, which was permitted, or at least not forbidden, by most of the state banking laws. Certified checks were sometimes issued to merchants in advance of their deposits, but it was in connection with security trading that such checks usually came into existence and they became an integral part of the financial machinery of New York. By 1868 it was estimated that three-fourths of the checks going through the Clearing House were certified checks issued in advance of deposits. Of

[31] *Commercial and Financial Chronicle,* Vol. 67, p. 56, July 9, 1898.

constructive proposals for eliminating this practice there were few. To use an uncertified check instead of a certified would have been unacceptable to the banks, for it would have transferred their trust from a known customer to many unknown persons. A stock exchange clearing house would have gone far towards solving the difficulty, but the conservative opinion of Wall Street refused to consider such an innovation at that time.[32] The comptroller of the currency discussed the subject in his annual report for 1868, and after condemning over-certification of checks, call loans, and interest on deposits, because they encouraged stock speculation, suggested that the over-certification, at least, might well be prohibited by law.[33]

On March 3, 1869, the recommendation of the comptroller was enacted into law, and it was made illegal for any national bank to "certify any check drawn upon said bank unless the person or company drawing said check shall have on deposit in said bank at the time such check is certified an amount of money equal to the amount specified in such check." The penalty for violation of the law was the appointment of a receiver for the bank, and the forfeiture of its charter. An effort to strengthen the law, by making bank officers individually liable for checks certified illegally, failed to gain the approval of Congress in 1870. Only two banks were prosecuted in the early days of this law. The National Bank of the Commonwealth was obliged to suspend during the panic of September, 1873, when it permitted a banking firm to overdraw its account by $200,000, and the New Orleans National Banking Association was closed a month later, although both banks had assets more than sufficient to cover their liabilities.[34]

In spite of these efforts to enforce the law, it had very little influence on the actual making of bank loans on collateral security. The national banks knew that unless they could accom-

[32] *Commercial and Financial Chronicle*, Vol. 4, p. 807, June 29, 1867. See pp. 299-305 below.

[33] *Commercial and Financial Chronicle*, Vol. 7, July 4, 1868, p. 6. Comptroller of Currency, *Annual Reports*, 1882, p. 25; 1884, p. 47: 1911, pp. 78-79.

[34] Huntington and Mawhinney, *Laws*, p. 368. Comptroller of Currency, *Report*, 1873, p. xxxii. *Commercial and Financial Chronicle*, Vol. 17, p. 410, September 27, 1873.

modate their customers in some way, business would go to the state banks, and various methods of circumventing the law were resorted to. Some of the banks stamped the checks "accepted" instead of "certified"; others granted the broker a loan on his unsecured note, the proceeds of which were then deposited in the bank and made the basis for a certified check.[35]

For a time after 1873, the agitation died down. In 1879 it was renewed because of the great increase in the volume of certified checks presented at the Clearing House. From a daily total of 30 million dollars in April of that year, it rose to 90 millions in October, nearly three-fourths of the total daily clearings. At the same time the national bank examiner reported that 9 of the city banks had at various times certified checks in violation of the law, 5 of them being accustomed to do so frequently. A quiet investigation was made and when it was learned that this over-certification had been materially reduced, the comptroller took no further action.[36]

The volume of certified checks continued to increase and by 1882 the situation had reached a point where 9 of the banks in a single day were certifying or accepting checks in larger amount than their combined capital. The law was thereupon made more stringent; not only the over-certification of checks was made illegal, but a penalty was imposed upon any one "who shall resort to any device or receive any fictitious obligation, direct or collateral, in order to evade the provisions" of the law. Under this phrase the attorney general ruled that the acceptance of checks, which had been widely adopted to take the place of certification, was equally without the law.[37] Two national banks in New York City, the Bank of the State of New York, and the Saint Nicholas, changed from national to state charters because of this ruling. A new state bank was organized under the auspices of the Produce Exchange in order to facilitate the certification of checks for brokers dealing in commodities. The movement towards the organization of a stock clearing house, toward

35 *Commercial and Financial Chronicle*, Vol. 8, p. 326, March 13, 1869.

36 Comptroller of Currency, *Report*, 1879, p. 25.

37 Comptroller of Currency, *Report*, 1882, pp. 28-29

which several unsuccessful efforts had been made in previous years, was now given encouragement by the comptroller, and succeeded in coming sufficiently alive to function for several weeks.[38]

Day loans

After this period of active agitation against over-certification the matter was quietly dropped and the banks succeeded in working out devices for providing the brokers with funds without running athwart the law. The stock clearing house which began operations in 1892 reduced the amount of funds which were required in security transactions and did much to solve the problem by that means. The banks developed a technique for making day loans which were quite as satisfactory from their point of view as the over-certification of checks. These loans are used only in the purchase and sale of securities which take place one day for delivery the next day. The broker first obtains from his bank authority to issue checks; this authority is usually for an amount five times as great as the broker's balance and it is issued, either upon the broker's demand note, or upon a contingency loan agreement. With this authority the broker proceeds to draw checks in payment of the securities, and these checks the bank is willing to certify. From the proceeds of the day's transactions, the broker obtains sufficient funds to make a deposit at his bank against the check already drawn. By three o'clock, when the receiving teller closes his window for the day, the broker's deposit is large enough to meet the checks sent through the Clearing House in the morning. The day loans are not entered in the regular loan books of the bank and they do not enter at all into the statement of condition drawn up at the close of the day. They do not therefore, affect the reserve position of the banks.[39]

The day loan, or clearance loan, as it is sometimes called, is quite different from the call loan, and is indeed only the first step in the making of a call loan, since it enables the broker

[38] *Bankers' Magazine*, Vol. 37, pp. 387, 546. Comptroller of Currency, *Report*, 1884, p. 47. See pp. 299-305 below.

[39] *New York Times Weekly Financial Quotation Review*, Dec. 16, 1912, p. 3.

to get possession of the securities on which he can borrow in the call market. The amount of day loans in 1912 was estimated at about 100 millions of dollars. It is probable that brokers asked for a greater amount of day loans than was really needed, since the only element of cost for them was the necessity of keeping bank balances up to one-fifth of the total.[40]

Liquidity of call loans

The call market was the market of last resort for the banks of the country. When funds could not be obtained, some emergency measure became necessary. These measures were of three general types. The first was coöperative action among the banks, which might take the form of a syndicate offering funds on call until the panic was allayed. This was the device used in December, 1899, when several suspensions announced after a period of uncertainty precipitated a sharp but short panic. The firm of J. P. Morgan loaned one million dollars at 6 per cent at the height of the excitement, and persuaded nine of the banks and one trust company to do the same. This was sufficient to bring the call rate from ½ per cent per day back to 6 per cent per year, and break the panic. Again in May, 1901, the corner in Northern Pacific demoralized the stock market and sent call rates from an opening of 40 to 75 per cent. The Chairman of the Clearing House Committee organized a syndicate of Morgan and fourteen banks, with 20 millions at their disposal, which effectually lowered rates.[41]

Where the panic seemed likely to be more serious in nature and of longer duration, the banks knew that throwing funds into the call market would not alone be sufficient and they made preparations more effectively to utilize their reserves by the issues of Clearing House loan certificates. These issues were made on five different occasions between 1863 and 1913.[42]

[40] The New York banks began to charge interest against day loans at the rate of 1 per cent in 1930 in order to reduce the amounts requested by brokers. See Volume II of these studies.

[41] *Commercial and Financial Chronicle*, Vol. 69, Dec. 23, 1899, p. 1277; Vol. 72, May 11, 1901, p. 901.

[42] See p. 419 below.

Besides the coöperative action of the banks during a money market crisis, there was the action of the treasury, which threw itself into the breach on many occasions, sometimes more effectively than at others. The relations between the treasury and the banks were continuous and important but they were not adequate to cope with a panic.

There remained a third possibility for assisting the money market—the importation of gold from abroad. Each of these three methods will be discussed in detail in later chapters, but it must already be clear that each was a method, not for preventing disaster, but for coming to the rescue of the banks after disaster had occurred.

Summary

Although part of the funds of the call loan market came from outside of New York, the banks of that city were the most important lenders on call and much of the importance attached to the call market arose from this close association. The rates for call loans and the reserve ratio of the banks moved inversely to each other through the year, call rates rising in the autumn as the reserves of the banks declined. A few changes in the technique of making call loans occurred, but without affecting the basic relations between the call loan market and the banks. When call loans were called, only a small portion could be liquidated, and the rest had to be shifted or the market became frozen. Certain emergency measures could be taken, but no completely satisfactory device was available.

CHAPTER XIV

THE EXPORT OF SECURITIES AND THE INVESTMENT MARKET

The half century after the Civil War was notable in the securities market chiefly because it marked the gradual diminishing of foreign domination in that field. In the ante-bellum period the United States, like every other new country, needed more capital than its own savings could provide and had to depend upon the importation of capital from older nations. In the years between 1863 and 1913 this dependence became gradually less, and by the turn of the century, the United States had begun to lend capital to other countries.

The loss of national credit occasioned by the outbreak of Civil War put a temporary stop to the influx of foreign capital, and the northern states were obliged to absorb enormous issues of government bonds without foreign aid. The national debt of the Federal government rose from less than 100 millions in 1861 to more than 2½ billions in 1866, an increase of about ½ billion per year. It would have been impossible to float so large an amount of government bonds at home if the currency had not been greatly inflated, and the further the inflation proceeded, the greater was the amount of money which the government had to raise by bond issues. The fact that the country could absorb the loans was also partly due to the fact that other issues were held in abeyance during the War. The Confederate government succeeded in borrowing a small sum at a high cost in England[1] but none of the issues of the northern government were floated abroad although they were bought and sold abroad to a limited extent and quotations on them appeared regularly in the foreign financial journals.

Growth of foreign investments after the War

Towards the close of the War, when it became apparent that

[1] Hirst, *The Credit of Nations*, p. 118.

Courtesy Manhattan Card Publishing Company

WALL STREET IN 1908

the Federal government was certain to be victorious, the European investor again began to buy United States government bonds, state bonds, and railroad stocks and bonds. By the year 1866 new purchases added to those held abroad before the War, brought the total to approximately 600 millions of dollars. Government bonds accounted for 350 millions, state and municipal bonds for 150 millions, and rail stocks and bonds for 50 millions. A few millions of government bonds were returned from Germany when war broke out there in 1866 and the crisis in London in the same year also reduced the demand for American securities, but these losses were soon wiped out by the increased demand. Europan capital made possible the refunding of the public debt and the resumption of specie payments. The amount of United States bonds held abroad increased rapidly. In 1866 it had been estimated at 350 millions; in 1868, it was set at 700 millions, and in 1869 at one billion.[2]

SECURITIES HELD BY FOREIGN INVESTORS, 1869

(In millions of dollars)

United States bonds	1,000
Railroad bonds	130
Railroad stocks	113
Municipal bonds	7.5
Canal bonds	5
Mining stocks and bonds	10
Mortgage bonds	25
Miscellaneous	125
Floating debt	50
TOTAL FOREIGN CAPITAL	1,465.5

The panic of 1873 administered another setback to the export of American securities. The depression which followed the panic and the uncertainty regarding the resumption of specie payments seriously impaired the market abroad. Of the 1½ billion dollars' worth of American stocks which were supposed

[2] Hunt's *Merchants' Magazine*, Vol. 59, pp. 245 ff.; 41 Congress, 2 Session, House Executive Document 27, p. xxviii. Secretary of Treasury, *Annual Report*, 1868, p. viii.

to have been held overseas before the panic,[3] 300 millions were returned to this country in the three years from 1876 to 1878 alone. Up to this time the greatest appeal to European capital had been made by government securities which had comprised two-thirds of the total foreign holdings in 1869. It was impossible for foreign investors to keep their government bonds, however, for a strong domestic demand drove the price up and the yield down, and brought them home again. The national banks purchased them to serve as a basis for their circulating notes; and Federal securities were among the few eligible investments for savings banks in many states. Moreover the government was rapidly redeeming the debt and thus reducing the amount of bonds in the market. By 1878 the amount of governments bonds held abroad had fallen to one-fifth the total of a decade before, and was put at 200 millions by the secretary of the treasury. In 1900 even state and municipal bonds were almost entirely absorbed by the home demand, and only two states, six cities, and one county, had their issues listed in London.[4]

Railroad securities held abroad

In these circumstances the foreign demand turned to railroad shares. The total foreign holdings of rails, which had been estimated in 1869 at 243 millions, increased by 1876 to 375 millions.[5] Many of the rail bonds were issued in sterling denominations rather than in dollars, and were payable in London.[6] The Atlantic and Great Western railroad, built during the Civil War, was almost entirely owned in England, and the Illinois Central was controlled by foreign shareholders who owned at least three-fourths of its stock.

The building of railroads was given new impetus by the revival of foreign interest. With this assistance 28,000 miles of new road were constructed between 1879 and 1882. By 1883

[3] *Commercial and Financial Chronicle*, May 18, 1872, p. 646.

[4] Secretary of Treasury, *Annual Report*, 1878, p. xviii. Bacon, "Capital Invested in United States from Abroad," *Yale Review*, 1900, pp. 265-66.

[5] *New York Journal of Commerce*, December 6, 1911.

[6] Thirty-three millions of such securities were outstanding in 1868, in addition to 9 millions of canal and water bonds in sterling.

foreign holdings of railroad securities alone were more than 1½ billions and the total of all American securities in foreign hands must have been at least 2 billions.[7] Unfortunately much of this new mileage paralleled tracks already in existence and the rate wars which began in 1882, coupled with generally depressed business, made American railroad securities again an unpopular investment from the foreign point of view. The net movement of securities turned against this country and about 25 million dollars worth were returned to America from Europe each year from 1882 to 1885, although this was not a large amount in comparison with the total amount of American securities held abroad at the time. The revival of trade in the years after 1885 had the usual effect upon the export of securities; German investors put enormous amounts into such railroads as Northern Pacific and English investors bought American rails and American mining shares. The new capital brought in from abroad in the next five years raised the total foreign investments to about 3 billions, or an increase of 50 per cent above 1883.[8]

This period of heavy capital importation was brought to a close, like most of its predecessors, by a business crisis. Indeed the tide of securities had turned even before the panic. The conflict over the monetary standard in the United States, combined with the depressing spectacle of a government treasury obliged to borrow on the lender's terms in order to avoid bankruptcy, lowered the value of all types of securities, and the scandals in the administration of certain railroads which came to light at the same time further depressed the rails. For the five years from 1890 to 1894 inclusive the average net withdrawal of capital and return of American securities was about 60 millions per year, with the heaviest returns in 1893 and 1894. Probably no previous period except that of the Civil War had seen so heavy a return of securities to this country.[9]

[7] Paish, *Trade Balance of the United States*, p 173.

[8] Bullock, Williams and Tucker, "The Balance of Trade in the United States," *Review of Economic Statistics*, 1919, p. 226.

[9] See p. 372 for further details of treasury and money market difficulties at this time. *Commercial and Financial Chronicle*, Vol. 60, April 13, 1895, p. 632; May 4, p. 769.

The improvement in America's credit after 1895 inaugurated a new phase of capital importation with only minor interruption during the panics of 1903 and 1907. But the rate of capital importation was materially lessened during these years; the American investor was becoming increasingly able to provide funds for American railroads and industries without calling upon Europe for assistance. By 1899 the total volume of securities held abroad had increased to only 3 1/3 billions as compared with 3 billions in 1890,[10] and by 1914 the total was only 4½ billions. These figures were reduced by the return of securities, not only during depression but during times of unusual prosperity as well. Particularly in the railroad mergers of 1899-1900 securities were repurchased by Americans and brought back to this country in great volume.[11]

New York begins to export capital

Coincident with declining importation of foreign capital, was the beginning of an exportation of American capital. In 1879 a New York banking house associated with the Bank of Montreal floated in New York a loan of 3 millions for the Province of Quebec which was heralded as a remarkable feat for the time. Canada was also the destination of about 100 millions of American capital invested during the years 1896 to 1900.[12] In 1900 American investors began to go farther afield; a large part of the British Exchequer loan was placed in New York during the Boer War; 30 million pounds of it were taken jointly by J. P. Morgan and the Rothschilds and public subscriptions to the remaining 30 million pounds were taken in New York by Morgan, and by Kidder, Peabody and Company. A German loan was also offered in New York during the same year and thereafter the flotation of foreign loans became more frequent.[13]

[10] Bacon, "Capital Invested in United States from Abroad, *Yale Review*, 1900, p. 275. The Paish estimate of 6 billions in 1910 is reviewed and judged too high, in, Bullock, Williams and Tucker, "The Balance of Trade in the United States," *Review of Economic Statistics*, 1919.

[11] Conant, "Securities as Means of Payment," *Annals American Academy of Political Science*, Vol. 14, p. 181.

[12] *Bankers' Magazine*, Vol. 33, p. 744. *London Economist*, January 26, 1901, p. 119.

New York began to take on the appearance of a world security market. Even more important than this was the fact that as New York ceased to borrow abroad it became less dependent upon foreign markets and foreign business conditions. The New York market did not reach financial maturity until the World War, but it was growing rapidly in the years from 1900 to 1914.

The issue of new securities was largely carried on by a few important private investment houses in New York City and only a few banks in New York took any direct part in such operations. Yet they were of the most vital importance to the security market and of the greatest public interest, since in the existing scheme it was almost impossible for any large issue to be floated without the backing of one or more of these houses organized as an underwriting syndicate. Kuhn, Loeb and Company, the Morgan house, and Speyer and Company, were foremost among the investment bankers and a large share of American issues, whether destined for the American or the foreign purchaser, went through their hands before they appeared at the Stock Exchange. The larger banks in New York, although forbidden by law to purchase common stocks, were able to take part in the underwriting of such issues through the security companies organized under their auspices and controlled by the same stockholders. The stock of the bank and the security company was usually sold together so that to all intents they were inseparable. The degree of control which was thus exercised over the money market was undoubtedly enormous. But with all the disadvantages which were inherent in this form of centralized control, it was a valuable stabilizing factor in what was otherwise a badly disorganized money market.

Lack of mortgage bonds in New York market

The market for investment securities in New York was preëminently the market for corporate obligations. Throughout its history the New York money market has been almost entirely lacking in facilities for the floating and sale of mortgage bonds.

[13] *Bankers' Magazine*, Vol. 61 pp. 329, 485. *Commercial and Financial Chronicle*, Vol. 72, April 27, 1901, p. 796.

In this it failed notably to follow the example of European money markets; where special banks have been organized to furnish credit on this type of security.

It is doubtful if the provision of the national banking act, which forbade national banks to lend upon real estate collateral, had very much to do with the situation. The law was occasionally evaded when evasion seemed profitable, and it might have been evaded more often by taking judgment notes and lending on personal security, had there been a real desire for such investment.[14] State banks, which were in nearly every state permitted to make such investment, utilized the privilege to a very slight extent. A proposed amendment in 1893 to the National Bank Act, repealing the clause against real estate loans, failed of passage.[15]

Perhaps the fundamental cause for the failure of a mortgage market to develop lay in the fact that during most of the nineteenth century there was free land available in the United States. Rather than mortgage a farm in the East for the purpose of adding improvements, the eastern farmer could pack up his goods and his family and take them West where they could settle on unencumbered ground and make a fresh start. Farm land in the eastern and middle states declined in value in some places as much as 25 per cent in the fifteen or twenty years before 1890.[16]

The first companies attempting to put mortgage security on the same basis as corporate security, by issuing their own bonds with mortgages as collateral, ended in such disastrous failure that further efforts were discouraged. A number of small mortgage loan companies were founded in the years from 1870 to 1876, but they did not issue debenture bonds, secured by the mortgages until 1881.[17] The issue of such securities went on rather rapidly during the next ten years and an effort was made to place them in the eastern markets. Thirty-nine companies

[14] Hearings of House Committee on Banking and Currency, 1913, 62 Congress, 3 Session, p. 500.

[15] Powell, *Evolution of the Money Market,* p. 284. Hearings of House Committee on Banking and Currency, 1893, 53 Congress, 1 Session, p. 7.

[16] Peters, "The Depreciation of Farming Land."

[17] Frederiksen, "Mortgage Banking in America."

from other states were licensed to sell mortgages in New York states in 1891 and almost as many more in Massachusetts and Connecticut together. Most of these companies were organized originally in states west of the Mississippi—Iowa and Kansas were particularly well represented.[18] The long decline in general prices affected farm products and had a depressing effect upon the New York sale of these bonds. During the year 1889-1890 sales in New York fell to one-fifth of the average during the preceding five years, and the market for mortgage bonds was given a setback from which it never entirely recovered. Such securities never advanced to the point where they were listed on an exchange, as was the case in Europe, and the trading in them became confined to a comparatively small class of specialized investors, such as savings banks and trust companies.

The development of security trading technique

The greater part of security trading took place at the New York Stock Exchange and it was that institution which symbolized Wall Street in the minds of many persons. Yet there have always been other exchanges, some of them important enough to be serious competitors of the New York Stock Exchange. The New York Mining Stock Exchange maintained a market for mining and other stocks from 1876 to 1883; then enlarged its scope and became the New York Mining Stock and National Petroleum Exchange. In 1885 it became the Consolidated Stock and Petroleum Exchange of New York, and added railroad securities to its list. For many years it carried on a considerable business, amounting in the nineties to about one-third as much as that of the New York Stock Exchange.[19] So serious was the rivalry that members of the latter were not permitted to buy or sell on the Consolidated Exchange. The Curb Exchange, which sacrificed picturesqueness for comfort by moving indoors in 1921, provided a market for securities unacceptable at other exchanges and was not a competitor. The amount of the sales on the Curb was not reported before 1921.

[18] *Annual Report* of the New York State Superintendent of Banks relative to Mortgage, Loan and Investment Companies, 1891-1899.

[19] *Annual Reports* of the Consolidated Exchange, 1886 to 1913.

The actual volume of trading appears absurdly small in comparison with modern standards. In November, 1879, during the revival which followed the resumption of specie payments, the highest sales at the New York Stock Exchange were 700,000 shares a day. It was not until December, 1886, at the peak of a two-year rise in stock prices, that the million-share mark was passed. On Tuesday, April 30, 1901, the sale of 3,281,226 shares established a new high record which stood until 1916. An average day, in the years from 1901 to 1913, was far below this figure.[20] The volume of trading was closely correlated with changes in business, reflecting four major cycles between 1897 and 1912.[21]

Increase of industrial securities

The greater part of the increase in volume of trading was due to the industrial security. The number of industrial issues listed by the Exchange rose from 15 to 191 between 1867 and 1913, while the rails increased only from 63 to 147. The corporate form of organization for industrial enterprises, which had made slow progress during the first three-quarters of the century, got under way with a great rush during the last quarter century. By that time the great period of railway construction was nearly over; after 1887 the new mileage constructed in each year declined almost steadily and the capital which had formerly gone into railroads became available for other types of security. Lax corporation laws, low interest rates, and the ease with which money could be raised by stock issues, were strong incentives toward the incorporation of business enterprises. Combinations and mergers drew many small companies into larger corporations of national scope, and improved the demand for their issues. These new companies listed their stock on the New York Exchange; others appeared on the Consolidated Exchange or on the curb, and a few on the exchanges in other cities.

[20] *Commercial and Financial Chronicle,* Vol. 29, Nov. 29, 1879, Supplement, p. iv; Vol. 43, Dec. 18, 1886, p. 739; Vol. 72, May 4, 1901, p. 865.

[21] A detailed analysis of seasonal and other changes in stock prices and the volume of stock trading may be found in Hardy and Owens, *Interest Rates and Stock Speculation.*

The proportion of stocks to bonds was much higher in the case of the industrial issues than it had been in the case of the railroads, and this gave the industrials a speculative tinge which caused them to be looked upon with great suspicion.[22]

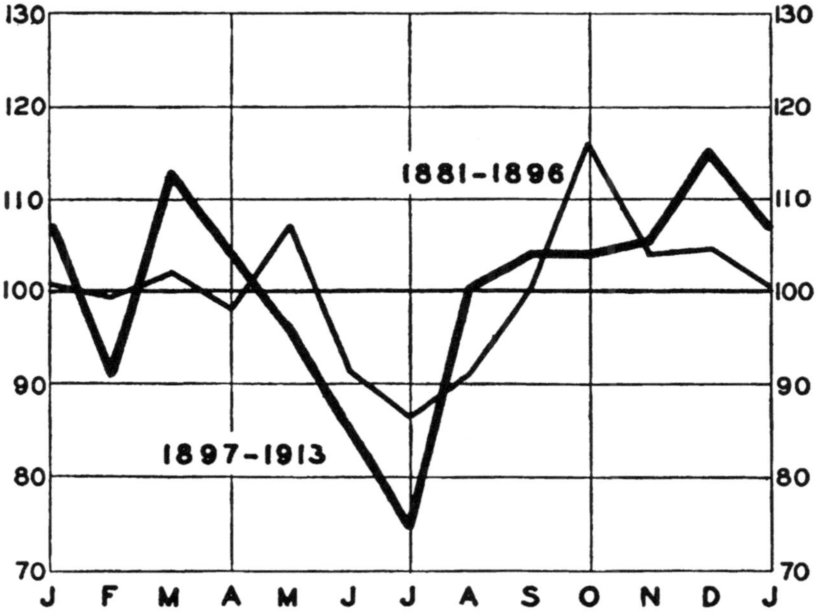

INDEX OF SEASONAL VARIATION IN THE NUMBER OF SHARES SOLD ON THE NEW YORK STOCK EXCHANGE.

SOURCE: OWENS AND HARDY, INTEREST RATES AND STOCK SPECULATION. DEVIATIONS FROM TWELVE-MONTHS' MOVING AVERAGE, ADJUSTED.

Many did not deserve a better reputation; they had little intrinsic value and their prices fluctuated widely at the mercy of speculators. Bankers refused to accept them on the same terms as railroad stocks as collateral for loans. It was not until the Stock Exchange grew much more severe in its listing requirements and demands for reports that the position of the industrials improved.

The steady upward trend in the volume of business transacted on the Exchange was a constant spur to the improvement

[22] *Bankers' Magazine,* Vol. 47, p. 410.

of trading technique. At the close of the Civil War this technique was still of the most primitive kind. Formal "calls" had not yet been abandoned by the New York Stock Exchange although more sales were made before and between, than during, them. The first was made at 10.30 A.M., the second at 1 P.M., and on full days it took more than an hour to get through the list. Calls were a hindrance rather than a help when trading was active and they were abandoned in 1875 for all but bonds and unlisted unsecurities, the slower-moving portion of the list.[23] The Consolidated Exchange followed the same principle for in 1899 it still retained calls for the mining shares in which transactions were very limited while there was no call in the more active rails and industrials.[24]

The ticker

To a certain extent the ticker took the place of the regular calls since it was a means of making public the market values of securities almost as rapidly as they were determined. The first ticker was installed in 1867 and with successive minor improvements proved adequate for many years. As business increased, accompanying the revival of 1896, it became necessary to omit the quotations for options; and in periods of unusually active business it was sometimes found necessary to omit the printing of quotations for odd lots and for bid and asked prices of inactive shares.[25] It is evident that pressure upon the stock ticker is not a new phase and that the necessity which culminated in the improvements of 1930 was similar to that which had been felt at other stages of the market's development.

It has always been a problem at the Exchange how to keep the actual trading confined within definite hours so that the bookkeeping and banking operations connected with security transactions may be performed, and that the details of the trading, with particular respect to undercutting of commissions, may

[23] *New York Times*, October 1, 1873, p. 2. Gibson, *The Stock Exchanges of London, Paris and New York*, p. 77.

[24] *Annual Report*, Consolidated Exchange, 1898-1899.

[25] *Commercial and Financial Chronicle*, Vol. 62, April 18, 1896, p. 713; Vol. 76, April 25, 1903, p. 894; Vol. 91, November 5, 1910, p. 1219.

be kept under close supervision. During the Civil War the activity in gold and securities was a strong temptation to brokers to lengthen business hours. It became their custom to spend the evenings in an uptown hotel and in 1865 a special building was erected for the express purpose of facilitating evening sales. Speculators in gold met in a basement room dubbed the Coal Hole which later became the Gold Exchange, with a corresponding gain in reputation. The Open Board of Brokers was organized from the brokers of the curb.[26] Both the Stock Exchange and the Gold Exchange forbade their members to attend the evening exchange and it was left to carry on its dealings on the outer fringe of the market. When the war boom was over it was abandoned, and the Open Board also gave up its independent existence and united with the New York Stock Exchange. In 1872 the New York Stock Exchange passed stringent resolutions against members guilty of trading on the street after the close of the Exchange.[27] The trading hours of the Stock Exchange at that time lasted until 5 o'clock on week days and 4 o'clock on Saturdays, which should have been long enough to satisfy any broker. In the next year the trading day was provisionally shortened, and lasted from 10 A.M. to 3 P.M.[28]

Stock clearing

The increase in the volume of trading on the Exchange brought forcibly into view the necessity of finding a more expeditious method of handling the transfer of securities from seller to buyer. Even more pressing than the physical delivery of shares was the problem of security credit with which to finance the sales.[29] The obvious form of relief was some sort of clearing house, following the principles which had been applied to bank checks by the New York Clearing House Association and to gold by the Gold Exchange Bank. The Civil War was hardly over therefore when the first published plan for a stock clearing

[26] Eames, *New York Stock Exchange*, p. 121.

[27] This rule did not apply to trading at the regular Curb market during legitimate hours.

[28] *Bankers' Magazine*, Vol. 20, pp. 26, 288; Vol. 26, p. 709; Vol. 28, p. 69.

[29] See p. 282 above.

house made its appearance. The *Bankers' Magazine* for August, 1868, carried the announcement that such an institution would soon be established. It had been chartered by the legislature on April 20, 1867, under the name of "The Bankers' and Brokers' Association." The capital stock was set at $500,000, in $100 shares, and the management was to be under a board of thirteen trustees, of whom the five incorporators were the first.[30] The process of organization was a slow one and all that was accomplished during the next year and a half was an agreement with the Open Board of Brokers, the current rival of the New York Stock Exchange, to coöperate with the latter in the clearing house. In May the clearing house was designated as the official agent of the Exchange in the settlement of stock transactions. It was planned to make a modest beginning with only three issues, *New York Central, Erie,* and *Michigan Southern.* Each broker was to send to the clearing house a list of his purchases and sales for the day, with his check for the difference. The clearing house was to make all deliveries and payments, and pay him any balance due by 12.30 P.M., for the modest commission of twenty cents per hundred shares.

The date of the opening was finally set for June 8, 1868, but the actual clearings did not begin until Thursday, June 11. During the first three days the clearings were 4,400 shares, 5,000 shares, and 16,500 shares respectively, and on Monday eight more stocks were added to the list to be cleared. By that time the opposition to the plan had rallied and succeeded in forcing through both the Open Board and the regular Stock Exchange resolutions which restored to members the right to choose their method of settlement. By the nineteenth, in consequence of this resolution, the business of the clearing house had fallen away to almost nothing. The chief basis of the objections was the requirement that dealers furnish statements of their dealings to the clerks of the clearing house. Many brokers had a morbid fear of publicity and were convinced that lists of their sales and purchases, even without the names of the principals, were a menace. Another reason for the failure of the plan was the

[30] Laws of New York, 90th Session, 1867, Vol. 1. Ch. 474, pp. 1167-69.

fact that it did not eliminate the difficulties in connection with the over-certification of checks. Deliveries of certificates and payments of certified checks were required before 12 o'clock, and many dealers found it difficult to obtain credit and furnish the certificate while most of their collateral security was locked up in the clearing house.[31]

So decisive had been the defeat of the first stock clearing plan that it was ten years before the effort was repeated. The Osterberg plan of 1879 was far less pretentious than the earlier scheme. Brokers who were interested in the project were asked merely to sign an agreement to settle their balances through the clearing house. The group was not incorporated, and it had no official connection with the Stock Exchange; it was a purely informal and voluntary arrangement. Operations were begun in February, 1880, but although more than one hundred brokers had agreed to use it, the new clearing house was even less successful than its predecessor and after two days the scheme was abandoned.[32]

In spite of this second failure the agitation for some form of stock clearing continued and the Stock Exchange was called upon for action. The pressure on the Governing Committee of the Stock Exchange became so strong that it felt obliged to publish a statement that the Committee itself had no authority to act in the matter and that the Exchange as a whole must take action if a clearing house were desired.[33] Meantime the over-certification of checks by national banks had been made illegal and it became more difficult for brokers to finance their purchases in the old way.[34] With this added incentive to action the New York Stock Clearing-house Association was organized in August, 1883, and put into operation under the direction of Mr. R. L. Edwards, president of the Bank of the State of New York, and with Mr. Osterberg as manager. It began by offering to clear four stocks free of charge for the first thirty days. Un-

[31] *Bankers' Magazine*, Vol. 23, pp. 145, 303, 472, 1006; Vol. 39, pp. 432, 587.

[32] *Bradstreets'*, November 1, 1879, p. 4. *Bankers' Magazine*, Vol. 34, p. 740; Vol. 31, p. 342.

[33] *Commercial and Financial Chronicle*, Vol. 35, p. 496, November 4, 1882.

[34] See p. 284 above.

fortunately the plan did not last even that moderate length of time and after two weeks it met the same fate which had overtaken its predecessors.[35]

The Consolidated Exchange by this time had an effective clearing system. The plan had been incorporated into the organization scheme when the New York Mining Stock and National Petroleum Exchange became the Consolidated Stock and Petroleum Exchange in 1885. When once installed the system functioned continuously for many years and seemed to escape the hazards which proved fatal at the New York Stock Exchange. The reason undoubtedly lay in the fact that the clearing house was under the direct control of a committee of the Exchange officers and that its prestige and financial standing were therefore superior to any organization which could exist outside the Exchange. The question of publicity seems not to have disturbed the Consolidated Exchange. Members were required to send to the clearing house a list of all their transactions of one day, before 10.45 the next morning, and with it cash or a certified check for the amount of the balance drawn on the Fourth National Bank (later the Bank of the State of New York). If the balance was in favor of the broker, he drew a draft in his own favor against the Fourth National Bank, and the clearing house had it accepted or certified by the bank. The charge for the clearing service was at first ¾ of one cent for each 10 shares bought or sold. This fee was later cut to ¼ of one cent for 10 shares, and to 2½ cents for 100 shares. The clearing service was available for railroad stocks only during the first years, but mining and industrial shares were also being cleared by 1890.

An interesting feature of the Consolidated clearing system was the weekly delivery of stocks. This device, which was probably an adaptation of the fortnightly settlement used in London, was not entirely satisfactory to the members. Daily delivery of two of the most active stocks—*Federal Steel common* and *Atchison preferred*—was begun in 1899 and in 1902 daily deliveries were instituted for all, the reason given being that it would bring the

[35] *Bankers' Magazine*, Vol. 38, p. 147; Vol. 39, pp. 432-35, 675.

usage of the Consolidated Exchange into conformity with the New York Stock Exchange. In 1906 however the daily delivery was also found unsatisfactory and a compromise plan of semi-weekly deliveries was adopted.[36]

In spite of the excellent example set by its competitors, the New York Stock Exchange continued to handle its transactions in the old clumsy manner. The genuine need for some method of clearing was proved by the informal arrangements frequently made between brokers for the payment of balances. A dealer who desired such service kept a minimum account with the broker. His purchases and sales were made in the usual manner, except that on his purchase slips occurred the notation that stocks were to be delivered to the clearing broker instead of to himself. The usual charge was one dollar for clearing one hundred shares.[37] In 1888 an attempt was made to centralize this rough clearing system in the Manhattan Trust Company, where forty Stock Exchange members agreed to send their stocks for clearance.[38]

It was not until 1892 that the New York Stock Exchange finally made up its mind that a stock clearing house was inevitable. The difficulties attending the heavy trading during the Baring panic in 1890 are said to have been instrumental in bringing about the decision. Once made it was carried out promptly. The Governing Committee appointed in February a special committee to report on a plan; in March the report was made, recommending a system similar to that of the Consolidated Exchange, which had already been copied by Philadelphia and Boston. In April the plan was adopted by the members of the Exchange, only 214 out of 1,100 having the temerity to vote against it; and in May, on the hundredth anniversary of the establishment of the Exchange, it was put into operation. With the previous failures in mind the start was made cautiously; only 4 of the most active securities were included in the clearing list during the first week: *Chicago, Milwaukee and St. Paul; Louis-*

[36] *Annual Reports* of the Consolidated Stock and Petroleum Exchange, 1886, p. 166; 1890, p. 63; 1891, p. 27; 1899, p. 56; 1902, p. 50; 1903, p. 51; 1906, p. 16.
[37] Fowler, *Ten Years in Wall Street*, p. 69. *Bankers' Magazine*, Vol. 39, p. 587.
[38] Cohen, *Evolution of Financial Clearance.*

ville and Nashville; Northern Pacific preferred, and *Philadelphia and Reading.* A week later, 4 more were added: *Atchison; Chicago, Burlington and Quincy; Rock Island,* and *Union Pacific.* Others followed, and by the end of the first year the total list for clearing numbered 22 stocks.[39] Gradually it was extended to include all of the issues in which trading was active. The clearing house was successful from the start.

The stock clearing system was extended in 1920 to loans and cash balances as well as to stocks. Under the old system a broker who purchased 1,000 *Steel* and sold 900 *Steel* received 100 shares from the clearing and paid only for them, while a broker who bought *Steel* and sold *Southern Pacific* did not benefit from the clearing. The new plan required the broker to pay only the difference in price between the two transactions.[40] By this means the volume of day loans necessary to carry each day's trading was reduced to about one-third of its previous figure. The volume of checks going through the New York Clearing House was also reduced and the total of bank clearings became less representative of stock transactions than it had been previous to the change since by far the greater part of stock transactions were cancelled and required no drawing of checks.

The saving which was thus effected in the matter of over-certification did not effect an equal economy in the total volume of bank loans outstanding. For the day loans are not now, and the over-certifications were not then, entered as loans upon the books of the bank. Nor was the total volume of bank deposits, against which reserves were computed, increased by the day loans so that there was no diminution in bank deposits by reason of the stock clearing house and its reduction in the amount of such loans. The reason for this may be explained briefly: a day loan is made without collateral security, either in the form of an overdraft against an account which is required to be kept at a certain minimum figure, or as an advance against the broker's

[39] *Commercial and Financial Chronicle,* Vol. 55, November 19, 1892, p. 836; Vol. 56, April 15, 1893, p. 605. *Bradstreet's,* February 13, 1892, p. 100; March 26, p. 193; April 9, p. 226; April 30, p. 280; May 14, p. 311.

[40] 66 Congress, 2 Session, Senate Document 262, Appendix by Mr. Streit.

unsecured promissory note. It is made by the bank to enable a broker to get possession of the securities he has purchased in order that he may secure a "call loan" with the securities as collateral. The call loan is made for the purpose of carrying the stock for a broker or a customer who has bought it on margin and the amount of such loans in existence is not affected by the method of settling balances between brokers. But the stock clearing house permits the broker to settle all his accounts, and therefore to secure possession of all his purchased stocks and bonds, by the payment of balances only, instead of payments for every purchase. The volume of these day loans is therefore greatly diminished by the clearing system; the volume of call loans practically not at all. On the other hand the reduction in the amount of day loans to brokers made it possible for them to reduce the bank balances which they had formerly been obliged to maintain for the purpose of securing such accommodation. Indirectly therefore the volume of bank credit outstanding was somewhat lowered by the new clearing arrangements.

Term settlement

Closely associated with the demand for a stock clearing house had been suggestions that term settlements be adopted in New York. It was natural that persons familiar with the English plan under which settlement was made only once in each fortnight should consider the possibility of its success in New York since it would obviously do what the stock clearing house alone did not do, reduce the amount of credit necessary to carry marginal stock transactions. If accounts between brokers as well as customers' accounts with brokers were permitted to accumulate and settlement and deliveries be made only at the end of the period specified, the short-term transactions would be entirely canceled. At a time of crisis the postponement of many of the transactions might avoid bankruptcies among brokers and traders although it might equally well serve to increase the total liabilities of brokers who, actually insolvent some days before the settlement period, were permitted to carry on until the end of the term.

A tentative suggestion that the rules of the New York Stock Exchange be amended to permit transactions "for the account," as in London, appeared in print as early as 1873 but no action upon the matter seems to have been taken. The change was not seriously advocated until 1887 when a marked decline in the volume of trading led to its recommendation by the "Committee on Dullness" as a method of attracting the public into the market.[41] It was, however, to be purely optional; the existing system of cash settlement was to be supplemented, not supplanted. Settlements were to be made on the fifth and the twentieth of the month through an auditing committee. The term transactions were given the advantage of a lower commission than cash trading, 1/16 of one per cent as compared with 1/8 for cash.

Little time was lost in putting the plan into operation for, in spite of the strong oposition to it among some of the members, the volume of business had so shrunk that many were willing to try any remedy. On September 20 the first "term" began. All trading which was done under the new system was reported to the auditing committee at the close of the day. Money balances were paid the next day through the bank selected as the depositary.[42] During the first period the total volume of sales "for the account" was 124,800 shares, in comparison with 3,687,579 the "regular way." The next fortnight's trial showed little gain. The difference in commissions, which had been expected to attract the public, was neutralized by a difference in quotations for stocks sold "for account" and "regular way." And the fear of publicity among professional traders was as potent in the case of term settlements as it had been in the case of the clearing house. There was also apprehension, not set at rest until a court decision of the following year, lest stock transactions settled by clearing rather than by actual delivery might be contrary to the anti-gaming law which required actual delivery of

[41] The fact that its rival, the Consolidated Exchange, had in 1886 adopted weekly settlements for all its transactions, may have been one of the motives behind the recommendation.

[42] This was the Manhattan Trust Company. Gibson, *The Stock Exchanges of London, Paris and New York*, p. 119.

stocks sold. After less than three months the new system was abolished.[43]

The matter was broached again in 1919 at the annual meeting of the American Acceptance Council, as a means of divorcing call loans from the security markets and establishing a new call loan market based on acceptances in the European manner. It was recognized, however, that the plan involved "changes of great importance both to banks and to members of the exchange,"[44] and the only recommendation was that further study of the subject should be made.

The Reform of the Stock Exchange

More far-reaching and significant than the technical improvements in trading were the reforms instituted from time to time either by legal enactment or by the Stock Exchange itself in the effort to forestall legal action. In spite of the continuous criticism which was directed at the activities of stockbrokers, it was found to be very difficult to secure effective legislative control over them. Whenever an outraged public opinion seemed about to be successful in securing the passage of a regulatory law, the Exchange hastened to change its rules and methods sufficiently to make unnecessary the proposed legislation.

The first piece of Federal legislation which applied to stock trading was a purely revenue measure adopted during the Civil War. Brokers were required to pay a license fee of fifty dollars each, and in addition all sales or contracts for sales of stocks or bonds were taxed 1/20 of one per cent of their par value. The tax was reduced in 1866 and at the end of the War it was abandoned.[45] During the decades which followed, when some of the worst examples of unregulated stock manipulations were taking place, Congress evidenced only sporadic interest in the Stock Exchange, being perhaps fully occupied with investigation of the scandals within its own precincts. In 1908 it was proposed that

[43] *Bradstreet's*, September 3, 1887, p. 581; September 17, p. 613; September 24, p. 629; October 8, p. 664; December 10, p. 815; February 4, 1888, p. 73.

[44] 66 Congress, 2 Session, Senate Document 262.

[45] *Annual Reports* of United States Internal Revenue Commissioner, 1864-1866; Secretary of Treasury, *Annual Report*, 1867, p. 291.

the Federal tax on stock sales be revived, not as a revenue measure, but as a means of penalizing speculation. The rate was set at 50 cents for each 100 dollar share, a figure purposely set high in order to discourage the frequent purchases and sales by which speculators made their profits. The bill raised a storm of protest; it was referred to Committee and never heard from again.[46]

The legislature of the state of New York followed the example of the Federal government in its attempts to control stock trading. In May, 1881, two separate proposals for taxing security transactions were introduced into the legislature. The first would have taxed all sales of stock brokers; the second, only dealings in futures and options. Neither of these bills was enacted,[47] but the subject was not immediately dropped. In 1882 the Senate ordered an investigation of all dealings in futures, with particular emphasis upon grain, and in 1882 and 1887 the annual report of the state comptroller again recommended a tax on stock sales.[48] It was not until twenty years later that such a tax was finally adopted. The tax of 2 cents on each 100 dollars of face value of shares transferred after June 1, 1905, paid, in the second year of its enforcement, one-fourth of all the expenses of the state. There was of course bitter complaint from the taxpayers. The shares selling far below their par value paid the heaviest proportionate tax, and it was said that many of the low-priced mining shares were being sold largely in New Jersey in order to avoid the tax. In spite of all protests the tax was retained.[49]

While these feeble legislative attempts were being made to keep the activities of the exchanges within bounds, the exchanges themselves were conscious, if not of their faults, at least of public disapproval, and were making serious efforts to correct the more flagrant violations of the current code of business ethics. The regulations of the exchange became increasingly more stringent as a result of these efforts and it must be admitted that the rules

[46] 60 Congress, 1 Session, House Bill 18,525. *Commercial and Financial Chronicle,* Vol. 86, March 7, 1908, p. 570.

[47] New York State Senate Documents, 1883, Vol. 5, No. 45. *Commercial and Financial Chronicle,* Vol. 32, May 14, 1881, p. 511; June 11, p. 644.

[48] New York State Documents, 1882, Vol. 6; Document 45, 1883, Vol. 5.

[49] *Commercial and Financial Chronicle,* Vol. 80, May 27, 1905, p. 2195. *Bradstreet's,* December 15, 1906, p. 785.

were enforced with admirable severity. In November, 1868, after several scandals in which overissue of stocks had been prominent, the Open Board of Brokers joined with the New York Stock Exchange in a resolution that on and after January 30, 1869, neither Board would call or deal in any stock of any company which did not keep a registry of its issues with some satisfactory agency, bank, or trust company. The number of shares then outstanding was to be given to the public and thirty days' notice was required before further issues might be made. The failure of the Erie Railroad Company to comply with this rule led to its being stricken from the list in February, 1869. Its defiant directors organized a new exchange popularly known as the "Erie Board," but it was not able to stand out alone. The rule for registry was complied with in September and it was readmitted to the Exchange. Reading stock was off the list from 1872 until 1879 for the same reason.[50]

The question of adequate corporation reports was not so easily disposed of. Business was still considered to be a private affair and corporations looked upon their reports as "concessions rather than rights" of stockholders.[51] The Stock Exchange carried on a long campaign before full and regular reports were obtained from the corporations whose securities appeared on its lists. The committee appointed in 1877 to work towards this end made a good start by requiring that every new company admitted to the list should furnish monthly returns, but over companies with stock already listed, it was unable to use the same sort of coercion. It sent out a modest request for reports, opened a book in which to collect them and then sat back to await results, which were inevitably unsatisfactory. The *Commercial and Financial Chronicle* was more successful simply by keeping at the task and began to publish special report supplements in 1875. Meantime it carried on a vigorous propaganda for better reports, as in the following editorial:

> Every railroad company having its stocks and bonds on the Stock Exchange list in New York or other cities ought certainly once a year

[50] *Bankers' Magazine*, Vol. 23, p. 757. *Commercial and Financial Chronicle*, Vol. 9, September 11, 1869, p. 332.

[51] *Commercial and Financial Chronicle*, Vol. 29, September 20, 1879, p. 289.

to make full report of its earnings, expenses and financial condition; and a failure to do so should fairly be accepted as an admission that there was something to be concealed from the public. Perhaps our readers are not aware of the extent to which some of the very largest railroad corporations conceal their affairs, even from the eyes of their own stockholders.

In the next year the railroad commissioners of New York state began to require quarterly reports under oath from all railroads operating in the state. The reports were to include earnings and expenses and were to be published in the newspapers immediately upon issue.[52]

The problem of industrial corporation reports was yet to be met. The *Chronicle* suggested in 1892 that, in view of their increasing importance on the Exchange, it was a suitable subject for legislative action; but none was taken. A Business Companies' Act, which would have regulated the corporations of the state and provided publicity for their regular reports, failed to pass in 1900. The publication of corporation reports did not become adequate until after the recommendations of the Hughes Committee in 1909 that

the Exchange should . . . adopt methods to compel the filing of frequent statements of the financial condition of the companies whose securities are listed, including balance sheets, income and expense accounts, etc., and should notify the public that these are open to examination under proper rules and regulations. The Exchange should also require that there be filed with future applications for listing, a statement of what the capital stock of the company has been issued for, showing how much has been issued for cash, how much for property, with a description of the property, etc., and also showing what commission, if any, has been paid to the promoters or vendors.[53]

This commission was appointed by Governor Hughes of New York state for the purpose of ascertaining what changes, if any, were "advisable in the laws of the State bearing upon speculation in securities and commodities." It carried on private hearings for six months and no record of them was kept or published.

[52] *Bankers' Magazine,* Vol. 32, p. 11. *Commercial and Financial Chronicle,* Supplement, February, 1882, p. iii; Vol. 34, April 15, 1882, p. 428; Vol. 49, November 16, 1889, p. 640.

[53] *Commercial and Financial Chronicle,* Vol. 55, November 26, 1892, p. 885. Report of Special Committee on Banks to Governor Hughes, 1907.

which seriously impaired their usefulness. But the report which was made in June, 1909, was careful and detailed and made specific recommendations covering the whole range of Stock Exchange activities.

The positive recommendations were largely directed to internal reforms to be put into effect by the Exchange itself; the requirement of larger margins, so that no business would be done on less than 20 per cent; the valuation of securities for margin purposes at average rather than at current prices; the adoption of a rule giving the Board of Governors of the Exchange power to decide when a corner in any stock existed and to fix a settlement price; the abolition of the unlisted department; the strengthening of listing requirements, with especial emphasis upon corporation reports; requiring trading to be carried on in reasonably small units, preferably of 100 shares, and the forbidding of offers for purchase or sale of large lots on an "all or none" basis. It was also recommended that the record sheets of the Clearing House be kept on file for six years, instead of being destroyed within the week, as was then customary.

The Commission put little faith in legislative action. It refused to go on record as condemning short selling and margin trading, pointing out that laws designed to stop them had never been successfully enforced, either in the United States or abroad. Nor did it recommend the passage of a law against the manipulation of stock prices; that which accompanied the issue of new securities they felt to be accompanied with certain advantages to investors, and that which was accomplished merely for the profit of the manipulators was difficult to reach by means of legislation and could better be attacked by the Stock Exchange itself.

The only legislation which was recommended outright was a statute to make it a misdemeanor for a broker to receive any securities or cash from a customer after he became insolvent; a statute giving the customer the right to recover three times the amount of any loss sustained through a broker because a purchase or sale was fictitious; and a statute making it larceny for a broker to sell securities purchased for a customer after they had been paid for in whole or in part. The Committee announced that it was not prepared to advocate the incorporation of the Exchange, a measure which had often been advanced as a necessary reform. But it pointed out that the only way in which the public demand could be satisfied was the reform of its practices from within so that legal regulation would be unnecessary.

The report of the Hughes Committee was taken with considerable seriousness by the Exchange and many of its recommendations were put into immediate effect. The unlisted department was abolished on April 1, 1910, when most of its 800 issues were admitted to the active list after meeting the requirements.[54] In April the Exchange resolved to amend its constitution so as to empower the Law Committee to examine into the dealings of any member whenever it should be deemed for the interest of the Exchange to do so. On March 30, 1910, the rule forbidding offers of large quantities on an "all or none" basis was passed; on May 19, 1909, members were forbidden to have business relations with "bucket shops."[55]

Quite different from the mildness of the Hughes investigations and report was the "money trust" inquiry of the Pujo committee of the House of Representatives. The tone which was adopted by the counsel for the committee gave the hearings the aspect of a trial and put the representatives of the Stock Exchange and other New York institutions on the defensive. The report of the hearings fills three volumes, and the report of the committee a fourth, and together they comprise a valuable source book on the financial organizationof American business in 1912.[56] That part of it which is of most concern at this point refers to the stock exchanges and the sales of corporate securities. The majority report of the committee proposed legislation to enforce:

> Incorporation of the Stock Exchange under state laws.
> Full reports from corporations desiring to list their securities on an exchange.

[54] *Commercial and Financial Chronicle,* Vol. 90, April 2, 1910, p. 891.

[55] 63 Congress, 2 Session, Hearings before the Senate Committee on banking and currency on . . . stock exchanges, pp. 544-49.

[56] 62 Congress, 3 Session, Investigation of financial and monetary conditions in the United States, etc. Hearings of Pujo Committee, 62 Congress, 3 Session, House Report 1593.

Margins of at least 20 per cent.
Prohibition of "wash sales" and price manipulation.
Prohibition of hypothecation of securities for amounts greater than unpaid balance of price.
Prohibition of lending of customers' securities by brokers, without consent of customer.
Judicial review of admission of securities to trading list, or exclusion from it.
Opening of brokers' books of account to Federal officials.

It will be noticed that the above proposals went far beyond those made by the Hughes committee four years earlier. The law which embodied these recommendations would have given the Post Office authorities power to exclude from the mails the quotations of any stock exchange which did not comply with the law in the points specified. The bill failed to pass but in the course of the preliminary hearings it became clear that the New York Stock Exchange had already made changes in conformance with the suggestions of the Pujo committee. In February, 1913, for example, the rule against fictitious transactions or "wash sales" was strengthened, and "reckless or unbusinesslike dealing" was included among the offenses punishable by the Exchange officers. At the same time the carrying of customers' accounts on less than "proper and adequate" margin and the use of customers' securities without permission was made an act "detrimental to the interest and welfare of the exchange," and subject to the penalty of expulsion for not more than one year. A month later a committee of five was appointed to watch the course of prices of securities and examine into the dealings of members whenever it appeared that improper transactions were being carried on.[57]

A number of laws were passed by the legislature of New York state during and after these hearings which were directly due to the demand for public regulation. In April and May, 1913, bucket shops, manipulation of stock prices and fictitious sales, false representation of securities, the publication of fictitious transactions in securities, the hypothecation of customers'

[57] 63 Congress, 2 Session, Hearings before the Senate Committee on banking and currency on . . . stock exchanges, pp. 586, 710.

securities by brokers without permission, unfair discrimination by exchanges or their members, and transactions by brokers after they had become insolvent, were all made crimes punishable under the penal code of the state. Another bill was introduced to compel Stock Exchanges to incorporate; it succeeded in passing the Assembly, but was defeated in the Senate after full hearings.

The reform wave had by this time pretty well spent itself, as far as speculation was concerned, and the center of interest was shifted to banking and the problem of credit organization. It was hoped that changes in that field would break the dependence of the banks upon the call loan market, and reduce, if not the amount of speculation, at least its bad effects. But there were many problems connected with the security markets which were left untouched and which would be little affected by banking reforms.

Summary

The importation of foreign capital through the sale of American securities abroad was one of the most important single factors in the investment market before 1913. Without it the exploitation of natural resources and the building of railroads would have been forced to proceed at a much lower rate. With it the prosperity of the country increased so rapidly that by the beginning of the twentieth century American investors were beginning to send small amounts abroad.

The increased volume of stock trading forced one improvement in technique after another upon the Exchange. The stock clearing plan, after many failures, went into operation in 1892; overcertification of brokers' checks gave way to day loans; the daily "call" of stocks was omitted, and the ticker speeded up. Besides these changes in mere technique, the Exchange introduced a number of innovations designed to protect the public and control the business of stock trading. By this means the demand for reform was appeased and the Exchange escaped more drastic legal regulation.

CHAPTER XV

THE COMMERCIAL CREDIT SYSTEM FROM 1863 TO 1913

Effect of Civil War on credit terms

The Civil War period produced far-reaching changes in the commercial credit system. The outbreak of war upset the normal course of business, completely cutting off from the market a large section of southern buyers and materially altering the needs of buyers in the northern states.[1] Inflation of the currency and the premium upon gold introduced an uncertainty into the future of prices which discouraged long credit terms and made cash settlements desirable. The effect of these alterations in the normal course of business was to reduce the length of credit terms, decrease the number of transactions conducted on credit, and increase transactions taking place on a cash basis.[2] The situation was summed up in the *Commercial and Financial Chronicle* in 1865:[3]

> It is desirable to know exactly to what extent credit is being given to Western and Southern buyers. After careful inquiries on the subject, we find that the great bulk of jobbing sales now being made are on short time, say from 60 days to 4 months, and since if the buyer pays up within the first 30 days, he is allowed a discount from his bill of 1% a month, which discount applies to the first 30 days also, the payment in most cases is anticipated; and the sum total of all is that very little credit is either asked or given. Currency is so plentiful and retail merchants have been so favored by the continual rise in prices, that they now possess all the facilities for buying on cash terms. . . .

[1] "In the first two years of the War . . . our internal credit system had broken down, and rural traders, no longer able to replenish their stocks on credit, bought little or nothing." Horace Greeley, *Political Economy*, p. 234. "In 1861, every dry goods jobber in this city doing a Southern business failed or compromised with his creditors," Edmund Page, address before National Association of Credit Men, New York, June 17, 1904.

[2] Secretary of the Treasury, *Annual Report*, 1865, p. 11: "It is undoubtedly true that trade is carried on much more largely for cash than was ever the case previous to 1861, and that there is a much greater proper demand for money than there would be if sales were made, as heretofore, on credit."

[3] Vol. 1, p. 325.

Goods are scarce. . . . On the part of the jobbers there is no pressure to sell. . . . Hence, there is no competition among sellers, and so long as this state of affairs exists, they can ask their own terms and get them. To be sure, old customers are still granted the old fashioned credit of six months if they require it, and some of them do, but this exception to the general rule does not prevail to any great extent. Half of the buyers pay in cash, and a large portion of the remainder average less than 3 months in their credits, while but a few obtain 6 or 8 months.

Cash discounts and open-book account

As a result of this stimulation to cash payments the cash discount and the open-book account gradually became a permanent part of American business methods. Two decades after the War they were so widespread that a writer in *Bradstreet's Weekly* declared: "All classes of staple goods in every branch of business are sold by first hands on what is called short time . . . and this largely on open account." And a western bank president, speaking in 1892, confirmed this statement, saying:

Three decades ago the sale of commodities by the manufacturer to the wholesale dealer was upon long time, the wholesale dealer giving long credit to the retailer, and the latter to the consumer and in nearly every case a note of hand closed each transaction. . . . Now the retail dealer . . . as a rule sells for cash or on thirty-day settlements and reports all of his outstandings as open-book accounts.[4]

The wide popularity attained by the cash discount and open-book account system of financing commercial transactions gave a stimulus to the development of a commercial paper market in the United States which was unlike any that existed in money centers abroad. The trade acceptance had been losing ground even before the War, and with the change in credit methods its decline was accelerated. By the end of the century it had fallen so low that it had become a method of forcing the collection of slow and doubtful accounts and was used in not more than 3 per cent of all domestic credit transactions.[5]

[4] *Bradstreets'*, April 22, 1882, p. 242; December 31, 1892, p. 838.

[5] *New York Times Annalist*, March 9, 1914, p. 293. J. J. Klein, "The Development of Mercantile Instruments of Credit," *Journal of Accountancy*, Vol. 13, p. 126.

Increased use of single-name promissory note

As the trade acceptance was relegated to the background in the commercial credit system, its place was filled by the promissory note, but in a new form. Before the War the most frequently used credit instrument had been the endorsed promissory note, two-name paper, which arose either from an actual sale of goods as an "endorsed receivable," or from a loan unrelated to a specific transaction as "accommodation paper." The new form of negotiable instrument which developed in connection with the cash discount and open-book account was the single-name, unendorsed, promissory note which became the "commercial paper" of the present money market. Such paper had not been unknown before the Civil War, but it required the disorganization of the war period to give it impetus. The cash discount system made it worth while for merchants to borrow in order to anticipate their bills, and the most convenient method of borrowing for this purpose was the issue of their own notes. An important factor in the increasing use of single-name paper was the possibility which it offered to large borrowers of obtaining a greater amount of credit than any single bank could make available. It became the custom for some of the best mercantile houses in New York to go to banks other than their own with their single-name paper, and if one of the bank directors was acquainted with the firm the paper could easily be discounted. This "acquaintance paper" paved the way for the development of a wider commercial paper market. The New York coffee jobbers whose warehouses lined Front Street in 1865 were among the first to offer their paper in the open market, and "Front Street names" were found frequently in the market by the end of the War. Wholesale dry-goods dealers were also among the early entrants into this field of borrowing. In one line of trade after another the financing of sales by this method was adopted in the decades after the Civil War. By 1892 it was stated that the only groups of wholesale dealers in which the endorsed promissory note was still preferred to single-name paper were those in the tobacco, jewelry, and rubber businesses.

There are very few large or reputable concerns doing business today without borrowing, and I am unable to recall more than one or two instances of a firm or company of any prominence which does not borrow directly, or use its credit in some other way. . . . It is now a prevalent idea among merchants that a concern which does not place its paper in the open market or use the facility of its bank is not in first-class credit. It almost seems, sometimes, as if a firm's credit were based on the amount of paper it is able to realize on, instead of its assets or liabilities.[6]

Rise of commercial-paper dealer

In the development of the commercial paper market the old-fashioned note broker was metamorphosed into the commercial paper dealer of the present day. Before the Civil War the broker had been a commission merchant, serving as agent in the placing of paper with the banks and only occasionally purchasing paper in his own name.[7] This type persisted even into the post-bellum period, as a description of the note-broker of the early seventies indicates:

Dressed in the very tall silk hat and frock coat of the period, he would each business morning stop in to see some merchant friend. The call usually ended in the consignment for sale of a small batch of bills receivable. The broker put the original paper inside the hat band of his "topper." Then he proceeded to the Chemical, the Importers, or one of the other few big New York banks, doffed his hat with great ceremony, took out of that inner hat band the paper, and bargained at some length with the venerable banker (for bankers were all venerable in those days) as to whether the rate should be 10 or 12 per cent. No balance sheets, no credit department—merchants' paper was judged according to the maker's character and standing in the business community.[8]

The change from the old status of broker to the new status of commercial paper house occurred gradually. The two kinds of business continued side by side for many years and were often carried on by the same firm so that it is impossible to fix the date of the change. A writer in the *Bankers' Magazine* in 1884

[6] Cannon, Address before Drexel Institute, Philadelphia, Nov. 17, 1892.
[7] See p. 55 above.
[8] Address of Walter E. Sachs, of Goldman, Sachs and Co., before the Kentucky Bankers' Association, Louisville, Kentucky, on August 24, 1921.

stated that occasionally brokers gave an immediate advance for a part of the value of the note, indicating that a large part of their business was still done on a commission basis. Frequently they did not have the note itself but merely a memorandum of it. Three years later, however, a speaker at the American Bankers' Association Convention said that the more responsible dealers bought their paper outright.[9] Some of them even went a step further and added their own endorsement.

Most of the brokers were located in New York City and banks of the interior bought commercial paper in the large cities, either direct from the brokers or on the recommendation of their city correspondent. In the southern states there were no note brokers at all and in the middle west Chicago seems to have been the only city where they could be found. The country banker, who usually lacked credit investigation facilities of his own, depended upon the source from which he bought paper for confirmation of its goodness and the large city dealer with a well-known name was considered more responsible than a smaller dealer. The business was therefore a highly concentrated one, and in the early days the situation was much like that of today, when about fifteen large houses with branch offices do almost all of the commercial paper business of the country. One of the New York companies was doing business at the rate of more than 40 millions of dollars a year as early as 1892 and in 1909 it was estimated that the total volume of paper sold by brokers throughout the country equalled 2 billions of dollars.[10]

Commercial paper as investment for banks

Single-name paper came into the market in large denominations and in round sums which made it a more salable product than the two-name paper rendered to pay a particular bill in an odd amount. Brokers were able to place a large loan among a number of banks and thus spread the credit risk. The advantage

[9] *Bankers' Magazine*, Vol. 39, p. 39. *Proceedings of Convention of American Bankers' Association*, 1887, p. 46.

[10] Speech of James G. Cannon at Drexel Institute, Philadelphia, November 17, 1892. *Proceedings of American Bankers' Association Convention*, 1887, p. 45. Phillips, *Bank Credit*, p. 264. Hearings and arguments before House Committee on banking and currency, 1897-1898; 55 Congress, 2 Session.

to the banks of this change in credit methods lay very largely in the more impersonal attitude which it introduced. Banks often found it difficult to refuse renewal on the notes of old customers but on paper purchased from a broker, made by a total stranger in another part of the country, payment at maturity was taken for granted. Moreover by purchasing from brokers and dealers banks were able to diversify their portfolios geographically and industrially, obtaining paper from a variety of industries, with different maturities, which also aided in reducing credit risks. The fact that the commercial-paper house was becoming an expert judge of credit positions was another safeguard to the bank purchasing the paper.

It must not be thought that single-name paper entirely superseded the older endorsed form. Banks with their accustomed conservatism continued to purchase endorsed receivables in large amounts but they gradually increased their holdings of open-market single-name paper. By 1884 a speaker at the American Bankers' Association spoke of the purchase of such paper by the banks as a practice "which has long prevailed" in the large financial centers, and which was "intimately bound up" with the financial habits of the community. Mr. James G. Cannon said, in 1892:

> The commercial paper business enters largely into the calculation of our large New York banks. There are seasons of the year when the regular demand from customers is so moderate that the large surplus held by the banks cannot be properly invested, and at such times, as a rule, call loans in Wall Street are placed very low, and time loans yield but very little. It is then that a thorough knowledge of commercial paper becomes very valuable, and it is a well known fact that the most successful banks in New York have achieved great prosperity by reason of intelligent purchases of commercial paper. They aim to make these purchases fit closely into their maturities, and arrange at all times, if possible, to have a few of them extend beyond a four months' limit, making a selection of four months' purchases so as to have equal amounts for the various months within that space of time. The custom of issuing single-name paper has grown largely within the last ten years, and although it was adversely criticised in former days, it has proven to be a profitable source of investment for our banks. . . . Many things have brought about a change in public opinion, and today two-thirds

of all the paper purchased by our New York banks, it is fair to say, is single-name.

Country banks were more conservative in their acceptance of single-name commercial paper than were the metropolitan banks. Many preferred to discount the notes of their own customers at the risk of an undiversified portfolio rather than to buy open-market commercial paper. A banker from Atlanta, in discussing the country banker and his investments in 1898, exemplified the older point of view when he said: "Lend your money to your regular customers, and do not make a rule of buying commercial paper. . . . Do not permit any loans to be made to any one on single-name paper, unless otherwise secured, no matter what the commercial rating may be."[11] On the other hand a western banker testifying before the House Committee in 1913 said it had been for thirty years the policy of his bank to buy commercial paper in sufficient amount to provide a margin for any fluctuation in deposits which might occur; and with the rest of their funds to buy bonds. The reason for the large proportion of bonds in his bank's portfolio was his experience in 1893 when he was able to sell the bonds for cash in Chicago but could not realize on his commercial paper.[12] Another western banker said that in the panic of 1907 bonds were practically unsalable and that commercial paper was the only form of investment that weathered the crisis satisfactorily.[13]

Regular publication of data relating to loans of national banks was begun by the Comptroller of the Currency in 1880 and from these figures it is possible to obtain definite information regarding the displacement of two-name by single-name paper in the portfolios of national banks. The total for single-name paper included some loans made directly to customers as well as paper purchased in the open market from brokers, but it is the only statistical series available which throws any light upon the

[11] Speech of W. S. Witham, *Proceedings of American Bankers' Association Convention*, 1898, pp. 128, 130.

[12] Testimony of Mr. Andrew Frame, of Waukesha, Wisconsin, before the House Sub-Committee on Banking and Currency Reform, 1913, p. 425; 62 Congress, 3 Session.

[13] Mr. Edward H. Sensenich, cashier of Northwestern National Bank, Portland, Oregon, in *Bankers' Home Magazine*, Vol. 8, p. 41.

growth of the commercial-paper market. For national banks in New York City between 1886 and 1900 the proportion of endorsed notes fell from nearly 50 to less than 20 per cent of the total loans and discounts and remained at that low level during

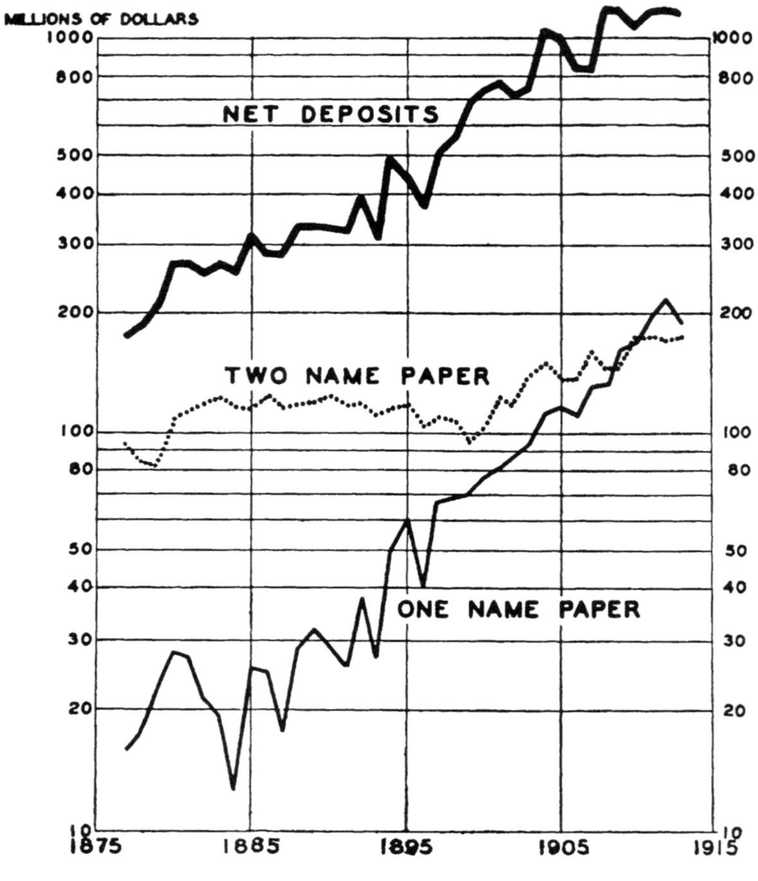

NET DEPOSITS AND HOLDINGS OF ONE-NAME AND TWO-NAME COMMERCIAL PAPER, AT NEW YORK CITY NATIONAL BANKS, AT THE FOURTH CALL EACH YEAR.

SOURCE: ANNUAL REPORTS OF THE COMPTROLLER OF THE CURRENCY.

the years from 1900 to 1913. Meantime single-name paper had increased from less than 10 to more than 20 per cent of the whole, rising steadily from an amount equal to 1/5 of the two-name paper to an amount equal to it. After 1900, while the proportion of double-name paper remained about stationary, that of single-name paper continued to rise.

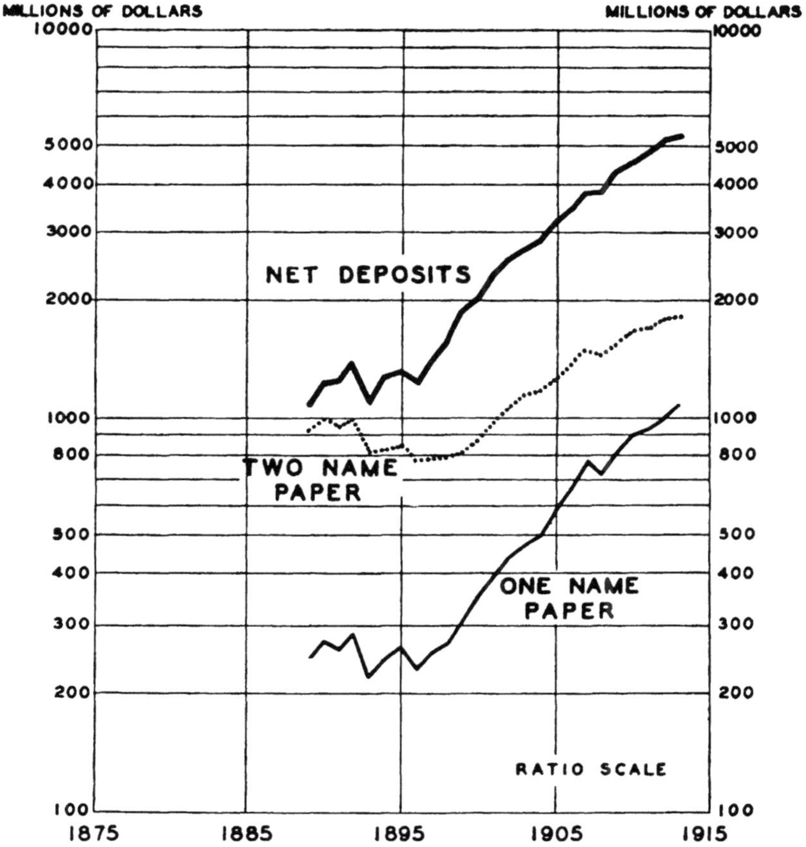

NET DEPOSITS AND HOLDINGS OF ONE-NAME AND TWO-NAME COMMERCIAL PAPER, AT NATIONAL BANKS OUTSIDE NEW YORK CITY, AT THE FOURTH CALL EACH YEAR.

SOURCE: ANNUAL REPORTS OF THE COMPTROLLER OF THE CURRENCY.

For the country banks the trends of the two types of paper were similar to that of the New York City banks. Two-name paper fell from more than 50, to about 33 per cent of the total by 1900, while single-name paper rose from about 10 to more than 20 per cent. Both trends changed at 1900, keeping their direction but with a lower rate of change.

When different sections of the country are considered separately with respect to their preference in regard to single-name and double-name paper, the variations are noteworthy. Country national banks of the eastern states in 1910 bought only ¼ as much single-name as double-name paper, while those of the western mountain states bought almost as much of the former as of the latter. Variations among the state were as wide as among the national banks; state banks in the South held only ¼ as much single-name paper as double, while those of the Pacific states held more than ¾ as much. The following table gives the percentage for each group but the reserve and central reserve cities are not included for the national banks. On this same date

PERCENTAGE OF SINGLE-NAME PAPER TO DOUBLE-NAME IN BANK PORTFOLIOS ON JUNE 30, 1910

	Country national banks	*State banks and trust companies (city and country)*
New England	46	53
Eastern	26	51
Southern	41	23
Middle-western	52	62
Western	98	73
Pacific	78	80
ALL	44	52

national banks of New York City were carrying slightly more single-name paper than double-name, and banks of other central reserve and reserve cities held exactly ¾ as much of single-name as of double-name.[14]

The place which single-name paper made for itself in this country is illustrated by the experience of the banks with the

[14] Comptroller of Currency, *Annual Report*, 1910, p. 750.

Aldrich-Vreeland Act. When the act was passed in 1908 national banks were authorized to issue circulating notes partly secured by "commercial paper," which was defined as paper which would "bear the names of at least two responsible parties and have not exceeding four months to run." The framers of the law intended by this definition to get the cream of the paper but experience soon proved that in many cases the best paper was the single-name paper which did not come within the letter of the law at all. In order to admit single-name paper Secretary MacVeagh was obliged to rule that single-name paper which bore the name of an endorsing bank should be classed as two-name paper and by this definition the banks were enabled to use the best paper they possessed, their single-name commercial paper, as collateral security for the notes issued under the Act.[15]

Bank credit departments

The appearance of single-name paper in bank portfolios in large amounts was accompanied by the development of credit investigation and the establishment in all large banks of credit departments similar to those which had long been customary in mercantile establishments. Their function was to pass upon the standing of applicants for this form of credit. To the president of the Importers' and Traders' National Bank of New York City is ascribed the achievement, during the 1880's, of the first of these departments. The idea progressed slowly; by 1890 there were only 6 in the country and as late as 1899, fewer than 10.[16] The mercantile reporting agencies of Dun and of Bradstreet had come into existence even before the Civil War but their chief function was the exchange of credit information between merchants one of whom wished to open an account with another. Data which they offered were not complete enough to meet the requirements of banks. With the development of a technique for

[15] Huntington and Mawhinney, *Laws Concerning Money, Banking, and Loans*, p. 461. Testimony of Dr. H. Parker Willis before Senate Committee on Banking and Currency, 1913, 63 Congress, 1 Session, Senate Document 232, p. 3035. *Commercial and Financial Chronicle*, Vol. 91, Sept. 3, 1910. p. 562.

[16] *New York Times Annalist*, March 23, 1914, p. 361. Kniffin, *Commercial Paper*, p. 4. Speech of James G. Cannon before American Bankers' Association, September 7, 1899.

judging credit standing of firms by such measures as ratios between items on the financial and income statements, a good general reputation in the business world was no longer sufficient and

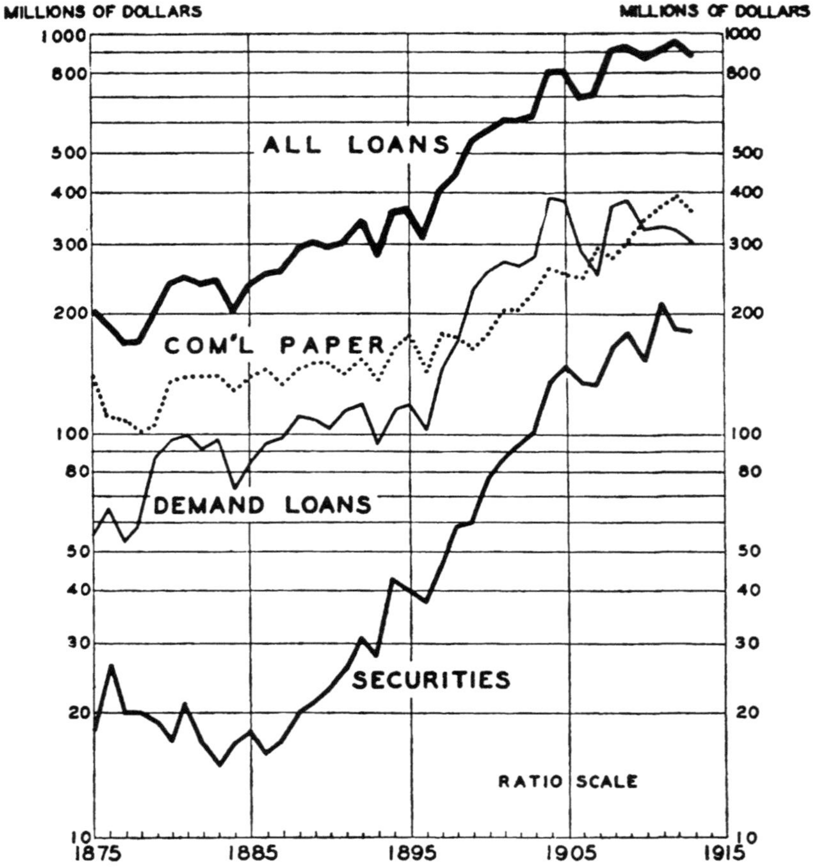

SECURITIES HELD, DEMAND LOANS AGAINST STOCK EXCHANGE COLLATERAL, LOANS AGAINST ONE- AND TWO-NAME COMMERCIAL PAPER, AND TOTAL LOANS, OF NEW YORK CITY NATIONAL BANKS, AT THE FOURTH CALL EACH YEAR.

SOURCE: ANNUAL REPORTS OF THE COMPTROLLER OF THE CURRENCY.

credit was made more impersonal than before. In line with the increased insistence of the banks upon publicity regarding financial conditions before credit should be extended, was the attempt made about 1885 to establish a clearing house for credit information among the banks of New York. The idea was born before

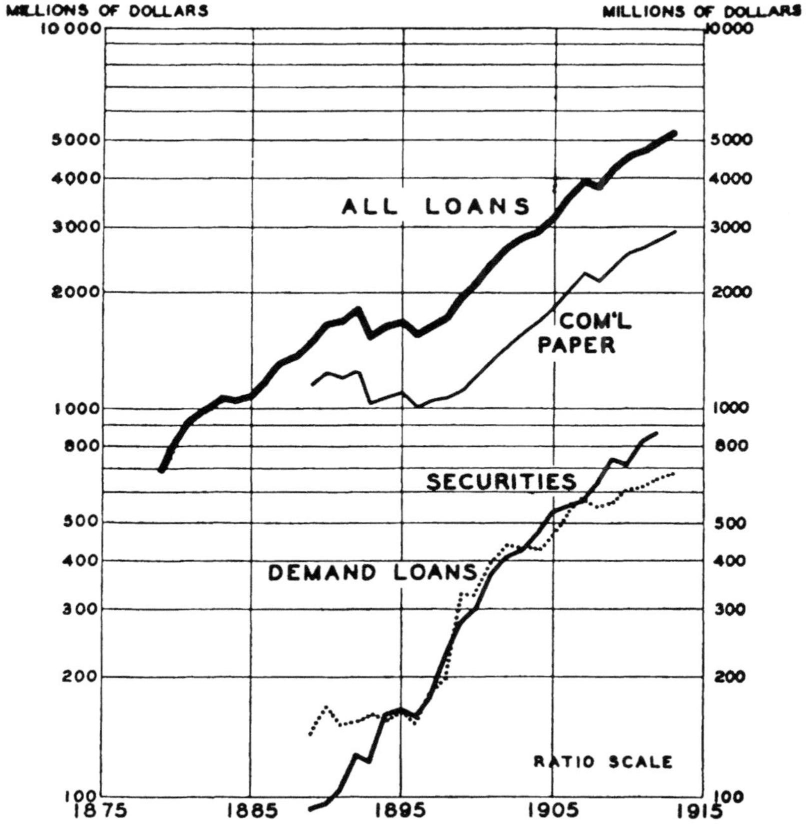

SECURITIES HELD, DEMAND LOANS AGAINST STOCK EXCHANGE COLLATERAL, LOANS AGAINST ONE- AND TWO-NAME COMMERCIAL PAPER, AND TOTAL LOANS, OF NATIONAL BANKS OUTSIDE NEW YORK CITY, AT THE FOURTH CALL EACH YEAR.

SOURCE: ANNUAL REPORTS OF THE COMPTROLLER OF THE CURRENCY.

its time; less than a dozen banks could be induced even to try the experiment and the small association actually formed for the purpose, lived for only two weeks.[17]

[17] *Bankers' Magazine*, Vol. 40, p. 359.

Sometime before 1894 banks began to insist that borrowers offer a statement of condition with each application for a loan. In 1895 the New York State Bankers' Association recommended that its members demand a written statement upon a uniform blank form prepared by the Association but it is difficult to discover how much progress was made in this direction or when such statements came to be taken for granted as prerequisite to a loan.[18]

A further step in safeguarding bank loans was taken when a credit bureau was organized by the bank examiners of New York to aid in determining the value of notes and investments and in judging the credit of borrowers whose paper they found in the portfolios of banks examined by them. All individual borrowers of large amounts at New York banks as well as group or corporate borrowers were recorded in this bureau. The usefulness of such a check was proved by the discovery that one individual was found to be borrowing from 29 different banks, each of which believed itself to be the only creditor; while another was borrowing in the name of 17 different individuals and corporations. In 1912 New York passed a law providing a penalty for false credit statements.[19]

About the same time the necessity of similar information for national banks brought about the establishment in Washington of a central credit bureau, similar to that of New York state, for the use of national bank examiners. It served to prevent a borrower from extending his loans beyond the limits of his legitimate line of credit by scattering his borrowings among many cities.[20] To protect their credit certain firms went to the trouble of having all their paper registered by a bank or trust company acting as registrar, but this movement did not gain headway.[21]

[18] Speech of James G. Cannon before New York State Bankers' Association at Saratoga, New York.

[19] New York State Superintendent of Banks, Report on Banks of Deposit and Discount, 1912, p. 8. Laws of the State of New York, 135 Session, Chapter 340, paragraph 1293-b; passed April 15, 1912.

[20] *Commercial and Financial Chronicle,* Vol. 91, October 1, 1910, p. 842.

[21] *Trust Companies,* March, 1911; April, 1912.

Rates of interest

The rates on open-market commercial paper in New York constituted such a valuable index of money market conditions that they were published at a very early date and the records on this point are more complete than for most financial data.[22] From 1866 until 1873 rates were on a very high level, the monthly average fluctuating between 5 and 16 per cent. This was the period when war inflation, uncertain credit conditions, and paper money, were the dominant factors in the money market. Cyclical movements were more prominent in these years than the trend. With the panic of 1873 and the passage in 1875 of the Resumption Act, the factors which had controlled the market after the War lost their influence and there began a period in which rates were definitely on a lower level. Between 1874 and 1892 the fluctuations of monthly average rates had a narrow range from 3½ to 7½ per cent. For these years, as in the earlier period, there was no general trend either up or down. In 1894, following the high rates of the panic in 1893, commercial paper fell to the lowest level of this period, and averaged about 3 per cent for the year. But from that date onward there was a steady rise to 1913, broken only temporarily by the panic of 1907.

Cyclical movements of commercial paper rates were closely correlated with those of general business, but with a lag of from three to twelve months. Every panic was marked by a violent rise in interest rates on commercial loans and the rates usually remained high until after the panic itself was well over; then they dropped even more rapidly than they had risen. These rates were one of the best indicators of business conditions, and were chosen by the Harvard *Review of Economic Statistics* as one of the three major indices of business conditions after 1875.

Seasonal changes in commercial paper rates are of especial interest because, like the trends, they show three distinct periods which closely coincide with the trend periods. For the years from 1866 to 1873, when rates were on a very high level, they were

[22] Figures were compiled by the *Commercial and Financial Chronicle*, and reprinted in the annual *Financial Review*. Monthly averages of these figures were compiled by the *Review of Economic Statistics*, 1923, p. 28, for the years 1866-1922.

also fluctuating widely from month to month with a range from 82 in June to 118 in November and a secondary peak in April at 107. In the next period, from 1873 to 1889 when rates were on a lower level, seasonal variation showed the same general movements as before in the matter of direction; there was a minor peak in the spring, a drop to the year's low point in June, and a high point for the year in October, as compared with November for the earlier period. But the range of variation was much diminished, 86 to 114, or only 28 points as compared with 36 before 1873. In the third period the range was reduced to 23 points, the low point of the year being 89 in June, and the high point 112 in October.[23]

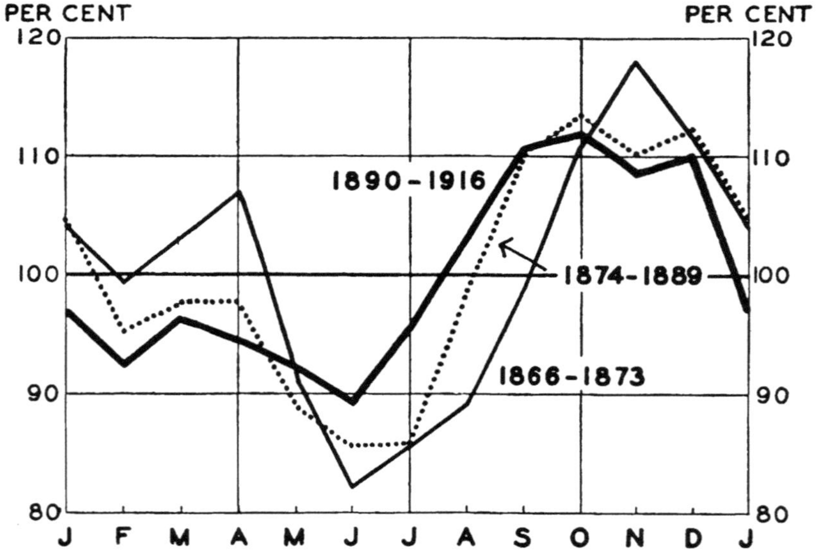

INDEX OF SEASONAL VARIATION IN COMMERCIAL PAPER RATES AT DIFFERENT PERIODS.

SOURCE: REVIEW OF ECONOMIC STATISTICS, 1923.

The narrowing range of seasonal variation in commercial paper rates was of great significance. It may have been influenced by

[23] *Review of Economic Statistics*, 1919, p. 120; 1923, p. 29.

the fact that agriculture, which was responsible for most of the seasonal change in the demand for credit, was becoming a relatively less important factor in production. There must also have been an adjustment between demand and supply of commercial credit; an increased supply made more available to borrowers as the banking system became widespread and the commercial paper market widened; and a more equable distribution of the demand for funds throughout the year as borrowers learned to anticipate their own needs and take advantage of the periods of lower rates.

Commercial paper rates, important as they were to a judgment of market conditions, were only one of the prices charged for commercial credit and should have been supplemented by bank lending rates in order to give a complete picture of the commercial credit market. Unfortunately these bank rates were not regularly published and even for New York there is no adequate information on the subject. Occasionally special studies were made with reference to variations in bank lending rates from one section of the country to another. One of the most serious indictments made against the American system of banking was that the rates on commercial credit varied widely from one part of the country to another, so that many districts were heavily penalized. In general rates of interest were proportionate to the distance from New York, although the size of the city was also a factor. Borrowers in western and southern states were obliged frequently to pay twice as much for commercial credits as borrowers in the East. In 1886 Boston and Philadelphia rates were slightly above those of New York; other large eastern cities came next, while Kansas City, the point farthest west for which figures were given, had the highest rate of all.[24] A compilation of rates on two-name paper for the years 1893 to 1897 which may be considered representative of bank lending rates lists the larger cities of the country in the order of their average rates and shows a striking dissimilarity between the lowest and the highest. As in the earlier period, two factors appear to govern the rates: the distance of the city from New York, and its size. San Francisco, although

[24] *Commercial and Financial Chronicle,* Vol. 42, March 20, 1886, p. 354.

one of the farthest from New York in miles, is higher on the list than smaller towns which are nearer. The rate in Boston was even lower than that in New York, 3.8 as against 4.4 per cent. The increase went steadily westward, from 4.6 in Philadelphia, Baltimore, and Hartford, up to 8.3 in Dallas, 9.3 in Tacoma, and 10 in Denver and Seattle.

RANGE OF RATES ON TWO-NAME PAPER, 1893-1897.*

	Low.	*High.*
Boston	3.83	5.05
New York	4.41	5.36
Baltimore	4.56	5.16
Philadelphia	4.64	6.01
Chicago	5.74	6.53
Pittsburgh	5.83	6.49
St. Louis	5.90	7.23
San Francisco	6.21	6.90
Milwaukee	6.27	7.02
Detroit	6.41	6.67
Kansas City	6.91	8.38
Galveston	7.31	8.00
Savannah	7.99	9.75
Dallas	8.34	9.90
Seattle	9.96	11.96
Denver	10.00	11.67

* *Bankers' Magazine*, Vol. 58, p. 44.

Another aspect of the geographical variation in rates was disclosed in 1879, when the comptroller of the currency made a detailed analysis of the loans of national banks by states, as they stood on October 2 of that year.[25] A total of 808,000 bills was included in the study and the amount of bank credit represented by them was 875 millions of dollars, so that the results may be considered fairly representative. The average amount of the bills varied widely from one part of the country to another. The

[25] Comptroller of the Currency, *Annual Report*, 1880, pp. 18, 90.

highest average was reported at San Francisco but, since that came from only one large bank, it is not included in the table. For other large cities of the country the averages, as one would expect, are roughly proportionate to the size of the city.

LOANS OF CITY NATIONAL BANKS ON OCTOBER 2, 1879.

	Average size	*Per cent of total number of bills*					
		Under $100	*$100–500*	*$500–1,000*	*$1,000–5,000*	*$5,000–10,000*	*Over 10,000*
New York City . .	$3,962	8	32	16	28	10	6
Boston	3,082	9	28	15	30	11	7
Chicago	2,244	9	34	19	26	8	4
Milwaukee . . .	2,260	10	35	14	29	8	4
New Orleans . . .	1,937	5	39	19	27	7	3
Philadelphia . . .	1,689	21	39	13	19	5	3

The awkward statistical grouping was evidently due to the presence of two distinct types of bill. The first group centers in the $100 to $500 class and probably consisted of small personal loans and endorsed promissory notes. In every city except Boston this group was the largest in point of numbers but, because of the small size, it accounted for a very small part of the total bank credit. The second concentration of bills occurred in the group from $1,000 to $5,000. Since these were the denominations in which single-name commercial paper was frequently drawn, this group probably represented purchases in the open market. There were very few bills of more than $10,000. Philadelphia, which had the greatest proportion of loans under $100, had the smallest over $1,000.

Country banks showed a much larger number of small, than of large, loans, indicating that the personal loan was still an important factor with them. New England states, as befitted their greater industrial activity, reported the largest average size for any of the groups; the southern, middle western, and mountain states averaged only half as large.

The real significance of this table appears when it is compared with the rates of interest in the same sections of the country. Where the average size of loans was small, the rate was high, and the lowest rates were to be found in conjunction with the highest average loans. This combination raises the question

LOANS OF COUNTRY NATIONAL BANKS, BY GROUPS OF STATES, ON OCTOBER 2, 1879.

	Average size	Per cent of total number of bills					
		Under $100	$100–500	$500–1,000	$1,000–5,000	$5,000–10,000	Over $10,000
New England . .	$1,203	22	38	13	20	5	2
Middle states . .	629	38	38	10	11	2	1
Southern states. .	722	28	42	13	14	2	1

whether the high rate of interest may not have included the higher cost of handling small bank loans. Some of the banks made a collection charge of ten to twenty-five cents for each small note, but this could hardly compensate them for the additional expense involved. Scarcity of bank capital was of course the primary factor in the high rates, but it may well have been exaggerated by the high overhead costs incident to the small loan business.

The differential in rates was due also to the increased risk of lending at such a distance, and to lack of adequate local supply of capital. Another factor in the higher rates in some of the states was the heavy taxation on bank capital, and restrictions as to the investment of bank funds.[26] The differential became somewhat less as the west became more closely linked with the east and better supplied with capital of its own. In Texas, for example, interest rates fell from 3 per cent a month, in 1872, to 6 and 8 per cent a year, in 1895.[27]

26 *Report of the Indianapolis Monetary Commission*, p. 378.

27 *Proceedings American Bankers' Association Convention*, 1895, p. 55.

Changes in commercial bank portfolios

While the rise of the commercial paper market was bringing about a change in the kind of commercial loans being made by banks, there was also under way a decline in the volume of commercial loans as compared with total loans and investments. The old form of endorsed promissory note was losing ground to the new form of single-name, open-market paper, but both together were losing ground to other forms of investment for bank funds.

Commercial loans as an investment for the funds of commercial banks had to compete against both call loans and securities, and on the whole they ran a losing race with other earning assets. This was especially noticeable at the New York City national banks, where the proportion of commercial paper, of both single-name and double-name variety, declined steadily in relation to total loans and investments. A net gain was realized by security holdings which, after falling off between 1876 and 1886, began thereafter an upward climb, raising the ratio of securities to deposits from 5 to 15 per cent. The increase in the holdings of securities by the New York banks, not including those which had been purchased to serve as collateral for note circulation and government deposits, was due in part to the increasing interest of the New York banks in what may be termed financial banking as distinguished from commercial banking.[28] Security companies, organized under the protecting care of a bank, borrowed as heavily as possible from it to finance the flotation of their issues and expected and received a preferential treatment.

Preference for securities was not, however, confined to the banks of New York. The same general trend with regard to investments of national banks was also apparent for the banks outside of New York. The ratio of commercial loans to net deposits fell from 105 per cent in 1889 to 56 per cent in 1913, while security investments increased during the same years from 8 to 17 per cent of deposits.

[28] Youngman, "The Growth of Financial Banking."

The state banks, which were for the most part the smaller banks of the country, invested about the same proportion of their total resources in commercial loans, as did the national banks.[29] State banks carried a smaller proportion of securities and a slightly larger proportion of paper than the national banks, while the reverse was true of the trust companies, owing to their different function.

RATIO TO NET DEPOSITS, OF VARIOUS INVESTMENTS OF BANKS

JUNE 30, 1909

	New York City Banks			*Banks outside New York City*		
	National	*State*	*Trust Companies*	*National*	*State*	*Trust Companies*
Demand loans . .	34	28	39	19	22	22
Two-name paper .	12	28	4	28	36	10
Single-name paper	13	17	6	14	16	5
Securities	20	10	46	26	20	33

The commercial credit situation evidenced by seasonal, cyclical, and geographic, fluctuations in interest rates which arose in the half century between the passage of the National Bank Act and the Federal Reserve Act, was due to the peculiar conditions of the American system. The lack of a central bank, which reacted unfavorably on every aspect of American finance, must be held responsible to a large degree. The large banks of New York and other cities during periods of seasonal strain, did a certain amount of rediscounting for the smaller banks, but their resources were too limited to be counted upon to any great extent. The lack of a large central bank was aggravated by the division of American banking capital among myriad small banks, unequally distributed about the country and functioning for the most part without branches.

[29] Comptroller of the Currency, *Annual Report*, 1910, p. 750; Aldrich, *Special Report from the Banks of the United States*, Tables 2 and 3.

Summary

The development of the commercial credit market after 1863 was marked by changes in credit practice, by the decline of the acceptance, and by the growth of single-name paper. The rise of commercial paper houses was a late stage of this development. Rates on commercial paper merit attention because of their significance for business conditions. Bank lending rates also showed a wide range of fluctuation. Differences between rates in New York and in other sections of the country were symptomatic of an immobility of funds which put a heavy penalty upon many borrowers.

CHAPTER XVI

THE FOREIGN EXCHANGE MARKET AFTER 1863

As New York moved towards its ultimate goal of world money market, the status of foreign bills was altered in two directions. In one respect they became less important to the financial community, since the latter was no longer so dependent upon foreign credit and security purchases as it had been in the past and the "state of the foreign exchanges" was no longer the sole compass by which the banker set his course. But in another respect the market for foreign bills gained greatly by the change in the international position of New York. Not only was the amount of the transactions greatly increased, but the New York market became linked with the international movement of funds, that constant ebb and flow by which conditions are equalized over the world. New York was climbing up from its position as financial center of a debtor nation, obliged to borrow on the lender's terms, and becoming an equal participant.

Reality of international transfers

Under the conditions which existed in the international money market between 1863 and 1913, the only transfer of funds between London and New York which affected banking reserves was the shipment of gold. Most of the so-called "transfers" consisted merely of a shifting of book credits by the banks from the accounts of nationals of one country to the accounts of nationals of another. When funds were being "sent" from London to New York, for example, sterling bills were being sold in New York by English agents, and purchased with American bank deposits. No gold would be shipped until this demand for dollars had driven the price up to a point where it was less expensive to ship the metal than to use sterling bills. Gold shipments entered only into the settlement of balances. In many respects this period furnishes an example of the unregulated gold standard at its simplest, at least from the point of view of New York.[1] There were no complications of bimetallism such as had existed in the early part of the nineteenth century and the introduction of the telegraph and improvements in shipping had made the gold market almost instantly responsive to changes in the balance of international payments.

Seasonal variation in sterling rates

Sterling exchange was the most conspicuous element in the foreign exchange market and rates on sterling reflected the condition of the market better than any other. The largest factor in the variation of these rates was seasonal conditions. The fundamental seasonal rhythm which was set by the predominance of agricultural production in this country was repeated in international, as well as in domestic, trade. Foreign exchange rates showed a regular course from month to month, depending directly upon the movements of the crops and the consequent changes in the international balance of trade.

Since exchange rates fluctuate above and below par, they can have no long-term trend, and the average of the mean rates for each week may be taken as a rough but fairly accurate representation of the seasonal variation of the series. The complications introduced by the gold premium during the suspension of specie payments make it undesirable to include the years from 1863 to 1879, so the period studied will include only the years from 1879 to 1913.[2] Average monthly exchange rates on London in 1901-1913 rose from January to February, and fell off to March, reaching a secondary low point in March when the exports from the United States reached a spring peak. From that low, the rates rose again for three months, reaching the high

[1] It may well be doubted whether on the English side the functioning of gold was as unregulated as it appeared to be.

[2] Exchange rates were published by the *Commercial and Financial Chronicle* each week, and in the *Financial Review* of that publication issued annually. For the years 1889 to 1908, a convenient compilation of these figures is to be found in Andrew, *Statistics for the United States*, pp. 188 ff.

point for the year in June. When the exports of merchandise got well under way during the summer, exchange rates fell again and continued downward to September, going directly from the highest to the lowest points of the year. During the last quarter rates rose again gradually, so that throughout the year there was an inverse correlation between exchange rates and movements of merchandise. The carefully computed index of Professor Cole, for 1897 to 1913, agrees with the rough averages as to the placing of high and low points. The steady, slight shifting of the seasonal, which was observed in the period before 1863, continued during this later period, although at a slower rate. The

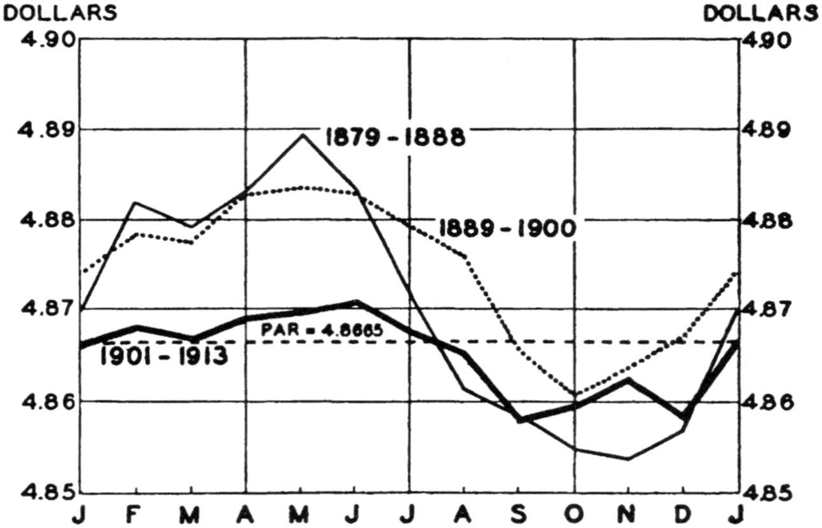

SEASONAL VARIATION IN STERLING EXCHANGE RATES AT THREE PERIODS, SHOWING SHIFT IN HIGH AND LOW POINTS, AND NARROWING RANGE.

SOURCE: REVIEW OF ECONOMIC STATISTICS.

low point of the year, by the years 1889-1900, had moved back to October. In the period before the Civil War the low point had occurred in the spring.[3]

[3] See p. 75 above.

As foreign exchange rates fluctuated between the export and the import points, the balance of gold shipments also changed. In the years between 1890 and 1908, March, in which sterling reached its spring low point, was the only month before August which showed a net importation of gold into New York. May and June, in which rates were nearest the export point, showed the heaviest net exports of gold, while every month from September to November, inclusive, had net imports. During December there was again a small net export. Like sterling rates, net gold movements also showed a change from decade to decade. The high point for imports during the years 1878-1889 came in September, while in the later period, 1890-1908, it fell in October.

The shifting of the high and low points was not the only change apparent in the seasonal variation of exchange rates. There was also a progressive narrowing of the range of variation, a continuation of the tendency which was observed in the ante-bellum period.[4]

Professor Cole found[5] that, besides this narrowing of the seasonal variation from 1865 to 1913, there was also a tendency for the relations between pairs of successive months, known technically as link relatives, to become more stable. Not only were seasonal changes becoming more regular, but month-to-month changes were becoming less pronounced. This was especially true of the years from 1900 to 1913, when finance bills were being used to a greater extent than before.

Export and import points

Daily quotations as well as seasonal averages give evidence of the tendency toward progressive narrowing of the range of variation in the rates. This tendency stands out clearly when the highest and lowest rates for each year are considered. The difference between the high and the low points during the last five years of the period is only a fraction of the difference which

[4] See p. 74 above.

[5] Cole, "Seasonal Variation in Sterling Exchange." *Journal of Economic and Business History*, Vol. II.

stood between them during the first five years for which the record was made. The principal factor in this movement was the drawing together of the specie points—the quotations above and below par at which it became, respectively, profitable to ship or to import gold, instead of making remittance by purchasing bills of foreign exchange. As the means of transportation across the Atlantic improved, the time lost in shipping was cut

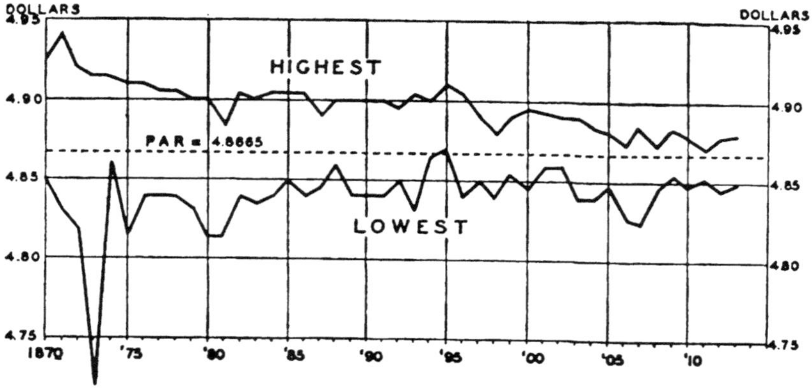

HIGHEST AND LOWEST QUOTATIONS EACH YEAR FOR STERLING EXCHANGE, BANKERS' SIGHT BILLS.

SOURCE: COMMERCIAL AND FINANCIAL CHRONICLE.

down and with it insurance costs and the interest for the time lost in transit. The expense of shipping gold from New York to London was greatly reduced and, although the true par of exchange remained the same, the "gold points" were brought closer together. It is difficult to set the export or import point for any specific time, since in extreme cases, gold might be shipped for other than profit motives, and even at a loss. The most reliable indications of the position of the gold points at any time are probably the statements of contemporaries as to the cost of shipping gold. In 1882, a writer in the *Bankers' Magazine*[6] remarked upon the fact that the shipping point had been recently reduced from $4.905 to $4.900 and then to $4.89125, where it was standing. In 1906, nearly a quarter of a century later, testimony

[6] Vol. 36, p. 232; Vol. 37, p. 287.

before the House Committee on Banking and Currency set the export point at $4.89, and two years later it was stated that it stood approximately at $4.88.

The import point, on the other side of par, was also moving nearer to it. In 1883, it was said to be at $4.8225.[7] The Secretary of the Treasury succeeded in reducing the interest cost of gold imports by an arrangement with the banks devised by him in 1906 when he felt that imports should be encouraged. The banks were at first permitted to count gold on the way to New York as part of their reserves, but the ingenious Mr. Shaw discarded this plan for another which was more nearly in line with the law. He permitted banks which had engaged gold for import to secure government deposits to 110 per cent of the amount of the gold, by depositing with the Treasury securities of the classes acceptable to the New York savings banks. The deposit made against this collateral was returned to the Treasury when the gold arrived. As a result of this scheme the banks had the use of the amount imported while it was on its way to New York, and the interest cost for the ten days in transit was thus eliminated. The point at which imports could be profitably undertaken was raised by this means from about $4.8290 to about $4.8515, since the total cost of importation, excluding interest, was at that time about 5/16 of one per cent. The same device was used in September and October, 1906, during another stringency, but seems not to have been used after Mr. Shaw left office.[8] In 1908, when there was no artificial aid being given to gold movements, the import point was said to be at $4.8375.

The drawing together of the gold points is still going on. Transportation time is being cut still further, and the interest charges as well as the risk will be proportionately diminished. Moreover the central banks may in the future absorb the interest charges altogether, as they are said to have done already in one or two instances,[9] thus taking the responsibility for keeping up

[7] *Commercial and Financial Chronicle*, Vol. 36, March 3, 1883, p. 232.

[8] *Commercial and Financial Chronicle*, Vol. 82, March 31, 1906, p. 719; April 12, p. 893; May 21, p. 1069; Vol. 83, October 27, 1906, p. 1002. *London Economist*, September 8, 1906, p. 1465.

[9] See Vol. II of these studies.

the gold supply at home even at the cost of importation. In mathematical language, par may be considered as the asymptote toward which both import and export points are tending.

Finance bills

The narrowing range of sterling exchange rates was due in part to the same factors which had brought about a smaller range of variation in commercial paper and call loan rates—a better adjustment within the market itself as the technique of trading improved.[10] But more important than either of these was the growth of the finance bill, which was drawn, not to pay for goods, but to obtain credit for other purposes. Finance bills were not an invention of the twentieth century; they had figured in the panic of 1837, and they were used constantly in varying amounts as a method of borrowing abroad. But there was undoubtedly a great development in the use of these bills in the boom years which followed the turn of the century. The amount of American finance bills in Europe at the beginning of 1903 was estimated at 300 to 500 millions of dollars.[11] During 1906 it increased rapidly until the Bank of England, in the last quarter of the year, gave notice that such bills must be paid as they matured, and must not be renewed. Berlin followed the example of London and the contraction of credit thus initiated was one of the forces which put an end to the prosperity of that year and paved the way for the crisis of 1907. The result of that crisis was materially to reduce the volume of such bills outstanding, so that the total for 1909 was far below that of 1906.[12]

The rate of discount on finance bills was usually higher than that on trade bills.[13] Consequently there was no profit in borrowing in New York by means of finance bills on London until

[10] Professor Cole points out the comparative slowness of foreign exchange dealers to utilize cable transfers. The first Atlantic cable was laid in 1866, but cable transfers were not quoted by the *Commercial and Financial Chronicle* until 1879. Arbitrage dealings did not begin until 1882. "Evolution of the Foreign Exchange Market of the United States," *Journal of Economic and Business History*, Vol. I.

[11] Margraff, *International Exchange*, p. 34.

[12] *Commercial and Financial Chronicle*, Vol. 83, October 13, 1906, p. 854; November 10, p. 1140; Vol. 89, October 30, 1909, p. 1110.

[13] Aldrich, *Interviews on the Banking and Currency Systems*, pp. 21, 109.

sterling rates were close to the export point. The summer months were those in which a large proportion of such bills was drawn, for the rapid drop in exchange between July and October made possible a quick return on the transactions.[14] Both the high and the low peak were flattened somewhat by the increased use of finance bills.

The rate on sterling bills was ordinarily the determining factor in shipments of gold, though if gold was at a premium in New York importation would begin when the sterling rate was still above the usual import point by approximately the amount of the premium. The long suspension of specie payments following the Civil War was accompanied by a constant fluctuation in the gold premium which demoralized the exchange market. Quotations had to be given in both gold and paper, and if the buyer preferred to pay in paper, the dealer was obliged at once to cover the sale by purchasing gold.[15] Since the settlement of all foreign balances had eventually to be made in gold, the gold premium was even more disturbing to foreign trade than to domestic.

In nearly every one of the panics the suspension of specie payments gave rise to a premium on gold which set in motion an import of the metal before sterling rates alone would have brought it about. The panic of 1873 occurred when a premium on gold was already in existence so that it does not provide a clear example, but in the panic of 1893 the currency premium began with the panic and its effect upon gold imports was clearly marked. From August 3 to September 2 all forms of currency were above par, gold being subject to wider fluctuations than other kinds of money because it arrived irregularly in large consignments. During the four weeks of the premium, more than 40 millions of gold were imported from abroad, although exchange rates were above the import point throughout that time. The Clearing House Loan Committee gave assistance to the movement by issuing loan certificates to banks which were making the importation. The currency premium in 1907 lasted

[14] Kemmerer, *Seasonal Variations*, etc., p. 141.
[15] Brown, *A Hundred Years of Merchant Banking*, pp. 228, 281.

longer than in any previous panic, through the months of November and December. Exchange fell to the import point at the end of October, when gold began to come in, but the movement of gold toward New York did not stop when exchange rates climbed beyond the import point nor even when they finally reached the export point. Altogether the imports of gold in the two months of the currency premium amounted to 96 millions.[16]

Both sterling rates and gold movements were correlated with domestic interest rates, not only because the latter were subject to the same seasonal influences as the former but because there was also a direct relation between the demand for funds at home and the importation of funds from abroad. When interest rates were relatively high in New York as compared with abroad, foreign funds came in and sterling rates hovered about the import point in spite of seasonal influences to the contrary or for longer periods than could be explained by seasonal changes in trade. This was the case in nearly every panic; high rates in 1895, 1896, 1903, and 1907 were accompanied by importations of gold and low sterling exchange rates. The low rates of interest which followed upon the panics were conversely usually marked by high rates for sterling and exports of gold. The most striking example of this occurred in the depression of 1894-1895, when the return of foreign-owned securities and the doubtful position of the gold standing in the United States depleted the country's gold stock. Sterling rates remained above par almost constantly during those two years and never touched the import point.

Quotations on sterling exchange

The old inaccurate method of making sterling quotations in percentages of par persisted down to January 1, 1874. The true par was $4.8665 to the pound but, following an old law, quotations were made on the basis of $4.44 as par so that the true par was not reached until the nominal par had been passed by 9.45⅝ per cent.[17] The range of quotations in the decade before

[16] Sprague, *History of Crises*, etc., pp. 192, 280. *Commercial and Financial Chronicle*, Vol. 57, August 5, 1893, p. 196.
[17] See p. 72 above.

1874 was approximately 106 to 111 per cent, never touching the nominal par of 100.

The law of March 3, 1873, as part of the general revision of the currency laws, required that the pound sterling should be deemed equal to $4.8665 and that contracts previously made at the old rate were to be voided. Since the true par and the nominal par were thus made the same, it was impossible to continue the old method of making quotations without confusion. The change had the further good effect, therefore, of causing sterling rates to be given in actual dollars and cents, and even the English papers adopted the new form early in 1874.[18] An attempt to revert to the old percentage method of quoting foreign bills as well as bonds was made in January, 1881, by some of the principle drawers of such bills in New York City. What their motives were is not known but they were unsuccessful in the attempt, and the plan was soon abandoned.[19]

As variations in rates grew less extreme it became customary to give quotations in smaller fractions. Before 1873, the unit was usually one-eighth of one per cent which approximated units of one-half of one cent. Following the change from percentage figures to dollars and cents, the unit was reduced to quarters and finally to eighths of one cent. Today it is customary for rates to be given in thirty-second parts of a cent, which permits a still closer degree of accuracy.

All other foreign exchange rates before the World War were quoted in the number of coins per dollar, German exchange in marks per dollar, French in francs per dollar, and so forth. One reason for the difference between the quotations for sterling and these other currencies was probably that the pound sterling was the only unit which was larger than the dollar. This awkward

[18] The London Stock Exchange had also made a change in its method of quoting American securities. Where it had formerly overvalued the dollar, so that true par was 91½, it now undervalued the dollar slightly by giving it a nominal value of four shillings, or about 97 1/3 cents. This valuation was about 2 2/3 cents below par, or equal to a quotable premium of 2¾ per cent. London quotations of American securities were therefore about 2¾ per cent above their actual value, a bond worth 100 here, being quoted at 102¾ there. *London Economist,* January 3, 1874, p. 12. *Bankers' Magazine,* Vol. 28, p. 311.

[19] *Financial Review,* 1886, p. 26.

contrast was not corrected until after the War, when quotations for all currencies were converted into dollars and cents.

Increased activity of banks in foreign exchange market

In the period before the Civil War the banks took very little part in the drawing of foreign bills of exchange. This business was left largely to the private banks and to the large commission houses which combined the functions of merchant and financier. A similar division of function persisted even after the Civil War and a list of the principal drawers of foreign bills in New York, published by the *Bankers' Magazine* in 1870, includes only four banks, the Bank of New York, the Chemical National, the National Bank of Commerce, and the National Park Bank. Agencies of four Canadian and Californian banks also drew such bills but the remainder of the 56 houses on the list were private bankers or brokers.[20] It was not until the turn of the century that it became common for national banks to undertake a foreign exchange business. In his annual report for 1904, the Comptroller of the Currency urged that the larger national banks be specifically authorized to buy and sell foreign exchange, issue letters of credit, open foreign branches, and accept bills of not more than four months maturity, since "many of the national banks are now engaged in handling foreign exchanges; some of them have large and successful foreign departments." Although there was no such change made in the law, the foreign exchange business continued to be taken out of the hands of the specialists who had formerly carried it and scattered among a great number of banking houses of all kinds, even the trust companies undertaking it on a large scale. The market became a much more complicated structure under the new conditions. Where it had formerly been a simple matter to estimate accurately the amount of short-term American indebtedness abroad, it was now almost impossible. Moreover, the credit and reputation of the few foreign exchange houses had formerly been so well known that it required little investigation to determine the worth of a bill issued by them but under the new system the

[20] *Bankers' Magazine*, Vol. 25, p. 719.

business of buying bills required expert knowledge and up-to-date credit information.[21]

Plans for international banking at New York

As New York became conscious of her growing strength in the field of foreign exchange operations, she became increasingly restive under the domination of London. Various plans were suggested for freeing American trade from the burden of paying tribute to English bankers. Especially in the exchange of goods with South America, it seemed absurd that credits could be obtained only through bankers in London. Drafts upon the United States could not be obtained at all in many South American cities and in others they were sold at a higher rate than sterling drafts. In order to procure the long credits which would form the basis for a dollar exchange market, it was proposed by the International American Conference of 1890 that a bank should be chartered by Congress with all the functions of a national bank except that of note issue and, in addition, the privileges possessed by private banks of issuing letters of credit and loaning upon commodities, accepting bills and so forth. Branches could be established in each of the important centers in South America, and direct banking relations between them and New York would thus be maintained. In spite of the enthusiastic recommendation of President Harrison and Secretary of State Blaine, Congress refused to favor the plan. During the next decade it frequently received the favorable reports of Congressional committees, but to no avail. The terse report of the minority of the House Committee on Banking and Currency in 1898, explains the ground of the objections: "We are opposed to this bill. The two predominating reasons are, first, that Congress has no power to grant such a charter; secondly, it is the most stupendous corporation ever offered to control the finances of the country."[22] It was not until the time

[21] *Bankers' Magazine*, Vol. 74, p. 340; Vol. 78, p. 761; *Commercial and Financial Chronicle*, Vol. 89, October 30, 1909, p. 1110.

[22] 51 Congress, 1 Session, House Report 2561. 55 Congress, 2 Session, House Report 1627, Part 2.

of the World War that international banking corporations were finally authorized.

Summary

The half century between 1863 and 1913 marked a growth in the status of New York to a world money market. Lowered costs of business and the greater use of finance bills cut down the former wide variations in exchange rates and stabilized the foreign exchange market. Dependence upon London became increasingly irksome to New York but it was not until after 1913 that this ceased to be the normal relation.

CHAPTER XVII

THE TREASURY AND THE NEW YORK MONEY MARKET FROM 1863 TO 1913

The Independent Treasury which had been established in 1846 found its legal status considerably altered by the passage of the National Bank Act and other legislation of the Civil War period. During the first fifteen years of its existence it had muddled along, escaping any thoroughgoing revision in spite of its obvious defects. Minor changes had been made in the administration of the law, but on the whole it had retained its essential form. Funds of the government were carefully sequestered; none were deposited in banks; no bank notes were received by the treasury, and although the spirit of the law was frequently violated, the letter which required treasury transactions to be conducted on a cash basis was observed with scrupulous care. It was not that the law worked well; it was simply that it had not worked badly enough to force a change.

In the years after 1863 the Independent Treasury was not so fortunate. It was altered in one respect after another until by 1913 it had lost most of its distinguishing characteristics. The story of its relations with the money market between 1863 and 1913 may be roughly divided into four periods. During the first years after the Civil War the treasury had a surplus and was obliged to resort to the usual devices for preventing it from causing a stringency. The operations during this period were complicated by the fact that gold was at a premium over paper, and that a large part of the surplus had to be devoted to strengthening the treasury's gold reserve in preparation for resumption.

In the second period, which lasted from the resumption of specie payments in 1879 to 1890, the surplus continued and the usual routine methods for meeting the needs of the money market in spite of the law were applied over and over again with little originality. When in 1890 the revenues fell below the expenditures of the government, a third period marked by serious deficit began, unlike any other the country has experienced. The treasury found its relations with the money market completely reversed and could not have carried on at all without the aid of the New York bankers. By 1899, when the reappearance of a surplus marked the beginning of the fourth period, the attitude of officials was changed. If they felt that the market required aid which the treasury was not specifically authorized to give, they reinterpreted the law to suit the occasion and then persuaded Congress to change the law. The Independent Treasury was actually defunct long before it was interred by the Act of 1921.

The first step in the long process of attrition had been taken in 1861, when the act authorizing an issue of war bonds made it legal for the proceeds of these bonds to be left on deposit with the banks which purchased them.[1] The National Bank Act as amended in February, 1864, took a second step in undermining the Independent Treasury. As an incentive to bond purchases the newly-formed national banks, after depositing "United States bonds and otherwise" with the comptroller for security, were given authority to serve as depositaries of any public moneys except receipts from customs. About one-third of the government's income was released from the treasury by this provision. Still a third law of the Civil War period affected the independence of the treasury; the first Greenback Act of February, 1862, made the notes issued under its provisions a legal tender in payment of all obligations to the government except customs duties and interest on the public debt by the government. A stream of paper currency was thus started through the treasury in comparison with which the flow of coin was a mere trickle.

To a limited extent these laws forced the treasury to behave like a normal member of the financial community but there were many points at which it still clung to its outmoded practices. It could not yet receive checks or make payments with them, but

[1] See p. 194 above.

was forced to transfer gold or notes or to use drafts drawn upon other treasury offices. Customs duties had to be paid in gold or in greenbacks. Prejudice against banks and the monied interests, which had been the motive in the establishing of the Independent Treasury, were still strong enough to prevent legal recognition of the actual coöperation which existed between the treasury and the banks. Only gradually, and in many cases after the practice had already been adopted, did the law recognize each departure from the tradition of independence. The history of the relations of the treasury and the New York money market between the years 1863 and 1913 presents therefore an amazing picture of extra-legal and sometimes illegal transactions by which coöperation between them was achieved.

First period of surplus, before resumption, 1863-1879

The relations between the treasury and the money market under the most favorable conditions require skillful management. The government at this time was still the largest single factor in the money market and the mere size of its operations produced a strain upon the financial mechanism unless precautions were taken. These difficulties were augmented by the fact that treasury operations were extremely irregular. The revenues came largely from customs; in some years duties made up as much as two-thirds of the total. They were collected in greatest amount in the spring and summer, when imports were heaviest, and they fell off during the last half of the year. The expenditures were also irregular and quite different from the receipts; payments of interest on the public debt came at the beginning of each half year in greatest volume, and many other payments were quarterly. For several months at a time it might be necessary for the treasury to hoard receipts against the day of heavy disbursement, and during that time the currency of the country would be contracted. On the interest date the currency would be thrown again into circulation, and the funds of the money market would be suddenly expanded.

If the total annual receipts of the government had been approximately balanced by its expenditures so that at the end of the year little remained in the treasury, the management of the funds would have been much simplified. But in every year from 1866 to 1890 and in nearly every year after 1899, there was a surplus of receipts over expenditures and the result was a locking-up of gold and legal-tender notes which was a constant menace to the reserves of the banks. Under these conditions the state of the balance in the subtreasury became one of the most important of the money market indicators. The reserves of the New York banks varied inversely with the treasury balance and the Secretary of the Treasury was obliged to undertake a long series of maneuvers to correct the situation and restore the funds to circulation. The existence of a large surplus revenue is always a bad thing for a government, but when this is combined with a system of safekeeping which attempts to segregate it from the regular current of financial life, its potentiality for danger is enormously increased. The money market becomes dependent upon the treasury, and treasury officials are given a power and responsibility for which they are seldom fitted and with which it would be unwise to endow the best of them.

Until specie payments were resumed on January 1, 1879, the normal obstacles to smooth relations between the government and the money market were augmented by the necessity which the treasury shared with the rest of the country of keeping its accounts in two separate media. Gold, which was received for customs duties and paid out for interest on the public debt, was at a varying premium over the legal-tender greenbacks and national bank notes used in all other transactions, and did not enter into ordinary commercial exchanges. In the days before the Civil War a treasury surplus had been disposed of in one of three ways: the purchase of bonds before maturity, the prepayment of interest on them, and the transfer of funds from one subtreasury to another. Now sales of gold were also available to serve as a link between the treasury and the money market. They were as effective in influencing the supply of funds in the market as were sales and purchases of bonds or the deposit of government funds in national banks.

These methods of providing contact points between the treasury and the money market were not separate devices used independently of each other but were closely interrelated. Sales of gold, made necessary by the accumulations of the metal in treasury vaults, brought in such a volume of currency that it became necessary for the government to purchase bonds in order to put the currency again into circulation. Sales of bonds on the other hand took so much money out of the market that the proceeds had to be left on deposit with the banks to be withdrawn gradually in order to avoid a sudden contraction. Transfers of funds to other districts were necessitated by the large receipts at New York from bond sales and from customs.

Deposits of government funds in the national banks were very small during these early years. Only the proceeds of internal revenue and miscellaneous taxes might be kept outside of the treasury itself and these could be put into banks only at the time of their collection; if they were once deposited in the treasury, they could not lawfully be transferred to a bank. Customs receipts of gold went directly to the various subtreasury offices and the proceeds of government loans were transferred gradually from the banks into the treasury. The total amount of government deposits in national banks under these circumstances fell from about 30 millions in 1866 to between 7 and 8 millions in the early seventies. The share of the total held by banks in New York City was seldom more than one-tenth.

A strict interpretation of the law in this respect was difficult to maintain in the face of the market's need, and it was gradually relaxed. A stringency in the market in the autumn of 1872 caused the treasury to sell gold in large amounts for the relief of New York importers and bankers, at their particular request. The deputation which went to Washington and persuaded the Secretary of the Treasury to take this action was also concerned about the resultant withdrawal of greenbacks from the market. The treasury agreed therefore to name banks as government depositaries for the purpose of receiving the proceeds of the gold sales, as it had done in connection with loans during the Civil

War.[2] The Bank of Commerce, the Fourth National, the Second National, and the Central National, after depositing bonds as collateral, were entrusted with nearly six millions of treasury funds and the reserves of the New York banks immediately rose. The deposits were drawn down gradually during the next three months, when the worst of the stringency was over. The banks somewhat reluctantly gave them up, their distress when the deposits were recalled overshadowing the relief which had been felt when they were made—a difficulty which constantly beset the treasury in its honest efforts to assist the market.[3]

This action of Secretary Boutwell, although commendable as a step in the restoration of natural banking relations between the treasury and the market, had been certainly without precedent and possibly without legal sanction. When the same question arose again in the administration of Secretary Sherman, in connection with the sales of bonds during 1877, he asked for a ruling from the Attorney-General as to what funds might be deposited in national banks. He was assured that under the funding and resumption acts his authority was sufficient to cover the making of such deposits, and he was therefore able to grant the request of banks purchasing the bonds that the proceeds be left on deposit for a time in order to avoid depleting their reserves. The purpose of these sales was the building up of a substantial reserve in the treasury for resumption of specie payments and since New York City was the only point at which greenbacks were actually to be redeemed in gold, two-thirds of the treasury deposits were left in that city. The First National Bank, the Bank of New York, the Chase Bank, and the Bank of Commerce, held large balances on treasury account and during 1878 the government deposits in the whole city were increased from less than ½ million on the first call to 26 millions on the fourth.[4] During the early part of 1879 the treasury deposits in New York were permitted to increase still further;

[2] See p. 194 above.

[3] *Commercial and Financial Chronicle*, Vol. 15, October 12, 1872, p. 480; November 30, 1872, p. 709; December 7, 1872, p. 749; December 21, 1872, p. 821.

[4] Sherman, *Recollections*, Vol. I, p. 601. 46 Congress, 2 Session, House Executive Document 9, pp. 135, 138.

on the second call, in April, they reached a high point of 249 millions, the greater part of which were in the First National Bank and the National Bank of Commerce. After that date they decreased rapidly. It was apparent by this time that resumption was not going to require any large sum and the volume of government funds in banks speedily sank back to the low figure at which it had stood before the preparations for resumption began.[5]

Closely associated with its deposits in banks were the treasury's sales of bonds. Until preparations for resumption had forced the treasury to depend upon banks, the larger part of the bond sales were carried on without an accompanying increase in government deposits. This was true of the new loans made by the government as well as of the refunding operations. More than half of the debt was in the form of treasury notes and other short obligations which had to be funded into bonds, and the long-term securities which had been issued during the war were at high rates of interest and required to be refunded. A surplus began to accumulate in 1869 and Secretary Boutwell began the regular retirement of the public debt in order to save the interest charges. While these operations were under way the state of the money market was of the most vital concern to the treasury. When for example the sale of bonds caused too rapid a contraction of the currency and a consequent stringency in the market, the Secretary of the Treasury ordered that thereafter bonds might be paid for with treasury notes as well as with cash. One lot of bonds was sold secretly abroad in order to avoid disturbance in the market at home.[6] Bond purchases were at first made irregularly and secretly through the agency of several brokerage houses. Again, as in the case of the sale of bonds abroad, public opinion forced a change, and after May, 1870, offers of bonds were made publicly once a week, 1 or 2 millions at a time. Later in the summer, when the reserves of the New York banks were low and the treasury surplus was high,

[5] 46 Congress, 2 Session, House Executive Document 9, pp. 750-51. *Commercial and Financial Chronicle,* August 23, 1879, Vol. 29, p. 183.

[6] *Commercial and Financial Chronicle,* Vol. 5, August 10, 1867, p. 165; November 9, 1867, p. 581. Secretary of Treasury, *Annual Report,* 1868, p. xliii.

the purchases rose to 3 millions at a time and the reserves of the banks gave immediate evidence of relief.[7]

The treasury surplus grew so rapidly that the original function of bond purchases, refunding the war debt, was overshadowed by the necessity of restoring to circulation the currency locked up in government vaults. The bulk of the purchases were concentrated in the late summer and early autumn months of the year in order to release currency when it was most needed. In 1872 what came very near to a panic was averted by the purchase of an extra 5 millions' of bonds for several weeks in succession and deposit of the proceeds in national banks.[8] When a more serious crisis came in September, 1873, the treasury had nothing to offer except its usual device of bond purchases, and this in limited amount. In this year, when help was to be needed in greater degree than ever before, the income of the government was so diminished by shrinking imports that the balance was lower than in the preceding year. The first of the brokerage failures which marked the beginning of the panic occurred on the thirteenth of September and there were other failures in the week which followed; the reserves of the New York banks had been falling for a number of weeks and it was plain that the market was in the throes of a severe reaction. Yet the treasury made no move towards assisting it until the twentieth, the day on which the Clearing House began the issue of loan certificates. Then it offered to buy bonds at prices not above par in gold. Thirteen million dollars' worth were brought in during the next four days, but by that time the treasury saw that its shrinking balance made it impossible to continue and the offer was withdrawn. The amount of currency paid for bonds was not even sufficient to restore the reserves of the New York banks. Indeed it was just about enough to replace the currency which, it was estimated, was hoarded during the panic.[9]

[7] *Commercial and Financial Chronicle,* Vol. 11, September 10, 1870, p. 325.

[8] *Commercial and Financial Chronicle,* Vol. 15, October 12, 1872, p. 480.

[9] *Commercial and Financial Chronicle,* Vol. 17, September 6, 1873, p. 313; September 27, 1873, p. 406. Secretary of Treasury, *Annual Report,* 1873, pp. x-xv, 30.

In the same crisis the treasury officials definitely refused to assist the market in two ways suggested to it by committees of distracted bankers from New York. One was that the government use its funds in the purchase of foreign exchange, which at the first sign of panic had collapsed. The other was the issue of treasury notes on terms very similar to those of the Clearing House loan certificates. Both of these actions were clearly *ultra vires,* but the treasury had not always found that to be adequate reason for non-interference in the money market, nor did it accept that reason on many later occasions. In the very next month certain of the legal-tender notes retired during 1866-1867 were reissued without the sanction of Congress.[10]

The purchases of bonds fell off after this time, for the treasury was building up its reserves against resumption of specie payments, and instead of buying bonds was selling them for gold during the years immediately preceding 1879. Public sales of gold had played a prominent part in treasury policy during the decade after the War. Like bond purchases and deposits in banks, they were another method of disposing of a surplus and meeting the currency needs of the country. The government had obligated itself to pay the interest and the principal of the public debt in gold, and it was to assure itself a supply of this metal during the period of depreciation when gold would otherwise have been driven out of the country that the customs dues were required to be paid in gold. More than half of the treasury revenues during the seventies, excluding proceeds of loans, arose from customs and consisted of gold coin. Since the total amount of gold specie in the country was 130 millions, of which only about 25 millions was in banks, the payment of 200 millions of duties annually necessitated a rapid turnover of the available specie. If it had not been sold back to the public at intervals there would have been a serious shortage in the market.

The first sales were made in 1863 to the modest amount of $89,000 in gold coin which with the premium netted the treasury

[10] The report of the Secretary of the Treasury for 1873 maintained a discreet silence on the subject but when the matter leaked out it created a great furor. Sherman, *Selected Speeches and Reports,* pp. 380-85.

nearly $125,000 in paper currency. The sales of gold increased rapidly and during the next five years averaged about 47 millions a year, bringing to the New York subtreasury about 70 millions in greenbacks annually.[11] The action of the treasury in the gold market was watched with interest and frequently with anxiety. At first the gold sales, like the bond purchases, were made secretly through various brokerage houses. Under these conditions the amount sold was not known until after the sale was completed, and the secrecy surrounding the whole matter added fuel to the speculative fires already raging.[12] The first indication of a sale was sometimes obtained in the contraction of legal tenders felt in the reserves of the New York banks when the treasury received payment for the gold it had sold.[13] City banks found this sort of unexpected demand upon their reserves a serious strain, and requested the Secretary of the Treasury to sell the gold as it came in, except for enough to meet the interest on the public debt. In this way it would have been impossible for any great amount to be sold at a time and the banks would have been protected against a sudden demand for greenbacks. But the Secretary of the Treasury preferred to keep the situation more closely in his own hands and continued to let the gold accumulate in the treasury until he felt that special conditions necessitated sales. In May, 1866, for example, during the Overend-Gurney panic in London, he sold more than 35 millions in order to meet the demand for gold to be sent abroad.[14] So serious were the complaints against the irregular and secret sales of gold that they finally influenced the secretary. In October, 1868, he announced that gold would thereafter be sold by public tender, at the rate of $300,000 daily until 3 millions had been sold.[15]

[11] 40 Congress, 3 Session, House Executive Document 84.

[12] Early in 1867, a rumor gained currency in New York that government officials were lending gold to speculators in defiance of the law; complaints were made to Washington, and a Congressional investigation was well under way before it was discovered that the whole matter was a mere rumor for the purpose of depressing gold. 39 Congress, 2 Session, House Report 14.

[13] *Commercial and Financial Chronicle*, Vol. 2, February 24, 1866, p. 234.

[14] *Bankers' Magazine*, Vol. 21, pp. 33, 239.

[15] *Commercial and Financial Chronicle*, Vol. 7, Oct. 24, 1868, p. 517. *Bankers' Magazine*, Vol. 23, pp. 416, 473.

Under the new administration of President Grant and Secretary Boutwell the amount of gold released at public sales was increased during April and May, 1869, to one million per week, and in June, to 2 millions. In July the sales were suddenly cut to one million every two weeks, in order to avoid a shortage of paper currency during the autumn. It was in September of this year that the disgraceful "Black Friday" occurred, when speculators, counting on the cessation of sales by the treasury during the crop-moving season, tried to corner the gold market. The secretary released 4 millions in the week following that episode, effectually ruining the plan, and for the rest of the year a million dollars' worth of gold was offered to the public twice each week.[16] In 1870 public sales of gold were further systematized by confining them to Wednesdays, when one, 2, or 3, millions were released, as the occasion seemed to demand. The chief disadvantage of this, as compared with the old method of secret sales, was that it concentrated the whole movement for the week into one day and caused severe contraction of greenbacks at the city banks on Thursdays, when the banks settled for their purchases. Unusual conditions in the money market or unusual accumulation in the treasury brought about special sales in addition to the regular amounts. In 1871, when the treasury was holding about 74 millions of gold while the whole sum available for the rest of the country was less than 15 millions, Secretary Boutwell doubled his sales of gold for a time until his balance was down to the more normal figure of 35 millions.[17]

A sale of gold had the same effect upon the money market as a sale of bonds. The gold had to be sold in order to restore it to the money market, but without the greatest care the result was a shortage of greenbacks. Frequently the treasury offset the sale of gold by an equivalent purchase of bonds. The situation of October, 1872, has already been described, when the banks needed the gold in the treasury but did not want to give up its

[16] 41 Congress, 2 Session, House Report 31, Vol. II, p. 366.

[17] *Commercial and Financial Chronicle*, Vol. 11, October 22, 1870, p. 517; Vol. 13, September 9, 1871, p. 325; September 16, 1871, p. 357; October 7, 1871, p. 454.

value in greenbacks and arranged instead to pay the government with deposit credit.[18] The sales of gold by the treasury were a necessary evil rather than a means of relieving the money market. It was essential to get the gold out of the treasury for the sake of the merchants and the banks, but the consequent absorption of greenbacks was almost as severe a strain upon the banks as the holding of the gold. The whole difficulty might have been avoided had the treasury been permitted to place gold customs receipts on special deposit in the banks, just as private individuals made their deposits of gold. The depreciation of the paper currency would still have been a burden to the community but treasury relations with the money market would have been simplified and one factor in the uncertainty of the time would have been eliminated.

As the date for the resumption of specie payments drew near the treasury began to hoard gold against the redemption of its notes.[19] Gold bonds bearing 4 or 4½ per cent interest were issued at the rate of 5 millions each month during eight months of 1877 through a group of bankers in New York and London. This, with the surplus revenue, gave a coin reserve of 63 millions by the end of the year. During 1878 more bonds were issued and the 50 millions of gold obtained in this way was added to the previous reserve. By the day of resumption the total reserve was more than 133 millions in gold coin.[20]

The whole question of sales of gold was solved by the resumption of specie payments which brought the paper currency to a par with gold. After January 1, 1879, the subtreasury at New York was required to redeem in gold all United States notes when presented in sums of 50 dollars or more. Greenbacks were thus made equivalent to gold for all commercial transactions. The law also made provision for correcting certain minor defects

[18] Secretary of Treasury, *Annual Report*, 1873, p. xi.

[19] *Commercial and Financial Chronicle*, Vol. 20, January 30, 1875, p. 75; May 8, 1875, p. 437.

[20] By the terms of the contract, the subscribers to this loan agreed to pay for it "in gold coin, matured U. S. coin coupons, 6% 5-20 bonds, or U. S. gold certificates." Secretary of Treasury, Annual Report, 1876, p. xi; 1877, p. xii; 1878, p. ix; 1879, p. ix. Sherman, *Recollections*, Vol. I, pp. 566-70, 574, 580; Vol. II, pp. 627, 636.

in the currency due to the suspension of specie payments during the War; a silver coinage in small denominations was to be issued in place of the fractional paper still outstanding, and the coinage charge on gold bullion was removed.

The treasury had had four years in which to get ready for the change and it was well prepared for resumption unless something akin to a run should develop. Actually resumption was accomplished in so undramatic a manner that it seemed almost an anticlimax to the elaborate preparations which had been made for it. When anxious treasury officials telegraphed from Washington to New York, after the first day of resumption, they learned that instead of a run on the subtreasury office only an "insignificant" amount of greenbacks had been presented for redemption in gold. Less than a million dollars per month were redeemed during the first year. So small was the demand for gold that in September, 1879, Secretary Sherman ordered that gold need no longer be hoarded but should be paid out for current government obligations along with notes and silver whenever it was convenient to do so.[21]

Several precautionary measures had been taken by the treasury to reduce the public demand for gold. The issue of gold certificates was stopped on the theory that if the public were put to the trouble of handling the actual coin the demand for it would be cut down. No more certificates were issued after December 1, 1878, and the 25 millions then outstanding were gradually withdrawn as they were paid in for customs dues and taxes.[22]

As a second step toward checking a possible drain of gold the treasury became a member of the New York Clearing House. There had previously been suggestions that the subtreasury at New York should join the Association,[23] but while gold was at a premium the accounting difficulties were too great. During the latter part of 1878, when the value of legal tenders was nearly

[21] Sherman, *Recollections*, Vol. II, p. 742. Secretary of Treasury, *Annual Report*, 1879, p. ix. 46 Congress, 2 Session, House Executive Document 9, p. 449.

[22] 46 Congress, 2 Session, House Executive Document 9, pp. 380, 414.

[23] Sherman, *Recollections*, Vol. II, p. 670.

equal to that of gold, an arrangement was made with the National Bank of Commerce whereby it was to collect all the checks due the treasury, convert the proceeds into coin, and make payment to the treasury—in other words, to act as its clearing agent. This saved the treasury much inconvenience, but there was still a loss of time in collection and difficulties over the correct rate of exchange between paper and coin which convinced the secretary that actual membership in the Clearing House and direct relations with the New York banks through that medium would be preferable to the use of a bank as agent. On November 7, 1878, therefore, a committee of bankers from New York went to Washington to arrange for the treasury's admission to the Clearing House and for coöperation with the treasury during the process of resumption. The banks were eager to secure the membership of the treasury in the Clearing House but stipulated for their own protection that in settling the clearing balances only gold and greenbacks should be used. Silver, which was legal tender equally with gold and greenbacks, was barred, not only because of its bulk and the consequent difficulty of storing it but also because the silver coinage act threatened to drive out gold and the banks did not want to run the risk of having large amounts of the cheaper metal left on their hands.[24]

This step did much to dissolve the difficulties which attended the payment of public dues under the Independent Treasury system since it eliminated much of the vexatious carrying back and forth of coin. With the resumption of specie payments, greenbacks became equal to gold and the Secretary of the Treasury ruled that they were acceptable for all public dues so that it was no longer necessary to obtain gold or gold certificates for payments to the government. Under the silver coinage act of 1878 the new silver dollars and the silver certificates were also legal tender and there were now three kinds of money acceptable at the treasury for customs.[25] Moreover drafts on

[24] 46 Congress, 2 Session, House Executive Document 9, pp. 319, 399; House Miscellaneous Document 34, p. 1.

[25] Secretary of Treasury, *Annual Report*, 1879, p. ix. 46 Congress, 2 Session, House Executive Document 9, pp. 401, 807.

a Clearing House bank could be used for all payments to the government except internal revenue and could be used by the treasury for all expenditures except interest on the public debt.[26]

In spite of these improvements the payment of customs duties was still an extremely awkward process. In January, 1879, Secretary Sherman instructed Assistant Treasurer Hillhouse of New York to confer with merchants and importers in an effort to devise a more expeditious method of settling customs duties. This group of business men recommended that the treasury conform to good commercial practice and accept the certified checks of banks. There was some doubt as to the legality of this course. Since it would have been a long and arduous task to persuade Congress to change the law and since Secretary Sherman had not the type of hardihood shown by some of his colleagues in interpreting the law to his own wishes, the certified check was abandoned. It was then suggested that the banks be permitted to make deposits with the New York subtreasury and draw against the credit thus built up as their customers needed to make payment for duties. This cumbersome scheme seemed equally unlikely to find sanction under the narrow interpretation of the law and no action was taken upon it.[27] But in 1888 it was revived and, by an elaborate arrangement with the banks, customs duties were at last permitted to be paid by check. Every morning certain banks largely used by importers made deposits with the assistant treasurer sufficient to cover payments of duties during that day. Importers drew against these deposits and had the drafts certified by the banks in the manner prescribed by the treasury. The total amount of checks drawn was deducted from the balance of the morning and the remainder was credited back to the depositor bank through the Clearing House at the regular daily settlement. Within a month two-thirds of the customs collections were being made in this way

[26] Secretary of Treasury, *Annual Report*, 1881, p. 428. *Commercial and Financial Chronicle*, Vol. 33, November 19, 1881, p. 554.

[27] 46 Congress, 2 Session, House Executive Document 9, pp. 452, 456.

and another modernization of the Independent Treasury had been effected.[28]

The period of the surplus, 1879-1890

With the great accomplishment of resumption fairly behind it the Independent Treasury found itself again faced with the problem which had been foremost in its relations with the money market in its earliest days, that of the surplus. From year to year the receipts of the government mounted above its expenditures. The principal source of these revenues was the tariff which had been permitted to remain at wartime levels long after the necessities of war had ceased to exist. A few changes were made in the rates in the revision of 1883 but the net effect was negligible.[29] Revenues continued to overbalance expenditures.

The money market was as sensitive as usual to the treasury's operations. Each change of policy was watched with apprehension and reported in detail by the financial journals. Every action of the secretary of the treasury was subjected to the most careful scrutiny and unsought advice was lavished upon him. The rapidly declining prices after the War had created serious maladjustments in the economic organization; the propaganda for free silver had penetrated to every district with its partly true, largely false, insistence upon the need for more money. To the group which demanded that the government issue more greenbacks and coin more silver in order to make money plentiful and the country prosperous, the locking up of currency by the treasury was an unmitigated evil and to every group it was an admitted problem.

The various secretaries of the treasury themselves protested against the responsibility which was put upon them. In report after report they begged Congress to stop the flow of funds which was threatening to inundate the government and pointed out the anomalous position in which they were placed by the

[28] *Bankers' Magazine*, Vol. 43, pp. 16, 81. *Commercial and Financial Chronicle*, August 4, 1888, Vol. 47, p. 120.

[29] The returns from customs receipts during the first nine months' operation of the new law was at the rate of 30.2 per cent, compared with 30.5 per cent during the same period under the old law. *Commercial and Financial Chronicle*, Vol. 38, April 5, 1884, p. 400.

laws.[30] They insisted either that the tariff rates should be reduced in order to cut the surplus revenue to a reasonable figure or that the Independent Treasury law should be changed so that the surplus could be handled without endangering the stability of the money market. But the high-tariff party was in control of Congress and refused to consider changing the rates. Neither would it make any fundamental change in the law which governed the relations of the treasury and the banks. The cheap money party, supported by the West and the South, introduced into Congress in 1886 a resolution which would have required the treasury to call in 10 millions' of bonds whenever the surplus exceeded 100 millions. But even those who were most opposed to the existence of the surplus were not willing to attempt so arbitrary a solution and it was defeated largely by the votes of New York and New England.[31]

One of the most unfortunate characteristics of the surplus was the fact that it was very difficult to tell from the published treasury reports just how large it was and how it changed from week to week. The hundred million dollar fund for the redemption of the greenbacks, for example, which was practically a trust fund, was reported in the total of current assets and gave a misleading impression of the surplus available for the relief of the money market. The "fictions of bookkeeping" led to still more erroneous reports; from October, 1882, to February, 1883, the government purchased 20 million dollars' worth of bonds prior to their maturity. The purchase was not however recorded in the cash account until the date of maturity and for a period of months the apparent balance of the treasury was 20 million dollars greater than the actual available balance. Again in December, 1888, the official treasury statement showed a net loss of 15 millions in currency because part of the current month's surplus had been pushed into the next month by the device of making a great number of payments in advance in

[30] Secretary of Treasury, *Annual Report,* 1883, p. xxx; 1887, p. xxv; 1889, p. xxviii.

[31] Congressional Record, 49 Congress, 1 Session, pp. 6921, 6945. *Bankers' Magazine,* Vol. 41, p. 144.

December. The month had actually been marked by a net gain of 5 millions instead of a loss of 15 millions.

Some improvement in the form of the statement was made in April, 1885, by setting down opposite each item of the assets its corresponding liability, with the net balance remaining. But it was not until 1903 that the treasury statement was finally put into such form that the difference between income and expenditure was equivalent to the change in the balance.[32]

Although it was not always possible to tell exactly how large the surplus was at any given moment, it was plainly evident by 1880 that something had to be done about it. The usual round of bond purchases and government deposits was begun again, varied occasionally by the transfer of funds from one subtreasury office to another. No new technique was developed during this period; the only method by which the funds could be finally disposed of was by spending them and the only purchases which the treasury was authorized to make, outside of the specific appropriations of Congress, were of bonds. But the public was not at all anxious to sell bonds; most of them stood at quotations well above par with prospects of a further rise. The treasury was empowered to meet the market price but even with this inducement the public did not respond. In 1881, when the market was in a very unsettled state, the secretary of the treasury offered to purchase 10 million dollars' worth of the 5 and 6 per cent bonds at prices not over par, but only 5 millions were presented. Again in 1882 the secretary offered to purchase 5 millions of the 5 per cent bonds weekly for a period of five weeks, in order to relieve the market, but the bonds came in at the rate of only 3 millions per week.[33] The same obstacle to treasury policy continued during 1883 and 1884, in the months preceding the panic of May, 1884, and the surplus balance grew steadily.[34]

[32] *Commercial and Financial Chronicle,* Vol. 33, September 17, 1881, p. 298; Vol. 36, June 9, 1883, p. 633; Vol. 40, April 4, 1885, p. 404; Vol. 48, January 5, 1889, p. 3.

[33] *Commercial and Financial Chronicle,* Vol. 30, February 14, 1880, p. 164; Vol. 35, October 14, 1882, p. 414.

The truth was that the market did not need money at this time; for months there had been such abundance of funds that call rates stood at one and two per cent, and fell back to that level a few days after the panic. The market was glutted with silver certificates and this brought about a curious situation. Ordinarily in a period when government receipts are in excess of expenditures the market is at the mercy of the treasury operations and unless the surplus is paid out the reserves of the banks will be impaired. But the issue of silver dollars and silver certificates under the law of 1878 reversed the normal course of events and for a time made the treasury dependent upon the banks in spite of a large surplus revenue. It will be recalled that the silver dollars and certificates had been made legal tender in payment of customs dues to the government but that the New York Clearing House banks had steadfastly refused to receive them.[35] The diagram of receipts for customs at the port of New York indicates what happened; the proportion of gold receipts fell from more than ¾ in 1882-1883, to less than 2/5 in the latter part of 1884 and the first half of 1885. But the treasury was still obligated to pay interest in gold and the gold balance in the treasury was so reduced after the payment of interest on July 1, 1885, that a complete cessation of gold payments at the treasury seemed inevitable. Rather than accept silver in settlement of its balances at the Clearing House, the New York banks offered to provide the treasury with 10 to 20 millions in gold in return for subsidiary silver. With this assistance the government continued to meet its obligations in gold and an increased receipt of gold customs duties during the following months prevented a recurrence of the dilemma.[36]

During 1887 and 1888 the abnormal ease of money ceased; the bank reserves of New York went back to a figure near the legal minimum, interest rates rose, and the operations of the

[34] *Commercial and Financial Chronicle*, Vol. 36, January 6, 1883, p. 3; March 24, p. 324; June 9, p. 633; Vol. 37, August 25, 1883, p. 195; November 10, p. 489; November 24, p. 556; Vol. 38, February 9, 1884, p. 157; May 10, p. 563; May 17, p. 582.

[35] See p. 364 above.

[36] *Commercial and Financial Chronicle*, Vol. 41, July 18, 1885, p. 61; July 25, p. 88.

treasury again became a factor of importance in the money market. The announcement by the treasury in April, 1888, that it would purchase more bonds gave relief to the banks at a time when they had been curtailing their commercial loans. More than 80 millions' of bonds came into the treasury during the next six months and the release of the currency permitted a more liberal policy on the part of the banks which had been nervously husbanding their resources.[37]

The treasury surplus was so large by 1887 that bond purchases alone were not sufficient to disburse it and the secretary of the treasury decided to increase the government deposits in national banks. In order to do so he found it necessary to relax the stringent rules which had been in force since the War. The National Bank Act had given the secretary the right to demand of depositary banks "satisfactory" collateral in the form of "United States bonds and otherwise," which had always been interpreted to mean government bonds. For many years the amount of deposits which could be placed in any bank had been set at 90 per cent of the par value of the collateral bonds. As a matter of fact the deposits were being constantly drawn down so that the average amount of the deposits was well under 90 per cent of the par value of the bonds. Government bonds since 1882 however had stood well above par, and many banks were unwilling to use them in so unprofitable a manner. In order to encourage banks to accept government deposits and get the funds out of the treasury a new ruling was made permitting deposits to be made to the full par value of the 4½ per cent bonds which were selling at about 105, and to 1.1 the par value of the 4 per cents which were selling at about 125. That amount moreover was to serve not as the maximum amount of the deposit, but as the average about which the deposit might fluctuate during the month. At the same time the upper limit for deposits in any one bank was raised from ½ to 1 million. Under the stimulus of these changes government deposits in national banks increased from less than 20, to 60, millions dur-

[37] *Bankers' Magazine*, Vol. 43, pp. 321-24. *Commercial and Financial Chronicle*, Vol. 46, April 21, p. 492. Comptroller of Currency, *Annual Report*, 1888, p. 34.

ing the year 1887. In New York City alone they rose from less than 1 million to 9 millions, and reached a maximum of 12 millions at the first call in 1888.[38]

The increase in government deposits had an interesting reaction upon the issue of national bank notes. As banks increased the amount of collateral against deposits they withdrew many of the bonds which had been used as security for note circulation. The volume of notes outstanding, which had been slowly declining for some years, now fell off at a more rapid rate. The designation of new national bank depositaries was therefore stopped early in 1888 in a futile effort to halt the decline in national bank note circulation. By 1892 the total of government deposits in banks was back at the low level of 1886, and there it remained for the new secretary of the treasury was opposed to deposits in banks except as far as was required for the needs of the public service.[39]

These years between the resumption of specie payments and the appearance of a deficit in the government balance sheet, from 1879 to 1890, were on the whole uneventful ones for the development of treasury technique in dealing with the money market. The usual problems connected with a surplus of government income arose: the question of how to spend it without flooding the market, and if it could not be spent of how best to put the money back into circulation in order to avoid strangling the market for lack of funds. The confusion caused by the operations of the treasury was aggravated by the currency legislation of the period. The surfeit of silver and silver certificates at New York was due to the silver coinage act of 1878 and much of the doubt and uncertainty regarding the financial future which assailed the money market was due to the long-dragged out debates in Congress over currency questions. On the whole the money market was at the mercy of the treasury during much of this time and the combined factors of govern-

[38] Comptroller of Currency, *Annual Report*, 1888, p. 32. *Commercial and Financial Chronicle*, Vol. 45, October 15, 1887, p. 488.

[39] See p. 405 below. Comptroller of Currency, *Annual Report*, 1888, p. 34. Secretary of Treasury, *Annual Report*, 1890, p. xli.

ment surplus and faulty currency legislation made it a serious drag upon the financial community.

The period of the deficit, 1890-1898

The period which began with the latter part of 1890 is unique in treasury history. It was the first time that the government was faced by a deficit in its income during a period when it was not at war. From the point of view of the independence of the treasury the result was appalling. The treasury found itself not only unable to help the market, but forced to seek help from it; its rôle reduced from patron to suppliant. Its independence, which had long been a fable, now became a bitter jest.

The forces which brought about this change need not be described here. A panic in 1890 followed by a prolonged business depression prepared the way for it; and the silver legislation, first of 1878 and then of 1890, was an important factor. Under the Act of 1890 the treasury was obliged to purchase 4½ million ounces of silver each month, with the effect that the currency was inflated at home and American credit destroyed abroad. Imports of goods into the United States began to fall off and, in spite of the increased rates of the McKinley tariff act of 1890, the net revenues from duties declined. The European demand for American securities which had been one of the chief items in balancing our foreign trade account was reduced at the same time, bringing about an export of gold larger than usual.

The high point of the treasury surplus balance had been reached in the middle of the year 1888 and its decline from that point had been rapid. It was soon apparent that the days of the surplus were drawing to a close. Secretary Windom announced late in 1889 that the depositary banks were holding larger deposits for the government than were necessary and that 10 per cent of the excess was to be transferred back to the treasury by January 15, 1890, and another 10 per cent on March 1.[40] It

[40] Secretary of Treasury, *Annual Report*, 1890, p. xli; *Commercial and Financial Chronicle*, Vol. 50, February 8, 1890, p. 186.

was also announced that the purchase of 4 per cent bonds would be discontinued until the balance of the treasury was larger.

During the early summer of 1890 the funds available to the treasury were increased by the transfer to it of 50 millions which had formerly been held in the bank-note redemption fund. With this amount the secretary of the treasury was able to resume the purchase of bonds, and during the stringency which developed in August took in 20 millions' of the 4½ per cents with prepaid interest. To the urgings that deposits in national banks be increased the secretary was adamant, insisting that the only legal method of doing so—designating depositaries, receiving bonds as collateral, and then permitting the proceeds of the internal revenue to accumulate—was too slow to be useful and was also not so effective as the purchase of bonds. The bonds continued to be called in and during the four months from August to November nearly 100 millions were redeemed. When the Baring crisis broke in London in the middle of November, the treasury had nothing left with which to aid the market. The banks were forced to resort to the usual Clearing House loan certificates in order to settle their balances and the panic ran its course without assistance from the government.

The balance in the treasury continued to fall off with the decline in receipts and by the last quarter of the year 1891 the disbursements were in excess of the receipts. It was especially the gold part of the treasury's funds which was being drawn out. The net exports of gold from New York increased from 9 millions during 1890 to 44 millions in 1891 and to 62 millions in 1892. By April of 1893 the gold in the treasury was reduced to less than 100 millions, the amount which had been set as the minimum compatible with safety. Accompanying the withdrawal of gold for export was a decline in the gold received for customs. Gold and gold certificates in the fiscal year 1889-1890 had formed 92 per cent of these receipts, but they fell to around 15 per cent in the middle of 1891. There was a brief period of increased gold receipts at the end of the year but through most

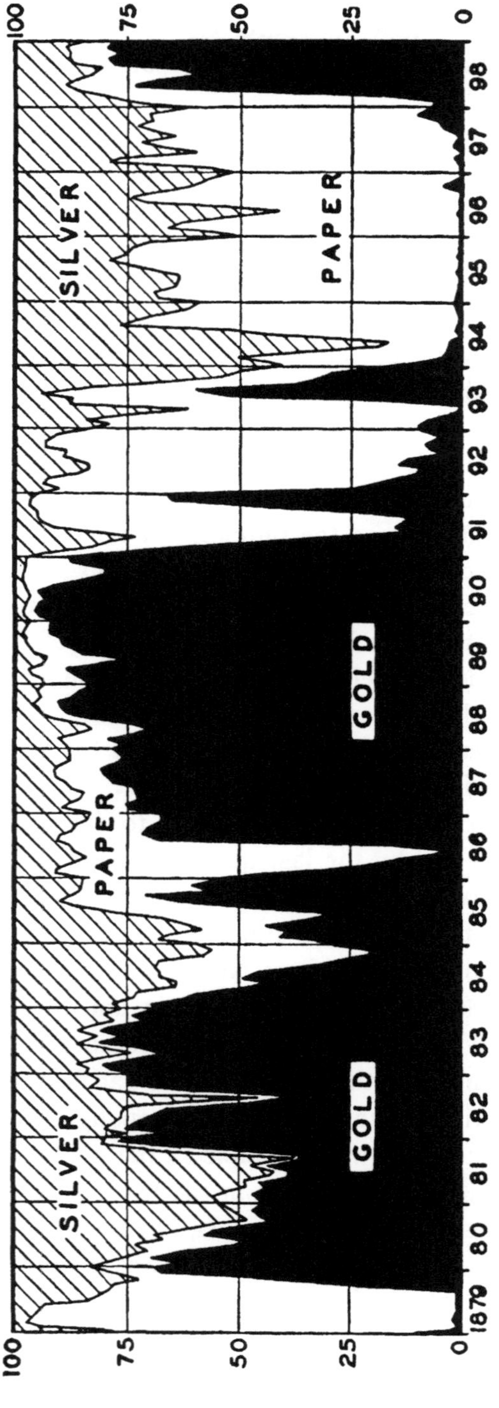

PERCENTAGE OF MONTHLY CUSTOMS RECEIPTS AT NEW YORK IN EACH FORM OF CURRENCY.

SOURCE: ANNUAL REPORTS OF THE SECRETARY OF THE TREASURY.

of 1892 they continued to fall and for the fiscal year 1892-1893 averaged only 7 per cent of the total.[41]

The combination of gold exports and smaller gold receipts bore such a threatening aspect that the secretary of the treasury felt obliged to limit the gold used in settlement of his balances at the Clearing House. He was severely criticized for this action but it seems to have been inevitable under the circumstances; the gold paid into the Clearing House was not sharply reduced in amount until after the gold customs receipts had fallen. The effect of the treasury's action upon the reserves of the New York Clearing House banks became apparent at once. During 1890 their gold reserve had averaged about 75 millions, their legal tender notes about 25 millions. During 1891 the legal tenders increased and the specie declined until at one time in September the two were almost equal in amount. The proportion of legal tenders in the reserve, although it fell off from the high point of September, remained above normal throughout 1892. The change was reflected also in the settlement at the Clearing House; during the fiscal year ending October 1, 1890, only 1 per cent of the balances had been paid in legal tenders; in the next two years the proportion rose to 35 per cent and then to 58.[42]

One of the major problems connected with this general shortage of gold was that of obtaining gold for export. During the period when the treasury had a large surplus of funds with an ample proportion of gold it was of little consequence whether the gold was obtained from the banks, which then applied to the treasury to replenish their reserves by exchanging legal tenders for gold; or from the treasury by the redemption of greenbacks. As a matter of fact few greenbacks had been presented at the treasury in New York to be exchanged for gold and in all the years from 1879 to 1891, the total amount was only 34 millions.[43] But in December, 1892, the demand for re-

[41] Secretary of Treasury, *Annual Report,* 1896, pp. 137, 138. Hearings before House Committee on Banking and Currency, 59 Congress, 2 Session, 1906-1907, p. 81.

[42] *Annual Report,* New York Clearing House.

[43] Secretary of Treasury, *Annual Report,* 1896, p. 131.

demption of greenbacks suddenly increased and during the next three months more gold was taken from the treasury by this device than in the preceding thirteen years.

In spite of the danger to their own reserves the banks felt obliged to respond to the demand of the secretary of the treasury in February, 1893, when he came to New York to confer with the leading bankers on the best plan for keeping the treasury gold at the 100-million mark. The banks which were strongest in gold made up a subscription and turned over more than 6 millions of gold in return for treasury notes and greenbacks.

It was clear that this sum could not permanently improve the government's income in the face of the continuing export of gold. In April for the first time the reserve against the greenbacks fell to less than 100 millions, and the treasury considered the flotation of a gold loan, similar to the issue which had been made before resumption. In order to avoid this the banks offered the treasury another 8 millions of gold, making 14 millions in all, or nearly one-fifth of their total reserve. Only the National City and the Hanover Banks refused to join in the offer, believing that it was as disastrous for the New York banks to be depleted of their gold, as for the treasury.[44]

The general breakdown of credit and business which was the culmination of this movement started in February with the failure of an important railway and brought a severe panic in the middle of the summer. The reserves of the city banks had fallen from 145 millions in February to 76 millions in August owing largely to the withdrawals of their deposits by interior banks. The treasury was quite unable to give assistance of any kind and the banks, which had already jeopardized their position by giving up gold, were entirely helpless.

The panic itself did not last long and after the usual issue of Clearing House loan certificates and the curtailment of loans the banks began to recover their lost reserves. From the low point of August, 1893, when they fell below 80 millions, they more than trebled, and were above 240 millions by February,

[44] *Commercial and Financial Chronicle*, Vol. 56, February 11, 1893, p. 224; April 29, p. 690. *New York Tribune*, February 12, 1893, p. 1. The banks of Boston also offered the Treasury one-half of their gold reserve.

1894. Even the gold portion of their reserves increased from 60 to 130 millions, as the low exchange rates for sterling brought in coin.

The treasury was not so fortunate. The general setback which had been received by trade was reflected in lower commodity imports at the port of New York, so that the average monthly customs receipts during 1893 and 1894 were one-third less than during the previous year. Matters were made worse by the fact that the proportion of gold in the payments also declined by the middle of 1894 to less than one per cent of the total. The gold income of the treasury was thus cut off just when the demand for gold from the treasury to redeem greenbacks and treasury notes of 1890 was heaviest. From August 10, 1893, when the treasury gold reserve had been restored to the 100-million dollar level, it declined until by the end of the year it stood at slightly less than 70 millions. Under these circumstances there seemed nothing to be done except to offer bonds for gold and an issue of 50 million dollars was announced by the treasury for subscription on February 1. These were to yield 3 per cent and to run for ten years or longer at the option of the government. But the public was in no mood to take the bonds. The credit of the treasury was very low; the promise to pay in "coin" did not definitely specify gold. Four or five days before February 1, the total of individual bids amounted to only 2 millions and it became apparent that the bonds were not going to be taken by public subscription. The secretary of the treasury himself visited New York to persuade the reluctant New York banks to come to his aid. Under the leadership of the presidents of several of the banks and trust companies, the subscription list was filled and the whole issue taken.[45] Although part of the coin with which the bonds were purchased had been previously withdrawn from the treasury, the net gain was sufficient to raise the reserves slightly above 100-million dollars, just about where it had been in February, 1893. The margin was as inadequate as it had been in the

[45] *Commercial and Financial Chronicle*, Vol. 58, January 20, 1894, pp. 96, 98, 105; February 3, pp. 196, 198.

previous year and lasted about as long; by August the reserve had fallen to a new low point of 52 millions.

The reserves of the New York banks reflected every change in the condition of the treasury throughout this period. The bond issue of February was accompanied by a sharp drop in the gold of the associated banks, which they did not regain. In June the treasury was obliged to ask the banks to provide all gold required for export; instead they offered to exchange their gold for legal tenders, and again there was a sudden drop in the gold portion of their reserves.[46] Fifteen millions were given up in this way. By November the treasury was again reduced to the necessity of a bond issue and the performance of January and February was repeated; the banks formed a syndicate and took over the issue and the effect upon their reserves was the same as before—a sharp drop from 90 to 60 millions. By the end of the year it was apparent that further appeal to the banks was futile, for the exports of gold in December were again large and even if the banks should give more of their gold to the treasury, it would not remain there.

During January, 1895, the redemptions of greenbacks and treasury notes for gold proceeded at a more rapid rate than ever before, not only for the purpose of exporting gold but also for hoarding at home. The situation of the treasury was extraordinary; by the first week in February the New York subtreasury had barely gold enough to maintain payments for one more day and the country waited to hear that the government had again suspended specie payments.[47] In the emergency the President himself took control. After a vain appeal to Congress for authority to issue bonds specifically payable in gold he summoned the heads of the international private banking houses to Washington to make terms for a bond issue to be repaid in lawful money, which might or might not be gold, according to the decision of Congress. They agreed, at a good price, to take the risk of floating the new bonds, to pay for them in gold at

[46] Secretary of Treasury, *Annual Report*, 1894, p. lxix. *Commercial and Financial Chronicle*, Vol. 58, June 23, 1894, p. 1050.

[47] A. D. Noyes, *Forty Years*, pp. 232-33.

least half of which should be drawn from abroad, and to keep up the treasury's gold reserve. The mere rumor of the negotiations was enough to stop the run on the treasury and the announcement of their successful completion turned the tide of gold. The syndicate included nearly all of the large drawers of exchange and by keeping the market well supplied with bills, they pegged the rate and protected the gold in the treasury.[48]

Date	*Redemptions of Treasury notes and greenbacks*	*Net movement in gold*	
		Import	*Export*
1894			
January	$0.4		$0.6
February	19.2		1.1
March	3.5		2.9
April	7.7		9.4
May	26.5		23.1
June	22.2		22.4
July	13.9		12.8
August	4.7		1.9
September	0.9	$0.4	
October	3.0	0.5	
November	7.8	1.5	
December	31.9		9.4
1895			
January	45.1		24.7
February	5.6	4.1	
March	1.1	4.1	
April	1.0	2.0	
May	1.2	3.3	
June	1.0	2.0	
July	3.8		3.3
August	16.6		15.1
September	17.4		16.7
October	2.2		0.1
November	16.0		13.5
December	20.2		14.2

Almost no gold was exported from February to June, 1895, and the treasury was obliged to pay out very little gold in

[48] *Commercial and Financial Chronicle,* Vol. 60, February 2, 1895, p. 205; February 23, p. 331.

redemptions. The table above indicates how the tide was turned.[49]

The part of the gold which the syndicate obtained at home for payment of the bonds came largely from the reserves of the New York banks which was the only large accumulation of the metal in the country. From the middle of February to the middle of April they lost nearly 20 millions, about one-fourth of their total stock. Altogether, since the high point in February when their gold reserve had been 130 millions, they had lost more than one-half and almost all of it had been sacrificed on account of the treasury. Fortunately they were not to be called upon for much more. In July, 1896, the banks of New York provided 20 millions to restore the treasury's gold reserve, as they had so often done before, but this was the last time that they were called upon for such aid. Their gold reserves reached a low point of 46 millions on August 1, 1896, but increased steadily thereafter. By October 1, 1897, the New York banks held more gold than paper in their reserves.[50]

The proceeds of the syndicate loans in 1895 were left for a time on deposit with the national bank members of the group. The First National held 15 millions; the National City, 2.6 millions; the National Park, 3.1 millions; the National Bank of Commerce, 1.2 millions; and the Hanover, 1 million. These deposits were transferred gradually to the treasury and by June 20, 1895, were entirely out of the banks. A year later, when the 100-million dollar bond issue was put upon the market, more than 30 millions were left with six of the New York national banks until the proceeds could be withdrawn without disturbing the money market. But the receipts of the treasury were not yet sufficiently in excess of expenditures to permit a large balance in depositary banks and by June, 1896, it was again at a low point.[51]

The revenues of the treasury were increasing during 1895 and gave promise of soon equaling expenditures; general business

[49] Secretary of Treasury, *Annual Report*, 1896, p. 130.

[50] *Commercial and Financial Chronicle*, Vol. 63, July 25, 1896, p. 130; August 1, 1896, p. 168.

[51] 56 Congress, 1 Session, House Document 264, p. 7.

conditions were improving after the long depression and the government's credit both at home and abroad had been greatly improved by its evident earnestness in maintaining gold payments. When gold exports increased again during the latter half of 1895, they bore a less alarming aspect than before. The operations of the syndicate had ceased but the treasury managed to fend for itself; the bold offer of a 100-million dollar bond issue was oversubscribed by the public in February, 1896, in sharp contrast to the issues in the same months of the two previous years. The proceeds of this loan were left with depositary banks. In July after several months of heavy exports, the members of the former syndicate took informal action together to prevent or diminish gold exports by furnishing bills on London and were again successful in their efforts.[52] By the opening of the year 1897 the crisis in the affairs of the treasury was past.

The period of reform, 1899-1913

An actual surplus appeared during the last half of 1899 and thereafter the net gold in the treasury kept almost constantly at 200 millions or above. The problems of the period from 1899 to 1913 were again therefore the problems connected with the management of a treasury surplus. For the first time in half a century, since the passage of the National Bank Act, positive changes in the technique of dealing with the surplus were instituted. The large size of the surplus in these years was in itself a potent factor in initiating changes but large surpluses had existed before without effecting any radical innovations. One influence was the general dissatisfaction with the whole banking and credit situation. The general feeling was reflected in the attitude of officials towards the Independent Treasury. In nearly every annual report of the secretary of the treasury, the comptroller of the currency, and the United States treasurer, and in many of their public utterances, there was expressed a matter-of-fact disapproval of the law and suggestions for its improvement. Nor did treasury officials stop at spoken criticism of the

[52] *Commercial and Financial Chronicle,* Vol. 62, February 8, 1896, p. 252; March 14, p. 476; Vol. 63, July 25, 1896, p. 130.

Independent Treasury; the administration of the law went frequently a step beyond the actual law and Congress was frequently called upon to amend it in order to cover the precedents already established.

The various secretaries of the treasury during this period came to have a much larger conception of their function than that which was comprised in Sherman's ideal of "watchdog of the Treasury." Secretary Gage, Secretary Shaw, and Secretary Cortelyou, in turn, indicated that they considered themselves to be guardians of the money market as well as custodians of the treasury. The treasury at this time was far less in need of a guardian than was the money market, since it was amply provided with funds while the very abundance of its resources was a menace to the money market. The treasury moreover was in itself a comparatively simple mechanism, collecting taxes and customs on the one hand and paying the government's bills on the other; while the money market was an intricate piece of machinery depending upon the coördination of many parts for its functioning. The treasury now became a sort of balance wheel providing elasticity in the currency by alternately hoarding and releasing funds, giving assistance when panic threatened, bringing in gold when the reserves of the banks grew low, although it was not always able to counteract the disharmonies in the system which were brought about by its own existence.[53]

From the very beginning of his administration in 1897, even before the treasury had begun to accumulate a surplus, Secretary Gage kept a watchful eye upon the money market with the avowed determination to guard it as far as lay within his power from the crises to which it had hitherto been subject. In justification of his attitude he declared that "for more than half a century it has been the established policy of the Government to endeavor, wherever it may, to contribute toward the avoidance of commercial disaster."[54] But during his term of office there was no spectacular incident in the relations between the treasury and the money market. When the large payments from

[53] An important device for smoothing the relations between the treasury and the money market, namely, short-term financing, was not developed until 1917.

[54] 56 Congress, 1 Session, House Document 264, p. 5.

the Union Pacific Railroad were made to the treasury in November and December, 1897, public deposits in national banks were permitted for a short time to increase in order to avoid withdrawing a large sum suddenly from the market. But this was no more than had been permitted by former treasury officials in connection with the floating of bond issues. The funds thus accumulated were utilized for the redemption of bonds and, by the middle of the next year, deposits in national banks were again at their former low level. The bond issues necessitated by the Spanish-American War were also accompanied by a temporary increase in the public funds held by banks during the latter part of 1898.

When a treasury surplus had once again appeared the usual devices were adopted by the secretary of the treasury—treasury funds in the form of small notes were hoarded during the summer in order that they could be released during the autumn demand for currency and interest payments were anticipated for the same purpose.[55] The treasury made frequent use of the banks of New York City on several occasions when the deposits were temporarily very large. The National City Bank alone sometimes held government deposits amounting to more than 20 millions of dollars at the invitation of the treasury, because other banks were unable to furnish the collateral required in order to qualify as depositaries.[56]

Government officials continued to coöperate with representatives of the New York banks to the full extent of law and precedent. In September, 1901, when call rates rose to a high point a committee of the Clearing House banks sent an urgent request to the treasury to release funds. The request met with instant response, the purchase of bonds was increased, and incoming internal revenue receipts were ordered to be placed with bank depositaries up to the full par value of the collateral.[57]

The secretary's dissatisfaction with the system under which the government's financial operations had to be carried on

[55] Secretary of Treasury, *Annual Report*, 1898, p. xxvii.

[56] 56 Congress, 1 Session, House Document 264, p. 4.

[57] Secretary of Treasury, *Annual Report*, 1901, p. 20. *Commercial and Financial Chronicle*, Vol. 73, September 14, 1901, p. 535.

had been voiced at the New York State Bankers' Convention in 1900.

I made an investigation on my own account, and discovered some salient facts. Taking the last thirty-two years, what was the average sum on hand in excess of an ample working balance locked up in the Treasury? It averaged about $50,000,000. Had this sum been placed out at interest in the banks, at 2% per annum, how much would the Treasury have been bettered? No less than $32,000,000. And the country would at present have at its disposal $200,000,000 of money now confined under lock and key in the Treasury vaults.[58]

But Secretary Gage did not at any time go beyond the precedents set by former secretaries. It remained for his successor to make a real innovation in the methods of dealing with the money market.

When the first annual report of Secretary Shaw appeared in 1902 it contained the radical suggestion that the secretary of the treasury be permitted to make deposits in banks without any security at all, after special examination of the banks and at a specified rate of interest. In this way the surplus revenue could be utilized to introduce a large element of elasticity into the banking system. Should this seem too startling a proposal for Congress to approve, he recommended that he be permitted to transfer funds already in the treasury to depositary banks offering the usual security, whenever the market needed relief.[59] As the law then stood the internal revenue receipts might be deposited in banks as they were paid to the government but if once received into the treasury vaults they could not be transferred to banks.

The balance of the treasury had been growing steadily ever since the close of the Spanish-American War. By the autumn of 1902 it stood at 250 millions and, with the reserves of the New York banks facing a deficit as currency was shipped to the interior, the secretary of the treasury came to the aid of the market. The traditional methods of increasing deposits in national banks and anticipating interest payments were tried but

[58] *Commercial and Financial Chronicle*, Vol. 71, December 22, 1900, p. 1248.
[59] Secretary of Treasury, *Annual Report*, 1902, p. 62.

found inadequate and he took a bolder course. After a conference with New York bankers on September 29 two new devices were announced. In order to make it possible for banks to qualify as depositaries of government funds, he ruled that securities other than Federal bonds might be used as collateral. Selected state and municipal issues were acceptable if they were used to free governments for use as security against national notes. During the next two months bank treasury deposits in banks increased by 15 millions, and the circulation by 18 millions. It was a device admirably adapted to preventing the contraction of the currency which had formerly accompanied increases of government deposits in depositary banks.[60]

In addition to this, the secretary ruled that government deposits collateralled by Federal securities need not be subject to the reserves requirements of national banks. The total amount of such treasury deposits in banks was at that time about 133 millions, and 40 millions were held in New York alone. But this action exceeded even the wishes of the banks and the New York Clearing House members agreed to continue the usual reserve requirements against all of their deposits, declining the aid which the ruling would have given them. Only the banks outside of New York took advantage of it.[61]

In 1903 the autumn pressure was more severe than usual. The floating supply of bonds was by this time nearly exhausted so that bond redemptions could not be counted upon to relieve the stringency. Internal revenue receipts amounted to only ½ million dollars per month, and depositing them in banks could not be counted upon for aid. Even the possibility of substituting other securities for governments and of leaving treasury deposits out of reserve computations would not, it was feared, provide adequate relief. The secretary of the treasury therefore found new ways of assisting the market. In his report for 1902 he had recommended among other things that Congress give him authority to transfer funds already in the treasury to national banks. When Congressional action was not forthcoming the

[60] Secretary of Treasury, *Annual Report*, 1902, p. 138. See p. 371 below.

[61] *Commercial and Financial Chronicle*, Vol. 75, October 4, 1902, pp. 700, 702; October 11, p. 759. Secretary of Treasury, *Annual Report*, 1902.

secretary surmounted the obstacle with his usual ingenuity. Receipts from internal revenue and miscellaneous sources were segregated as they were received and permitted to accumulate during the spring and summer until the expected stringency had developed. Then they were "restored to circulation" by deposit in banks to the amount of 14 millions during the autumn of 1903. The law certainly did not authorize the transfer of the funds from the treasury to the banks, but because they had been thus set aside the legal fiction was maintained that they had never really been in the treasury.[62] The law had been circumvented, and the secretary had been able to use the funds of the government to assist the market.

The panic year of 1907, with its near-panic in 1906, brought the new policy to its fullest fruition. The midwinter pressure of early 1906 was lightened by the deposit of 10 millions in the banks, to be called in July when the market was usually easy. Payment of 50 millions to the government of Panama and the Panama Canal Company in May was carefully prepared for by a transfer of government deposits to New York and payment through the Clearing House in such a way that only a few thousand dollars actually changed hands. The money market was not at all disturbed and rates showed no evidence of the enormous transaction. As the autumn stringency of 1906 approached 60 millions of surplus were accumulated and deposited in banks against any collateral security which would have been acceptable for savings bank investment under the laws of New York state.

When this did not prove sufficient to maintain the reserves of the banks, the treasury made a fourth innovation. It offered to place deposits in banks which should engage gold for importation, the deposit to be made as soon as the gold was shipped so that the bank would have the use of the funds immediately. The net result was to make the importation an interest-free transaction, and thus enable banks to import gold at less cost. The National City Bank imported 31 millions under this plan;

[62] Secretary of Treasury, *Annual Report*, 1906, p. 37. *Commercial and Financial Chronicle*, Vol. 77, September 5, 1903, p. 471.

while the Chase, the Hanover, the First, the Fourth, and the Commerce, Banks brought in an additional 18 millions.[63] This was the most revolutionary of all the actions of Secretary Shaw for it was furthest from the intention of the law. When similar action had been requested during the panic of 1873, Secretary Richardson had declined to consider it because unquestionably beyond his authority.[64] No better proof could be found of the changing attitude towards the Independent Treasury than the fact that this action of the secretary of the treasury was defended by many persons.

Even Congress at last became impressed by the necessity of making some alterations in the law and on March 4, 1907, passed an act which gave specific authority for several things which the secretary had already done. The collateral required of depositary banks was left to the discretion of the secretary, and the restriction which had forbidden the deposit of customs receipts in banks was repealed. Thereafter all government funds without distinction could be placed in properly qualified national banks. Three weeks later the new secretary of the treasury ordered the customs dues to be deposited in the banks of New York day by day and for the first time since 1846 they ceased to be a fund set apart.

The new provisions of the law were fully utilized during the panic of 1907 and the months immediately preceding it. Government deposits in national banks reached a high point during this year. The number of depositary banks was increased from 927 to 1,255 during the twelve months between June, 1906, and June, 1907. The total volume of deposits reached 173 millions during May, 1907, fell off to 143 millions during the summer, and rose again in the autumn. Beginning August 23, deposits were made in banks throughout the country at the rate of about 5 millions weekly. An effort was made to deposit the funds where they were most needed, and the New York banks felt some resentment that they did not receive more.

[63] Secretary of Treasury, *Annual Report*, 1906, pp. 38, 39, 118. House Representatives Hearings on Banking and Currency, 1906-1907, p. 110. *Commercial and Financial Chronicle*, Vol. 82, April 21, 1906, p. 893; May 12, p. 1069.
[64] See p. 359 above.

When the panic actually came an additional 35 millions was transferred within four days from the treasury to the banks of New York City on state, municipal, and railroad, collateral. Besides these deposits in New York, 3 millions were placed in the banks of Chicago, 1½ millions in Pittsburgh and in Cincinnati, and ½ million in Saint Paul and Minneapolis. By the middle of November the working balance of the treasury was down to 5 millions and no more deposits could be made for a time, particularly as the customs revenue had been seriously curtailed during the panic.

There is no denying that the banks of New York had needed assistance. Their reserves fell off sharply during the panic and by November 16 showed a deficit of more than 50 millions. Nearly 300 millions of currency were absorbed by the country during the panic and of this sum more than 200 millions were supplied by the banks of New York. It was not until January, 1908, that they were able to restore their reserves. But the difficulty with the relief which was provided by the treasury was that so much of it served merely to counteract the harm which was being done by the treasury in the absorption of currency. Interior banks which had to make payments to the government were accustomed to draw on their New York correspondents and expected them to provide currency for the payment. During the panic the banks of New York felt unable to meet such demands and drew down upon themselves serious criticism because they refused to give up their currency for the benefit of the treasury.[65]

Bonds were purchased during 1907 also, but these played a much smaller part in the treasury's efforts to relieve the market than during earlier panics. There was also a curious issue of 30 millions in Panama Canal bonds designed to aid the market. Since an actual sale of the bonds would have taken money out of the market the device of leaving the proceeds on deposit with the banks was used, but here again it seems doubtful if more

[65] Secretary of Treasury, *Annual Report*, 1907, pp. 10, 52, 124. *Commercial and Financial Chronicle*, Vol. 84, March 30, 1907, p. 715; Vol. 85, September 7, 1907, p. 550. 60 Congress, 1 Session, Senate Document 208, p. 31.

was accomplished than to undo damage caused by the tying up of funds in long-term investments.[66]

In 1908 Congress legalized another step which had already been taken by the secretary of the treasury and definitely authorized the exclusion of government deposits from the total deposits against which reserves were to be carried. Offsetting this privilege however was the requirement that at least one per cent interest be paid upon the average monthly balance. Two of the New York City banks immediately surrendered their deposits altogether, because they had never paid interest on deposits and would not begin.[67] The secretary of the treasury was now legally entitled to do almost everything that he had been doing during a panic and the Independent Treasury had abandoned one by one nearly all of the features which made it at once distinctive and dangerous. One further reform was introduced into the technique for managing the treasury. Customs dues were still being paid by the plan adopted in 1888 of permitting banks to deposit with the subtreasury in the morning funds against which importers drew during the day. In 1911, after an urgent appeal to Congress for a change in the law, the secretary of the treasury was successful in obtaining permission to accept certified checks drawn on national or state banks or trust companies.[68]

The close watchfulness with which treasury officials followed the money market and adjusted their operations to its needs during this period is indicated by the average figures for New York bank reserves and for treasury deposits in the years 1900 to 1908.[69] In the early part of each year, when the reserve ratios of the city banks were fairly high and there was no special need for cash, the treasury permitted its funds to accumulate in its own offices and its deposits in banks were moder-

[66] Secretary of Treasury, *Annual Report*, 1907, pp. 144-46.

[67] The required rate was raised to 2 per cent by order of the secretary of the treasury on July 12, 1912. *Commercial and Financial Chronicle*, Vol. 86, June 20, 1908, p. 1503; Vol. 94, April 27, 1912, p. 1156. Huntington and Mawhinney, *Laws concerning money, banking and loans*, p. 468.

[68] Secretary of Treasury, *Annual Report*, 1910, p. 7; 1911, p. 14.

[69] Kemmerer, *Seasonal Variations in the Relative Demand for Money and Capital.*

ate, even falling off during June and July. By that time the reserve percentage of the banks was declining and the treasury began to increase its deposits in banks, nearly trebling it on the average between July and December. The transfers of funds from New York to the interior also increased during the same months, the treasury taking over a large part of the burden of supplying the cash for crop-moving.

The years immediately after 1907 passed uneventfully for the treasury and the money market. During this period of comparative peace the officers of the government were able to concentrate their energies upon plans for permanent reform. The National Monetary Commission published a voluminous report in 1910, one part of which was devoted to the subject of the treasury's relations with the money market. When in 1913 the Federal Reserve Act was drafted and forced through Congress it seemed that the time had finally come for a complete reform of the Independent Treasury. But so strong was its hold that although the new Federal Reserve Banks were made the fiscal agents of the treasury, the outward form of the Independent Treasury was still retained and not until 1921 was it finally done away with as an anachronism which even the government could no longer tolerate.

The treasury obliged to exercise many of the functions of a central bank

The regulation of the money market is usually considered to be the function of the central bank, but in the United States where there was no central bank many of its duties devolved upon the officials of the treasury. When money rates were high, when gold was being exported, and in half a dozen other contingencies, the treasury was expected to step in. It was supposed to provide elasticity for the currency on the one hand and to prevent inflation on the other, to ward off panics and to assist in maintaining prosperity—and all under a law which had as its foremost purpose the complete separation of the treasury from the money market. Of those powers by which the central banks of other countries assisted the banks, the treasury possessed none with the possible exception of the purchase of securities. It could not issue notes, rediscount commercial paper, or lend on securities, and so it was put to all sorts of shifts. The wonder is, not that it was obliged to resort to such devious methods, but that it managed to survive at all.

Summary

It is difficult to understand why the Independent Treasury system lasted as long as it did. For three-quarters of a century it had maintained its existence against constantly increasing criticism and against a process of attrition which took away one after another of its prerogatives. Certainly it could be defended on no rational grounds and it was only because it was bound up originally with the strong emotions of partisan politics and became associated in the public mind with certain stock political catchwords that for a long time no one dared to raise the issue. The time when it should have been done away with was at the establishment of the national bank system when the necessities of war finance could have been urged as justification—as they were urged to justify far less worthy actions. But this opportunity was permitted to pass. One of the chief functions of the secretary of the treasury therefore became the task of technical obedience to the law without permitting its hostile spirit to endanger the stability of the money market.

CHAPTER XVIII

MONEY AND THE MONEY MARKET

The elements of instability which were inherent in the structure of the New York money market in the period before the passage of the Federal Reserve Act have been discussed in previous chapters. Chief among these were the reserve situation which put unwanted responsibilities on the banks of New York and the close connection between the reserves and the speculative markets. In addition there were other disturbing factors which were due less to the organization of the market than to the monetary basis upon which it rested. The faults of the circulating media accentuated the difficulties under which it was already laboring. Many aspects of the development of the New York money market during this period are inexplicable without an understanding of the monetary situation.

Lack of stability the chief problem before resumption of specie payments

The two worst defects in the monetary system of the United States, from the point of view of the money market as well as from a larger social viewpoint, may be roughly classified as instability and inelasticity. Instability was at first the more apparent. The War had left the country with enormous issues of paper money, a suspension of specie payments, a new kind of bank note replacing the familiar state bank issues, and an opposition to deflation which made the return to a specie basis difficult and even doubtful. In spite of this the price level fell rapidly. The result of all these factors was the creation of uncertainty regarding the future course of prices and money rates which had an adverse effect upon every phase of financial activity. The suspension of specie payments in 1861 had immediately put gold at a premium over paper and made necessary two moneys of account.[1] Banks were obliged to carry separate accounts for gold deposits and paper deposits and to clear separately the checks drawn against each. Eventually a specialized banking business grew up about the sales of gold. The Bank of New York began to issue certified checks against its gold deposits in order to guard against fraud and avoid physical transfers of the metal about the city. As the demand for such services increased a Gold Exchange Bank was established. This took over many of the gold accounts, and made clearings for the Gold Exchange, continuing its activities until the falling premium on gold in 1877 made them no longer profitable.[2]

Business dealings were as much hampered as banking by the two kinds of money. Merchants were unwilling to extend credit at a time when the value of money was changing rapidly, and showed a preference for cash settlements. The effect of this upon the commercial paper market was to encourage the cash discount system and the use of promissory notes rather than acceptances.[3] Merchants engaged in foreign trade were even more affected than those occupied chiefly with domestic trade, for settlement of foreign accounts had to be made in gold. Quotations for foreign exchange were always given both in gold and in currency and, if the buyer was paying in currency, it was necessary for him to cover the transaction at once by the purchase of gold. The fluctuations in the gold premium were so wide and so rapid that serious losses often occurred and a new element of speculation was introduced into foreign exchange transactions.

The premium on gold affected also the long-term security market, particularly because of repercussions upon the foreign demand for American securities. In 1866 for example the sudden decline in the gold premium produced so wide a margin between the value of American government bonds at home and in London that during one week of April nearly one million of the 5-20s were returned from Europe, and the continuation of the move-

[1] Mitchell, *Gold, Prices and Wages Under the Greenback Standard.*

[2] *Bankers' Magazine*, Vol. 20, p. 250, September, 1865; Vol. 31, p. 645, February, 1877.

[3] See p. 197 above.

ment finally necessitated the shipment of an unusual amount of specie with a consequent drain upon the banks and a derangement of the loan market.[4]

There was also a question in the minds of many investors as to whether American bonds would be paid in gold at all. The action of the Chicago and Southwestern Railroad Company in refusing to redeem in gold the coupons on their first mortgage bonds in 1872 had an adverse effect upon the eagerness of European investors[5] and when to that was added the suspicion that even the government might decide to pay its debts in silver the importation of capital was decisively checked. Secretary Sherman and his representative in London complained in 1877 that the continued discussion of silver coinage in Congress made it impossible to arrange for further refunding operations abroad. The passage of the Bland silver act sent the price of government 4's down to 98¼ and it was not until the amount of silver to be coined under that act was definitely limited that it was again possible to sell them at par.[6]

Resumption of specie payments and return to the gold standard was advocated by the secretary of the treasury and the comptroller of the currency in many of their reports just after the close of the War. The early efforts to push a bill for resumption through Congress met with failure and its chances became even less as a powerful popular movement against contraction of the currency arose. The question was debated in Congress over a period of nearly fifteen years, and its probable action "kept business in a state of palpitating uncertainty" and was "a prime factor in every business man's risks, but one which he had no data for conjecturing."[7] The Supreme Court added to the confusion by deciding first that debts made before the passage of the legal tender law were payable in coin and then reversing its decision, in January, 1872, and making greenbacks legal tender for any debt.

[4] *Commercial and Financial Chronicle*, Vol. 2, April 14, 1866, p. 450; May 26, 1866, p. 650.

[5] *Bankers' Magazine*, Vol. 27, p. 495.

[6] Sherman, *Recollections*, Vol. I, pp. 578-80; Vol. II, pp. 604, 626. 46 Congress, 2 Session, House Executive Document 9, p. 211.

[7] *Commercial and Financial Chronicle*, Vol. 23, August 12, 1878, p. 146.

A bill providing for the resumption of specie payments was finally passed in 1875, setting the date nearly four years ahead on January 1, 1879, and the secretary of the treasury began to redeem legal tender notes in preparation. But the question was not settled. Almost at once bills to repeal the resumption act were introduced into Congress and during the presidential campaign of 1876 resumption was the chief issue of the "Greenback" party. It demanded more legal tender notes and abandonment of resumption plans. Although the party was not successful at the polls, it kept up a constant agitation in Congress. The steady decline in prices and in general business after the panic of 1873, which had serious consequences for industrial and agricultural workers, was used as an argument for abandoning altogether the attempt to get back to a specie basis. There was undoubtedly need of reforming the monetary laws, but the adoption of an irredeemable paper currency has never proved a solution for such ills. The possibility of such action aggravated the trouble, for financial commitments of all kinds were postponed until the monetary question should be settled. A contemporary observer summed up the situation in 1877 as follows:

> It was a misfortune that . . . Congress . . . was engaged for months in the agitation of bills for the repeal of the specie resumption act, the unlimited coinage of silver dollars as a legal tender, the discontinuance of the further retirement of greenbacks, and other matters of minor importance, but all of an unsettling character. It was not until summer that the uncertainty was finally terminated by the adjournment of Congress.[8]

The actual resumption of specie payments was accomplished on January 1, 1879, with a minimum of disturbance to the money market.[9] In many ways it brought relief to the market; no longer was it necessary for the banks to keep two sets of accounts for their customers, one in gold and one in legal tenders; no longer was it necessary for the exporter and importer to discount the future course of gold in making plans for trade

[8] *Commercial and Financial Chronicle,* Vol. 28, January 4, 1878, p. 5.
[9] See p. 362 above.

with foreign countries. The stability of the money market was measurably improved.

But it did not unfortunately put an end to the monetary difficulties from which the money market was suffering. Other elements of instability were still present and the twenty years following resumption were if anything more beset than the fifteen years preceding. Prices continued to fall almost steadily. This general downward movement of prices was linked up with the decline in the production of gold and was not peculiar to the United States; it was felt also in England and Europe. But in the United States it was aggravated by several factors which affected only this country: the forced coinage of silver after 1878, the decline in the volume of national bank notes in circulation, and the export of gold. Resumption of specie payments had been attained at a heavy price, the passage of a law which required the treasury to purchase and coin from 2 to 4 million dollars' worth of silver each month. The silver coin and certificates in circulation increased from 70 millions in 1879 to 408 millions in 1890. Under other circumstances this increase in coinage might have been of great service, filling the gap created by the increasing value of gold and keeping prices at a stable level. These possible advantages were offset by two factors, a decline in the circulation of national bank notes and agitation for repudiation of the gold standard.

The withdrawal of national bank notes began in 1882 and continued to 1891, with a total reduction from 363 millions to a low point of 168 millions, cutting in half the circulation of the national banks. The reason for this decline was briefly that it was no longer profitable for the banks to buy United States bonds and deposit them with the comptroller of the currency for the privilege of issuing less than that amount of notes. The prices of the bonds were high, the yield was low, and the margin requirements of the comptroller were high. There was also a tax upon the notes issued. If the law had not required national banks to invest in government bonds, the volume of notes would have been reduced even further. The New York City banks, which had never placed a high valuation upon the circulation privilege, permitted the notes issued by them to fall from 22 millions to less than 4 millions in the decade after 1882 and several of them, the Chemical, the City, the American Exchange, and the Mechanics', had no notes outstanding.[10]

Difficulties due to dispute over standard

The silver legislation of 1879 was not enough to satisfy the cheap money party. Prices were still falling, and business and agricultural conditions had not improved. Southern and western states were as dissatisfied with the situation as was New York but their remedy for it was quite different. New York would have stopped the coining of silver altogether while the agricultural states, where the cheap money element was strong, insisted that more money would solve their problems. The latter were in sufficient majority in Congress to change the law. Instead of coining from 2 to 4 million dollars' worth of silver each month, the treasury was to buy 4½ million ounces of silver per month and issue against it the treasury notes of 1890 which it was hoped would be more acceptable to the public than the heavy silver dollars. Not content with having diluted the currency, the party carried on a constant agitation for repudiation of the gold standard altogether. The effect of this new demand was more serious than the silver coinage act and it was felt first in the market for securities. Foreign investors did not care to take bonds which might not be redeemed in gold at maturity. The export of securities, which had always been a large factor in the settlement of the foreign trade balance, was therefore diminished and its place had to be taken by gold. The export of gold increased and at the same time the proportion of gold in customs receipts, upon which the treasury relied for its own supply of the metal, fell off sharply because importers preferred to use silver and save gold. The loss of the foreign market for securities had an adverse effect also upon the railroads and other corporate borrowers. Stock prices, which had dropped

[10] Comptroller of Currency, *Annual Report*, 1882, p. 21; 1888, p. 62; 1893, p. 106. The Act of July 12, 1882, reduced this requirement from one-third to one-fourth of capital for banks of $150,000 capital or less. For larger banks, the requirement of $500,000 under the Act of June 20, 1874, was still in force. See also p. 89 above.

sharply from 1881 to 1885, were fairly stable between 1885 and 1892 but the volume of trading was so low that brokers made extraordinary efforts to stimulate buying. The American investing public was in no position to take the place of the lost European market and instead of a recovery there was a further drop in prices in 1893.

The constant forcing of silver into circulation prevented the export of gold from having its normal contracting effect upon credit and prices. Sterling rates, which should have been brought down towards the import point by the constant outward movement of gold, remained for months near the export point. The fluctuations in rates were unusually wide and the movement from month to month irregular. Steady deterioration in the quality of the circulating medium as the result of forcing into circulation treasury notes based upon silver alone, nearly bankrupted the government and intensified the panic of 1893. The silver purchase act was repealed during the panic and the recovery of the treasury was assured by the syndicate loan in 1895 but these measures solved only the immediate difficulty and did not settle the question of the ultimate monetary standard.

Even after the treasury had recovered from its well-warranted fear of failure and had accumulated sufficient gold reserve to make a repetition of the events of 1894-1895 unlikely, the unsettled matter of the standard metal caused perturbation in other parts of the market. The argument was not finally settled until the passage of the gold standard act on March 14, 1900. So much was the issue in doubt until the very eve of the election in 1899 that it is said that savings were withdrawn from the banks and hidden away in the form of gold or invested in foreign exchange for fear that the silver party might win and the currency be depreciated by the event.[11]

The first years after the passage of the gold standard law were unusually prosperous ones in the United States. Indeed, they were the first of the "new eras" which were to occur in the new century. The cessation of silver coinage and treasury note issues, the assured position of gold as the basis for the money

[11] *New York State Report on Banks of Discount and Deposit*, 1900, p. xiii.

and credit of the country, introduced into the financial system a stability which it had not enjoyed since the Civil War and freed the money market from a great part of the strain under which it had been laboring.

Inelasticity of money

There still remained the problem of elasticity of the circulation. It was set in clearer relief by the settlement of the issue between gold and silver but it had been in existence since the passage of the National Bank Act, if not before. There is no doubt that in the matter of security the national banking system was a great improvement over the state bank issues of the antebellum period. Whether or not it was equally superior in the matter of elasticity is another question. It is certain that the note issues of the state banks—and the greater part of their credit took the form of notes rather than deposits—showed a wider variation from one phase of the business cycle to another than those of the national banks. In the expansion phase of every one of the major cycles before 1863 there was a great increase in the note issues of the banks and the panic period was as invariably marked by a sharp contraction. There were few legal safeguards about either notes or deposits and the limit to expansion was set only by the banker's willingness to sacrifice profits for safety. On the downward movement the banker was equally dependent upon himself and contracted his loans ruthlessly in order to recover specie.

The freedom from legal restrictions made it possible for the state banks to meet the seasonal variations in currency needs. Again the weekly reports of the New York City banks after 1853 give unmistakable proof of the seasonal changes in their note circulation.[12] By 1853 however the deposits of the New York banks had come to be a more important part of their credit issues than notes. There was also by that time a close supervision over the New York banks although there was no legal reserve requirement. For these two reasons it is probable that

[12] Cole, "The New York Money Market, 1847-1862," *Review of Economic Statistics*, 1930.

the country banks' circulation varied more widely in response to seasonal needs than that of the New York banks and that both varied more than the later national bank circulation. Before 1863 the monetary system seems to have possessed elasticity at the sacrifice of security; after that date, security at the expense of elasticity.

The amount of money required for hand-to-hand circulation and use as bank reserves was constantly changing, yet none of the forms of money in circulation was responsive to changes in demand. There was needed first of all an annual increase. The growth of trade, production, and employment, increased the demand for cash more rapidly than declining bank reserve ratios and increased use of checks could offset it. At the close of the Civil War the necessary deflation was accomplished as much by letting the trade of the country grow up to the money in circulation as by an actual withdrawal of currency from circulation. State bank notes were taxed out of existence in 1865 and the greenbacks were reduced by about 100 millions between 1866 and 1878 when further reduction was forbidden by Congress but offsetting these reductions there was an issue of 300 millions of national bank notes. Even after prices had come back to normal levels and the post-war deflation may be considered to have been completed, the price level continued to fall, indicating that money and bank deposits were not increasing as rapidly as the growth of the country required. During periods of expanding business activity, on the upward swing of the business cycle, the shortage of money was accentuated, while on the downward swing, as trade and employment declined, there was frequently a plethora of cash in spite of the fact that the actual amount had not increased. Besides these long-term factors in the demand for money seasonal changes occurred in trade and employment which brought about a seasonal variation in the demand for money. A high degree of elasticity was required of money to meet all the variations in demand to which it was subject, but not one of the kinds of money in circulation in the United States between 1863 and 1913 could be said to possess that quality in more than the slightest degree.

Metallic coin cannot be expected to meet sudden, short changes in demand, but the trend of its growth should parallel that of business. The hard money in use during this period consisted of silver dollars, and of gold coins in larger denominations. Gold and silver certificates were frequently used in their stead merely as a matter of convenience, but did not differ from the actual coin and need not be considered separately. There were also silver subsidiary coins, but they were only a small part of the total.

Under ordinary conditions the circulation of gold would have been increased gradually by coinage, as the demand for money increased, but it did not follow the usual rule in this period. From 1863 until resumption of specie payments in 1879 gold was at a premium which made it too valuable for use in circulation. For several decades after that, the world demand for gold was increasing faster than production and it was impossible for the United States to increase its share. This situation, coupled with the silver coinage laws, kept the amount of gold in circulation almost stationary from 1881 to 1896. Not until after that year did gold circulation begin to increase normally and maintain a fair proportion to the total money of the country.

The circulation of silver was more erratic than that of gold. In the first years after 1863, while large amounts of greenbacks were outstanding, there was little coinage of silver and in 1873 the free coinage of silver dollars was completely abandoned. After five years of no silver coinage, the law of 1878 required 2 to 4 million dollars' worth of silver to be coined monthly and put into circulation as coin or certificates. The treasury resorted to many strange devices to stimulate its use. These certificates were received at the New York subtreasury in large amount in payment for customs duties but could not be used for the settlement of balances at the Clearing House. They accumulated in such volume that they became a problem at the New York subtreasury office. In September, 1880, an arrangement was made whereby a deposit of gold at New York entitled the depositor to receive silver certificates at some interior office without paying the usual charge for transfer. Two years later the New York office was so put to it to dispose of the certificates that it offered to pay the express charges on any shipped to interior banks. The Mint had made the same offer in connection with the unpopular silver dollars.[13] The difficulty was not overcome until the repeal of the purchase act in 1893 and the enactment of the gold standard law in 1900 reduced the proportion of silver in the monetary total.

The elasticity in the circulation is usually expected to be provided by paper money, since it is less expensive than coin and can be retired more easily. There were only two kinds of independent paper money in use after the Civil War, ignoring the "shinplasters" which took the place of subsidiary coins and the gold and silver certificates which were mere substitutes for metal. These were the greenbacks, or legal tender notes, and the notes of the national banks, and neither one could be speedily increased when a stringency arose or easily withdrawn when it had past. The amount of greenbacks was determined by political rather than economic considerations. Successive acts of Congress had authorized a total issue of 450 millions. Mr. McCulloch and other secretaries of the treasury reduced this to 346 millions by 1878 when further retirement of the notes was prohibited. That amount of legal tenders is still outstanding to the present day. In 1872 the secretary of the treasury reissued greenbacks already retired in order to increase the currency during a stringency, but this attempt to inject a measure of elasticity into an essentially inelastic form of paper was severely criticized and was never repeated.

National bank notes were at first as definitely fixed in amount as the greenbacks. In its effort to avoid further inflation the original act set the total at 300 millions of dollars. It soon became evident that this limit would be reached long before the demand for national bank charters had been satisfied and that the later applicants would be at a serious disadvantage in the matter of circulation. The greater part of the first banks organized were located in the northern and eastern sections of

[13] Secretary of Treasury, *Annual Report*, 1881, pp. x, 430. *Commercial and Financial Chronicle*, Vol. 35, September 2, 1882, p. 248; Vol. 49, August 17, 1889, p. 186.

the country, and banks in the southern and western states, organized at a later date, found it impossible to secure the note-issue privilege in the amounts which they wished. They were further handicapped by the minimum capital requirements which set $50,000 as the smallest capital with which a national bank could be organized, and that only in towns of 6,000 population or less. Since the large centers of population were concentrated in the North and East, the number of national banks, as well as their possible circulation, was limited.

Several attempts were made by changes in the law to equalize the differences between North and East, on one hand, and West and South on the other. The act of March 3, 1865, reenacted into the law the complicated system for allocation of the national bank notes among the states, half according to population and half according to banking capital. This had been a part of the original National Bank Act but had been omitted in the revision of 1864. The act of July 12, 1870, took even more drastic action in the same direction. Not only did it increase the amount of the total issue by 54 millions but it gave the comptroller of the currency authority to withdraw 25 million dollars of notes from banks in states having more than their share and to allot it to banks in sections which had less. In 1874 the amount which could be thus withdrawn by the comptroller was increased to 55 millions. The law was difficult to apply and it was no more successful than the others had been in meeting the demands of the agricultural sections for more money. The whole system was repealed by the Resumption Act of January 14, 1875, and there was no longer any restriction on the total amount of national bank notes to be issued.

It is a valuable sidelight upon the monetary situation of the time that while a large part of the country was agitating for more bank notes, the banks of New York were finding such an accumulation of them on their hands that they were hard put to it to be rid of them. They were not legal tender, and so could not be counted as part of the reserves and for the same reason they were not acceptable at the Clearing House in settlement of balances. They could not even be sent home for redemption fast enough to get them out of the way, for there was at that time no central redemption office and country national banks might redeem their notes at any one of a number of places. Although as a matter of fact 1,320 out of the 1,647 national banks existing in 1866 had chosen New York, Boston, or Philadelphia, as their redemption center,[14] the labor of sorting out the notes and sending the issues of each bank for separate redemption made the process a slow and expensive one. The banks of New York organized in 1865 a National Bank Note Redemption Association, with its office in the Clearing House, to save the banks the trouble of sorting redemption items, but the attempt was not successful and the old method had again to be resorted to. Many of the city banks felt an unwillingness to send notes back to their correspondents for redemption because they feared it would cause resentment. Instead they sold notes to brokers at a discount of 1/10 to ¼ of 1 per cent, letting the broker bear the onus of returning the notes to the bank of their origin. The "note-broker" had always been anathema to the country banker anyway. The accumulations of national bank notes grew so large at certain times of year that the New York banks resorted to loans without interest for as long as two weeks, on condition that the loan made in national bank notes be repaid in greenbacks.[15] The notes continued to accumulate in New York City and there was frequent complaint from the banks until the change in the law of June 20, 1874, abolished the system of redemption agents and put the responsibility upon the treasury. Thereafter any bank might make up national bank notes into packets of $1,000 each and send them to Washington, where they were redeemed in greenbacks. This solved the immediate problem for the New York banks.

The removal of the restrictions upon the total issue of national bank notes in 1875 made it possible for that type of currency to grow with the increase in demand, but there were other

[14] Comptroller of Currency, *Annual Report,* 1866, p. 68.

[15] *Commercial and Financial Chronicle*, Vol. 1, September 16, 1865, p. 354; October 14, p. 489; Vol. 3, July 7, 1866, p. 9; Vol. 10, May 14, 1870, p. 622; Vol. 12, January 21, 1871, p. 78; May 20, 1871, p. 613.

obstacles in the way. The requirement that national bank notes be collateraled by government bonds to an amount in excess of their par value, when bonds were selling in the market at a premium, made banks unwilling to tie up their funds in what was for them an unprofitable investment. From 1882 to 1892 the amount of national bank notes fell steadily and the proportion of national bank notes to the total money of the country also declined. It is evident that the expansible element in the country's currency was not to be found in the national bank notes. They were as unsatisfactory during a crisis as in a long-time movement. During a stringency, when notes were especially needed, no bank could afford to reduce its lending power in order to buy bonds as collateral for notes although special inducements were often given. In 1900 notes were permitted to be issued up to the full par value of the bonds; in 1907 bonds other than governments were permitted to be used as collateral for government deposits in order to release the governments for use as note collateral. In spite of these concessions it was possible to increase note issues only after a delay of from 30 to 60 days,[16] by which time the immediate need had passed. Contraction of the circulation was as laborious and time-consuming as expansion. The Act of 1882, which was in force until 1907, forbade the retirement of national bank notes at the rate of more than 3 millions per month, and denied to a bank which had retired part of its currency the right to increase it again for a period of six months. The slowness with which national bank notes could be increased and the still greater slowness with which they could be retired prevented them from meeting seasonal changes in the demand for currency.

It is evident from the chart that national bank notes did not expand and contract with the rhythm of trade. There was a slight increase in the autumn but, as Professor Kemmerer pointed out, it was small in amount and was not followed by a seasonal decrease in the winter. All that can be said of it is that banks which planned to make a permanent addition to their

[16] Hearings before House Committee on Banking and Currency, 53 Congress, 3 Session, 1894.

circulation were apt to do it in the autumn months. The autumn increase in national bank notes was hardly larger than the fortuitous autumnal increase in gold coinage arising from the

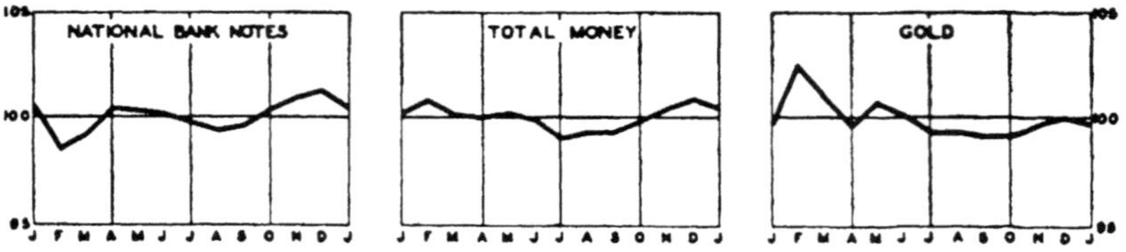

INDEX OF SEASONAL VARIATION OF NATIONAL BANK NOTES, OF GOLD, AND OF ALL MONEY IN CIRCULATION IN THE UNITED STATES, 1895-1909.

SOURCE: ANDREW, STATISTICS FOR THE UNITED STATES, ETC.

mechanics of production and transportation of the metal, which had no relation to the needs of the country for money.[17] This conclusion is confirmed by an index of variations computed by Professor Allyn A. Young for the dates of the comptroller's calls. His results are as follows:

INDEX OF SEASONAL VARIATION, 1900-1913*

	National bank notes	*Total money in circulation outside banks*
First call	100.3	98.7
Second call	99.7	99.4
Third call	99.6	98.0
Fourth call	100.0	99.9
Fifth call	100.3	103.9

* Young, *Analysis of Bank Statistics for the United States.*

The fact that the calls of the same number actually fell upon dates which were as much as two months apart tends to average out the fluctuations and reduce their apparent range. But even so it is apparent that the range of seasonal variation for

[17] Kemmerer, *Seasonal Variations*, etc., pp. 145 ff. The monthly changes in national banknotes outstanding were not reported before 1890. Since the year 1891 was marked by an upward turn in the trend of growth, the index of seasonal variation was computed from that year.

national bank notes, which should have been the most elastic part of the circulation, was less than that of total money outside the banks.

The inability of the national bank notes to expand and contract expeditiously caused them to be compared unfavorably with Canadian bank notes and brought about numerous proposals to institute a similar form of note issue in the United States. Canada had a seasonal variation in trade very similar to that of the United States but its currency expanded about 30 per cent in the autumn, proportionately six times as much as that of the United States. Canadian notes were based upon the general assets of banks rather than upon bonds and they could be put into circulation promptly as loans increased and retired as promptly when the need for additional funds had gone. The comptroller of the currency recommended such a change in his annual report for 1894, and elaborated it in the hearings of the House Committee on Banking and Currency in the same year.[18] Each national bank was to be permitted to issue notes up to 75 per cent of its capital stock, secured by its general assets and by a fund of legal tenders to 30 per cent of the notes issued, deposited with the secretary of the treasury. The American Bankers' Association at its convention in Baltimore in the same year drew up a plan which differed only in detail from that of the comptroller. Known as the Baltimore Plan, it served as a focal point for public discussion. It would have permitted the issue of circulating notes up to 50 per cent of capital, and in place of the 30 per cent guarantee fund, would have required a 5 per cent safety fund with the government standing behind the notes as ultimate guarantor. In spite of the prestige of these advocates no change was made in the law until after the severe panic of 1907.

Because the currency of the country was almost completely inelastic, the operations of the independent treasury took on an importance which they would otherwise not have had and became on occasion almost equivalent to the functions of a central

[18] 53 Congress, 3 Session. Secretary of Treasury, *Annual Report*, 1914, pp. 11, 481.

bank. It was the treasury which was called upon in any stringency to put funds into the market by buying bonds or by making deposits with banks.[19] Inevitably the action of the treasury was most often in the direction of increasing the funds of the market; little complaint was made when there was a plethora of funds, and if there had been the treasury officials would seldom have dared to produce a tightening. But the treasury was not qualified to fulfill all the functions of a central bank and it could not provide a sufficient degree of elasticity to ward off recurrent crises. It was then that the lack of elasticity in the monetary system became most apparent for the shortage of gold and legal tender currency created a low reserve ratio and forced the banks to contract their loans. Banks of the interior which felt the pinch at the same time began to withdraw their balances from New York and accelerated the contraction movement already under way. If there had been a central bank to provide increased currency and credit at this juncture, the panic might have been warded off or at least mitigated.

Clearing House loan certificates

When a shortage of currency went to such lengths that the New York banks found their reserves declining and no help to be obtained from any outside source, they resorted to the device which had been first developed during the crisis of 1860, the issue of Clearing House loan certificates. The first real panic after 1863 and the first occasion upon which it was necessary to make use of loan certificates occurred in 1873. The general causes of this panic were speculation and expansion, especially in the railroads, and the immediate cause was the failure of several brokerage and banking houses. The currency situation became acute early in the course of the crisis. The banks had been losing deposits throughout August, as the interior bankers withdrew their balances in preparation for the autumn crop movement, and the shipment of specie brought down their reserves in almost equal amount. By September 20, the date of

[19] See the preceding chapter.

the last weekly bank report before the actual panic, the Clearing House banks had seen their reserves fall off from the 80 millions of August to 53 millions—a loss of 27 millions in gold and legal tenders which had accompanied a decline from 238 to 198 millions of deposits. The reserve percentage was still above the legal minimum, but the surplus reserve was small and when a series of failures brought on a panic in the next week a reduction in deposits began which carried them to the low point of 150 millions by the end of October and brought reserves to 20 millions, representing a ratio of 13 per cent instead of the legal reserve of 25 per cent. The Clearing House weekly reports did not give separate totals for individual and bankers' deposits and it is therefore impossible to say how much of the decline was due to the increased demand for money in the interior and consequent drawing down of bankers' balances. For September 13 and October 15 however there are reports for the national banks which include these important details. In that period of slightly more than a month the national banks suffered the following losses:

DECLINE BETWEEN SEPTEMBER 13 AND OCTOBER 15*

(Amount in millions of dollars)

		Per cent loss
Individual deposits	$36.5	22
Bankers' deposits	35.0	39
Reserves	30.7	65

* Comptroller Currency, Annual Report, 1873, p. LXXXIII and 19.

It is noteworthy that the decline in bankers' deposits was almost equivalent to the decline in reserves. The withdrawal of bankers' deposits frequently entailed an actual shipment of currency or transfer of bank funds. Individual deposits on the other hand were often drawn out for the purpose of paying off bank loans and the two items on the opposite side of the balance sheet offset each other without affecting the absolute amount of the reserves.

The New York banks, faced with panic in the money market, with falling reserves, and with no resource except the importation of gold from abroad or the coining of gold at home, resorted again to the device which had served them in the crises of the Civil War, the Clearing House loan certificate. This action was not taken until the panic had already been in control of the market for a day, but when the issue of the certificates was once decided upon it went forward rapidly. A committee of five persons was appointed to accept securities or bills receivable from member banks and to issue certificates up to 75 per cent of the value of the bills or up to the full par value of the bonds. The certificates were charged interest at the rate of 7 per cent and were to be used for settlement of balances at the Clearing House. The committee was also given the very important power of equalizing the legal tender reserves of the member banks, by assessment or otherwise.[20] A limit of 10 millions was set for the first issue, but this was soon passed and the total of the certificates reached nearly 27 millions by November 30, when the last were taken out. The facts regarding the issue were not published at the time however and the regular weekly reports of the Clearing House banks were suppressed through October and November so that no one could tell which banks were making use of the loan certificates to keep up their reserve ratio and which banks were benefitting from the equalizing of the legal tenders.

The Clearing House had acted, not quite promptly perhaps, but courageously, particularly in the matter of equalization of reserves; but in spite of its efforts specie payments could not be fully maintained. On September 24, two days after the first issue of the loan certificates, the New York banks adopted a measure of partial suspension when they resolved not to certify checks unless they were stamped "Payable through the Clearing House." Individual depositors were still able to obtain cash at bank windows. When the interior banks could no longer withdraw cash balances from New York they felt obliged to suspend also. During the following week many other cities and clearing

[20] Comptroller of Currency, *Annual Report*, 1873, p. xxvi.

houses adopted the New York plan and it was not until the end of October that specie payments were resumed throughout the country.

The result of this suspension was a premium upon currency over certified checks which rose to 5 per cent on the last days of September and persisted at a diminishing rate until the third week in October when specie payments were generally resumed. During this time there was a general shortage of currency in circulation. Factories found it difficult to meet their pay rolls and buyers were unable to pay for goods purchased.[21] This shortage of currency occurred in spite of the fact that the New York banks, strengthened by the issue of Clearing House loan certificates, did not reduce their loans in the same degree that deposits had been drawn down. While the former went from 198 to 151 millions between September 20 and October 25, the loans went from 278 to 255 millions, a drop of only 9 per cent in loans compared with 24 per cent in deposits. The diagram showing the changes in the principal items reported weekly by the Clearing House member banks indicates the relative reductions.

CHANGES IN CASH RESERVES OF NATIONAL BANKS*

	September 12, 1873	*October 13, 1873*	*Change*
Country banks	$48.0	$50.4	Plus $2.4
Reserve city banks	39.5	34.7	M nus 4.8
New York City banks	47.2	16.5	Minus 30.7
TOTAL	$134.7	$101.6	Minus $33.1

* Comptroller Currency, Annual Report, 1873, p. LXXXIII:

It is interesting to see what happened to the millions of legal tender notes and specie which were being taken out of New York during the panic. The reserves of the country and reserve city national banks are shown in the table above. Much of the

[21] Sprague, *History of Crises*, p. 71; Comptroller Currency, *Annual Report*, 1873, p. lxxxiii.

currency of the country had been taken entirely out of the banks during the month and had either entered into circulation, which always required a greater amount of funds during the crop-moving season, or else was being hoarded because of the panic.

The panic of 1884

General business had been declining for nearly a year and large gold exports had somewhat depleted the gold reserve of the New York banks and the treasury but there was no such overexpansion of credit as had characterized the period before the panic of 1873. It was a series of breaks in stock prices and the consequent failure of several brokerage houses, coupled with news of fraudulent activities at two banks, which precipitated the panic.[22]

NET MOVEMENT OF GOLD AND CURRENCY BETWEEN NEW YORK AND THE INTERIOR

(In thousands of dollars)

	Week ending				
	May 2	May 9	May 16	May 23	May 30
Currency	3,070	3,797	673	−1,036	1,576
Gold	60		−1,780	−1,290	− 650
TOTAL	3,130	3,797	−1,107	−2,326	926

Although the crisis was largely confined to New York, the alarm which was felt by interior banks was sufficient to bring about a withdrawal of their deposits from New York, and the consequent decline of cash reserves at the New York banks. The movement of funds reported weekly by the *Commercial and Financial Chronicle* had been in favor of New York during the first two weeks in May, as was normal for that season, but shifted abruptly during the third and fourth weeks and did not recover until the end of the month.

[22] See p. 368 above.

The result of this drain from New York was a sharp decline in the reserves of the banks. Between May 10 and May 24, when the movement was most strongly against the city, reserves fell from 87 to 67 millions accompanying a decline in net deposits from 330 to 296 millions. The shortage in reserves was immediately reflected in a contraction of bank loans and an advance of money rates, call loans going to 4 per cent per day on Wednesday, May 13.[23]

The circulation remained constant throughout this period. An increase in national bank notes could not have been effected in time to give relief even if the banks had attempted it. The secretary of the treasury prepaid a few bonds but did not supply enough currency to ease the pressure when it was at its worst. The only effective relief came through the issue of Clearing House certificates, which had now become almost a routine measure in crises. It was made more promptly in 1884 than in 1873 and so rapidly did the market recover its balance that only 20 of the 82 member banks applied for certificates and more than one-fourth of the total issue of 25 millions was taken by the Metropolitan Bank. The chief difference between the issue of the certificates in 1873 and 1884 was that in the latter year the committee in charge of the issue was not given power to equalize reserves as in 1873. Banks which were not themselves in difficulty felt they should not be required to make sacrifices in order to save banks which had been none too scrupulous.[24] If the emergency had lasted longer they might have been forced into the use of equalization in order to prevent a general suspension, but when the issue of Clearing House certificates alone served to allay the panic nothing further was done.

The panic of 1890

The panic which occurred in 1890 was shorter and less serious than many others but it too was marked by a withdrawal of cash from New York and an issue of loan certificates. Until the week which ended on August 9, 1890, there had been a small surplus reserve held by the Clearing House member

[23] *Commercial and Financial Chronicle*, Vol. 38, May 16, 1884, p. 589.
[24] Sprague, *History of Crises*, pp. 121-23.

banks. During July and August the exports of gold had been unusually heavy and in August the usual demand from the interior began to make itself felt. The result was that by the middle of August the combined bank reserves had fallen below the legal figure, and there they remained for five successive weeks during which the call rate fluctuated violently and commercial loans were contracted. No action was taken by the Clearing House however and the stringency was finally relieved by the action of the secretary of the treasury in purchasing bonds.[25] Loans increased during September and the reserve ratio went above 28 per cent for a few days. In October it fell again, and when the resulting contraction of loans began to be felt in the stock market a real panic accompanied by the usual failures of brokerage houses and banks made its appearance. The Clearing House committee met on November 11, the day on which the first failures occurred, and made the first issue of the loan certificates on November 12. Their issue alone did not stop the panic in the face of adverse news from London but suspension of specie payments was avoided. It was not until November 20 that the monetary situation ceased to be serious. No attempt to equalize the reserves of the member banks was made, although the banks did agree to divide any loss resulting from the issue of the loan certificates. The reserves of the individual banks varied widely and those which held a surplus were not willing to share it with those which were deficient.

While the reserves of the New York banks were being drawn down to a point below the legal minimum, the cash reserves of the country banks actually increased by 6 millions between July and December although their deposits fell off by 15 millions in the same time and they had need of less reserves than before. New York lost nearly 5 millions of specie and legal tenders, and other reserve cities lost 4 millions.

The panic of 1893

The rôle played by currency during the panic of 1893 again demonstrated how important cash became when there was any

[25] See p. 373 above.

doubt of its being obtainable and how ineffective were the existing provisions for expansion and contraction of the currency. In this case it was the quality as well as the quantity which was in doubt. Heavy exports of gold had almost denuded the country and both banks and treasury had difficulty in keeping up gold payments. An unusually rapid outward movement of gold during the early part of the year was followed by a stock market crash in May and there was continuous pressure in the money market thereafter. The usual return of funds from the interior continued however and by the end of May the reserves of the Clearing House banks were as high as they had been in February. Widespread failures of commercial banks in the West and Southwest again created such serious distrust that heavy balances had to be shipped out of New York during June, and the reserve percentage declined steadily.

Although there was not yet an actual panic, the Clearing House committee realized the seriousness of the situation and began to issue loan certificates at once. Their use enabled the banks to keep up loans and discounts to a fair amount. In July 78 per cent of the balances at the Clearing House were settled with certificates, and in August 95 per cent. The issue of loan certificates in larger amount than ever before warded off the suspension of specie payments for a time, but was unable to prevent it altogether. Country banks continued to draw down New York balances to such an extent that their reserve percentages actually increased and the pressure in New York grew worse as the New York banks saw their reserves fall from 135 millions, where they had stood in May, to a low point of 77 millions in August. By the middle of August currency was selling at a premium of from 2 to 4 per cent; pay rolls were being made up in checks instead of in currency; and banks in many cities had suspended specie payments, requiring their customers to mark checks, "Payable through the Clearing House only." Some banks went to the extreme of opening special currency accounts for customers who were able to make deposits in that medium, as gold accounts had been kept before 1879.

Bank credit also suffered a severe contraction. The equalization of reserves, which had saved the banks from general suspension in 1873, was not used in 1893. It was not until large gold imports had arrived that the reserves of the banks came back to normal; certainty that the silver purchase act would be repealed was also of assistance in restoring confidence,[26] and by the beginning of September the banking phase of the crisis was over. During the long and disheartening trade depression which followed the banks had no difficulty in maintaining reserves.

The intense demand for money brought about an increased issue of national bank notes, although the increase did not get under way until the peak of the demand was passed, and it continued during September when the premium on currency had disappeared and there was practically a glut in the market.[27] One-fourth of the new notes issued were due to the banks of

NATIONAL BANK NOTES OUTSTANDING IN 1893*

(In millions of dollars)

Date	All banks	New York City banks
June 1	$177.2	$5.5
July 1	178.7	5.5
August 1	183.8	6.3
September 1	199.0	9.9
October 1	208.7	14.3
November 1	209.3	14.6
December 1	208.9	13.8

* Comptroller Currency, Annual Report, 1893, p. 151. Weekly statements of New York Clearing House banks, in *Commercial and Financial Chronicle*.

New York which formerly had shown little interest in the circulation privilege. Since the law of 1882 forbade the retirement of the circulation at a rate of more than 3 millions per month, it was impossible for this emergency issue of more than 30 millions to be reduced within less than ten months. As a matter of fact

26 The Act was repealed on November 1, 1893.

27 *Dun's*, August 12, 1893, p. 3; August 26, p. 1; September 23, 1893, p. 3.

most of it remained outstanding and never was retired, since the repeal of the silver purchase act in November, 1893, stopped the issue of treasury notes which had been pouring into the market and made a place for national bank notes.

The panic of 1907

The last serious panic of this period occurred in the autumn of 1907. There had been a sharp break in stock prices in 1903 but it was unaccompanied by the currency stringency and contraction of loans usual to the American crisis and hardly deserves to be classified as such. The panic of 1907 ran the full gamut of disturbance. Arising out of the rapid speculation which followed recovery from 1903, the immediate crisis was precipitated by the difficulties of several banks and trust companies which had become involved with some of the less reputable speculators of the time. During the third week in October the Knickerbocker Trust Company was in difficulties and runs on two other trust companies produced a general feeling of uneasiness. A few small banks in the city had to suspend and, what was of more significance, the banks out of town began to draw down their deposits in New York. The net loss of currency to the interior during the first part of the month had been at the rate of about 4 millions of dollars weekly; for the week ending on Friday, the twenty-fifth, the net withdrawal was more than 16 millions and it continued at this rate or higher throughout the month of November. The total withdrawn by December 6 was more than 100 millions. The reserves of the New York Clearing House banks had been declining slowly ever since the middle of the year and with this sudden demand they started down much more rapidly. The ratio of specie and legal tender to deposits declined to less than 20 per cent during November.

No issue of Clearing House loan certificates was made until Saturday, October 26, although bank runs had begun on the preceding Tuesday. One reason for postponing the issues seems to have been that the New York bankers took for granted that they would be equivalent to a suspension of specie payments Because of the delay, their fears were justified and suspension occurred simultaneously with the issue of loan certificates. If the first issues in New York had been made as soon as the runs began, before the panic had spread to the interior, they might have been more effective.

In spite of later denials[28] New York banks did restrict their cash payments during this time. The *Chronicle* affirmed that whenever an interior bank had a balance in the city, drafts upon it would certainly be met although the demands would be scaled down if they seemed disproportionate. But it is certain that some of the city banks refused to honor drafts drawn upon them in favor of the subtreasurer at New York because they would have had to be met in gold instead of being settled through the Clearing House. Other such drafts were met by the purchase of gold in New York and the charging of the premium to the account of the drawee bank. The city banks were afraid to pay out cash.[29] The shortage of currency was reflected in a premium which appeared on October 31 and continued until the end of the year. The rate during the first week of November was sometimes as high as 4 per cent.

Other cities, when they found themselves unable to get the amount of currency from New York which would tide them over the crisis, began to issue Clearing House loan certificates and also introduced the much more radical innovation of Clearing House checks which were certainly beyond the intention of the law, if not in actual violation of it. The country was flooded with paper intended for local circulation only, to an amount estimated at 500 millions of dollars.[30]

The issues of Clearing House loan certificates in New York City were made at a rate and for a length of time which exceeded those of any previous panic. The total amount reached 101 millions and on December 16, 1907, the date on which the greatest amount was outstanding, more than 88 millions were held by the banks. The certificates continued to be issued until

[28] Sprague, *History of Crises*, p. 260. *Commercial and Financial Chronicle*, Vol. 85, November 2, 1907, p. 1110; November 9, p. 1172.

[29] 60 Congress, 1 Session, Senate Document 435, pp. 14, 15.

[30] A. Piatt Andrew, "The Treasury and the Banks under Secretary Shaw," *Quarterly Journal of Economics*, 1908. Comptroller Currency, *Annual Report*, 1908.

January 30, 1908, and the last one was not cancelled until the end of March. The Clearing House banks used the loan certificates in practically all of their settlements at the Clearing House during the last few days of October and through November and December. The treasury alone required gold and it made every effort to avoid embarrassing the banks by insisting upon prompt payment. With this active economizing in the use of cash, it is not remarkable that the reserves of the Clearing House banks showed steady improvement during December and reached the legal minimum again early in January.

Although the amount of loan certificates used in New York was greater during 1907 than on any previous occasion, the proportion of loan certificates to total deposits of the banks was less than that in 1873 and 1893. On the other hand, except for the minor panic of 1890, the length of time for which the certificates were outstanding was steadily increasing.

Year	*Total amount (In millions of dollars)*	*Maximum amount (In millions of dollars)*	*Period of issue (Months)*	*Per cent of loan certificates to deposits*
1873	$26.6	$22.4	3.75	14.7
1884	24.9	21.9	4.25	7.3
1890	16.6	15.2	2.75	4.0
1893	41.5	38.3	4.66	10.2
1907	101.1	88.4	5.00	8.6

In this brief survey of the currency aspects of the chief panic periods between 1863 and 1913, it has been apparent that the issue of Clearing House certificates could not compensate for the lack of elasticity. The usefulness of the loan certificate was very definitely limited. It was powerless to ward off a panic or stop one which had got under way. It could not increase the reserves of the banks when they had been reduced and it did not assist New York banks in meeting the demand of the interior for specie and legal tenders. But it did perform two very valuable functions in an emergency. Banks could continue to make loans in spite of falling reserves, without fear of losing the last of their reserves in the Clearing House settlement of balances as the result of the increased deposits arising from the loans. If all the banks together had agreed to expand, as was attempted in 1857, they would have secured the same result but it was impossible to get the banks to act together without some such instrument as the loan certificate to assure them of protection. This effect of the certificates was so well known that the mere announcement they were to be issued tended to relieve a stringency.

One other result of the loan certificates was of great benefit. This was the partial equalization of reserves which resulted from their use. The banks which had large reserves in effect shared them with those which were below the minimum by guaranteeing to divide any losses resulting from their use. All the banks were thus enabled to lend after some would have been obliged to stop had it not been for the certificates.

Emergency currency of Aldrich-Vreeland Act

If New York had been an ordinary large commercial city, with no special responsibility in the way of bankers' reserve balances, the issue of loan certificates which enabled local loans to be increased would have been a very satisfactory device for meeting panics. Under the existing circumstances New York's ability to meet the demands of interior depositors was of far greater importance than her ability to assist local borrowers and for this purpose the loan certificate was practically useless. A more comprehensive scheme was needed and the first step in that direction was made by the Aldrich-Vreeland Act of May 30, 1908. It made provisions for a currency secured by assets of banks rather than by bonds in order to introduce elasticity. The act permitted the national banks of each city or district to form "national currency associations." Membership in such a body carried with it the right to issue additional bank notes based upon any securities, including commercial paper. The bank applying for this type of bank note must already have issued the old bond-secured notes up to at least 40 per cent of its capital stock. It had to satisfy the secretary of the treasury also that additional circulation was demanded by business conditions in its locality, and that the "character and value" of the securities and the assets of the banks in the currency association were sufficient. Notes might then be issued up to 75 per cent of the cash value of the securities and commercial paper deposited as collateral. The total of old and new types of bank notes issued by any national bank could not exceed the amount of its unimpaired capital and surplus, and the aggregate of the new type of note for all the banks in the country could not exceed 500 millions of dollars at any one time. The notes issued against commercial paper could not amount to more than 30 per cent of the unimpaired capital and surplus of the issuing bank. The term "commercial paper" was defined as "notes representing actual commercial transactions, which when accepted by the association shall bear the names of at least two responsible parties and have not exceeding four months to run."[31]

Forms for the new type of bank note were to be prepared in advance, and held in the treasury to be ready for an emergency demand. Under this new plan the increase of bank notes was greatly facilitated and their retirement was also made easier. The limit of 3 millions monthly, which had applied to the old national bank notes, had been raised to 9 millions monthly by a law of 1907 and no restrictions were put upon the retirement of the new emergency notes. With both the issue and the retirement of bank notes speeded up by these provisions, bank notes might have enjoyed a large measure of elasticity. The banks were very slow to put it to a test. Organization of the currency associations proceeded slowly and only at the insistence of the comptroller, and the only occasion upon which notes were issued by them was in 1914 when the outbreak of war in Europe produced a panic in New York. In November of that year the Federal Reserve system went into operation and Aldrich-Vreeland notes were no longer needed. The passage of the Federal Reserve Act ended the long struggle with monetary problems which had

[31] See p. 317; *Commercial and Financial Chronicle,* Vol. 91, July 23, 1910, p. 178; Secretary of Treasury, *Annual Report,* 1914, pp. 11, 481.

harassed the New York money market and the rest of the country throughout its history.

Summary

Both the stability and the elasticity of money were probably less after the passage of the National Bank Act than before: stability was less because of the political controversies over silver and the standard rather than because of the National Bank Act itself; and elasticity because of the requirement that bank notes be secured by government bonds, and the obstacles which were put in the way of their retirement. The problem of stability was solved by repeal of the silver purchase act in 1893 and passage of the gold standard act in 1900, but the money market continued to struggle with the problem of elasticity up to 1913. Issues of Clearing House loan certificates enabled the New York banks to meet local demands during the recurrent panics of the period but they were of no avail in meeting the larger responsibilities of their position as holders of the central banking reserve of the country. The emergency currency of the Aldrich-Vreeland Act was a great improvement over the loan certificate but it was never put to a serious test. It was superseded by the more comprehensive Federal Reserve Act, which provided not only for an emergency elasticity but also for a constant elasticity which tended to make emergencies less frequent.

CHAPTER XIX

THE NEW YORK MONEY MARKET—A REVIEW

The roots of the present-day money market lie deep in the past. Those features which seem to be most arbitrary and least logical are frequently adaptations to peculiar American conditions which have left their mark upon financial history. The isolation of America from the monetary centers of Europe, the early conditions under which American goods were produced and transported and sold, the early poverty of the country in "money" and its richness in resources, were vital factors in making the history of the New York money market significantly different from that of the European markets which developed before it. The American preference for small unit banks rather than large banks with branches, and the fear of a banking monopoly which prevented establishment of a central bank for three-quarters of a century and was then instrumental in the establishment of a regional form of central banking under the Federal Reserve system, is still reflected in the laws which prevent branch banks in certain states and in the fervid enthusiasm for the independent banker which reminds one of the old ditty in praise of the "independent farmer."

The National Bank Act itself, although it was in one sense a departure from past tradition, was an outgrowth of banking principles which had been developed in the more advanced states, and introduced no drastic innovation. Bond-secured circulation, legal reserve requirement, regular reports, had all been enacted into the laws of one or more states before the national law was drafted, and the pyramiding of reserves in New York, which was first crystallized into law by the National Act, had been in existence as a part of banking practice for decades before.

Close integration of all institutions of money market

The New York money market is a closely integrated structure, in which every part is dependent upon every other for its own smooth functioning. No one of the institutions of the money market can stand alone and it needs to be reiterated that the money market must be thought of in its entirety, though the desirability of organizing this study on other than a chronological basis led to a separate consideration of each portion. The development of each one of the different institutions of the money market affected in a greater or less degree the development of every other. The fact that bankers' balances came to New York in large volume, in the absence of a controlling central bank, resulted in the development of a call loan market closely associated with security transactions. The existence of a call market gave an impetus to the daily settlement of Stock Exchange sales and relegated the older form of time settlements to a small fraction of trading. The failure of the National Bank Act to recognize the acceptance was one of the factors in the continued use of promissory notes, while the wide popularity of single-name paper grew out of changes in the commercial credit market.

Bank reserves have always formed the basis of the credit employed in the money market. They were closely tied up with call loans and the Stock Exchange. Security transactions in turn, because of the large sale of American shares abroad, were linked with the foreign exchange market, and the foreign exchange market related to all the other markets because through it passed the foreign funds flowing here for investment and, later, American funds for investment abroad.

There was a constant flow of funds from one part of the market to another, between the market and the rest of the country, and between the market and Europe. Differences in interest rates, different prospects of earnings, differences in liquidity and risk, were responsible for such movements. These movements have been accelerated by every improvement in the technique of handling funds and especially by the closer connections between New York and foreign money markets. Foreign funds have always played a large part in the New York money market and a large part of our securities found a market abroad just as a large part of our commercial credit originated abroad. The transfer of these funds became increasingly less expensive and more sensitive to slight fluctuations in interest rates.

All parts of the money market were affected by the monetary difficulties which have beset America, the insecurity of the old state bank note issues as well as the instability and inelasticity of the period following the passage of the National Bank Act. All parts were at the mercy of the funds held by the Independent Treasury when it had a surplus and all were influenced by its method of raising revenues when it faced a deficit or a war expenditure. Even closer was the bond which held the money market in common disaster when panic conditions arose. It is impossible to separate the different aspects of the financial structure in such considerations as these.

Lack of control and coördination due to unit type of banking with no central bank

The great need of the New York money market was an instrumentality of coördination and control. Development of methods of control had been a problem for every large financial center. In London, it was only gradually that the Bank of England assumed leadership. The charters of the first and second Banks of the United States were modelled upon that of the Bank of England and if they had lasted it is probable that they would have followed a similar course of evolution. The records of the first Bank of the United States are incomplete but it seems to have felt a heavy responsibility for the commercial banks and to have coöperated closely with them, on the one hand, and with the treasury on the other. The second Bank, under the enthusiastic leadership of Nicholas Biddle, fairly outdid its English prototype, taking the lead in the development of a domestic acceptance, in the foreign bill market, and acting also as a sort of clearing house for state bank notes by sending them home promptly for redemption. If the second bank had secured a renewal of its charter there is no doubt that the money market would have been subject to a large measure of control and the whole course of our financial history would have been altered. The development of New York as the principal market of the country would probably have been somewhat delayed, although eventually Philadelphia would have had to yield. When finally the central office of the Bank of the United States had been transferred from Philadelphia to New York, the banks in the latter city would have found themselves firmly gripped in a comprehensive system which would have saved them from many of their difficulties, but would have left them far less individual freedom.

Unfortunately the Bank of the United States overplayed its hand and the bank lost its national charter in 1836. From that time until the establishment of the New York Clearing House in 1853, the money market was completely without guidance. Since this was also the period when the Independent Treasury was being established, it lacked even so much direction as a secretary of the treasury like Alexander Hamilton or Mr. Shaw would have felt it incumbent upon him to give.

Treasury an unsatisfactory substitute for a central bank

The establishment of the national banking system set under way once more the movement towards national regulation and control of financial institutions which had been in abeyance since the administration of Andrew Jackson and the establishment of the Independent Treasury. The needs of Civil War finance gave the initial impetus but it was carried on by the logic of the situation. The relations between the treasury and the money market became steadily closer. Not only was the treasury looked to by the market to provide relief even in the minor stringencies, but in their turn the banks and investment houses came to the aid of the treasury. The technique developed by the treasury was similar in many respects to that of a central bank. The treasury, however, was subject to so many legal limitations that it was never a satisfactory substitute for a central bank.

Another aspect of the movement towards national regulation was the desire on the part of legislators to stop what were considered undesirable practices in the market. The inquiry into the conduct of the banks of New York in 1873 was a definite attempt to discover if they had lived up to their responsibilities in the matter of returning the reserve balances of country bankers during the panic of that year. The Banking and Currency Committees of both House and Senate carried on frequent investigations after that time, some of them directed towards a reform of the monetary legislation which had always been the concern of the national legislature, but others directed towards provinces which were a new field for national regulation. Such was the Pujo investigation in 1912-1913, when the whole problem of control of the money market was aired, and the existence of a "money trust" was wrangled over. Little direct legislation resulted from these hearings, although a bill to prevent fraudulent stock exchange quotations was introduced into Congress. However, the light thrown upon the workings of the money market by the Pujo Committee was reflected in the increased insistence upon banking reform which led up to the Federal Reserve Act.

The organization of the Clearing House gave the banks of New York an instrument by which they could have achieved a large measure of control over the money market with proper initiative. Its actual accomplishments were valuable and its action during at least some of the panics was admirable but it did not go far enough. Until a bank was known to be in difficulties or a panic actually appeared, it was content to perform the purely routine task of clearing checks. After a panic, it is true, the Clearing House committee frequently made excellent recommendations for the future course of action, but these were seldom carried into effect and were apt to be forgotten until the market was again in trouble. The agreement made by New York banks after 1857, to keep a cash reserve of at least 20 per cent against deposits, was the sort of action which the Clearing House was well fitted to undertake but it showed less and less disposition for it as the years passed. Even its action during panics became less decisive. It dropped the equalization of reserves which had been utilized in 1860 and 1873 and depended only on the issue of loan certificates. The banks were hostile and suspicious of each other, and coöperation between them through the Clearing House became more difficult with the growth of this attitude. In many of the later periods of crisis, it was the large private bankers and investment houses which took the lead in organizing relief for the market, rather than the Clearing House banks.

New York not equipped to be international money market until passage of Federal Reserve Act

It became more and more evident that a centralization of reserves was the only solution for American financial difficulties and the Federal Reserve Act was passed in 1913. It marked the end of an era. The period in which national banks and their reserves had been the controlling factor in the money market gave way to one in which the discount and open-market operations of the central bank became paramount. Every part of the money market was affected by the change; banking, the Stock Exchange, the commercial paper market, even the call loan market, is now dependent upon the functioning of the Reserve Banks.

The establishment of the Federal Reserve system made it possible for New York at last to take its place among the money markets of the world and indeed, by virtue of war conditions, to become their leader. This was the last step in a process which had been visible during the preceding half century when New York ceased gradually to be an importer of capital and became an exporter. As the New York money market has developed from a provincial money market to a world power, it has taken on a certain European sophistication of dress and manner but it has by no means lost its Yankee individuality. Many of its peculiarities must seem incomprehensible until they are considered in the light of its history.

APPENDICES

SECURITIES TRADED ON THE NEW YORK STOCK EXCHANGE IN 1835 AS LISTED IN CURRENT NEW YORK *EVENING POST*

New York City Banks

United States
National
Commercial
Phenix
Leather Manufacturers
Merchants'
Union
Bank of America
Mechanics
Butchers and Drovers
Tradesmens
Chemical
Dry Dock
Seventh Ward
Manhattan
Fulton
Greenwich
City
Long Island
North River
Lafayette
Brooklyn

Outside Banks

City Bank of New Orleans
Mechanics and Traders, N. Or.
Commercial of New Orleans
Franklin of Cincinnati
Lafayette of Cincinnati
Planters of Tennessee
Planters of Mississippi
Kentucky Bank
Louisiana Bank
Mobile Bank
Charleston Bank
Illinois
American Trust, Baltimore
Clinton Bank, Ohio
Vicksburg
New Haven

Railroads

Berkshire
Boston and Providence
Boston and Worcester
Boston Trans.
Camden and Amboy
Grand Gulf
Harlem
Hartford
Jamaica and Brooklyn
Long Island
Mohawk
New Haven
New Hope and Delaware
New Jersey
Norwich
Patterson
Philadelphia and Trenton
Saratoga
Stonington
Utica and Schenectady
Whitehall

Miscellaneous

Manhattan Gas
New York Gas
New York and Schuylkill Coal
New Orleans Gas

Delaware and Hudson Canal
Morris Canal and Banking
New Orleans Canal and Banking

INSURANCE COMPANIES

Aetna
American Fire
American Marine
Atlantic
Bowery
City Fire
Commercial
East River
Equitable
Farmers Loan
Firemans
Franklin
Globe
Guardian
Howard
Jackson Marine
Jefferson
Life Insurance and Trust
Long Island
Merchants
Mutual
National Marine
Neptune Marine
New Orleans
New York
North River
Phenix
Ohio Life Ins. and Trust
Ocean Marine
Sea
State Marine
Union Marine
Washington

SECURITIES TRADED ON THE NEW YORK STOCK EXCHANGE DURING 1856 AS LISTED IN CURRENT NEW YORK *EVENING POST*

RAILROADS

Baltimore and Ohio
Chicago and Rock Island
Cincinnati, Hamilton and Dayton
Cleveland, C and Cincinnati
Cleveland and Pittsburg
Cleveland and Toledo
Eighth Avenue
Erie (many issues)
Galena and Chicago
Harlem (many issues)
Hudson River
Illinois Central
Illinois and Toledo
Illinois Lake Shore
Indianapolis and C R
Lake Erie and Wabash
Little Miami
Long Island
Macon and W
Mad River and La E.
Michigan Central
Michigan Southern and N. Indiana
Michigan and Mississippi
Milwaukee and La Crosse
New Jersey
New Jersey Transfer
New Jersey Central
New York Central
New York and New Haven
Norwich and Worcester
New Haven and Hartford
Northern Indian and Goshen
Nic Transit
Panama
Reading
Rome and Watertown
Sixth Avenue
Stonington
Terre Haute and Richmond
Third Avenue
Toledo, Wabash and Western
Wisconsin and Lake Shore

BANKS

American Exchange
Atlantic Bank
Bank of America
Bank of Commerce
Bank of New York
Bank of North America
Bank of Republic
Bank of State of N. Y.
Broadway
Butchers and Drovers
Chatham
City
Commonwealth
Continental
Corn Exchange
Fulton
Manhattan
Market
Mechanics
Merchant's
Merchants Exchange
Metropolitan
Hanover
Importers and Traders
Indiana State
Nassau
Ocean

Peoples
Park
Phenix
Shoe and Leather
Saint Nicholas
Tradesmans
Union
United States Trust

Industrials

Alleghany Mining
Brunswick City Land
Canton
Cary Imp.
Chirque Coal
Cumberland Coal
Delaware and Hudson Canal
Florence Joint
Gardiner Gold Mine
Gold Hill Mine
Long Dock Co.
Manhattan Gas
Morris Canal
New Creek Coal
New Jersey Zinc
Pacific Mail S. S.
Penn Coal
Portsmouth Dry Dock
Susquehanna and El. Coal
Ward Coal and Iron

Insurance

Arctic
Excelsior
Great Western
Hanover
Home
Howard
Ohio Life and Trust
Rutgers Fire
Washington

BIBLIOGRAPHY

I. CONTEMPORARY LITERATURE

1787—Anon. *Case of the British Merchants Who Traded to America Previous to the Late War,* etc.

1791—Webster, Pelatiah. *Political Essays.*
Philadelphia; Joseph Crukshank.

1794—Coxe, Tench. *A View of the United States of America.*
Philadelphia; W. Hall.

1802—Webster, Noah. *A Sketch of the History and Present State of Banks and Insurance Companies in the United States.* Miscellaneous Papers, Vol. IV.
New York; E. Belden & Co.

1806—Citizen Talleyrand. *Memoir Concerning the Commercial Relations of the United States with England.*
London; Longman, Hurst, Rees and Orme.

1810—Atwater, Jesse. *Considerations on the Approaching Dissolution of the United States Bank.*
New Haven; Sidney's Press.

Bollman, Eric. *Paragraphs on Banks.*
Philadelphia.

Carey, Mathew. *Desultory Reflections upon the Ruinous Consequences of a Non-Renewal of the Charter of the Bank of the United States.*
Washington.

——— *Nine letters to Dr. Adam Seybert.*
Philadelphia; Published by the author.

1811—Chalmers, George. *Consideration on Commerce, Bullion, and Coin, Circulation and Exchanges.*
London; J. J. Stockdale.

1812—Anon. *The Ruinous Tendency of Auctioneering and the Necessity of Restraining it for the Benefit of Trade, Demonstrated in a Letter to the Right Honorable Lord Bathhurst, President of the Board of Trade.*
London; J. M'Creery, Black-Horse-Court.
(also printed in New York, 1813, Eastburn Kirk and Co.)

1815—A Citizen. *An Appeal to the Public on the Conduct of the Banks in the City of New York.*
New York; New York Courier.

Publicola. (Ferris Pell). *Letter to Albert Gallatin on Doctrine*

of Gold and Silver and the Evils of the Present Banking System in Effect and Tendency.
New York; Gould and Van Pelt.

1816—Carey, Mathew. *Essays on Banking.*
Philadelphia; published by the author.

1817—A friend to trade. *The Beneficial Tendency of Auctioneering and the Danger of Restraining It.*
New York; J. H. Sherman.

Corrector. *Six Numbers on Banking and the Shaving Operations of Directors.*
New Haven; printed for the author.

1818—Seybert, Adam. *Statistical Annals of the United States.*
Philadelphia; Thomas Dobson and Son.

1819—Aristides. (W. P. Van Ness). *A Letter to the Secretary of the Treasury on the Commerce and Currency of the United States.*
New York; C. S. Van Winkle.

1827—A New Yorker. (John McVickers, D.D.) *Hints on Banking in a Letter to a Gentleman in Albany.*
New York; Vanderpool and Cole.

Anon. *Letter on the Use and Abuse of Corporations, Addressed to the Delegation from the City of New York in the Legisture by One of Their Constituents.*
New York; G. and C. Carvill.

Jacob Barker. *Disclosure of the Real Parties to the Purchase and Sale of the Tradesmen's Bank.*
New York.

1828—Anon. *Facts Important to be Known by the Manufacturers, Mechanics and All Other Classes of the Community.*
New York.

Anon. *Reasons Why the Present System of Auctions Ought to Be Abolished.*
New York; Alexander Ming, Jr.

"A plain practical man." *Remarks on the Auction System.*
New York; 1828.

Buchanan, James. *Report and Observations on the Banks and Other Incorporated Institutions in the State of New York.*
New York; Wm. A. Mercein.

1829—A stockholder. *An Examination of Some of the Provisions of the Safety-Fund Act, Particularly as to Its Effects on the City of New York.*
New York; Ludwig and Tolefree.

Letter of John Forman to Martin Van Buren, Albany, January 24, 1829.
Albany; Croswell and Van Benthuysen.

1831—Carey, Mathew. *Brief View of the System of Internal Improvements of the State of Pennsylvania.*
Philadelphia; Society for the Promotion of Internal Improvements.

Gallatin, Albert. *Considerations on the Currency and Banking System of the United States.*
Philadelphia; Carey and Lea.

1832—Clark, M. St. Clair and Hall, D. A. *Legislative and Documentary History of the Bank of the United States.*
Washington.

1833—Bronson, Isaac, and others. *Outline of a Plan for a National Bank, with Incidental Remarks on the Bank of the United States.*
New York; Newcomb and Cropsey.

Cooper, Thomas. *Essays on the Present United States Bank.*

Report of a Committee of Directors of the Bank of the United States on Removal of Deposits.
Philadelphia; December 3, 1833.

1834—Lord, Eleazor. *Credit, Currency and Banking.*
New York; G. and C. and H. Carvill. (2d edition.)

Moulton, R. K. *Legislative and Documentary History of the Banks of the United States, 1781-1834.*
New York; G. and C. Carvill and Company.

Report of the "Union Committee" Appointed by the Meeting of the Signers of the Memorial to Congress.
New York; Harper and Brothers.

1835—A citizen of New York. (Theodore Sedgwick) *What is a Monopoly? or Some Considerations Upon the Subject of Corporations and Currency.*
New York; George P. Scott and Company.

Aristides. (Thomas L. McKinney) *Essays on the Spirit of Jacksonism as Exemplified in its Deadly Hostility to the Bank of the United States and in the Odius Calumnies Employed for its Destruction.*
Philadelphia.

Gouge, Wm. M. *An Inquiry into the Principles of American Banking System.*
Philadelphia; B. and S. Collins. (2d edition.)

——— *A Short History of Paper Money and Banking in the United States.*

New York; B. and S. Collins. (2d edition)
Pitkin, Timothy. *A Statistical View of the Commerce of the United States of America.*
New Haven; Durrie and Peck.

1836—A citizen of New York. *Thoughts on Banks and Banking.*
Seneca Falls, N. Y.; John H. Child.

1837—Biddle, Nicholas. *Two letters to J. Q. Adams.*
London; P. Richardson, 1837.

Chibborn, Edward. *American Prosperity, an Outline of the American Debit or Banking System.*
London; Richard Groombridge.

Fisk, Theophilus. *The Banking Bubble Burst; a History of the Enormous Legalized Frauds Practiced upon the Community by the Present American Banking System.*
Charleston, S. C.

Franklyn. (pseud.) *Letters to the Honorable Levi Woodbury.*
New York; E. B. Clayton.

Gilbart, James Wm. *The History of Banking in America.*
London; Longman, Rees, Orme, Brown, Green and Longman.

Gouge, Wm. M. *An Inquiry Into the Expediency of Dispensing with Bank Agency and Bank Paper in the Fiscal Concerns of the United States.*
Philadelphia; Wm. Stavely.

Hare, Robert. *Suggestions Respecting the Reformation of the Banking System.*
Philadelphia; John C. Clark.

Minutes of the Proceedings of the Bank Convention held in the city of New York, November 27, 1837.
New York; Bowne and Company.

Palmer, J. Horsley. *The Causes and Consequences of the Pressure upon the Money Market.*
London; P. Richardson.

Rafinesque, Constantine S. *Safe Banking—Enquiry into Principles and Practices of Safe and Unsafe Banks or Monied Institutions in North America.*
Philadelphia; Divitial Institution in North America.

Report of the Committee Appointed by the Legislature to Visit and Examine the Banks in Connecticut.
Hartford; Russell and Jones.

1838—Carey, Henry C. *The Credit System in France, Great Britain, and the United States.*
Philadelphia; Carey, Lea and Blanchard.

Duane, William J. *Narrative and Correspondence Concerning*

the Removal of the Deposits and Occurrences Connected Therewith.
Philadelphia.

Stillwell, Silas M. *A System of Credit for a Republic and the Plan of a Bank for the State of New York.*
Albany.

Vethake, Henry. *The Principles of Political Economy.*
Philadelphia; P. H. Nicklin and T. Johnson.

1839—A citizen of Ohio. *Money and Banking, or Their Nature and Effects Considered.*
Cincinnati; M. Beck.

Martineau, Harriet. *Society in America.*
London; Saunders and Otley.

1840—A citizen of Boston. *Remarks on Banks and Banking and the Skeleton of a Project for a National Bank.*
Boston; Torrey and Blair.

Narragansett. (Thomas Robinson Hazzard) *Facts for the Laboring Man, by a Laboring Man.*
Newport, R. I. James Atkinson.

Navillus. (pseud.) *Plenty of Money and the United States of America Independent of all Foreign Money Markets.*
New York; Samuel Colman.

Raguet, Condy. *A Treatise on Currency and Banking.*
Philadelphia; Grigg and Elliott. (2d edition.)

The Great Question of the Day. Letter from President Thomas R. Dew, of William and Mary College, to a representative in Congress . . . on the subject of the financial policy of the administration. (Originally published in the Madisonian)
Washington; T. Allen.

1841—Appleton, Nathan. *Remarks on Banking and Currency Having Reference to Present Derangement of the Circulating Medium in the United States.*
Boston; Little and Brown.

Duer, W. A. *A National Bank; Its Necessity and Most Advisable Form.*
New York.

Duncombe, Charles. *An Essay on Banking, Currency, Finance, Exchanges and Political Economy.*
Cleveland; Sanford and Company.

Gallatin, Albert. *Suggestions on the Banks and Currency of the Several United States.*
New York; Wiley and Putnam.

One of the people. *A Letter on Currency Matters to the People of the United States.*
New York; T. and C. Wood and Company.

1842—Hammond, Jabez D. *The History of Political Parties in the State of New York.*
Albany; C. Van Benthuysen.

1844—Forbes, Robert Bennett. *China and the China Trade.*
Boston; Samuel N. Dickinson.

Junius. (Reverend Calvin Colton) *The Junius Tracts.*
New York; Greely and McElrath.

Middleton, Henry, Jr. *The Government and the Currency.*
Philadelphia; Printed for the author, by King and Baird.

1845—Cary, Thomas G. *A Practical View of the Business of Banking.*
Boston.

1846—Goodwell, Godek. (Edward Kellogg) *Currency: The Evil and the Remedy.*
New York; Wm. H. Graham.

1848—A reformed Stock Gambler (William Armstrong) *Stocks and Stock-Jobbing in Wall Street, with Sketches of the Brokers and Fancy Stocks.*
New York; New York Publishing Co.

Bonnefoux, L. *Vindication of the Free Banking System.*
New York; Jared W. Bell.

1850—Johnson, Alexander Bryan. *A Treatise on Banking.*
Utica, N. Y.; Seward and Thurber.

Macgregor, John. *Commercial Statistics of America.*
London; Whittaker and Co.

1852—A New York merchant. *Remarks on the Usury Laws.*

1853—Baker, Henry F. *Banks and Banking in the United States.*
Boston; Ticknor, Reed and Fields.

Silex. *Letters on Banks and Banking.*
Boston; Wright and Hasty.

1854—Cunningham, John. *Suggestions on the Causes of the Present Scarcity of Money and in Favor of Essential Reforms in Our Banking System.*
Charleston; James, Williams and Gitsinger.

1855—A merchant of Boston. (Samuel Hooper) *Currency or Money: Its Nature and Uses.*
Boston; Little, Brown and Company.

1856—A New York merchant. *Banks, Banking and Currency.*
New York; Hall, Clayton and Company.

1857—Bank Crash, Esq. (George Dutton) *The Present Crisis of the Currency.*
Rochester; Darrow and Brother.
Cleaveland, John. *The Banking System of the State of New York.*
New York; John S. Voorhies.
Members of the New York Press. *'37 and '57. A Brief Popular Account of All the Financial Panics and Commercial Revulsions in the United States from 1690 to 1857.*
New York; J. C. Haney.
Snowden, James Rees. (Director United States Mint.) *A Measure Proposed to Secure to the People a Safe Treasury and a Sound Currency.* (Letter to Honorable Howell Cobb, Secretary-Treasurer.)
Philadelphia; Benjamin F. Mifflin.
Walker, Amasa. *Nature and Uses of Money and Mixed Currency.*
Boston; Crosby, Nichols and Company.

1858—Dealtry, William, Mechanic. *Money; Its History, Evils and Remedy.*
Albany; Baker Taylor.
M. B. C. *Remarks on New York Banking.*
New York; John M. Amerman.
Opdyke, George, Chairman of Committee on the Currency. *A Report on the Currency.*
New York; John F. Trow.
Report on the Subject of Paying Interest on Current Deposits. Presented to the banks in New York.
New York; W. N. Arthur and Company.

1859—Colwell, Stephen. *The Ways and Means of Payment: a Full Analysis of the Credit System, With Its Various Modes of Adjustment.*
Philadelphia; J. B. Lippincott and Company.
Gibbons, James S. *The Banks of New York.*
New York; D. Appleton and Company.

1860—Hooper, Samuel. *An Examination of the Theory and the Effect of Laws Regulating the Amount of Specie in Banks.*
Boston; Little, Brown and Company.
Peters, Richard Editor. *The Public Statutes at Large of the United States of America.* 1789-1845.
Boston; Little, Brown and Company.

1861—Gallatin, James. *Two Letters to the Honorable S. P. Chase.*
New York; Hosford and Ketcham.

Stillwell, Silas. *A System of National Finance; Notes of Mr. Chase's Plan of National Finance.*
Washington; Government Printing Office.

1862—Bigelow, Erastus Brigham. *The Tariff Question Considered in Regard to the Policy of England and the Interests of the United States.*
Boston; Little, Brown and Company.

Dwight, Edmund. *A National Currency and Banking System.*
New York; John W. Amerman.

1863—A bank Director. *An Examination into the Prospective Effects of the National Banks upon the Public Welfare.*
New York; Hall, Clayton and Medole.

Proceedings of the Meeting in Relation to the Establishment of a Large National Bank in this City.
New York; Wm. C. Bryant and Company.

Wiliams, John Earl and Everitt, John L. *Reports of a Committee on the National Bank Currency Act, Its Defects and Its Effects.*
Published by order of the New York Clearing-House.
New York; C. S. Westcott and Company.

1864—A member of Congress. *A Reply to the Report of a Committee of the New York Clearing House Association on the National Bank Currency Act.*

Bonnefoux, L. *The National Currency.*
New York; Sanford, Harroun and Company.

Colwell, Stephen. *Remarks and Suggestions upon the State and National System of Banks.*
Philadelphia; Sherman and Company.

Gallatin, James.. *The National Debt, Taxation, Currency and Banking System of the United States.*
New York; Hosford and Ketcham.

Walker, Robert J. *American Slavery and Finances.*
London; William Ridgway.

1865—*Circular in Regard to Interest on Deposits Issued by Culver, Penn and Company, bankers.*
New York; E. S. Dodge and Company. December, 1865.

Newcomb, Simon. *A Critical Examination of our Financial Policy During the Southern Rebellion.*
New York; D. Appleton and Company.

Wilkeson, Samuel. *How Our National Debt May be a National Blessing.* Issued by Jay Cooke, general subscription agent of the government loans.
Philadelphia; M'Laughlin Brothers.

II. BOOKS AND PERIODICALS

Adams, Charles F. and Henry. *Chapters of Erie, and Other Essays.* Boston; James R. Osgood and Company. 1871.

Adams, Henry C. *Public Debts.* New York; D. Appleton and Company. 1890.

Aldrich, Nelson W. *Interviews on the Banking and Currency Systems of England, Scotland, France, Germany, Switzerland and Italy.* Publications of the National Monetary Commission. Washington; Government Printing Office. 1910.

———*Special Report from the Banks of the United States.* Publications of the National Monetary Commission. Washington; Government Printing Office. 1910.

American Quarterly Review. Philadelphia; Carey, Lea and Carey. 1827-1837.

American Railroad Journal and Advocate of Internal Improvement (later the *Railway Mechanical Engineer*). New York; D. Kimball Minor, 1832.

Andrew, A. Piatt. *Statistics for the United States, 1867-1909.* Publications of the National Monetary Commission. Washington; Government Printing Office, 1910.

——— "The Treasury and the Banks under Secretary Shaw." *The Quarterly Journal of Economics,* Vol. XXI, August, 1907.

Angell, Joseph K. *Treatise on the law of fire and life insurance.* Boston; Little, Brown and Company. 1855.

Anon. *History of the Chemical Bank.* New York; Privately printed. 1913.

Anon. *The Bank of America.* New York; De Vinne Press. 1887.

Bacon, N. T. "Capital Invested in the United States from Abroad." *Yale Review,* 1900, Vol. 9, p. 275.

Bagehot, Walter. *Lombard Street.* London; Smith, Elder and Company, 1915 edition.

Baldwin, Simeon E. "American Business Corporations before 1789." *American Historical Society, Annual Report,* 1902, Vol. 1, pp. 255-273.

Bankers' Magazine. Baltimore and New York. 1846-1913.

Barnett, George E. *State Banking in the United States since the Passage of the National Bank Act.*
Baltimore; Johns Hopkins Press. 1902.

Barrett, Walter. *The Old Merchants of New York City.* (4 vols.)
New York; Carleton. 1864.

Beckhart, B. H. *Discount Policy of the Federal Reserve System.*
New York; Henry Holt and Company, 1924.

Benton, Thomas. *Thirty Years View.*
New York; D. Appleton and Company. 1862.

Bisschop, Willem Roosegarde. *The Rise of the London Money Market 1640-1826.*
London; P. S. King and Son. 1910.

Blair, William Allen. *A Historical Sketch of Banking in North Carolina.*
New York; B. Rhodes and Company. 1899.

Bogart, Ernest R. *Internal Improvements and State Debt in Ohio.*
New York; Longman, Green and Company. 1924.

Bourne, Edward G. *History of the Surplus Revenue of 1837.*
New York and London; G. P. Putnam's Sons. 1885.

Bowers, Claude G. *The Party Battles of the Jackson Period.*
New York; Houghton, Mifflin Company. 1922.

Bradstreet's. New York. 1879-1913.

Brown, John Crosby. *A Hundred Years of Merchant Banking.*
New York; Privately printed. 1909.

Bryan, A. C. *History of State Banking in Maryland 1790-1864.*
Johns Hopkins University Studies, Series 17, Nos. 1-3. 1899.

Buck, Norman S. *The Development of the Organization of Anglo-American Trade, 1800-50.*
New Haven; Yale University Press. 1925.

Bullock, Charles J., John H. Williams, Rufus S. Tucker. "The Balance of Trade in the United States," *Review of Economic Statistics*, 1919, p. 215.

Cable, John R. *The Bank of the State of Missouri.*
Columbia University Studies in History, Economics and Public Law, Vol. CII, No. 2.
New York. 1923.

Callender, G. S. "The Early Transportation and Banking Enterprises of the States in Relation to the Growth of Corporations."
Quarterly Journal of Economics, Vol. 17, November, 1902.

Cannon, James G. *Addresses.*
New York; J. S. Babcock. 1899.

Cannon, James G. *Clearing Houses.*
Publications of the National Monetary Commission.
Washington; Government Printing Office. 1910.

Carey, Henry C. *Miscellaneous Works,* Vol. II.
Philadelphia; Henry Carey Baird and Company. 1883.

Catterall, Ralph C. H. *The Second Bank of the United States.*
Chicago; University of Chicago Press. 1903.

Chaddock, Robert E. *The Safety Fund Banking System in New York 1829-1866.*
Publications of the National Monetary Commission.
Washington; Government Printing Office. 1910.

Chamber of Commerce of the State of New York. *Report of the Special Committee on Railroad Transportation, on Watering the Stocks of Corporations.*
New York; Press of the Chamber of Commerce. 1883.

Chamber of Commerce of the State of New York, Annual Reports of. 1858-1913.

Clark, Victor S. *History of Manufactures in the United States.*
Washington; Carnegie Institution of Washington. 1916.

Cleveland, Frederick A. *The Bank and the Treasury; Bank Capitalization and the Problem of Elasticity.*
New York; Longmans, Green and Company. 1908.

Clews, Henry. *Fifty Years in Wall Street.*
New York; Irving Publishing Company. 1908.

Cohen, H. H. *The Evolution of Financial Clearance.*
Unpublished manuscript in the library of New York University.

Cole, Arthur H. "Cyclical and Sectional Variations in the Sale of Public Lands, 1816-60." *Review of Economic Statistics,* 1927, p. 41.

——— "Evolution of the Foreign Exchange Market of the United States." *Journal of Economic and Business History,* Vol. 1, p. 384.

——— "Seasonal Variation in Sterling Exchange." *Journal of Economic and Business History,* Vol. 2, p. 203.

——— "Statistical Background of the Crisis Period, 1837-42." *Review of Economic Statistics,* 1928, p. 182.

——— "The New York Money Market of 1843 to 1862." *Review of Economic Statistics,* 1929, p. 164.

——— and Edwin Frickey. "The Course of Stock Prices, 1825-66." *Review of Economic Statistics,* 1928, p. 117.

Commercial and Financial Chronicle.
New York. 1865-1913.

Commercial Review of the South and West. 1847-1880.
J. B. D. DeBow, editor and proprietor.
New Orleans; J. C. Morgan.

Conant, Charles A. "Securities as Means of Payment." ***Annals of the American Academy of Political Science,*** 1899, Vol. XIV, p. 181.

Cornwallis, Kinahan. *The Gold Room and the New York Stock Exchange and Clearing House.*
New York; A. S. Barnes and Co. 1878.

Curtis, Benjamin R. "Debts of the States."
North American Review, 1844, Vol. 58, p. 109.

Dallas, George Mifflin. *Life and Writings of Alexander James Dallas.*
Philadelphia; J. B. Lippincott and Company. 1871.

Davis, Andrew McFarland. *The Origin of the National Banking System.*
Publications of the National Monetary Commission.
Washington; Government Printing Office. 1910.

Davis, Joseph Stancliffe. *Essays in the Earlicr History of American Corporations; Eighteenth Century Business Corporations in the United States.*
Cambridge; Harvard University Press. 1917.

DeKnight, Wm. F. *History of the Currency of the Country and of the Loans of the United States.*
Washington; Government Printing Office. 1900.

Depew, Chauncey M. (editor). *One Hundred Years of American Commerce.*
New York; D. O. Haynes and Company. 1895.

Dewey, Davis R. *Financial History of the United States.*
New York; Longmans, Green and Company. 1903.

——— *State Banking Before the Civil War.*
Publications of the National Monetary Commission.
Washington; Government Printing Office. 1910.

Domett, Henry W. *History of the Bank of New York, 1784-1884.*
New York; G. P. Putnam's Sons. 1884.

Dowrie, George M. *The Development of Banking in Illinois, 1817-1863.*
University of Illinois studies in the social sciences, Vol. II, No. 4.

Duke, Basil W. *History of the Bank of Kentucky, 1792-1895.*
Louisville. 1895.

Dunbar, Charles F. *Chapters on the Theory and History of Banking.*
New York; G. P. Putnam's Sons. 1904. (2d edition.)

——— *Economic Essays.*
New York; The Macmillan Company. 1904.

Dunbar, Charles F. *Laws of the United States Relating to Currency, Finance, and Banking from 1789 to 1891.*
Boston; Ginn and Company. 1893.

Eames, Francis L. *The New York Stock Exchange.*
New York; Thomas G. Hall. 1894.

Eliason, Adolph Oscar. *The Rise of Commercial Banking Institutions in the United States.*
Minneapolis; The University Press. 1901.

Ellis, Arthur. *The Rationale of Market Fluctuations.*
London; Effingham Wilson, Royal Exchange. 1879.

Esarey, Logan. *State Banking in Indiana, 1814-1873.*
Indiana University Bulletin, Vol. X, No. 2.
Bloomington, Ind. 1912.

Emery, Henry Crosby. *Speculation on the Stock and Produce Exchanges of the United States.*
Columbia University Studies in History, Economics and Public Law, Vol. VII, No. 2.
New York. 1896.

Financial Register of the United States.
Philadelphia; Wirts and Tatem. July, 1837 to Dec., 1838.

Financial Review.
New York; William B. Dana Co. 1873-1921.

Flagg, Azariah C. *Banks and Banking in the State of New York from 1777 to 1864.*
Brooklyn; Rome Brothers. 1868.

Fowler, William Worthington. *Ten Years in Wall Street.*
New York; Worthington, Dustin and Company. 1870.

Frederiksen, D. M. "Mortgage Banking in America."
Journal of Political Economy, Vol. 2, p. 210, March, 1894.

Frickey, Edwin. "Bank Clearings Outside New York City, 1875-1914."
Review of Economic Statistics, 1925, p. 252.

Garrett, Charles Hunter. *State Banks of Issue in Illinois.*
University of Illinois. 1898.

Gibson, George Rutledge. *The Stock Exchanges of London, Paris and New York.*
New York; G. P. Putnam's Sons. 1889.

Goss, John Dean. *History of Tariff Administration in the United States.*
Columbia University Studies in History, Economics and Public Law, Vol. 1, No. 2.
New York. 1891.

Greeley, Horace. *Essays Designed to Elucidate the Science of Political Economy.*
Philadelphia; Porter and Coates. 1869.

Griffiss, Bartow. *The New York Call Money Market.*
New York; Ronald Press Company. 1925.

Hamilton, Alexander. *The Works of Alexander Hamilton.* Ed. by Henry Cabot Lodge.
New York; G. P. Putnam's Sons. 1904.

Hamilton, Andrew. *Statutory Revision of the Laws of New York Affecting Banks, Banking and Trust Companies.* New Edition (1908) by Charles J. Hailes.
Albany; Banks and Company. 1908.

Hamilton, James Alexander. *Reminiscences.*
New York; C. Scribner and Company. 1869.

Hardy, Charles O. and Richard N. Owens. *Interest Rates and Stock Speculation. A study of the influence of the money market on the stock market.*
New York; The Macmillan Company. 1925.

Hart, Albert B. *Salmon Portland Chase.*
(American Statesmen Series.)
Boston and New York; Houghton Mifflin Company. 1908.

Hemming, H. G. *History of the New York Stock Exchange.*
New York; H. Glover and Company. 1905.

Hepburn, A. Barton. *History of Currency in the United States.*
New York; The Macmillan Company. 1924. (Revised edition.)

Hinchman, T. H. *Banks and Banking in Michigan.*
Detroit; M. Graham. 1887.

Hirst, Francis W. *The Credit of Nations.*
Publication of the National Monetary Commission.
Washington; Government Printing Office. 1910.

Hobson, C. K. *The Export of Capital.*
London; Constable and Company. 1914.

Hobson, John Atkinson. *An Economic Interpretation of Investment.*
London; The Financial Review of Reviews. 1911.

Hollander, Jacob H. *Bank Loans and Stock Exchange Speculation.*
Publications of the National Monetary Commission.
Washington; Government Printing Office. 1910.

Huntington, A. T. and Robert J. Mawhinney. *Laws of the United States Concerning Money, Banking, and Loans, 1778-1909.*
Publications of the National Monetary Commission.
Washington; Government Printing Office. 1910.

Huntington, Charles C. "A History of Banking and Currency in Ohio Before the Civil War."
Ohio Archaeological and History Quarterly, Vol. 24, 1915.

Jefferson, Thomas. *The Writings of Thomas Jefferson*. Ed. by H. A. Washington.
New York; J. C. Riker. 1853-1854.

Jenks, Leland Hamilton. *The Migration of British Capital to 1875.*
New York; A. A. Knopf. 1927.

Jevons, W. Stanley. *Investigations in Currency and Finance.*
London; Macmillan and Company. 1884.

——— "On the Frequent Autumnal Pressure in the Money Market, and the Action of the Bank of England."
Journal of the Statistical Society of London, Vol. XXIX, June, 1866.

Johnson, Emory, and others. *History of the Domestic and Foreign Commerce of the United States.* (2 vols.)
Carnegie Institution of Washington. 1915.

Kemmerer, Edwin Walter. *Seasonal Variations in the Relative Demand for Money and Capital in the United States.*
Publications of the National Monetary Commission.
Washington; Government Printing Office. 1910.

Keyes, Emerson W. *History of Savings Banks in the State of New York, 1819-1869.*
Albany; Argus and Company. 1870.

Kilburn, F. D. *Interest on Deposits.*
Privately printed, May, 1905.

Klein, Joseph J. "The Commercial Importance of Single Name Paper."
New York Times Annalist, Vol. III, No. 62, March 23, 1914.

——— "The Development of Mercantile Instruments of Credit in the United States."
Journal of Accountancy, Vols. 12, 13, 1911.

Kinley, David. *The Independent Treasury of the United States.*
Publications of the National Monetary Commission.
Washington; Government Printing Office. 1910.

Kniffin, W. H. *Commercial Paper.*
New York; The Bankers Publishing Company. 1920.

Knox, John Jay. *A History of Banking in the United States.*
New York; Bradford Rhodes and Company. 1900.

——— *The National Banking System.*
Address before the American Bankers' Association.
New York; Bankers' Publishing Association. 1879.

——— *United States Notes.*
New York; Charles Scribner's Sons. 1884.

Lamb, Martha. *History of the City of New York.*
New York; A. S. Barnes and Company. 1876.

——— *Wall Street in History.*
New York; Funk and Wagnalls. 1883.

Lanier, Henry Wysham. *A Century of Banking in New York.*
New York; The Gilliss Press. 1922.

Lavington, Frederick. *The English Capital Market.*
London; Methuen and Company, Ltd. 1921.

Leach, J. G. *History of the Girard National Bank of Philadelphia, 1832-1902.*
Philadelphia.

Leonard, John W. "History of City of New York, 1609-1909."
New York; *Journal of Commerce and Commercial Bulletin.* 1910.

Lewis, Lawrence. *History of the Bank of North America.*
Philadelphia; J. B. Lippincott and Company. 1882.

Lockhart, Oliver C. "The Development of Interbank Borrowing in the National System, 1869-1914."
Journal of Political Economy, Vol. XXIX, February and March, 1921.

McCulloch, Hugh. *Men and Measures of Half a Century.*
New York; Charles Scribner's Sons. 1900.

McCulloch, J. R. *Essays on Exchange, Interest, Money and Other Subjects.*
Boston; W. Crosby and H. P. Nichols. 1850.

McGrane, R. C. *The Correspondence of Nicholas Biddle, 1807-1844.*
Boston; Houghton, Mifflin Company. 1919.

McMaster, John B. *History of the People of the United States.*
New York; D. Appleton and Company. 1866.

——— *Life and Times of Stephen Girard.*
Philadelphia; J. B. Lippincott and Company. 1918.

Margraff, Anthony. *International Exchange.*
New York City. 1912.

Martin, Joseph G. *A Century of Finance.*
Boston; The author. 1898.

Matthews, Ada M. "New York Bank Clearings and Stock Prices, 1866-1914."
Review of Economic Statistics, 1926, p. 184.

Medbury, James K. *Men and Mysteries of Wall Street.*
Boston. 1870.

Meeker, Edward J. *The Work of the Stock Exchange.*
New York; Ronald Press. 1930.

Merchants' Magazine and Commercial Review.
New York; Freeman Hunt, editor and proprietor. 1839-1870.
Merritt, Fred D. *The Early History of Banking in Iowa.*
Iowa City, Ia.; The University Press. 1900.
Meyer, B. H. *History of Transportation in the United States before 1860.*
Washington; Carnegie Institution. 1917.
Miller, Harry Edward. *Theories of Banking in the United States before 1860.*
Cambridge; Harvard University Press. 1927.
Mitchell, Wesley Clair. *A History of the Greenbacks.*
Chicago; University of Chicago Press. 1903.
——— *Business Cycles.*
Berkeley; The University Press. 1913.
——— *Gold, Prices, and Wages under the Greenback Standard.*
University of California Publications in Economics, Vol. I.
Berkeley; The University Press. 1908.
Monetary Commission of the Indianapolis Convention, *Report.*
Chicago; University of Chicago Press. 1898.
New York Daily Express. 1836-1877-.
New York Evening Post. 1801-.
New York Herald. 1833-.
New York Journal of Commerce. 1827-.
New York Times. 1851-.
New York Times Weekly Financial Quotation Review. 1897-1914.
New York Tribune. 1841-.
New York World. 1860-.
Niles' Weekly Register.
Baltimore; Hezekiah Niles, Editor. 1811-1849.
Norton, John Pease. *Statistical Studies in the New York Money Market.*
New York; The Macmillan Company. 1902.
Noyes, Alexander Dana. *Forty Years of American Finance.*
New York; G. P. Putnam's Sons. 1909.
——— "The Banks and the Panic of 1893."
Political Science Quarterly, Vol. IX, No. 1, March, 1894.
Oberholtzer, Ellis P. *Jay Cooke, Financier of the Civil War.*
Philadelphia; G. W. Jacobs and Company. 1907.
Osborne, Algernon A. *Speculation on the New York Stock Exchange, September, 1904-March, 1907.*
Columbia University Studies in History, Economics and Public Law. Vol. 65, No. 1.
New York; Longmans, Green and Co. 1913.

Page, Edward D. *Character and Credit:* An address before the National Association of Credit Men, New York, June 17, 1904.
New York; Published under the auspices of the business literature committee of the National Association of Credit Men.

Paine, Willis S. *The Laws of the State of New York Relating to Banks, Banking, Trust Companies, etc.*
New York; L. K. Strouse and Company. 1894.

Paish, George. *The Trade Balance of the United States.*
Publications of the National Monetary Commission.
Washington; Government Printing Office. 1910.

Patchin, Sydney Allen. *The Development of Banking in Minnesota.*
Minnesota History Bulletin, Vol. 2, pp. 111-168.
Saint Paul. 1917.

Patterson, E. M. "Certain Changes in New York's Position as a Financial Center."
Journal of Political Economy, Vol. XXI, June, 1913.

Patton, Eugene B. "Secretary Shaw and Precedents as to Treasury Control over the Money Market."
Journal of Political Economy, Vol. XV, February, 1907.

Peake, Edward G. *An Academic Study of Some Money Market and Other Statistics.*
London; P. S. King & Son. 1923.

Persons, Warren M. "Cyclical Fluctuations of the Ratio of Bank Loans to Deposits."
Review of Economic Statistics, 1924, p. 260.

——— Pierson M. Tuttle, and Edwin Frickey. "Business and Financial Conditions Following the Civil War in the United States.'"
Review of Economic Statistics, 1920, Supplement.

Peters, Alfred H. "The Depreciation of Farming Land."
Quarterly Journal of Economics, Vol. 4, October, 1889.

Phillips, J. B. *Methods of Keeping the Public Money of the United States.*
Publications of the Michigan Political Science Association, Vol. IV, No. 3.

Platt, Sereno S. *The Work of Wall Street.*
New York; D. Appleton and Company. 1916.

Poor, Henry V. *Influence of the Railroads of the United States in the Creation of Commerce and Wealth.*
New York; Journeymen Printers' Coöperative Association. 1869.

——— *Sketch of the Rise and Progress of Internal Improvements.*
New York; H. V. and H. W. Poor. 1881.

Porter, Robert P. "State Debts and Repudiation."
International Review, November, 1880.

Powell, Ellis T. *The Evolution of the Money Market (1385-1915).* London; The Financial News. 1915.

Preston, Howard Hall. *History of Banking in Iowa.* Iowa City, Iowa. 1922.

Ravell, Charles H. *Sixty Years of Banking in Michigan.* Battle Creek; Old National Bank. 1910.

Reed, George B. *Sketch of the Early History of Banking in Vermont.* Boston. 1879.

Ross, Victor. *A History of the Canadian Bank of Commerce.* Toronto; Oxford University Press. 1920.

Royall, William L. *A History of Virginia Banks and Banking Prior to the Civil War.* New York and Washington; The Neale Publishing Company. 1907.

Ryner, Ira. *On the Crises of 1837, 1847, and 1857, in England, France, and the United States.* University of Nebraska Studies, Vol. V, No. 2. Lincoln, Nebraska. 1905.

Scott, William A. *The Repudiation of State Debts.* New York; Thomas Y. Crowell Company. 1893.

Seltzer, Lawrence H. and Seward L. Horner. "The Relation of the Percentage of Bank Reserves of National Banks in New York City to the Call Money Loan Rate on the New York Stock Exchange." *Journal of Political Economy,* Vol. XXX, No. 1, February, 1922.

Sherman, John. *Recollections of Forty Years.* New York; The Werner Company. 1895.

——— *Selected Speeches and Reports on Finance and Taxation, from 1859 to 1878.* New York; D. Appleton and Company. 1879.

Smith, James G. *The Development of Trust Companies in the United States.* New York; Henry Holt and Company. 1927.

Smith, Matthew Hale. *Twenty Years Among the Bulls and Bears of Wall Street.* Hartford; J. B. Burr and Company. 1870.

Smith, Walter Buckingham. "Money and Prices in the United States from 1802 to 1820." (Unpublished thesis of Harvard University, Division of History, Government and Economics.) Cambridge. 1928.

——— "Wholesale Commodity Prices in the United States, 1795-1824." *Review of Economic Statistics,* 1927, p. 171.

Snider, Joseph L. "Wholesale Prices in the United States, 1866-91." *Review of Economic Statistics,* 1924, p. 93.

Spahr, Walter E. *The Clearing and Collection of Checks.* New York; The Bankers Publishing Company. 1926.

Spaulding, Elbridge G. *History of the Legal Tender Paper Money.* Buffalo; Express Printing Company.

Spicer, Ernest Evan. *The Money Market in Relation to Trade and Commerce.* London; H. Foulks Lynch and Co., Ltd. 1922. (3d edition.)

Sprague, Oliver M. W. *History of Crises Under the National Banking System.* Publications of the National Monetary Commission. Washington; Government Printing Office. 1910.

——— "The New York Money Market." *Economic Journal,* Vol. XIII, March, 1903.

Squire, Newton. *The New York Clearing House, Its Methods and Systems.* New York; Livingston Middleditch and Company. 1883.

Stanwood, Edward. *American Tariff Controversies.* Boston and New York; Houghton, Mifflin Company. 1903.

Stedman, E. C. *History of the New York Stock Exchange.* New York; Stock Exchange Historical Company. 1905.

Stevens, John Austin. *Albert Gallatin.* Boston; Houghton, Mifflin Company. 1884.

Stillwell, Silas M. *Private History of the Origin and Purpose of the National Banking Law.* New York; Trow's Printing and Bookbinding Company. 1879.

Stone, Edwin A. *A Century of Boston Banking.* Boston; Rockwell and Churchill. 1894.

Sumner, William G. *Andrew Jackson.* New York; Houghton, Mifflin Company. 1882.

Swanson, William Walker. "The Crisis of 1860 and the First Issue of Clearing House Certificates." *Journal of Political Economy,* Vol. XVI, February and April, 1908.

——— *The Establishment of the National Banking System.* Kingston; Printed at the Jackson Press. 1910.

Taussig, Frank W. *The Tariff History of the United States.* New York; G. P. Putnam's Sons. 1923.

Taylor, William George L. *The Credit System.* New York; The Macmillan Company. 1913.

Tooke, Thomas and Newmarch, William. *The History of Prices, 1792-1856.* London; Longman, Brown, Green, Longmans and Roberts. 1857.

Tuckerman, B. (editor). *Diary of Philip Hone.*
New York. 1910.

United States Democratic Review: United States Magazine and Democratic Review, 1837-1851; *Democratic Review,* 1852; *United States Review,* 1853-1856; *United States Democratic Review,* 1856-1859; Washington; New York.

Van Buren, Martin. *Autobiography of Martin Van Buren.* Annual Report of the American Historical Association of 1918, Vol. II.
Washington; Government Printing Office. 1920.

——— *Political Parties in the United States.*
New York; Hurd and Houghton. 1867.

Veblen, Thorstein B. "The Use of Loan Credit in Modern Business." *University of Chicago Decennial Publications,* 1903, Series 1, Vol. 4, p. 31.

Watkins, Leonard L. *Bankers Balances; A Study of the Effect of the Federal Reserve System on Banking Relationships.*
Chicago; A. W. Shaw and Co. 1929.

Westerfield, Ray B. *The Early History of American Auctions.*
Transactions of the Connecticut Academy of Arts and Sciences, Vol. 23, May, 1920.

White, Horace. *Money and Banking.*
Boston; Ginn and Company. 1904. (2nd edition.)

——— *Money and Banking Illustrated by American History.*
Boston; Ginn and Company. 1904. (2d edition.)

Wildman, M. S. "Independent Treasury and the Banks."
Annals of the American Academy of Political Science, 1910, No. 604.

Woodlock, Thomas F. *The Stock Exchange and the Money Market.*
New York; Columbia University Press. 1908.

Woodward, Joseph G. *Currency and Banking in Connecticut, 1635-1838.*
Boston; D. H. Hurd and Company. 1897.

Young, Allyn A. *An Analysis of Bank Statistics for the United States.*
Cambridge; Harvard University Press. 1928.

Youngman, Anna. "The Growth of Financial Banking."
Journal of Political Economy, Vol. XIV, July, 1906.

III. OFFICIAL DOCUMENTS.

A. Serials

American State Papers on Finance, Vols. 1-5, incl.
Washington; Gales and Seaton. 1834.

American State Papers on Foreign Relations, Vol. 1.
Washington; Gales and Seaton. 1832.

Annals of Congress, 1789-1824.

The Congressional Globe, Vols. 1-60, 1833-1863.
Washington; Blair and Rives.

United States Treasury, Annual Report of the Secretary on the State of the Finances, 1821-1913.

United States Treasury, Annual Report of the Secretary on the Condition of the State Banks, 1833-1863.

United States Comptroller of the Currency, Annual Report, 1865-1913.

United States Census, 1840, 1850, 1880, Vol. VII.

B. Non-Serials (By Date)

Letter from the Secretary of the Treasury . . . communicating his reasons for not transferring public moneys . . . to the Bank of the United States.
December 12, 1817. 15 Congress, 1 Session, House Document 9, Vol. II.

Report of the Committee appointed on the 30th of November, 1818, to inspect the books and examine into the proceedings of the Bank of the United States, etc.
January 16, 1819. 15 Congress, 2 Session, House Document 92, Vol. V.

Letter from the Secretary of the Treasury . . . showing amount of money standing to the credit of the United States . . . in every bank in which the public moneys have been deposited.
March 1, 1823. 17 Congress, 2 Session, House Report 105, Vol. VIII.

Report of the Committee of Ways and Means on Bank of the United States.
April 13, 1830. 21 Congress, 1 Session, House Report 358.

Report from the Secretary of the Treasury . . . respecting the relative value of Gold and Silver, etc.
May 29, 1830. 21 Congress, 1 Session, House Document 117.

Report of the Secretary of the Treasury . . . concerning orders drawn by the Bank of the United States and its branches.
February 29, 1832. 22 Congress, 1 Session, Senate Document 78, Vol. II.

Letter from Secretary of Treasury transmitting the information . . . in relation to the Bank of the United States.
March 2, 1832. 22 Congress, 1 Session, House Report 147.

Documents from N. Biddle.
March 12, 1832. 22 Congress, 1 Session, Senate Document 98.

Report of the committee . . . to inspect the books, and examine into the proceedings of the Bank of the United States.
April 30, 1832. Majority and minority reports. 22 Congress, 1 Session, House Report 460.

Letter from the Director of the Mint, Transmitting . . . a report of the Relative Value of Gold and Silver Bullion in the principal countries of Europe and the United States.
January 14, 1833. 22 Congress, 2 Session, House Document 38.

Report from the Secretary of the Treasury on the removal of the Public Deposits from the Bank of the United States.
December 4, 1833. 23 Congress, 1 Session, Senate Document 2.

Report from Secretary of the Treasury in reply to a resolution . . . requiring copies of certain correspondence relative to the removal of the public deposits, and the funds in the Bank of the United States.
December 30, 1833. 23 Congress, 1 Session, Senate Document 16.

Report of the Secretary of the Treasury . . . transmitting statements in relation to the condition of the Bank of the United States, etc.
January 14, 1834. 23 Congress, 1 Session, House Report 51.

Abstracts, returns and estimates of the condition of the several State banks compiled under the direction of the Clerk of the House of Representatives . . . read June 24, 1834.
23 Congress, 1 Session, House Report 498.

Report from the Secretary of the Treasury on the present system of keeping and disbursing the Public Money. December 15, 1834.
23 Congress, 2 Session, House Report 27.

Report from the Secretary of the Treasury with monthly statements of the affairs of the Bank of the United States, and of those State Banks selected as depositories of the public money.
December 9, 1834. 23 Congress, 2 Session, Senate Document 8.

Report of the Senate Committee on Finance.
December 18, 1834. 23 Congress, 2 Session, Senate Document 17.

Report from the Secretary of the Treasury . . . relative to Deposits and Transfers of Moneys derived from the Public Lands from the West to the Eastern cities.
May 3, 1836. 24 Congress, 1 Session, Senate Document 356.

Letter transmitting a statement of the several amounts deposited in the several deposit banks of the government.
May 6, 1836. 24 Congress, 1 Session, House Report 252.

Report from the Secretary of the Treasury . . . transmitting statements of transfers of public moneys.
December 26, 1836. 24 Congress, 2 Session, Senate Document 29.

Letter from Secretary of the Treasury transmitting statements showing the condition of certain State banks, etc.
January 4, 1837. 24 Congress, 2 Session, House Report 65.

Report of the select committee to which was referred certain memorials suggesting an amendment of the constitution of the United States in relation to banking companies and against the re-issuing of the notes of the United States Bank.
March 3, 1837. 24 Congress, 2 Session, House Report 306.

Letter from Secretary of the Treasury transmitting his annual report on the state of the Finances. September 5, 1837.
25 Congress, 1 Session. House Report 2.

Letter from the Secretary of the Treasury transmitting . . . information . . . in relation to the methods which have been adopted for the safe keeping of the public funds.
September 22, 1837. 25 Congress, 1 Session, Senate Document 29.

Letter transmitting information in relation to the transfers and payments of the instalments to the states; the condition of the deposite banks.
September 26, 1837. 25 Congress, 1 Session, House Report 30.

Report transmitting returns of the Bank of the United States (from 1817 to 1837).
January 24, 1838. 25 Congress, 2 Session, Senate Document 128.

Report of Committee of Ways and Means, to whom were referred various memorials relating to the Currency and a National Bank.
March 5, 1838. 25 Congress, 2 Session, House Report 634.

Report from the Secretary of the Treasury . . . transmitting statements of the rates of exchange and the prices of bank notes.
May 28, 1838. 25 Congress, 2 Session, Senate Document 457.

Message from the President of the United States . . . in relation to the banks which have recently suspended specie payments.
January 13, 1840. 26 Congress, 1 Session, Senate Document 72.

Report from the Secretary of the Treasury . . . showing in compliance with a resolution of the Senate, the losses by the General Government and by the people of the United States from the use of banks and bank-paper.
February 12, 1841. 26 Congress, 2 Session, Senate Document 180.

Letter from Secretary of the Treasury . . . transmitting information relative to the manner in which . . . the sub-Treasury law has been carried into effect.
July 15, 1841. 27 Congress, 1 Session, House Document 35.

Report . . . in relation to the custody of the public deposits since the repeal of the independent system.
July 19, 1842. 27 Congress, 2 Session, Senate Document 386.

Report of Wm. Cost Johnson, of Select Committee . . . to whom were referred memorials for the Relief of the States.
March 2, 1843. 27 Congress, 3 Session, House Report 296.

Elliott, Jonathan. The Funding System of the United States and of Great Britain.
28 Congress, 1 Session, Executive Document 15.

Report of the Secretary of the Treasury in relation to depositories of the public money.
February 10, 1845. 28 Congress, 2 Session, Senate Document 88.

Report of the Secretary of the Treasury in answer to a resolution of the Senate calling for the amount of American securities held in Europe and other foreign countries on June 30, 1853.
March 2, 1854. 33 Congress, 2 Session, Executive Document 42.

Joint Select Committee on Retrenchment, who were instructed by a resolution of the House of Representatives of January 15, "to inquire why, in the present stringent condition of the New York money market, the currency balance in the sub-treasury in that city is constantly increasing, etc."
February 7, 1867. 39 Congress, 2 Session, House Report 14.

Letter from the Secretary of the Treasury in answer to a resolution of the House of 6th ultimo, transmitting various statements of gold coin sold by the government since January, 1863, in each year.
February 13, 1869. 40 Congress, 1 Session, House Executive Document 84.

Report of Special Commisioner of the Revenue.
December 17, 1869. 41 Congress, 2 Session, House Executive Document 27.

Report of the committee on banking and currency on the gold panic.
March 1, 1870. 41 Congress, 2 Session, House Report 31, Vol. II.

Report of the Committee on Banking and Currency, to whom were referred "A bill to substitute United States notes for the issues of the national banking associations" and . . . "A bill to provide for the retirement of national bank notes and the substitution in lieu thereof, of Treasury notes, etc."
March 3, 1875. 43 Congress, 2 Session, House Report 328.

Notes of a conference between the committee on banking and currency of the House of Representatives and the Hon. John Sherman, Secretary of the Treasury.
April 1, 4, 1878. 45 Congress, 2 Session, House Miscellaneous Document 48.

Testimony before the committee on banking and currency in relation to the resumption of specie payments.
1878. 45 Congress, 2 Session, House Miscellaneous Document 62.

International Monetary Conference, held . . . in Paris, in August, 1878.
1879. 45 Congress, 3 Session, Executive Document 58.

Report of Mr. Davis, of West Virginia, from the Select Committee to Investigate the Finance Reports, Books, and Accounts of the Treasury Department.
April 28, 1880. 46 Congress, 2 Session, Senate Report 539.

Notes of a conference between the committee on coinage, weights, and measure, the Secretary of the Treasury, and the Treasurer of the United States, concerning the arrangement with the New York Clearing House, and in regard to the circulation of silver.
March 20, 1880. 46 Congress, 2 Session, House Miscellaneous Document 34.

Loans by national banks on real estate.
March 31, 1880. 46 Congress, 2 Session, House Report 636.

Report of the Committee on Banking and Currency on the International American Bank. (To accompany House Bill 11159.)
June 26, 1890. 51 Congress, 1 Session, House Report 2561.

Hearings before the Committee on Banking and Currency, of the House of Representatives.
1893. 53 Congress, 1 Session.

Notes of hearings before the committee on banking and currency of the House of Representatives, on bill (H. R. 8149) to amend the law relative to national banking associations.
1894. 53 Congress, 3 Session.

Hearings and arguments before the committee on banking and currency of the House of Representatives, 1896-97.
Washington: Government Printing Office. 1897. 54 Congress, 1 and 2 Sessions.

Views of the Minority of the House Committee on Banking and Currency, on the International American Bank. (To accompany H. R. 10807.)
June 30, 1898. 55 Congress, 2 Session, House Report 1627, Part 2.

Report of the special sub-committee of the committee on banking and currency of the United States House of Representatives on the bill drafted by it, etc.
1898. 55 Congress, 2 Session. Washington; Gibson Bros.

Hearings and arguments before the committee on banking and currency of the House of Representatives on proposed changes in the currency system of the United States, 1897-98.
1898. 55 Congress, 2 Session.

Letter from the Secretary of the Treasury . . . as to communications and agreements between the Secretary of the Treasury and the officials of the National City Bank of New York.
January 26, 1900. 56 Congress, 1 Session, Senate Document 121.

Transactions with certain national banks.
January 10, 1900. 56 Congress, 1 Session, House Document 264.

Hearings and arguments before the committee on banking and currency of the House of Representatives on proposed currency legislation.
1907. 59 Congress, 2 Session.

Response of the Secretary of the Treasury to Senate Resolution No. 33 of December 12, 1907, calling for certain information in regard to Treasury operations, United States depositaries, the condition of national banks, etc.
January 29, 1908. 60 Congress, 1 Session, Senate Document 208.

Letter from the Secretary of the Treasury . . . relative to the refusal of the national banks in New York City to furnish currency for the needs of interior banks.
April 13, 1908. 60 Congress, 1 Session, Senate Document 435.

Hearings on House resolution No. 314, authorizing the appointment of a committee to investigate as to whether there are not combinations of financial and other concerns who control money and credits, and operate in restraint of trade through that control—before the committee on rules, House of Representatives.
December 15, 1911. 62 Congress, 2 Session.

Investigation of financial and monetary conditions in the United States . . . before the sub-committee of the committee on banking and currency of the House of Representatives.
1912. 62 Congress, 3 Session.

Report of the committee appointed . . . to investigate the concentration of control of money and credit. Submitted by Mr. Pujo, February 28, 1913.
1913. 62 Congress, 3 Session, House Report 1593.

Hearings before the sub-committee of the committee on banking and currency, House of Representatives, charged with investigating plans of banking and currency reform and reporting constructive legislation thereon.
1913. 62 Congress, 3 Session.

Hearings on Federal Reserve Act. United States Senate Banking and Currency Committee. 3 Volumes.
1913. 63 Congress, 1 Session, Senate Document 232.

Hearings before the committee on banking and currency of the United States Senate on . . . a bill to prevent the use of the mails and of the telegraph and telephone in furtherance of fraudulent and harmful transactions on stock exchanges.
1914. 63 Congress, 2 Session.

Letter from the Governor of the Federal Reserve Bank transmitting, in response to a Senate resolution of March 8, 1920, a communication concerning the rates of interest on collateral call loans.
March 29, 1920. 66 Congress, 2 Senate, Senate Document 262.

C. By Locality

Connecticut—Annual Report of the Bank Commissioners. 1841-.

Illinois—Report from Joint Select Committee to Enquire into the Condition of the State Bank of Illinois.
January 21, 1840. 11 Assembly, 2 Session.

Louisiana—Report from the Joint Committee on Banks and Banking of the Senate and House of Representatives of the State of Louisiana. February, 1857.

Massachusetts—Schedule exhibiting the Condition of the Banks in Massachusetts from Secretary of the Commonwealth. 1803-1837, inclusive. 1838. Senate Number 38.
Annual Reports of the Banking Commission. 1851-1865.

Missouri—Report of the Committee Appointed by the Governor to Examine into the General Condition of the Bank of the State of Missouri, House of Representatives. November 24, 1840.

New York—Annual Reports of the Bank Commissioners, 1831-1841.
Annual Reports of the New York State Comptroller, 1842-1851.
Annual Reports of the Superintendent of Banks on Deposit Banks, 1852-.

Annual Reports of the Superintendent of Banks relative to Savings Banks, Trust Companies, Safe Deposit Companies and Miscellaneous Corporations, 1858-.

Annual Reports of the Superintendent of Banks relative to mortgage, loan and investment companies, 1891-1899.

Annual Reports of the New York State Tax Commissioners, 1905-1913.

Quarterly Reports of Banks, published by the New York State Banking Department, 1887-.

New York State Assembly Journals.

New York State Senate Journals.

Report by Committee on Banks, Vindication of State Currency and a Review of Assembly Report.
New York State Assembly Documents, 1818.

Report of the Bank Committee on the Safety Fund Act.
February 13, 1829.
New York State Assembly Documents, 1829.

Report of the Committee on Banking and Insurance Companies on so much of the Governor's Message as relates to the currency.
February 2, 1835.
New York State Assembly Documents, 1835, Vol. 3, No. 229.

Memorial and Remonstrance of the board of stock and exchange brokers of the city of New-York.
March 23, 1836.
New York State Assembly Documents, 1836, No. 291.

Report of the Banking Committee on the System of Private Banking.
March 18, 1837.
New York State Senate Documents, 1837, No. 55.

Report of the Select Committee appointed to investigate the banks.
May 11, 1837.
New York State Assembly Documents, 1837, No. 328.

Report of the Select Committee on the subject of money.
March 1, 1851.
New York State Senate Documents, 1851, No. 40.

Report of the Committee on Banks and Insurance Companies on petitions praying for an enlargement of the basis of circulation for bank notes.
March 1, 1853.
New York State Assembly Documents, 1853, No. 46.

Message from the Governor, returning with objections a certain bill in relation to banking privileges.
January 1, 1853.
New York State Assembly Documents, 1853, No. 113.

Report on the effect of payment of interest on deposits of foreign banks in banks of this state.
February 29, 1856.
New York State Senate Documents, 1856, Vol. 2, No. 58.

Report of the Committee on Banks and Insurance Companies to the State Legislature.
April 1, 1864.
New York State Assembly Documents, 1864.

Preamble and resolutions relating to grain and other articles.
March 22, 1882.
New York State Senate Documents, 1882, Vol. 6, No. 73.

Majority and minority reports of the committee appointed to investigate the cornering of grain and other articles.
April 20, 1883.
New York State Senate Documents, 1883, Vol. 5, No. 45.

Report of Special Committee on Banks to Governor Hughes.
December 15, 1907.

Message from the Governor, on stock exchange.
January 27, 1913.

Report of the Senate Committee on Banks, relative to private banking business.
February 17, 1914.
New York State Senate Documents, 1914, Vol. 11, No. 28.

OHIO—Series of reports made on the condition of the Ohio Stock Banks.
Ohio Public Documents, 1854, Vol. XVIII, No. 9.

RHODE ISLAND—Report of Committee to visit and examine Banks in this State.
June, 1836.
Newport, General Assembly, 1836.

GREAT BRITAIN—Parliamentary Papers
1808, (119) X, 81.
1810, Vols. 2 and 3.
1819, Vol. 3.
1821, Vol. 6, Nos. 635, 746; Vol. 7, No. 476.
1847-48, (395) VIII, Part I; (565) VIII, Part III.

INDEX

INDEX

COLUMBIA UNIVERSITY PRESS
Columbia University
New York

FOREIGN AGENT
OXFORD UNIVERSITY PRESS
Humphrey Milford
Amen House, London, E. C.

Bei Fragen zur Produktsicherheit wenden Sie sich bitte an:
If you have any questions regarding product safety,
please contact:

Walter de Gruyter GmbH
Genthiner Straße 13
10785 Berlin
productsafety@degruyterbrill.com